LOCOMOTIVES
I HAVE
KNOWN

LOCOMOTIVES

I have known

by

J. N. MASKELYNE

MODEL & ALLIED PUBLICATIONS

ARGUS BOOKS LTD

Argus Books Ltd,
Argus House,
14 St James Road,
Watford Herts,
England

First published by Percival Marshall, 1959
Combined volume, Facsimile edition Published by Argus Books, 1980.

Copyright © 1959 J. N. Maskelyne

ISBN 0 85242 636 4

Printed in Great Britain by Redwood Burn Limited, Trowbridge & Esher
Bound by Webb Son & Co, Ltd., Ferndale, Glamorgan

CONTENTS

INTRODUCTION

TO enthusiasts of my generation, J. N. Maskelyne needs no introduction. Editor of 'Model Railway News', President of the Stephenson Locomotive Society, locomotive draughtsman and historian of renown, he loomed large on everyone's horizon. His most lasting memorial is almost certainly the collected locomotive drawings which appeared, first as a series of articles in 'Model Engineer' then published in two volumes.

When I was asked to collate the two into one, I approached the task with enthusiasm. Not only has my own career roughly paralleled his, but it was his example that set me to draw locomotives in a substantially similar style.

Mechanical drawing is largely looked on as a means of presenting information; for this purpose it is certainly supreme, since the basic conventions bypass language: it is truly international in its concept. It is clear that it can be made attractive to the eye by the use of certain techniques and, more particularly, the avoidance of a number of basic conventions. One specific area where this applies in force is the preparation of locomotive elevations.

The steam locomotive lends itself to this art, because its basic shape is produced by the assembly of varied cylindrical and plane surfaces. As will be seen in the following pages many designers have succeeded in producing a harmonious blend of these essentially simple elements. J. N. Maskelyne's meticulous draughtsmanship has highlighted their beauty.

This collection is not an absolutely definitive assembly of all J. N. Maskelyne's locomotive drawings; I know of at least one other published example which, probably because he never knew the locomotive personally, he omitted from his reminiscences. I have resisted the temptation to include it, furthermore, I have not carried out a detailed, pettifogging check on the information herein. Since this book was written, the excellent RCTS locomotive histories, generally accepted as the last word in this arcane branch of scholarship have covered most of the locomotives described in considerable detail, and I would hope any ardent seeker of fact would refer to these. As a near lifelong admirer of JNM's work, I would not alter a word. This is essentially one man's view of British locomotives, a glorious book of personal reminiscences, much as JNM spoke when one was fortunate enough to meet him. Let the record stand.

One locomotive in this book has memories for me. 7007 'Great Western' turned up so frequently on my trains during a glorious week of train travel in Devon during 1948 that I began to wonder if it were the only 'Castle' west of Exeter. The others were, in the main, just names to me; thirty years and more ago, I envied JNM's chance to see these magnificent machines. Today I am more philosophical as younger enthusiasts listen avidly to my own reminiscences. To those who feel envious, I say 'stick around'. Already the 'Westerns' and 'Warships' have passed into legend and the Deltics are being phased out. By 2000 the 45's and 47's will be a memory. Then the present generation can lovingly recall their merits, while quietly ignoring their faults, which is exactly what JNM has done for the locomotives in this book.

The steam locomotive was not perfect. It was the product of an age when skilled labour was cheap, unskilled labour dirt cheap. Most of the machines in this book were designed and built around the turn of the century, an age of elegance created by a social order that has been swept away. To a large extent J. N. Maskelyne remained at heart, an Edwardian; he practised the old world courtesies, and a locomotive engineer received the title 'Mr' whereas today we award him his initials, if that. Perhaps the old way was best.

'Locomotives I have known' and 'A further Selection of Locomotives I have Known', each followed a different arrangement of companies. It seemed impossible to slot one satisfactorily into the other so I have completely recast the order, setting out the locomotives roughly in ascending order of size so that the contents page can effectively act as an index, since in arranging steam locomotives, the wheel formula is the most convenient rough guide. This was tedious rather than difficult: there are one or two places where I have juggled twice with the order, since here there is no hard and fast 'right' arrangement. The separation of the 'Brighton' line from the rest of the Southern Group is of course a deliberate tribute to JNM's love of that railway, and follows the style set by the first volume which, I suspect, is JNM's own choice.

It has been a great pleasure studying, yet again, this fine collection of locomotive drawings by a man whose work in this field inspired me to follow suit. In closing one can perhaps feel relieved that JNM did not live to see the diesel locomotive supplant steam, for he was most vehemently opposed. Electric traction he could just tolerate but internal combustion almost roused this most gentle of men to anger. Let his own work remain as a tribute to the machine he loved, the British steam locomotive.

C. J. Freezer.

Hemel Hempstead 1980

Author's Preface

TO the railway enthusiast, the steam locomotive has always been an object of veneration; but the inherent attraction of the machine itself must surely be unique among machines, for there can be no other that has commanded so much respect from the human race. The reasons for this are many, involved, intangible and need not be discussed here; but mention may be made of the fact that most people are subtly aware that, unlike the majority of modern scientific inventions, the influence of the steam locomotive has been for the good of mankind; it has never been used as an instrument of deliberate destruction; always it has been applied to furthering the wellbeing and progress of human civilisation, by promoting rapid transit of freight and passengers from one community to another. At its inception, nearly 150 years ago, it was the only means of achieving that object, and for almost a century it remained alone and unchallenged to serve us in that capacity.

I admit to having succumbed to the attractions of the steam locomotive at a very early age. I was born in south-west London at the beginning of the last decade of the nineteenth century, and so came upon the scene in time to enjoy the steam locomotive when it was at the zenith of its influence, usefulness and popularity. About 1910, the influence and usefulness began to show signs of waning a little, due to the increase of efficiency and reliability of other forms of motive power; but the popularity remained, because of the advances made in steam locomotive design to meet the growing challenge.

Locomotive engineering, as a profession, attracted many eminent men whose scientific knowledge, technical ability and practical experience were of the best. Some of their work is illustrated and described in the following pages, presented as a locomotive enthusiast with technical training of his own can remember it. The preparation of the drawings has provided me with much pleasurable occupation over many years. It was my long-standing association with the model engineering hobby and its needs that prompted me to undertake the work involved, and the fact that my drawings have been of interest and use to many of my fellow-enthusiasts is its own reward for my efforts.

A physical disability, which became permanent in early youth, prevented my taking part in the more normal outdoor pastimes and games enjoyed by boys; therefore, I gave much of my spare time to the study of locomotives and their work. What I learned from books and magazines was supplemented by what I saw and heard during many hours of observation at railway stations, locomotive running sheds and other points of vantage; or, in later years, during railway journeys to various parts of Britain, in the normal course of my professional duties.

My drawings, however, could never have been made without the very generous help received from professional locomotive men, with many of whom it has been my privilege to be personally acquainted. Often they must have been surprised and not a little disturbed by the queries and requests that I made when searching for detailed information. In all the years, I cannot remember an occasion when I was " sent empty away "; this patient, courteous treatment, so cheerfully and readily given, is hereby most gratefully acknowledged.

The following articles appeared in MODEL ENGINEER, between February, 1957 and April, 1959. To the managing editor of that magazine, Mr. C. E. Waller, I am much indebted for his enthusiastic efforts in making this reprint possible; his expert advice and co-operation in planning the layout of the book are deeply appreciated.

I leave the book to speak for itself, but not before tendering my warmest thanks to Mr. R. A. Riddles, C.B.E., Past President of the Institution of Locomotive Engineers and the first Mechanical and Electrical Engineer of British Railways, for the Foreword. Also, to my friend of many years' standing, George Dow, Assoc.I.Loco.E., Divisional Traffic Manager, West Midlands, British Railways, London Midland Region, for his unstinting co-operation in enabling me to include the coats-of-arms, crests or emblems of the various railways and for his never-failing help whenever I wanted official information about some of the lesser-known locomotives; he was, in fact, self-appointed liaison officer between the various Locomotive Departments and myself, for which service I gratefully acknowledge my indebtedness to him.

J. N. MASKELYNE.

Midgham, Berks.
MAY, 1959.

THE DRAWING BOARD BY THE WINDOW

Iɴ *Locomotives I Have Known*, J. N. Maskelyne set down but a fraction of his vast historical knowledge of the locomotive, gained over a period of more than 60 years. His enthusiasm for his

---

This appreciation of the late J. N. Maskelyne, by his brother Noel, appeared in Model Engineer *on May 18, 1960, soon after his death. This volume is complementary to J.N.M.'s earlier " Locomotives I Have Known " and is published in response to a wide demand.*

---

subject and everything connected with it began in the days when, at a very early age, he would be taken for walks on Wandsworth Common. These walks, as he used to say, would always lead in the direction of the railings atop the cutting on the London side of the station.

In those days he would have seen locomotives of the LBSCR in all the glory of Stroudley's livery. Then followed more than 60 years of enthusiasm for the locomotive. That he lived to see the last locomotive built for British Railways must have been a bitter satisfaction for him.

* * *

To have the distressing duty of looking through a brother's collection and library is something which I had not foreseen. The task gave me an insight into a side of J.N.M. that even a brother had never suspected. I knew that his outline drawings of locomotives were appreciated the world over, but the meticulous care with which they were executed had never dawned on me. At least, not until I came across what appeared to be two identical drawings of the experimental locomotive *The Great Bear* built for the GWR in 1908. To my inexperienced eye the

drawings appeared identical, but on one of them were some pencilled notes headed " errors." So slight were these errors that only one of J.N.M.'s knowledge of locomotive detail would have noticed them. In the second drawing the errors had been corrected. A labour of love indeed. . . .

There were, of course, many locomotives that he did not know personally; although on these he was able to give most of the information for which an enquirer could ask. I have beside me, as I write, an album of photographs taken at random from his library. It contains photographs of locomotives of a bygone era. The pages are annotated in J.N.M.'s handwriting as well as that of someone else whose identity I cannot even guess.

One of the earliest dated photographs in the album is that of the LBSCR 2-2-2 *Seaford* No 292, built in 1845. But an undated and much earlier photograph is annotated " Old Wylam engine *Lady Mary*." The engine has to be seen to be believed. I imagine it to be contemporary with Stephenson's *Rocket* and its building might have been in 1825-29, or even earlier. The two photographs indicate astonishingly the development of the locomotive in a matter of 20 years. One human touch is common to both photographs; the crews are well and truly bearded ! Though most of the locomotives illustrated in the album he would not have known, such was the life

For J. N. Maskelyne a locomotive had to be drawn perfectly or not at all. The drawings on this page failed to satisfy him. He redrew them as on the next page.

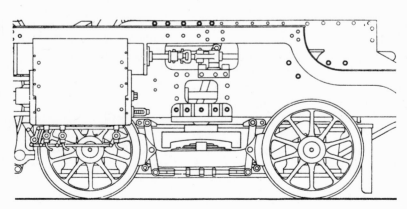
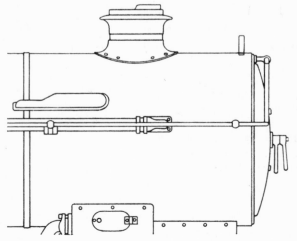
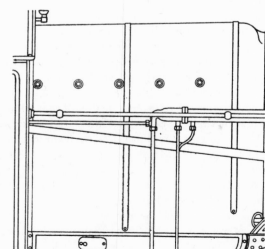

2

of the best of them that he may have seen some of them at work.

Looking through J.N.M.'s library set me thinking along the lines of the layman's view of the locomotive's development. Lack of technical knowledge in this field, leads a layman to compare external appearances and try to assess the degree of development that has taken place, even to speculating on what a locomotive is in terms of basic essentials. While *Lady Mary* has her works scattered indiscriminately all over her, naked for all to see and giving her an appearance of uninhibited abandon, the locomotives of recent years are discreetly clothed. The essentials are hidden from the gaze of the common herd by an all-enveloping metal cloak, which creates an air of aloofness and detachment. Gone are the details so beloved of the earlier locomotive enthusiast. Gone are the points of breeding that gave the earlier ones their personality, the polished brass steam-dome, the copper cap to the chimney and the beautiful liveries. Now we see only a metal monster with no more concession to personality than a name-plate on the side and, perhaps, a five figure number savouring suspiciously of a code.

*   *   *

The two are, of course, worlds apart in terms of speed and development. No doubt it mattered little what sort of efficiency figures *Lady Mary* had, even if anyone ever thought about it. What did matter was that she would go, if she were provided with water and coal.

Basically, what is the similarity or the difference between the two? In the broadest possible terms they are, as the layman interprets them, little different. Both are steel frames with a boiler mounted above and wheels below. Both require two men to work them. The difference is one of degree and development. It is curious that a basic design, so broadly stated, was formulated for the first locomotives and holds good for the latest and last of the race. In engineering it is so often the same story; original basic conceptions remain. The earliest motor cars were steel frames with a wheel at each corner, an engine in front and seats behind. And so, broadly speaking are those of today.

*   *   *

Conversation along these lines would produce in J.N.M. the greatest disgust, and how could it not have done? His life had been spent in the accumulation of knowledge of the locomotive, and a visit to his work-room reflected his enthusiasm for his subject. Three of the four walls were occupied by bookcases and cabinets and the fourth, with the window, contained his drawing board and all that went with it. The three shelves of a sort of tea trolley were filled to overflowing with hundreds of his drawings, so familiar to those whose interests were akin to his own. The whole room had about it an air of well-ordered chaos. But in a matter of seconds only, J.N.M. could turn up any information he might require; whether from his collection of some 12,000 postcard illustrations, 40 years and more of periodicals, or a satisfactory library of locomotive reference books, not to mention the many thousands of photographs of locomotives taken by him throughout his life.

As a parallel part of his life he was a keen locomotive modeller. Much of his time was devoted to models of locomotives. His model of *Plumpton*, the LBSCR Stroudley 2-2-2, built and developed in conjunction with Mr Norris, is apparently quite famous.

Though his work as a modeller is known to many, if not all, of those of similar interest, it is not generally known that his first models, built to scale and perfect in every detail, were made entirely of paper. I well remember a paper *Stephenson*, painted of course in the original Stroudley livery, long before the *Plumpton* model was ever thought of. The building up and cutting out of the wheels from successive layers of Bristol board was, I remember, a difficult and lengthy task. But the final product was, for him, satisfactory.

The passing of J.N.M. will leave a serious gap in the ranks of locomotive historians. His loss to locomotive modellers may be even greater, and he will long be remembered by many as one to whom the locomotive was an essential part of life.

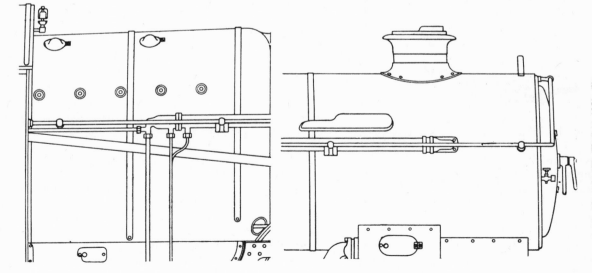

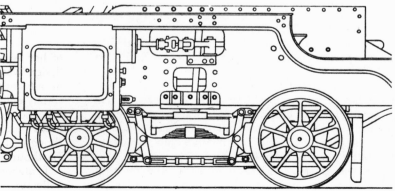

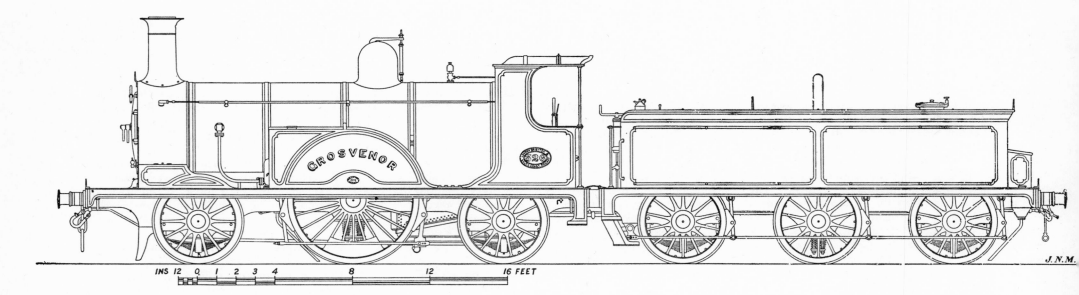

2-2-2 GROSVENOR

IN my young days, the old London Brighton and South Coast Railway was still in possession of 26 very attractive 2-2-2 type express engines which were universally referred to as the " Stroudley singles."

They were great favourites among locomotive enthusiasts of those days, mainly because of the steady reliability of their work; years later, when I came to know some of the older drivers of the Brighton line, I discovered that these engines were well liked by the men who had charge of them.

Originally, the 26 engines had been divided into three separate classes, officially designated B, F and G; B and F each consisted of one engine only, *Grosvenor* and *Abergavenny*, respectively, while G was made up of 24 engines that were built about five years later than class F. Afterwards, all the 26 engines were put together under one class letter G. This chapter deals with engine No 326, *Grosvenor*, originally class B, later B2.

She was built at Brighton in 1874, and for that period she was a very fine engine, one of the largest

of her type in the country, and every detail of her design was, at least, right up to date if not actually in advance of the times. With it all, she was a stately engine, a real aristocrat, and she was loved by all who knew her. Even in my time, she worked crack express trains, mostly Portsmouth trains, though she often worked some to Brighton and Eastbourne.

I always associate her with that most amusing collection of headboards which signified " Victoria

to Eastbourne via Quarry Tunnel." This consisted of a plain white disc above the left-hand buffer, another, often a square-shaped board, with a pair of horizontal parallel black lines on it set over the middle of the bufferbeam, and a third with a black, vertical cross mounted above the right-hand buffer. To all and sundry, this glorious combination, read across the bufferbeam, announced that " nothing equals plus."

All the best Eastbourne and Hastings trains carried it, and it usually raised a smile. *Grosvenor* was the first engine on which I noticed it, one afternoon, as she approached sedately towards me at the head of a long train passing Wandsworth Common, and I do not think that a more intriguing headcode was ever seen. The discs were 15 in. dia.

Incidentally, it was *Grosvenor* that worked the first through train from London to Portsmouth on 13 August 1875; the train was a Royal special conveying the then Prince and Princess of Wales (afterwards King Edward VII and Queen Alexandra) to a naval occasion. The 87 miles from Victoria to

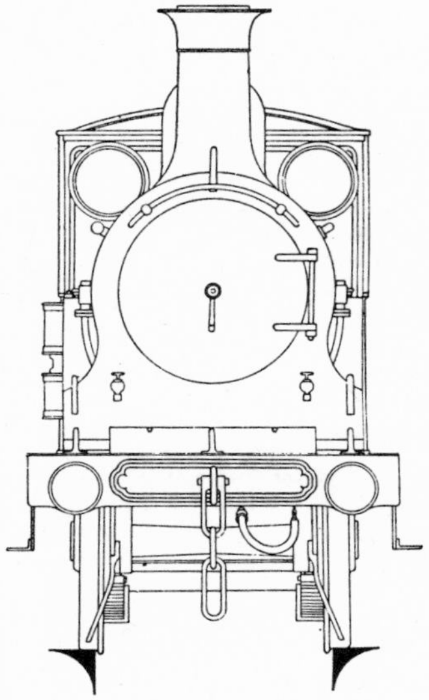

GENERAL SPECIFICATION

CYLINDERS		TUBES	
Diameter	17 in.	Number	206
Stroke	24 in.	Diameter	1¾ in.
BOILER			
Length, between tubeplates	10 ft 5 in.	HEATING SURFACE	
		Tubes ...	1,022 sq. ft
Maximum diameter ...	4 ft 5 in.	Firebox ...	110 sq. ft
		Total ...	1,132 sq. ft
FIREBOX LENGTH			
Inside ...	5 ft 7¾ in.	GRATE AREA	
Outside ...	6 ft 2¼ in.	Square feet ...	19.3

Portsmouth were run in 110 minutes at an average speed of 48 m.p.h.

Two months earlier, however, this fine engine was her owners' representative at Newark, where some trials of various braking systems were held. She had an unusual arrangement of two brakes, one steam and the other hand-operated, in the cab, immediately accessible to the driver. In addition, the tender was equipped with the normal handbrake operated by the fireman.

As a result of the Newark trials, the LBSCR decided to adopt the expensive, but very effective, Westinghouse air brake, which remained standard practice at Brighton ever after. It was one of the first of the continuous, automatic power-operated brakes, operating throughout the length of the train as well as on the engine, regardless of the number of vehicles in the train.

Originally, the brake rigging on *Grosvenor* included two massive wooden shoes per side, working on the driving and trailing wheels; but at a later date this was altered to the clasp arrangement with cast-iron shoes on the driving wheels only, as seen in the drawing.

For some time, *Grosvenor* worked the heavy 5.0 p.m. train from Victoria to Brighton, with its numerous company of regular season-ticket holders returning home from business, and taking 70 min. on the journey. At that period, she was stationed at Brighton; later she was moved to Battersea and became what today we should call a popular star; everybody seemed to know her. She was never rebuilt, and was withdrawn early in 1907, after running a total of 1,048,000 miles.

Her principal dimensions were: cylinders, 17 in. dia. by 24 in. stroke; they were placed at 26 in. between centres, with the steamchest, 4½ in. wide, between them, set vertically. The ports were 1½ in. and 2 in. wide, respectively, for admission and exhaust; their extreme length was 15 in., but they were divided on the horizontal centre line so as to form two sets of ports, upper and lower, per cylinder. The valves had ⅞ in. steam lap and ⅛ in. exhaust lap, and were set with ⅛ in. lead; their travel in full gear was 4 in.

An interesting feature was the placing of the whole group of ports 1¾ in. ahead of the vertical centre line through the steamchest, viewed in side elevation. The effect of this was that the length of the back steam passage, from port face to cylinder bore, was 3½ in. greater than that of the front steam passage; but the idea was to compensate for the inequality of the admission periods, due to the angularity of the connecting rods, and to ensure the supply of equal volumes of steam to the front and back of each cylinder. Lever reverse was employed.

The boiler was made in three rings, 4 ft 3 in., 4 ft 4 in. and 4 ft 5 in. dia., respectively; the length of the barrel was 10 ft 5 in. and its pitch was 7 ft 3½ in. The firebox casing was 6 ft 2¼ in. long by 4 ft 1 in. wide, and the grate area was 19.3 sq. ft. There were 206 tubes of 1¾ in. dia., providing 1,022 sq. ft of heating surface, to which the firebox added 110 sq. ft, making the total 1,132 sq. ft.

The driving wheels were the largest ever used by Stroudley, 6 ft 9 in. dia., and the leading, trailing and tender wheels were all 4 ft 6 in. dia., after the standard passenger tender shown in the drawing had been substituted for the smaller outside-framed tender originally fitted.

Grosvenor's wheelbase was 8 ft plus 7 ft 9 in., with overhang of 5 ft 8¼ in. at the front and 3 ft 8¼ in. at the back. The tender wheelbase was 14 ft equally divided, with overhang of 4 ft 2 in. at each end. The width of the engine footplating was 7 ft 2 in. while that of the tender was 7 ft 6 in. The cab and tender body were both 6 ft 0½ in. wide outside.

The tractive effort, calculated at 85 per cent. of the 150 lb. boiler pressure and with 14 tons on the driving wheels, was 10,918 lb. Here, undoubtedly, was a fine engine, quite a landmark in the history and development of locomotive design; yet no more exactly like her were ever built. Her original number was 151, which was altered to 326 in 1880.

In 1907, the year when this fine engine was withdrawn, a story got about that she, together with two of the G-class proper, had been sold to the Italian State Railways. Two years or so later this tale was augmented by another rumour that *Grosvenor* was destroyed in the great earthquake at Messina in December 1908.

In 1926, I made very careful enquiries through the ISR offices in London, but no trace could be found of any information that could account for the story; but there is a very detailed account of the subsequent history of 40 Midland Railway 0-6-0s that were sold to Italy a few years prior to 1907. For this reason, I discredit the tale about the Brighton engines.

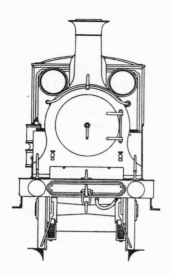

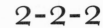
GENERAL SPECIFICATION

CYLINDERS			TUBES		
Diameter	...	17 in.	Number	...	262
Stoke	...	24 in.	Diameter	...	1½ in.
BOILER					
Length, between			**HEATING SURFACE**		
tubeplates	10 ft 2 in.		Tubes	...	1,084.51 sq. ft
Maximum dia-			Firebox	...	99.8 sq. ft
meter	...	4 ft 3 in.	Total	...	1,184.31 sq. ft
FIREBOX LENGTH					
Inside	...	5 ft 1½ in.	**GRATE AREA**		
Outside	...	5 ft 8¼ in.	Square feet	...	17

IT seems that Stroudley, after trials with the big, imposing *Grosvenor* and the small, but altogether delightful *Abergavenny*, decided that there was plenty of scope for singlewheelers on the LBSCR, but that the best design would be a compromise between classes B and F.

Consequently, in December 1880 engine No 327, *Imberhorne*, was put to work; she was the first of the 24 jolly little sisters which comprised the original Class G. I knew them all, in spite of the fact that some of them seldom, if ever, worked trains through Wandsworth Common, which made them difficult to "cop." Perhaps the one which, in course of years, I came to know best was No 329, *Stephenson*; and, in any event, she outlasted all the others.

No 345, *Plumpton*, is the prototype of an experimental 7 mm. scale model that I built in 1933, to test the possibilities of exact-scale wheels. I chose her because I have memories of many runs behind her, and also because—breathe it gently !—her name seemed to be about the easiest of all of them to reproduce in 7 mm. scale !

In their early years, the G class engines were stationed at New Cross, Battersea, Brighton and Portsmouth, being fairly evenly distributed between the four depots; and they were set to work main-line services over the principal routes. They did well; in fact, on the London-Portsmouth line they did

extremely well, in view of the trying gradients encountered on that line.

The timetables, however, did not then demand average speeds of more than about 40 m.p.h., but the trains were not of the lightest, so that the work required was of a high standard. To see these engines at their best, one had to go to a place like Forest Hill, a station at the top of 2¾ miles of 1-in-100 gradient that begins only about 2¾ miles from the point of departure (London Bridge).

To see a G class engine hauling a long trail of assorted coaches, four-wheeled, six-wheeled and eight-wheeled, resolutely topping that bank was to realise that those Stroudley singles had something which some other singles had not got. True, at the top of the Forest Hill bank, their speed was often down to around 20 m.p.h.; but once over the top, they were away.

It was apparent that, although these engines, like all singles, often indulged in a good deal of slipping when starting, they had a very firm grip on the road when running; and it stood them in good stead on the Portsmouth line with that Ockley bank and other rather testing gradients to negotiate.

When I came to know the G class really well, they had mostly given way to larger and more powerful types on the best main line trains; but there was a great deal of secondary passenger traffic between London and the south coast on which these engines gave satisfactory service for several years. Semi-fast trains to and from Tunbridge Wells were frequently worked by these engines, and between 1909 and 1912, I enjoyed many runs with No 342, *St Lawrence*, 345 *Plumpton* and 329 *Stephenson*.

The first two of these were then stationed at Tunbridge Wells, while *Stephenson*, then renumbered 329-A, was a Battersea engine, and had an interesting turn; for she regularly ran the 6.3 p.m. on Fridays only, from Victoria to Tunbridge Wells and returned on the 8.25 p.m. from the latter town. I found out that the reason for this was to make sure that she was in proper trim for working the Eastbourne Pullman Limited on Sundays, a duty for which she was specially reserved, in summer months only, until 1912.

I was travelling to London daily from Edenbridge

then, and, needless to say, always went home by the 6.3 p.m. from Victoria on Fridays, so as to enjoy a run behind *Stephenson*! She never failed; though one evening, during a terrific thunderstorm, she very nearly stuck in the deep cutting between Woldingham and the Oxted tunnel, but recovered herself just in time to prevent a stall.

On the Eastbourne Pullman she was well known, and ran her last trip on it in September, 1912. After that, she was kept as a sort of odd-job engine at Battersea sheds, pottering about on any job that offered itself, until May 1914, when she, the last survivor of her class, was withdrawn for scrap, still with her *original* boiler, then 33 years old.

I have already mentioned some runs I had behind either No 342, *St Lawrence* or No 345, *Plumpton*. These two engines were then taking it in turns to work a fast morning train from Tunbridge Wells to London; it left Edenbridge Town at 11.25 a.m., and, stopping at Oxted and East Croydon only, was due at Victoria at 12.8 p.m. I was learning engineering at King's College at that time, and on Wednesdays had no lecture to attend before 2.0 p.m. So the 11.25 a.m. ex-Edenbridge was my normal train on that day, though a later one would have sufficed!

Either of the two singles timed that train without trouble, and I always enjoyed the trip. The load was made up in the following order: one six-wheeled van, one eight-wheeled third, one six-wheeled first, one eight-wheeled third, two six-wheeled vans with another eight-wheeled third bringing up the rear; the tare weight would be about 125 tons, and the gross about 140 tons. This was a comfortable load for a single, and there was never any trouble in working it. But the chief excitement of the trip usually occurred on the run down from Woldingham to Sanderstead, where speed would often rise into the seventies.

The dimensions of these engines were: cylinders, 17 in. dia., 24 in. stroke and 26 in. apart; they were horizontal and with the steam chest between them; the valves were provided with $\frac{7}{8}$ in. steam lap and $\frac{1}{8}$ in. exhaust lap; the lead was $\frac{1}{16}$ in. and the full-gear travel was $3\frac{3}{4}$ in., the valve-gear being Stephenson's, with the weighshaft above.

The diameter of the leading and trailing wheels was 4 ft 6 in.; that of the driving wheels was 6 ft 6 in. The wheelbase was 15 ft 11 in. divided into 8 ft plus 7 ft 11 in., and the overhang was 5 ft 8$\frac{1}{4}$ in. in front and 3 ft 3$\frac{1}{4}$ in. at the back. The length of the frame plates was 24 ft 10$\frac{1}{2}$ in. and their thickness $\frac{7}{8}$ in.; they were of steel.

The boiler was made in three rings, the diameter of the largest being 4 ft 3 in., while the length of the barrel was 10 ft 2 in. and the centre line was pitched 7 ft 1$\frac{7}{16}$ in. above rail level. There were 262 tubes of 1$\frac{1}{2}$ in. dia., their heating surface being 1,084.51 sq. ft; the firebox heating surface was 99.8 sq. ft, so that the total amounted to 1,184.31 sq. ft. The original working pressure was 140 p.s.i., but this was later increased to 150 p.s.i. In 1913, however, *Stephenson* was running with the pressure reduced to 120 p.s.i., due to the age of her boiler.

These engines weighed 33 tons 8 cwt and the tenders 27 tons 7 cwt. The driving wheels carried 13 tons 10 cwt, the leading wheels 12 tons, and the trailing 7 tons 18 cwt. The capacity of the tender was for 2 tons of coal and 2,250 gallons of water.

My old fried, the late E. L. Ahrons, had quite an affection for these engines, but he used to say that all the wheels being outside gave the engines the appearance of being "all legs," and when they were running they always reminded him of centipedes! I have often wondered what he would have thought and said about some modern engines. But, so far as I am concerned, it is enough that I knew all the Stroudley singles and found so much delight in their elegance and in their work.

INS 12 6 0 1 2 3 4 5 6 7 8 FEET.

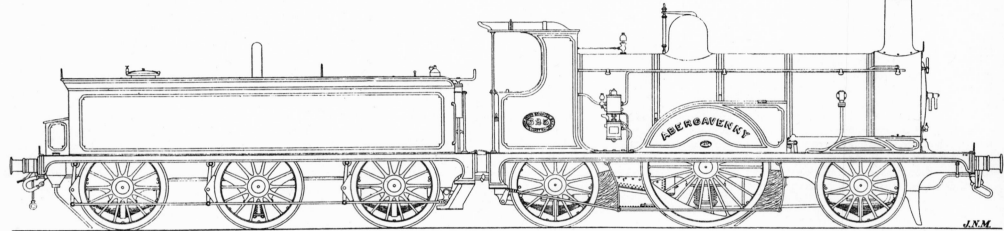

ABERGAVENNY 2-2-2

THIS engine was a considerable contrast to the magnificent *Grosvenor*. At first glance, the two engines were very similar, but *Abergavenny* was smaller and she always seemed to be more alert and lively. She was a delightful little engine and gave me a lot of pleasure.

It is a bit odd to recall that her construction took about two years and was regarded as a sort of stock job in the Brighton Works. It seems that Stroudley was carefully weighing up the feasibility of building single-wheelers for service on a line like the LBSCR; but his predecessor, J. C. Craven, had had no compunction in the matter and had provided the

line with many such engines of all sizes for passenger duties all over the railway.

Abergavenny was eventually completed in January 1877 and was given the number 325; she was the only example of the original Class F. Some years later, she, with *Grosvenor*, was transferred to Class G.

In her early years, her principal job was the working of the night Continental boat train from London Bridge to Newhaven; she was consequently stationed at New Cross for the purpose, and was never seen at Wandsworth Common during the years in which she worked that particular job. This, however, was before my time.

When I knew *Abergavenny* she was stationed at Tunbridge Wells, which was her station for the last nine years of her existence. Her regular duty then was a trip to London via Three Bridges in the morning, returning on the 3.45 p.m. from Victoria via the direct line, running non-stop to Groombridge.

She seldom missed this turn, and when we moved to Edenbridge just before Easter 1909 she was still on it. So I was able to continue my acquaintance with a lovable little friend, though for only a short while.

At Whitsun 1909 I saw the 3.45 *ex* Victoria pass Edenbridge Town; it was being hauled by a large 0-6-2 tank engine, No 399, *Middleton*, and I never

8

saw *Abergavenny* again. She had been withdrawn and, I regret to add, in rather ignominious circumstances.

It appears that during that Whitsun week, a rush of traffic had caused a shortage of engines at Tunbridge Wells shed, and one afternoon *Abergavenny*, just arrived off the 3.45 from Victoria, was immediately called upon to work a train from Tunbridge Wells to Brighton via Lewes.

This is not a road that is exactly suited to single-wheeled engines, for it has some severe gradients and

No 325

awkward curves. However, after a few trying moments at certain places and hauling a load that was rather more than she could comfortably cope with, she succeeded in reaching Lewes. But the somewhat formidable Falmer Bank lay ahead, and on it *Abergavenny* stalled and could not be persuaded to go any farther.

Now it so happened that Mr D. E. Marsh, the then locomotive superintendent, was travelling by that train and, exasperated by the delays, he gave orders that *Abergavenny* was to be destroyed forthwith. So ended her gay life! I believe that she had never before given trouble, having always worked well and punctually; so the circumstances of her end were particularly unfortunate.

Abergavenny's driving wheels were originally like

Grosvenor's, but only 6 ft 6 in. dia. They were of wrought-iron with the spokes welded into the rim and hub, and with the wrought-iron tyres shrunk on and held by setscrews placed between each alternate pair of spokes. The balance-weights had square-shaped ends. At a later date, these wheels were replaced by a cast-steel pair having crescent-shaped balanceweights, as shown in the drawing; the new tyres were of steel, shrunk on and setscrewed, as before.

The wheelbase was 8 ft plus 7 ft 9 in., and the overhang was 5 ft 8¼ in. at the front and 3 ft 5¼ in. at the back. The length of the main frames was

GENERAL SPECIFICATION

CYLINDERS				TUBES			
Diameter	...	...	16 in.	Number	...	...	244
Stroke	...	...	22 in.	Diameter	...	...	1½ in.
BOILER							
Length, between				HEATING SURFACE			
tubeplates ...		10 ft 2 in.		Tubes	...	1,006 sq. ft.	
Maximum diameter		4 ft 3 in.		Firebox	...	103 sq. ft.	
				Total	...	1,109 sq. ft.	
FIREBOX LENGTH							
Inside	...		—	GRATE AREA			
Outside	...		—	Square feet		...	—

24 ft 10½ in. The cylinders were small, being only 16 in. dia. × 22 in. stroke. But, to judge from her general sprightliness, the engine did not find these small cylinders any serious handicap. They were horizontal, with the centres 2 ft 2 in. apart, but I have never been able to find any particulars of the ports and valve events.

The boiler was made in three rings with the dome, as usual, on the back ring; the diameter of the largest ring was 4 ft 3 in. and the length of the barrel was 10 ft 2 in. Originally, there were 202 tubes of 1¾ in. dia., giving 971 sq. ft of heating surface, but this was afterwards altered to 244 tubes of 1½ in. dia. having 1,006 sq. ft of heating surface.

The firebox heating surface was 103 sq. ft which, with the later tubing, made the total heating surface

1,109 sq. ft. The pitch of the boiler centre line was 7 ft 1½ in. above rail level.

In my time, the tender was one of the standard passenger type with inside frames, 4 ft 6 in. wheels and a 14-ft equally-divided wheelbase. An interesting feature was that this tender was lined out as one big panel instead of the usual two. I have shown this on the drawing, but nobody has ever been able to explain to me why this alteration was made, as it was done long before the adoption of the later practice of putting the initials LB & SCR on tenders.

In working order, *Abergavenny* weighed 32 tons 13 cwt, with 10 tons 9 cwt on the leading wheels, 14 tons 9 cwt on the driving wheels, and 7 tons 15 cwt on the trailing wheels.

This engine retained her original brake gear, with its massive wooden blocks on driving and trailing wheels, unaltered throughout her existence; but the tender had the later standard brake rigging with cast-iron blocks.

I omitted the fact, when dealing with *Grosvenor*, that the delivery clacks were mounted each side of the boiler, on the front ring and about 18 in. to the rear of the smokebox; *Abergavenny* had exactly the same arrangement.

In the engines of the G class proper the clacks were mounted very low down on the boiler barrel and were out of sight behind the driving-wheel splashers. I raise this matter because of a certain model in one of our technical museums; it is named *Shanklin*, but has the clacks on the front ring of the boiler barrel. Its proportions suggest that its general dimensions were scaled down from the *Grosvenor*! In other words, it is a *muddle* rather than a model.

This is a pity, because the little engine, which is to ¾ in. scale, is not at all bad in other respects; even the painting is creditable—and that was not an easy feature to reproduce accurately in a small scale. I have tried it in 7 mm. to the foot and know how difficult that was.

It is of interest to recall that when *Abergavenny* was new, the tyres of her wheels were left bright and unpainted. So far as I know, this was the only instance of the kind on the LBSCR, and there does not appear to have been any particular reason for it. When I knew the engine, however, the wheels were painted in the normal style, with black tyres.

WILLIAM STROUDLEY'S
CELEBRATED GLADSTONE CLASS

EXPRESS PASSENGER ENGINES

FOR the first 13 years of my life, I lived with my parents at Wandsworth Common, within sight and sound of the old London Brighton and South Coast Railway, 4½ miles from Victoria on the main line to Brighton.

During that time, I got to know every type and class of engine on the line and, to me, the pick of the bunch was the celebrated " Gladstone " class of 0-4-2 express passenger engines, the first of which, No 214, *Gladstone*, had been completed in December 1882.

There were 36 of these engines, the last one having been put on the road in April 1891, just nine months before I came on the scene. They were most attractive engines and, for some reason that I cannot recall, No 180, *Arundel*, was my particular pet. I was always on the lookout for her and always felt an extra thrill of pleasure whenever she passed by.

Many years later, this engine gave me an added reason for feeling proud of her, as I will recount at the end of this article.

The " Gladstone " class was designed by William Stroudley, who had a very difficult problem to solve at the time,

because a really powerful and speedy express passenger engine was badly needed. The track would not allow an exceptionally heavy engine to run over it and the existing turntables at most of the principal locomotive depots were not long enough to accommodate an engine of more than about 50 ft. total length. Added to this, the cost of the engines had to be kept down to an absolute minimum.

To solve this problem, Stroudley produced a most unorthodox design, but it met all the exacting requirements successfully. Compared with the prevailing practice of the period, the four coupled wheels of large diameter placed at the front end of the engine were the most striking feature; but Stroudley maintained that this arrangement put the driving and coupled wheels under the heaviest part of the engine and so ensured that ample adhesion was available.

Another feature, unique at the time, was that the two cylinders with their steamchests were produced as a single casting, thereby considerably reducing their cost.

The boiler was of conventional type, but was remarkable on account of the

GENERAL SPECIFICATION					
CYLINDERS			**TUBES**		
Diameter	...	... 18¼ in.	Number	... ...	333
Stroke	...	... 26 in.	Diameter	... ...	1½ in.
BOILER			**HEATING SURFACE**		
Length, between tubeplates ...		10 ft 2 in.	Tubes	...	1,378.2 sq. ft.
Maximum diameter		4 ft 4 in.	Firebox	...	113.9 sq. ft.
			Total ...	...	1,492.1 sq. ft.
FIREBOX LENGTH					
Inside	...	—	**GRATE AREA**		
Outside	...	—	Square feet ...	...	20.65

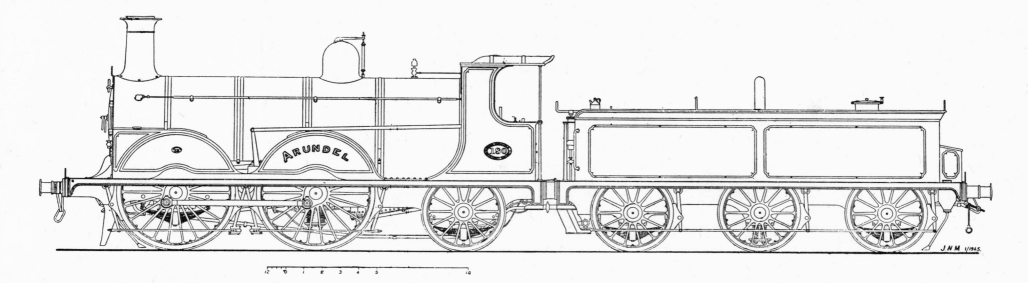

large amount of heating surface in such a comparatively small space. It was an excellent steamer and, because the coupled wheels were at the front end of the engine, there was plenty of room for a good deep firebox, which allowed a deep fire to be built up and become fully incandescent at the beginning of a trip and require little, if any, more feeding during the run.

The principal dimensions of these fine engines were: cylinders, 18¼ in. dia. by 26 in. stroke; coupled wheels 6 ft 6 in. dia.; trailing and tender wheels, 4 ft 6 in. dia.; wheelbase, 7 ft 7 in. plus 8 ft; overhang of frame, 5 ft 10 in. at the front, 4 ft 4 in. at the back; inclination of cylinders, 1 in 11½; inclination of the steamchest (which was underneath the cylinders) 1 in 15; boiler barrel dia. (max.), 4 ft 4 in.; length of barrel 10 ft 2 in.; grate area, 20.65 sq. ft; the barrel contained 333 flue tubes of 1½ in. dia., the heating surface of which amounted to 1,378.2 sq. ft. To this the firebox added 113.9 sq. ft, making the total no less than 1,492.1 sq. ft, which was a remarkable amount for the period. The pitch was 7 ft 5 in.

The beautiful, deep golden-yellow colour, with its dark olive-green bordering and red, black and white lining-out, produced an effect that can never be forgotten and I was somewhat horrified when in 1906, that wonderful livery was replaced by umber brown with black and yellow lining, and most of the old familiar names were removed.

The engines worked the principal expresses to Brighton, Eastbourne, Hastings and more rarely, to Portsmouth. They could go like the wind when necessary, and they could haul prodigious loads. Which brings me back to *Arundel*, the hero of an incident that is indelibly fixed in my memory.

On the Thursday before Easter of 1913, I took a train from Victoria to East Croydon, where I had to change into another train. At Victoria, there was a tremendous crowd and the train was so long that I could not see the engine. I secured a corner seat, however, and in due course we started. Up the half mile of 1 in 64 grade outside Victoria the speed dropped until we were only just moving but our engine struggled over the summit and, very gradually, began to accelerate.

The tussle was over and speed was mounting steadily. Approaching Clapham Junction, the engine cast her shadow on a lineside hoarding, and I saw that she was a "Gladstone." We stopped at East Croydon—10¼ miles, in 17 min. 40 sec. from Victoria—and I went to the front of the train to find that the engine was No 180, my old friend *Arundel*, now repainted but otherwise in original condition.

I had a word with the driver, and commented on the length of the train and the ascent of the Grosvenor Road incline. "Yes," he said, "we've got about twenty on and if I'd given her more steam up the bank, that would have stalled us; it was just touch and go!"

As No 180 left to continue her trip, I counted the coaches; there were six eight-wheelers, nine six-wheelers and eight four-wheelers, totalling about 350 tons tare and at least 380 tons gross. A tidy load for a "Gladstone" unassisted on the Grosvenor Road bank!

This performance showed what these fine engines were capable of doing; on the average, they had about 45 years' service, the first withdrawal being in 1908 and the last in 1933.

The 'GRASSHOPPER' Class

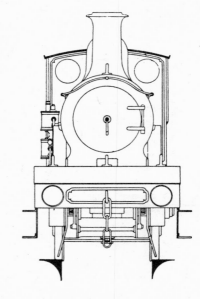

UNTIL 1895, the largest express passenger engines on the London Brighton and South Coast Railway had been six-wheelers of three different types: 2-4-0, 0-4-2 and 2-2-2. During the previous few years, however, the company, realising that the time was approaching when larger engines would be needed, went to the trouble and expense of installing longer turntables at the principal locomotive depots. Consequently, the B2 class 4-4-0 engines, now to be described, inaugurated a new era in which no more six-wheeled passenger tender engines were built. Henceforth, the only tender engines larger than 4-4-0s to be built for the LBSCR, until 1923, were Marsh Atlantics, which first appeared in December, 1905. These will be described later.

The B2 class engines were designed by Robert J. Billinton as his first express passenger engines for the LBSCR. They were also the first 4-4-0 tender engines that the old line possessed, and were quite a new departure for the Brighton.

They were graceful, slender-looking engines—which is really about all that can be said in their favour. Not that they were wholly bad, but their work was never outstanding. They were not particularly vigorous pullers and they seemed to have difficulty in getting a move on, as we say today.

The rather small boiler, combined with the four big coupled wheels produced an effect that suggested grasshoppers, and to the men—and many other people besides—the engines were known as " Grasshoppers " ever afterwards. In addition the prominent exposure of the big driving wheels was regarded at the time as rather overstepping the bounds of decorum !

The design was prepared in 1893 and, be it said, included a *smaller* boiler ! It was subsequently much improved and the first three engines, Nos 314, *Charles C. Macrae*, 315, *Duncannon* and 316, *Goldsmid*, were put to work in June 1895. Exactly 12 months later the first of 21 further engines of the class came out, the last one being put to work in January, 1898. They were intended to replace the valiant little Stroudley single-wheelers on the Portsmouth line, but did not entirely succeed in this project, as some of the singlewheelers managed to hold their own against the newcomers for nearly 12 years afterwards.

I have drawn *Goldsmid* in her original condition; she was later fitted with the automatic vacuum brake in addition to the standard Westinghouse air brake, and it entailed some extra piping which did not improve her appearance. No 202, *Trevithick*, No 206, *Smeaton* and No 208 *Abercorn* were fitted in 1901 for burning oil fuel on Holden's system which was so successful on many Great Eastern Railway locomotives at that time.

No 206 was also noteworthy for two other events in her career; on 2 October 1898, she worked the first 60-minute all-Pullman train from Victoria to Brighton, while on 24 December 1900 she was at the head of the express which, during thick fog, came into violent collision with a train that was standing on the same track in Wivelsfield station, causing some deaths and many injuries to passengers.

From about 1906 Mr D. E. Marsh turned his attention to these engines and in the endeavour to improve their performance he gradually fitted the whole lot with much larger boilers. This, however, achieved only partial success and nothing like the general improvement that had been expected; that suggests that the fundamental trouble was in the engine rather than in the boiler.

I can never forget the wonderful musical ringing given out by the coupling-rods when these engines were running; it was a characteristic of all the Billinton 4-4-0s, but was for some reason especially noticeable in the B2s. It inspired my boyish efforts as a mimic of loco noises, and was not very difficult for me to imitate.

It is strange how from time to time a locomotive engineer has seemed to lose his courage temporarily. R. J. Billinton was one of these; he had been under Stroudley at Brighton years before and then moved to the Derby Works of the Midland Railway as chief

---

```
             GENERAL   SPECIFICATION

CYLINDERS                           TUBES
   Diameter    ...     ...  18 in.     Number   ...     ...    267
   Stroke      ...     ...  26 in.     Diameter ...     ...    1⅝ in.

BOILER
   Length, between                  HEATING SURFACE
      tubeplates  10 ft 7¼ in.         Tubes   ...  1,227.34 sq. ft
   Maximum dia-                        Firebox ...   114.74 sq. ft
      meter   ...     4 ft 5 in.        Total   ... 1,342.08 sq. ft

FIREBOX LENGTH
   Inside   ...    5 ft 7¾ in.       GRATE AREA
   Outside  ...    6 ft 2¼ in.          Square feet  ...    18.73
```

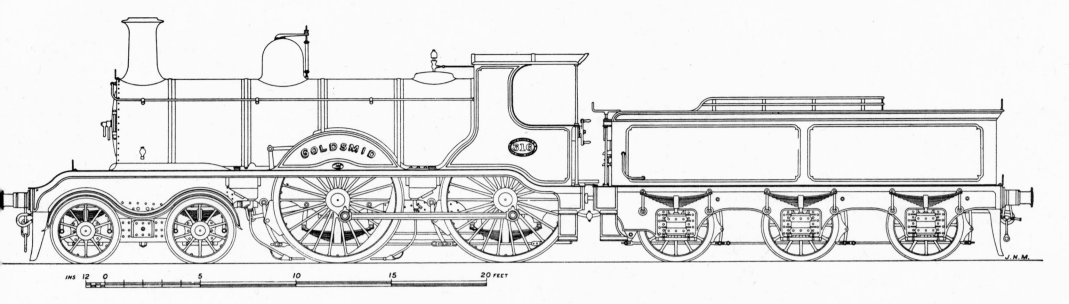

draughtsman under S. W. Johnson. Therefore, he must have been familiar with the general trends of locomotive design at that time. Yet when he returned to Brighton to become locomotive superintendent and found that there was a need for a new class of express passenger engines to follow on his predecessor's Gladstone class, he produced a design which at first was about 10 years out of date. He then modified the design, bringing it only just into line with contemporary practice before building the new engines.

His ideas changed quickly, however, because in only four years his basic 4-4-0 engine became transformed from the none-too-successful B2 class into the magnificent B4 class, of which No 70, *Holyrood*, described in the next chapter, was one. The intermediate B3 class of January 1898 consisted of only one engine, No 213, *Bessemer*, which was merely a B2 with a slightly larger boiler. She was a successful engine, but she showed quite clearly that a larger boiler was not all that was required.

The B2 class engines may not have merited a place among England's best 4-4-0s, but I had a great affection for their pleasing, graceful lines and their attractive variety of noises.

Their principal dimensions were: cylinders, 18 in. by 26 in., inclined at 1 in 20; the diameters of the wheels were 3 ft 6 in. for the bogie and 6 ft 9 in. for the four coupled wheels; the wheelbase was 6 ft

plus 7 ft 2 in. plus 10 ft 9 in., totalling 23 ft 11 in. The boiler was made in three rings, the largest of which was 4 ft 5 in. dia. outside; the length of the barrel was 10 ft 7¼ in. between tubeplates and the pitch was 7 ft 7 in. above rail level. The firebox casing was 6 ft 2¼ in. long and 4 ft 1 in. wide, and the depth was 5 ft 3 in. in front and 4 ft 9 in. at the back. There were 267 tubes of 1⅝ in. dia., the heating surface of which was 1,227.34 sq. ft. The firebox heating surface was 114.74 sq. ft, making the total 1,342.08 sq. ft. The grate area was 18.73 sq. ft.

The weight of the engine in working order was 42 tons 16 cwt, of which 28 tons 16 cwt rested on the coupled wheels. The tender wheels were 4 ft dia. and the wheelbase 13 ft equally divided, the overhang at the leading end being 4 ft 4 in. and at the back 3 ft 10½ in. The capacity was for four tons of coal and for the first three engines 2,420 gallons of water which, on the later engines was increased to 2,600.

The position of the reversing screw beyond the cab pillar applied to the first three engines only; on all the others it was 6 in. farther forward.

In all my long association with the model locomotive hobby I have never seen a model of one of these quite attractive-looking 4-4-0s. I have sometimes wondered why. There is no insurmountable difficulty to be tackled, and a model in any size from 3½ in. gauge upwards could be made to give at least as good

a performance as can be obtained from many a less attractive engine of the 4-4-0 type.

For those who believe that the small boiler could not be made to give the required amount of steam, the Marsh rebuild with a 5 ft dia. boiler offers a possible alternative, with the added advantage of greater weight for adhesion.

One of the tricky details to reproduce in a model would be the fitting of the chimney. In the prototype, the bottom flange fitted down flush with the smokebox wrapper plate. This was due to the fact that the smokebox was actually double, with a thickness of lagging between the inner and outer plates. The chimney, therefore, stood on the inner plate and projected through a hole cut in the outer plate.

So neatly was this done that I never saw a suspicion of a misfit between smokebox and chimney.

This method of fixing the chimney was used on all the Billinton engines of the LBSCR in the early 1900s and it fascinated many people. To achieve it nicely in a model calls for some careful fitting but I think it could be managed without going to the trouble of making a double smokebox.

The smokebox could be made in the usual manner and a hole cut in the upper part to take the base of the chimney. The latter could rest on a ring silver soldered to the inner surface of the wrapper-plate. The ring itself could be part of a petticoat-pipe.

B4 Class
EXPRESS ENGINES
4-4-0
The
'BUSTERS'

To the schoolboy's mind, the idea of a locomotive, aeroplane, ship or motor car being a record-breaker is irresistible, and whatever may have succeeded in breaking the record becomes, forthwith, an object of admiration and even adoration. So it was with the fine 4-4-0 engine, No 70, *Holyrood*, one of a class of 36 large and handsome express passenger engines officially styled Class B4 on the old London, Brighton and South Coast Railway.

I shall never forget Sunday, 26 July 1903, because, to a number of my very youthful friends and myself, it was one of the highlights of our very young lives; and it happened in this way:

During 1901 and 1902, these B4 class engines,

known as Busters, or Scotchmen, were being delivered to the railway, 30 of them from Sharp, Stewart and Co. of Glasgow, and six from Brighton Works. We boys were immensely impressed; we had seen nothing like them before, with their noble proportions, big

boilers, big wheels and deep, rich yellow colour. At the same time, there was a good deal of newspaper publicity about a proposed electric railway from London to Brighton, and talk about electric trains running to and from Brighton in anything between 30 and 45 minutes.

We were not in the least interested because we were seeing for ourselves that our fine, new engines were beginning to show that they could run the *Brighton Limited*, a splendid all-Pullman train, from one place to the other in considerably less than the booked 60-minute schedule.

In fact, engines 58 *Marlborough*, and 70 *Holyrood*, were openly engaged in a sort of friendly competition

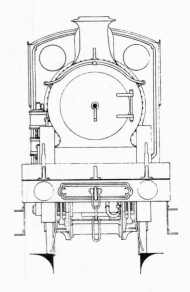

GENERAL SPECIFICATION					
CYLINDERS			**TUBES**		
Diameter	... ... 19 in.		Number	... ...	315
Stroke	... ... 26 in.		Diameter	... ...	1⅝ in.
BOILER					
Length, between			**HEATING SURFACE**		
tubeplates	10 ft 10 in.		Tubes	...	1,507 sq. ft
Maximum dia-			Firebox	...	120 sq. ft
meter	... 4 ft 10 in.		Total	...	1,627 sq. ft
FIREBOX LENGTH					
Inside	... 6 ft 11¾ in.		**GRATE AREA**		
Outside	... 7 ft 7 in.		Square feet	...	23.75

in this enterprise, and we boys heard of times of 55, 53½, 53 and 51 minutes for the journey, the last-mentioned time going to the credit of No 58 on Christmas Day, 1901. This "racing" continued throughout 1902 and into 1903, but the railway authorities appeared to take very little notice of it.

Then, at last, came an official announcement that a very special effort would be made on Sunday, 26 July 1903. The road was purposely cleared throughout, and *Holyrood*, in charge of Driver Tompsett and Outdoor Superintendent J. J. Richardson, was allowed to get to Brighton in the quickest time she could. A group of schoolboys, myself among them and all agog with excitement, had the thrill of our lives as *Holyrood*, hauling three Pullmans and two six-wheeled Pullman "pups" (special accumulator vans with electric light equipment), roared past Wandsworth Common to get to Brighton, 51 miles, in 48 minutes 41 seconds.

She returned later that day in 50 minutes 21 seconds, to become something like sacrosanct in our estimation! We talked about this memorable day for months afterwards; and so far as I am concerned, *Holyrood* still holds a place among my "special"

locomotives, remembered with an affection which, I am sure, can never be aroused by anything but a steam locomotive.

But the class as a whole, with its reputation established by exploits such as those just described, enjoyed much popularity among enthusiasts and the travelling public for nearly 40 years. For much of that time, the engines were subjected to many experiments and some considerable rebuilding; but there was no marked change in their performance.

The timetables did not call for any record-breaking speeds in the ordinary course of events; but if a special job was to be done well, then a B4 was usually selected to do it. The Brighton main line did not offer much opportunity for recovering lost time; but in my own experience, I have twice known a B4 to regain four minutes lost by delays in the early part of a run from Victoria to Brighton. In the opposite, and harder, direction, No 42, *His Majesty*, on one occasion, left Brighton with a 275-ton train all but seven minutes late and stopped in Victoria station within 15 seconds of right time, covering the 51 miles of really hard going in 54¼ minutes.

These engines had cylinders 19 in. by 26 in.,

inclined at an angle of 1 in 9½; the valvechest was between them, and the valves were of the flat type operated by Stephenson link motion. The wheel diameters were, bogie 3 ft 6 in., coupled 6 ft 9 in., and the wheelbase was 22 ft 2 in., divided into 6 ft plus 7 ft 5 in. plus 8 ft 9 in.; the overhangs were 2 ft 9 in. at the front and 4 ft 6 in. at the back.

The boiler was pitched 8 ft 3 in. above rail level; the barrel was made in two rings, the outside diameter of the larger of which was 4 ft 10 in.; the barrel length was 10 ft 10 in., and the diameter outside the clothing plates and smokebox wrapper was 5 ft 1½ in. The width over the cab sides was 6 ft 10¼ in.; over the driving splashers it was 5 ft 11¾ in., and the maximum over the running plate was the somewhat odd dimension of 7 ft 11⅝ in.

The tender was large enough to carry six tons of coal and 3,000 gallons of water; it was mounted on six 4 ft wheels spaced 6 ft 6 in. centre to centre, and the overhangs were 3 ft 3 in. at the front and 3 ft 9 in. at the back.

All these fine engines are now scrapped, the last one in 1951; but to all who can remember them in 1903, the memory is evergreen!

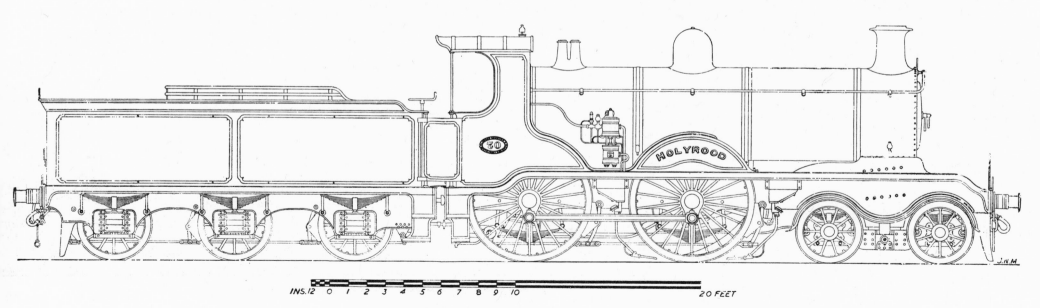

INS. 12 0 1 2 3 4 5 6 7 8 9 10   20 FEET

The BRIGHTON ATLANTICS

IN January, 1905, Mr D. E. Marsh was appointed Locomotive Superintendent at Brighton in succession to Robt J. Billinton, who had died in the previous November. Unlike his predecessor, Mr Marsh designed a new class of express passenger engine which appeared to be far larger than was required for any traffic that the old Brighton Railway was operating.

Mr Marsh's previous job had been that of chief assistant to Mr H. A. Ivatt, at Doncaster on the Great Northern Railway, and his first design for the Brighton was, apart from a distinctly Brightonian chimney, cab and tender, practically identical with Mr Ivatt's large-boilered Atlantics for the GNR.

Five of the new engines, built by Kitson and Co. of Leeds, were delivered to the LBSCR between December 1905 and February 1906. They created quite a sensation, and the first reaction of Brighton enthusiasts was: What on earth can the Brighton line find for such engines to do ? The engines themselves soon supplied the answer to that question; for it was found that they were capable of keeping time on the best and fastest trains, with the loads augmented by

anything up to about 200 tons. They were designated Class H1.

Five years later, in 1910, an order was placed in the Brighton Works for a further six of these engines. Mr Marsh, however, retired at the end of that year and was succeeded by Lawson B. Billinton, son of Robt J., who assumed office under the title of Chief Mechanical Engineer, and was the first and last officer of that title on the LBSCR. Work on the new Atlantics was temporarily suspended while Billinton ran his eye, so to speak, over the Marsh design. He tidied up the external details somewhat, by substituting a chimney of his own design, extending the cab roof by about 15 in. to the rear of the pillars, and, more particularly, smoothing out the run of the footplating which, in the March engines, contrived to reach five different levels in its progress from front to back of the engine ! Billinton's footplating reached only three, and being continuous, the effect was neater and more pleasing.

The construction of the new engines was resumed, and the opportunity was taken of providing them with superheaters, which the earlier engines had lacked. These six engines were Class H2; they were numbered 421 to 426, and the first one has been taken as the subject of my drawing. She is seen to be not quite in her original condition ; in 1911, she had been turned out with brakes on the bogie, and with a small steam cylinder mounted on the side of the smokebox, for the purpose of operating dampers for the superheater. I have shown her as she was when

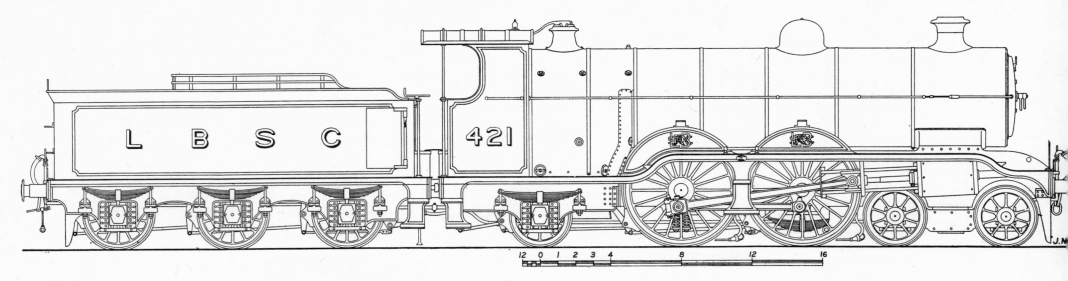

I got to know her really well about 1919, by which time the bothersome bogie brakes and superheater dampers had long since been discarded—which is just as well, because those two monograms with which her splashers were adorned have given me trouble enough in drawing! They were later replaced by coats-of-arms.

The following dimensions were common to both classes H1 and H2. The wheel diameters were: bogie and trailing, 3 ft 6 in.; coupled, 6 ft 7½ in.; wheel-base, 6 ft 3 in. plus 5 ft 3 in. plus 6 ft 10 in. plus 8 ft, totalling 26 ft 4 in. The overhang was 2 ft 6½ in. at the front and 5 ft 7 in. at the back. The boiler was pitched 8 ft 8½ in. above rail level; the barrel was made in two rings, the larger of which was 5 ft 6 in. outside diameter; the barrel length was 16 ft 3⅞ in. The firebox was 6 ft 9¾ in. long and 5 ft, 11 in. wide outside, and the grate area was 30.95 sq. ft.

The tender was carried on six wheels, 3 ft 9 in. diameter, the wheelbase being the usual 13 ft equally divided; its overhang was 4 ft 10 in. in front and 3 ft 10½ in. at the back. The capacity was for 4 tons of coal and 3,500 gallons of water, and the weight in working trim was 29 tons 10 cwt. The total length of engine and tender over buffers was 59 ft 9 in.

The variable dimensions, as between the two classes, are best given separately. For Class H1, the boiler contained 248 tubes, 2¼ in. dia.; they were of steel, but each had a length of 6 in. of copper welded on at the firebox end, to forestall any possible electrolitic action between the steel tubes and the copper firebox tubeplate. The total heating surface was 2,473.5 sq. ft, the tubes accounting for 2,337.1 sq. ft and the firebox for 136.4 sq. ft. The working pressure was 200 p.s.i.

The engine weighed 68 tons 10 cwt, distributed thus: 16 tons 5 cwt on the bogie, 38 tons 10 cwt equally divided between the coupled wheels, and and 13 tons 15 cwt on the trailing wheels.

For Class H2, the boiler contained 143 tubes of 2¼ in. dia., and 24 superheater flues of 5½ in. dia., the heating surfaces of which were 1,348 and 547 sq. ft respectively. The heating surface of the firebox was as before, 136 sq. ft, so the total amounted to 2,031 sq. ft. The working pressure was 170 p.s.i.

The cylinders were 21 in. dia., 26 in. stroke and had 10 in. piston valves operated, as before, by Stephenson link-motion arranged to give a travel of $4\frac{11}{16}$ in. The weight of the engine remained unaltered at 68 tons 10 cwt, but the distribution was now 17 tons 10 cwt on the bogie, 37 tons 10 cwt on the coupled wheels and 13 tons 10 cwt on the trailing wheels.

These fine, big, bold, smooth-surfaced locomotives greatly appealed to me, right from the beginning. Eventually, however, they achieved rather a melancholy record; for they were the last Atlantics to be designed for a British railway, the last and only express passenger tender engines designed by Mr Marsh, and No 424, as British Railways No 32424, *Beachy Head*, was the last Atlantic to run in Britain.

The work of these engines was always good, but I feel that, on a line like the LBSCR, they had no chance to show what they really could do, and it is a pity that there was never any opportunity to arrange an exchange-trial between an H2 and one of her ever-celebrated Great Northern sisters.

No 39, of Class H1, seemed to carry off most of the honours won by these engines. On Sunday, 30 June 1907, she made a splendid run from Victoria to Brighton with the Pullman Limited made up of five 8-wheeled and two 12-wheeled cars plus two 6-wheeled Pullman " Pups," totalling about 245 tons. In spite of severe checks near Earlswood, due to widening of the line being then in progress, she ran the 50½ miles in 51 min. 48 sec., start to stop, reaching a maximum speed of 86½ m.p.h. between Balcombe and Wivelsfield.

On 1 November 1908, the same engine was used to work the inaugural trip of that most-beloved luxurious and ever-popular all-Pullman train, the Southern Belle, and she was often to be seen on it for many years afterwards. In those days, the " Belle " was a train well worth seeing and travelling in; its successor, the present-day " electric ' Belle ' " is a mere travesty!

In 1909, No 39 was honoured by being given a name, *La France*, for working the special train which conveyed M. Raymond Poincare, President of France, on a State visit to London. No 39 retained her name until 1923, and for several years, was always used for any Royal specials on the LBSCR.

No 421, of Class H2, ran for about three years, after she first took the road in July 1911, painted dove-grey picked out with black bands and white lining; she looked very well like that, but was subsequently re-painted in the standard umber livery. But no matter what they were painted, they were all grand engines that I was pleased to know. In 1923, the Southern Railway named all these Atlantics after south-coast headlands.

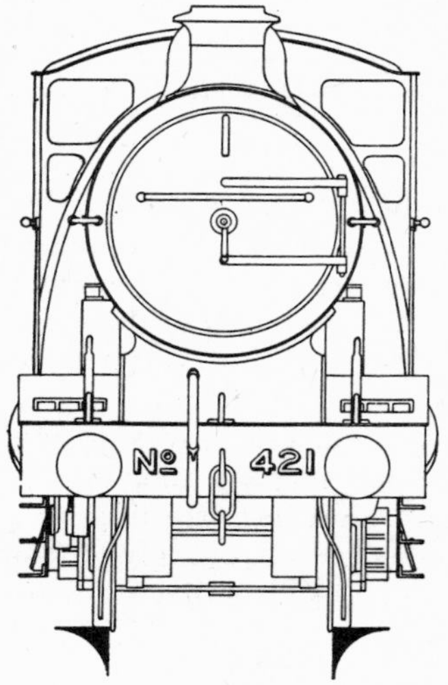

GENERAL SPECIFICATION

CYLINDER		**TUBES**	
Diameter	21 in.	Number ...	143 & 24
Stroke	26 in.	Diameter	2¼ in. & 5½ in.
BOILER		**HEATING SURFACE**	
Length, between tubeplates	16 ft 3⅞ in.	Tubes ...	1,895 sq. ft
Maximum diameter ...	5 ft 6 in.	Firebox ...	136.47 sq. ft
		Total ...	2,031.47 sq. ft
FIREBOX LENGTH		**GRATE AREA**	
Inside ...	5 ft 11 in.	Square feet ...	30.95
Outside ...	6 ft 9¾ in.		

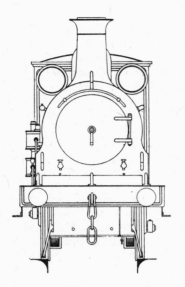

STROUDLEY'S 'BIG JUMBO'
Goods Engines

GENERAL SPECIFICATION			
CYLINDERS		**TUBES**	
Diameter ... ... 18¼ in.		Number ... ... ·317	
Stroke ... ... 26 in.		Diameter ... ... 1½ in.	
BOILER			
Length, between tubeplates 10 ft 2 in.		**HEATING SURFACE**	
		Tubes ... 1,312 sq. ft	
Maximum dia-meter ... 4 ft 8 in.		Firebox ... 101 sq. ft	
		Total ... 1,413 sq. ft	
FIREBOX LENGTH			
Inside ... 5 ft 7¾ in.		**GRATE AREA**	
Outside ... 6 ft 8¼ in.		Square feet ... 20.95	

BETWEEN 1882 and 1887, W. Stroudley, who loved to do things on a big scale, built 12 very fine 0-6-0 tender engines, primarily for working the heaviest goods trains on the LBSCR.

The engines, known as the Large C class, were numbered 421 to 432 and were built in three batches: Nos 421 to 426 between June and November, 1882; Nos 427 to 429 in May, 1884, and Nos 430 to 432 in June 1887. At the time, these were the largest 0-6-0s that had been seen on a British railway, and their advent caused considerable interest in railway circles.

Officially, this class was designated C1; to the staff the engines were known as Jumbos, with a certain amount of justification. They were the most powerful engines on the line, if not in the country, when they were new, and they worked the heaviest goods trains with unqualified success. At the same time, they were all fitted with the Westinghouse air brake so that they could be used on passenger trains when required.

As a boy, I was much impressed by these engines; their boilers were the largest that Stroudley ever designed, which gave the engines a grand, massive aspect that could hardly fail to attract attention. In later years, I often regretted that nobody, apparently, thought of rebuilding the 0-4-2 Gladstones with C1

boilers; there would have been no difficulty, from the technical point of view, but probably the weight would have been too great for the frames. In any case, the centre line would have had to be pitched higher, so as to clear the 6 ft 6 in. coupled wheels, and that may have been one of the reasons why the big Jumbo boiler was never used for the Gladstones.

The C1 class engines had the following dimensions: cylinders 18¼ in. dia. and 26 in. stroke, cast together in one piece with the steam chest which was underneath the cylinders; it was, in fact, the same casting as was used in the Gladstone class. The inclination of the cylinders, downwards from the front, was 1 in 11½, while that of the valves, upwards, was 1 in 15; this arrangement gave a direct drive from the main cranks, as well as from the valve eccentrics to the valves, and did away with any necessity for rocking shafts.

The steam ports were 1⅜ in. × 15 in. and the exhaust ports 2 in. × 15 in., the latter being somewhat on the small side for such large cylinders; but since the engines were not intended to run at express train speeds, the comparatively small exhaust ports would probably be no handicap.

The main frames were of steel, 1 in. thick, and the wheels were 5 ft dia. The wheelbase was 15 ft 3 in.

divided into 7 ft 9 in. plus 7 ft 6 in., and the overhangs were 5 ft 1½ in. at the front, and 5 ft 10¼ in. at the back, the total length of the frames being 26 ft 2¾ in.

The boiler barrel was made in three rings, 4 ft 5¾ in., 4 ft 6⅞ in. and 4 ft 8 in. dia., respectively; its length was 10 ft 2 in. and its centre line was 7 ft 1 in. above rail level. A big firebox, 6 ft 8¼ in. long and 4 ft 1 in. wide, was provided; the grate sloped steeply, being 5 ft deep at the front, rising to 3 ft 4 in. depth at the back so as to clear the trailing axle. The grate area was 20.95 sq. ft.

There were 317 tubes of 1½ in. dia., giving a heating surface of 1,312 sq. ft; the heating surface of the firebox was 101 sq. ft so that the total amounted to 1,413 sq. ft. As was customary on Stroudley's engines, the dome was mounted on the back ring of the boiler barrel, and carried two salter spring balanced safety valves set to blow at 150 p.s.i.

In working order, the engine weight was 40 tons 7 cwt, the leading axle supporting 13 tons 14 cwt, the driving axle 14 tons, and the trailing axle 12 tons 13 cwt; these weights are surprisingly low for such a large engine, but none of Stroudley's engines was really heavy.

Another interesting point was that the 12 engines

of this class had only ten tenders between them, and all these were secondhand. This was due to the fact that the singlewheelers *Grosvenor* and *Abergavenny*, four of the 6 ft 6 in. 0-4-2 engines of Class D3 and four of the 5 ft 6 in. engines of class D2 had all acquired new tenders of the standard inside framed passenger type, releasing the former outside framed tenders for use on the C1 goods engines. About ten years later, C1 class engine No 423 was supplied with one of the inside framed passenger tenders from an engine that had been scrapped, thereby reducing the deficiency to one. Fully loaded, the outside framed tender weighed 32 tons 15 cwt, so that the total weight of an engine and tender, was 73 tons 2 cwt.

These tenders, by the way, were quite interesting, and it is worth noting that, when Dugald Drummond left the post of Stroudley's chief draughtsman at Brighton, to become locomotive engineer of the North British Railway, he adopted precisely the same type of tender. The capacity was for 2,520 gallons of water and 6½ tons of coal; the wheelbase was 12 ft equally divided, and the overhangs were 4 ft 3¼ in. in front and 3 ft 9¼ in. at the back. The overall length of engine and tender was 48 ft 7 in.

The C1 class engines were painted in the usual goods engine livery, which was a dark olive green picked out with black striping, having a fine red line

on each side of it in the case of those engines equipped with the Westinghouse brake. Except for the fine copper cap for the chimney, decoration was not lavish. The wheels were olive green with black tyres, and the axle ends, where they showed in the bosses, were black. A nice little touch was that the coupling rods were painted olive green along their length up to within 3 in. of the coupling rod pins, where they were left bright.

The reach rod was bright steel, and I must add that in engines 421 to 426 it was behind the firebox lagging, emerging into view just above the driving splasher; in engines 427 to 432, it was outside the lagging, as seen in my drawing. The buffer-beams were vermilion with a narrow black margin having a white line on its inner edge, the buffer sockets were olive green with black striping and red lines.

The numberplates were brass castings, the company's title set between two oval black lines, being rendered in sunk black letters on the polished border; the figures of the engine's number were slightly raised and polished on a sky blue background. On the tender coping, at the back, the engine's number appeared in beautiful little hand painted miniatures of the figures on the numberplates.

The main frames of the engine were black; those of the tender were olive green with the edges and

cutouts bordered with a narrow black stripe and red line. The coal well, top of the tender tank and the exhaust steam dome were painted red oxide colour, just the plain shop colour without any special finish. The inside of the cab was light brown, down to waist level, and black below that.

These very fine 0-6-0s were not very often to be seen; they seemed to do most of their work at night, and matters were not helped by the fact that by no means all the class was stationed in London. A few were at Battersea and New Cross, but the rest were at Brighton and Portsmouth (Fratton), and possibly some of these did not come nearer to London than Norwood yards.

No 428 was sold to the Stratford-on-Avon and Midland Junction Railway in 1920, eventually becoming LMSR No 2303; I used to see her sometimes at Fenny Compton, when on my way to Birmingham. On the SMJR she was No. 7.

In December 1914, No 430 was used to work a special troop train all the way from Brighton to Doncaster, Yorks, via London Bridge, Metropolitan Junction, Farringdon Street and Kings Cross. The same engine was the last survivor of this class, remaining in service until 1925, whereas all the others, except No 428, had been withdrawn between 1907 and 1911.

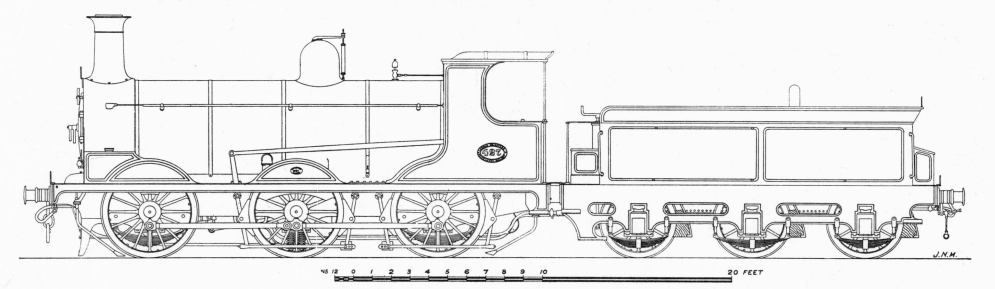

NS 12 0 1 2 3 4 5 6 7 8 9 10   20 FEET

THE BRIGHTON CLASS K MOGULS

WHEN, in 1911, G. J. Churchward brought out the first of his 4300 class 2-6-0 type mixed-traffic locomotives on the Great Western Railway, he inaugurated a type that appealed very strongly to the chief mechanical engineers of several other railways, who were not slow in noting the advantages of a moderately dimensioned general-purpose engine with a very wide scope; large numbers of such engines were built for British railways during the next 25 years or so.

Among the locomotive chiefs who were attracted by the engine was L. B. Billinton, of the London Brighton and South Coast Railway. He was contemplating the introduction of some engines to cope particularly with the fast Continental freight trains between London and Newhaven; their loads were rapidly becoming more than the existing goods engines could manage successfully.

Billinton saw in the new GWR engines exactly the sort of thing he needed, and he set to work on the preparation of the design for his 2-6-0 engines of Class K; meanwhile his choice was fully vindicated

by the excellent results that were obtained, not only from the GWR engines, but also from ten 2-6-0 fast freight engines that H. N. Gresley put into service on the Great Northern Railway in 1912.

The first Brighton example of this type was No 337, which was put into traffic in September 1913. . She was followed by No 338 in December of the same year, and by 339 in March, 340 in July, and 341 in November of 1914, the last taking the road some two months after the 1914-18 war had broken out. The engines proved to be so successful that special

permission was obtained from the Government for the construction of some more of the same class, with the result that another five, numbered 342 to 346, were added to the class between October and December 1916.

These ten proved to be invaluable on war work, for they were capable of hauling trains of munitions and other military equipment weighing up to 1,000 tons or more at speeds of 35-40 m.p.h.; moreover, they were unusually economical in fuel consumption, and their ability to accelerate rapidly from a standstill was especially remarkable.

After the war, and with the return of something approaching normal peacetime conditions the engines proved themselves thoroughly efficient on fast passenger trains; so much so that another four, Nos 347 to 350, were built in 1920, to be followed by a further three, Nos 351 to 353, in 1921.

After the grouping of railways in 1922, all 17 of Class K were taken into Southern Railway stock. They made themselves thoroughly useful to their new owners.

20

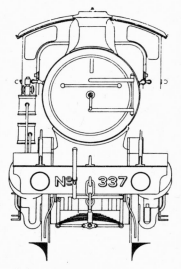

No 337

Drawing unfinished

GENERAL SPECIFICATION

CYLINDERS			TUBES		
Diameter	...	... 21 in.	Number	...	110 & 21
Stroke	...	... 26 in.	Diameter	2¼ in. & 5½ in.	
BOILER			HEATING SURFACE		
Length between		—	Tubes	...	1,155 sq. ft.
tubeplates ...			Firebox	...	139 sq. ft.
Maximum diameter	5 ft 3 in.		Total (including		
			superheater)	1,573 sq. ft.	
FIREBOX LENGTH					
Inside	...	7 ft 4½ in.	GRATE AREA		
Outside	...	... 8 ft.	Square feet	...	... 24.8

To widen the scope of their operations, R. E. L. Maunsell lowered the chimney height, flattened the top of the dome, and radiused the cab roof into the top of the cabsides, so as to clear the minimum loading gauge of the Southern Railway; but so far as I know, Class K was seldom seen far outside what had formerly been the LBSCR system, except at Salisbury, on the through trains from Brighton to South Wales. On heavy extra trains to the south-coast resorts at holiday times and week-ends, the engines were particularly useful; at such times, I noted as many as 12, out of the 17 engaged on such work in the course of not more than six hours' observation.

The Ks were the most powerful engines on the Brighton Railway, in practice as well as in theory. Their leading wheels were 3 ft 6 in. dia., the coupled 5 ft 6 in., and the tender 3 ft 9 in. The wheelbase of the engine was 23 ft 9 in., divided into 8 ft 3 in. plus 8 ft plus 7 ft 9 in.; that of the tender was 13 ft equally divided, and the total for engine and tender

was 47 ft 11 in. At the front, the overhang of the engine was 2 ft 6½ in., and at the back 5 ft 9 in.; for the tender, the overhang was 4 ft 9 in. at the front and 3 ft 9 in. at the back. Over the bufferheads, the total length was 57 ft 10 in.

The cylinders were large, with a diameter of 21 in. and a stroke of 26 in.; they had 10 in. piston valves actuated by Stephenson link motion with the weighshaft above and the expansion links suspended on the centre-line of drive. The link pins were 1 ft 6 in. apart on the curved centre-line of the link.

I have based my drawings on the working drawings published in *The Engineer* for January 30, 1914, from which it is clear that certain modifications were decided upon during construction. For example, the drawings show, in elevation and plan, a large sandbox incorporated in the leading splasher, but the engines did not have this; and the drawings show no forward extension of the piston-rods, whereas the engines were provided with it.

The boiler was pitched 8 ft 6 in. from rail level; the barrel was made in two rings, 5 ft 1¾ in. and 5 ft 3 in. dia. outside. There were 110 tubes of

2¼ in. dia. and 21 of 5½ in. dia., their combined heating surface being 1,155 sq. ft. The superheater tubes were 1½ in. dia., outside. They had a heating surface of 279 sq. ft.

It was on these engines that the Belpaire firebox was first introduced on the Brighton Railway. Its outer casing was 8 ft long, and the inner one 7 ft 4½ in.; the width, inside, was 3 ft 4¹¹⁄₁₆ in. at the grate, and the heating surface was 139 sq. ft, while the grate area was 24.8 sq. ft.

The tender was of quite a new design for the Brighton; it had outside slotted frames and its capacity was for 3,940 gallons of water and four tons of coal. It was provided with a tall steam dome where some of the exhaust steam from the engine was led into a pipe that reached almost to the top of the dome, inside, and allowed the steam to flow down outside the pipe to spread over the surface of the water in the tanks, and so heat the water for feeding the boiler, as in Stroudley's system.

In working order, the engine weighed 63 tons 15 cwt, of which no less than 55 tons 5 cwt was available for adhesion. The tender weighed 41 tons 10 cwt, making the total 105 tons 5 cwt.

In 1916, Billinton introduced his system of top-feed for the boilers. It had two distinct arrangements. The first consisted of mounting the clacks on top of a manhole about 3 ft ahead of the dome; the second consisted of providing a second dome mounted on the boiler barrel, exactly on the vertical centre-line through the leading coupled-wheels, with the clacks placed high up on its back. Engines 342 to 346 were built with the first arrangement, and 337, 338, 340 and 341 were fitted with it later. No 339 was given the second arrangement in February 1920, and 347 to 353 had it when they were built later in that year.

They passed to British Railways ownership in 1948.

(The class Ks were still in service in 1961 having recently undergone major overhauls.)

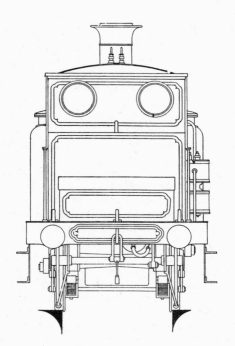

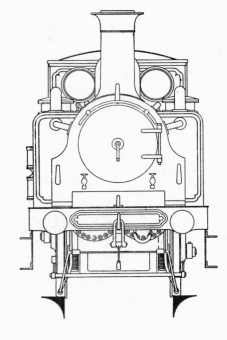

GENERAL SPECIFICATION

CYLINDERS				TUBES			
Diameter	...	...	17 in.	Number	...	...	175
Stroke	...	...	24 in.	Diameter	...	...	1¾ in.

BOILER			HEATING SURFACE			
Length, between			Tubes	...	952 sq. ft
tubeplates		10 ft 2 in.	Firebox	...	91 sq. ft
Maximum diameter		4 ft	Total	...	1,043 sq. ft

FIREBOX LENGTH			GRATE AREA			
Inside	...	4 ft 7 in.	Square feet	...	...	15
Outside	...	5 ft 2¼ in.				

The D1 Class 0-4-2 TANKS

O F all the smaller tank locomotives that at one time worked the intensive local services in the London suburbs, William Stroudley's 0-4-2 type for the LBSCR can be given a prominent place among the favourites.

To me, perhaps the best-loved were the very smart little 2-4-0 tank engines of the Great Western Railway, though the Brighton engines ran them a close second, for I knew so many of them long before I became familiar with the GWR engines.

On 25 November 1873 No 1 *Sydenham*, the first of Stroudley's D1 class 0-4-2 tanks was completed at Brighton Works and put into traffic; subsequently, batches of them, varying from six to 12 or more a year, were built until March, 1887, when the last one was completed, bringing their total number to 125. Of these, 34 were constructed by Neilson and Company, of Glasgow, in 1881-2; all the others were built at Brighton.

Although these engines were primarily intended for working the London suburban passenger service, they were to be found in numbers a l over the Brighton system, working local passenger traffic and, very often,

some of the longer-distance secondary passenger trains.

It did not seem to matter what sort of traffic these engines worked; they always did it with complete success. Their limited water supply, however, meant that when they were on long-distance main line work they had to stop to take water about every 30 miles or so. On purely suburban work, however, they gave exemplary service, even when working against later more powerful engines.

There was nothing particularly outstanding in their dimensions. They were simply good examples of the engine required for the kind of work they did.

Their long life is evidence enough of the soundness of their design and the very fine quality of workmanship put into their construction. With it all, they were endearing little engines loved by passengers, specialists and enthusiasts for more than 40 years.

The Brighton was a railway that carried an enormous number of regular passengers who were quick to give vent to their disapproval of anything that displeased them, but were ready to defend their railway to the last ditch against any criticism from outsiders. Anyone rash enough to make derogatory remarks about the D1 tank engines, for example, would soon be told enough to cause him to change his mind !

The mere fact that there were 125 of this class, is a sufficient indication of their general excellence.

The dimensions were quite normal: Cylinders, 17 in. dia. by 24 in. stroke, inclined at an angle of 1 in 11½ and spaced 2 ft 2 in. apart; the ports were arranged in two groups, one above the other, and each 7½ in. long; the steam ports were 1½ in. wide and the exhaust ports 2½ in. The exhaust from the lower ports was taken round the outside of the cylinders, and this arrangement, coupled with the fact that half the exhaust steam was turned into the tanks so as to heat the feed water, accounted for the very characteristic soft-sounding exhaust beats.

The diameter of the coupled wheels was 5 ft 6 in., and of the trailing wheels 4 ft 6 in. The wheelbase was 15 ft, divided into 7 ft 7 in. and 7 ft 5 in.; the overhang at the front was 5 ft 11¼ in. and at the back 7 ft 10¼ in. The total length over buffers was 31 ft 7½ in., and the height to the top of the chimney 13 ft.

The boiler was made in three rings, the diameter of the largest being 4 ft. The length of the barrel was 10 ft 2 in. and its pitch 6 ft 11 in. Originally, there were 175 tubes of 1¾ in. dia., giving 952 sq. ft of heating surface, to which the firebox added 91 sq. ft, to make a total of 1,043 sq. ft. The grate area was 15 sq. ft. and the working pressure 150 p.s.i.

Subsequently, these boilers were replaced by new ones of the same diameter and length as the old ones, but containing 207 tubes of 1⅝ in. dia., giving 924.57 sq. ft of heating surface augmented by 82.06 sq. ft. for the firebox and totalling 1,006.63 sq. ft. The pressure was unaltered.

The first dozen or so of these new boilers had the dome, with the safety valves on it, mounted on the middle ring; but in later ones the dome reverted to its original and more logical position on the back ring.

When these new boilers were fitted, the feed-heating pipes were usually removed and the whole of the exhaust steam from the cylinders was turned up the chimney. But even so, many years later, when boilers of Mr D. E. Marsh's design were fitted, it was noticeable that many of the engines so treated managed to retain the feed-heating arrangement.

The capacity of the tanks was 860 gal., and of the coal bunker 30 cwt. The total weight in working order was 38 tons 10 cwt, 27 tons being equally divided between the driving and coupled wheels.

The running numbers of this class were: 1 to 36; 221 to 297 and 351 to 362. Of these, Nos 233 to 267 were built by Nielsons. The names were entirely characteristic, being after London boroughs, suburbs, country towns and villages, with one or two engineering notabilities put in as make weight!

It is worth mentioning that engine No 25, *Rotherfield*, was the first on the LBSCR to be fitted with the Westinghouse air brake when she was new in March 1876, after which it was fitted to all passenger engines and most of the goods engines on the line.

I enjoyed many runs behind engines of this celebrated class—on slow as well as fast trains—especially during my years at Edenbridge.

Their work was generally excellent, though sometimes, when running fast, they set up an uncomfortable fore-and-aft surging that could be felt even in the rear coaches of the train, and I have often speculated on the cause. Probably, the reversing gear was wound up a little too far—beyond the " kicking point," as it is called—but if that was the case, why didn't the driver correct it? He must have felt it as much as, if not more than, the passengers. There is, of course, the possibility that the rather steep inclination of the cylinders may have had some influence in causing the surge, in which case there was little the driver could do.

However, these engines and their work were one of the real highlights of my long experience as a locomotive enthusiast, and I always recall them with pleasure. The last survivor, No 252, was withdrawn in August, 1950.

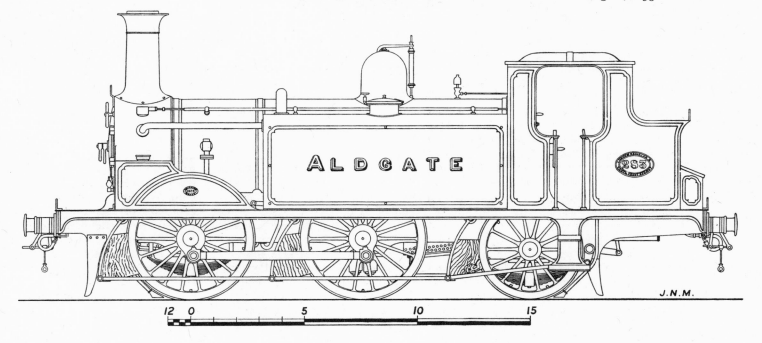

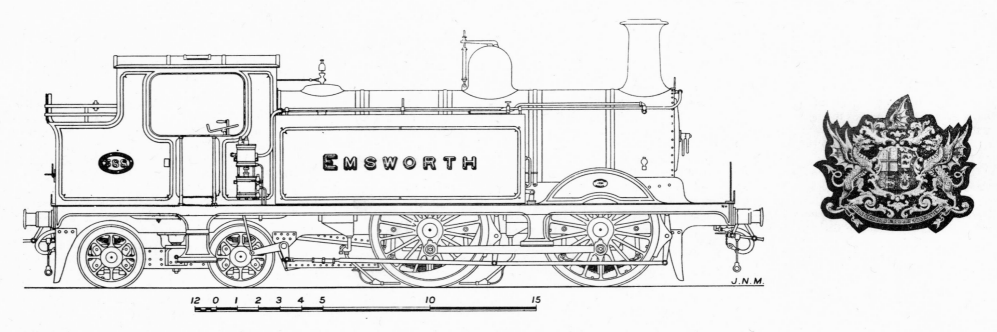

12 0 1 2 3 4 5   10   15

J.N.M.

BILLINTON'S 0-4-4 TANKS—*One destroyed an enemy aircraft*

AMONG the various designs of 0-4-4 tank engines that were employed on several British railways, R. J. Billinton's D3 class for the old London Brighton and South Coast Railway were well known and not without interest, if only because, in having four coupled wheels in front and a trailing bogie, they were an entirely new type for the Brighton line, and were the first locomotives to be designed and built by R. J. Billinton.

There were 36 of them, all built at Brighton, the first in May 1892, and the last in November 1896. While they were officially styled class D3, they were more often referred to as the " D bogie " class. They were principally used on outer suburban and secondary main line passenger trains, some of them travelling quite considerable distances in the course of a day's work. For example, No 388 *Emsworth* was stationed at New Cross for many years, and she frequently worked a morning semi-fast train to Brighton; in the afternoon she would take a train from Brighton

to Portsmouth and back, returning to London in the evening. On this turn she covered something like 180 miles per day.

The engines were numbered 363 to 398 and, with certain exceptions, were named after places in Surrey, Sussex and Hampshire. Until September 1895, No 363 was named *Goldsmid*, and a representation of her was embossed on the copper cap-badge worn by LBSCR enginemen from 1893 until 1923. When the 4-4-0 express engine No 316 *Goldsmid* was built in 1895, No 363 had her name changed to *Havant*; but the cap-badge remained unaltered.

No 366 was unfortunate in being named *Crystal Palace*, one of the really ridiculous examples of engine naming; but it was never altered, in spite of its frequently arousing sarcastic comment ! Perhaps it is as well that this engine was not often seen in London ; she was stationed at Portsmouth, and seemed to confine her activities to the Portsmouth-Brighton-Eastbourne traffic.

No 365, formerly *Victoria*, achieved unique distinction, in her last years, by becoming the only railway engine ever known to have destroyed an enemy aircraft. It happened on November 28, 1942, when she was working a train on the coast line between Brighton and Chichester ; she was seen by the pilot of a raiding enemy aircraft who, with his machine gun in action, came down low to attack. Apparently he misjudged his altitude, and as he swooped over the train some projection on the aeroplane collided with No 365's dome, which was knocked off. The explosion of steam from the engine's boiler overturned the plane which crashed in a nearby field and was totally wrecked ; the pilot died of injuries. I am glad to be able to add that No 365's crew were not seriously hurt and the engine sustained only superficial damage; she was repaired and, a few months later, was back in service.

On these rather attractive engines the cylinders had a diameter of 18 in. and were inclined at an

24

angle of 1 in 9½; the stroke was 26 in. The steamchest was between the cylinders, but to gain a little room it was inclined at 1 in 7¾. While the arrangement of the Stephenson link motion was the same as on the Stroudley 0-4-2 tank engines, it had two balance-weights carried on arms integral with the weighshaft, and was reversed by wheel-and-screw gear.

Leading and driving wheels were 5 ft 6 in. in diameter, and the bogie 3 ft. The wheelbase was 22 ft 10 in., divided into 8 ft plus 8 ft 10 in. plus 6 ft, and the overhang was 6 ft 1½ in. in front and 2 ft 7½ in. at the back. The frame length was 31 ft 7 in. Over buffers, the length was 34 ft 7 in.

The boiler was made in three rings of ½ in. plate, 4 ft 1 in., 4 ft 2 in. and 4 ft 3 in. in diameter, while the length of the barrel was 10 ft 4¼ in.; between tubeplates, the length was 10 ft 7¾ in. The firebox casing was 5 ft 8¼ in. long and 4 ft 1 in. wide; the inner box was 5 ft long and 3 ft 5¾ in. wide, and the grate was 5 ft 2 in. deep at the front and 4 ft 8 in. at the back. Grate area was officially given as 17.083 sq. ft and working pressure as 160 p.s.i.

There were 242 tubes of 1⅝ in. dia., with a heating surface of 1,106.44 sq. ft, to which the firebox added 99 sq. ft, making the total 1,205.44. The boiler became a standard one and was incorporated in the original design of Billinton's 4-4-0 express engines of class B2 (*Locomotives I Have Known*); but Billinton changed his mind and adopted a rather larger one for the B2s. On the 0-4-4 tanks the boiler centre-line was 7 ft 4⁵⁄₁₆ in. above rail level.

Bunker capacity was for 2 tons of coal; but the official figures for water capacity were unusually meticulous and I quote them as a matter of interest: the side tanks carried 884.86 gallons, and the tank under the bunker 262.25 gallons. The tanks were connected together by three pipes, whose combined capacity was 14.3 gallons; therefore, a total amount of 1,161.41 gallons of water was carried. I cannot think of any other instance where water capacity was officially given to two places of decimals, and I can only believe that the figures are the result of drawing-office calculations !

The weight of the engines in working order was 48 tons 9 cwt, divided into 14 tons 17 cwt on the leading wheels, 16 tons 13 cwt on the driving wheels and 16 tons 19 cwt on the bogie. Adhesion weight was 31 tons 10 cwt, not quite two-thirds of the total weight. The engines were equipped with duplex injectors, Gresham and Craven steam sanding gear and the Westinghouse air brake. Nos 367 to 374 and 379 had the automatic vacuum brake in addition. The class was the only one of R. J. Billinton's design to have the brake rigging outside the wheels.

All the engines were reboilered by D. E. Marsh after 1905. They received boilers of Marsh's design, but of very similar dimensions to the original ones, and the Billinton chimney was replaced by Marsh's standard cast-iron one. In 1909, Nos 397 and 398 were rebuilt with large Marsh boilers, to become class D3X, but these were the only two.

The engines all became Southern Railway property at the grouping in 1923. No 366, formerly *Crystal Palace*, was fitted with push-pull gear in 1933, for trial on auto-train working, and she was so successful that most of the other engines of the class were similarly altered; the exceptions, other than Nos 397 and 398 of the D3X class, were 369, 375, 381, 382 and 392, withdrawn from service. The rest continued for several years on auto-trains, mainly in the Brighton, Eastbourne, Portsmouth, Three Bridges and Tunbridge Wells districts; but they were gradually withdrawn until the last survivor, No 390, was taken out of service in 1955. By that time she was BR No 32390 and was stationed at Brighton for working on the Horsham line; she had outlived all her sisters by more than three years when she was withdrawn in September 1955.

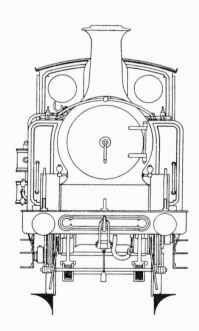

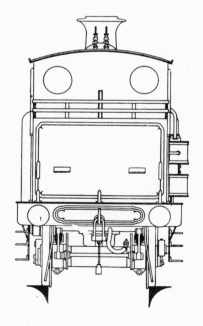

GENERAL SPECIFICATION

CYLINDERS			TUBES		
Diameter	...	... 18 in.	Number	...	... 242
Stroke	...	... 26 in.	Diameter	...	... 1⅝ in.
BOILER			HEATING SURFACE		
Length between			Tubes...		1,106.44 sq. ft
tubeplates ...		10 ft 7¾ in.	Firebox	...	99 sq. ft
Maximum diameter		4 ft 3 in.	Total ...		1,205.44 sq. ft
FIREBOX LENGTH			GRATE AREA		
Inside	...	5 ft 0 in.	Square feet	...	17.083
Outside	...	5 ft 8¼ in.			

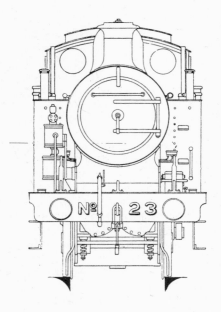

4-4-2
TANK ENGINE
No 23

Mr Douglas Earle Marsh, who was locomotive superintendent of the Brighton line from 1905 until 1910, seems to have formed the idea that, on such a line on which the longest run was less than 80 miles, there should be some scope for a tank locomotive designed for express passenger work; cost of construction and maintenance would be less than for a comparable tender engine and enough coal and water could be carried without making the engine too heavy. This idea was put to the test and proved successful; the result was the building of 27 fine 4-4-2 tank engines, known officially as Class I 3.

These engines were built in batches at Brighton between September 1907 and February 1913, the final ten being turned out by Marsh's successor, L. B. Billinton, who introduced a few slight, superficial modifications.

The engines were numbered 21 to 30 and 75 to 91, and it was No 23 which was destined to make a name for herself. I knew her very well and delighted in her fame; for she it was who showed the London and North Western Railway that there were many advantages in superheated steam!

Before we come to that, however, it will be as well to refer to certain differences that were to be noted, as the engines were not all exactly alike. No 21, the pioneer of this class, was really an odd one with dimensions and certain other details that were her own. To all intents and purposes, she was a B4 class 4-4-0 engine—exemplified, in this book, by No 70, *Holyrood*—but with side tanks, all-over cab, bunker, lengthened frames and a pair of carrying wheels at the rear end. Her running plates were flat from one end to the other; her smokebox and chimney were the same as those for *Holyrood*; but her dome was like that on No 23, while her Ramsbottom safety valves were enclosed in a plain rectangular casing. Her coupled wheels were 6 ft 9 in. dia. and her wheelbase was 30 ft 11 in., divided into 6 ft 3 in. plus 7 ft 5 in. plus 8 ft 9 in. plus 8 ft 6 in. The overhang was 2 ft 6½ in. at the front and 4 ft at the rear.

GENERAL SPECIFICATION			
CYLINDERS		**TUBES**	
Diameter ... ... 21 in.		Number ... 165 & 21	
Stroke ... ... 26 in.		Diameter 1⅝ in. & 4¾ in.	
BOILER			
Length, between		**HEATING SURFACE**	
tubeplates 11 ft 5 in.		Tubes ... 1,082 sq. ft	
Maximum dia-		Firebox ... 120 sq. ft	
meter ... 4 ft 10 in.		Total ... 1,202 sq. ft	
FIREBOX LENGTH			
Inside ... 6 ft 11¾ in.		**GRATE AREA**	
Outside ... 7 ft 7 in.		Square feet ... 23.75	

back. Nos 22 to 30 and 75 to 91 had slightly different dimensions, as will be noted in detail later, while Nos 82 to 91 had spiral springs for the driving wheels and no ventilators on the roofs of the cabs.

In 1909, a train called the *Sunny South Express* provided a through service between Crewe, Wolverhampton and Birmingham on the LNWR, and Brighton, Eastbourne and Hastings on the LBSCR. Engines were normally changed at Willesden Junction, until, towards the end of the year, arrangements were made for engines of each railway to work the train alternately in each direction between Rugby and Brighton. The LNWR allotted a 4-4-0 tender engine, No 7, *Titan*, to this job and the Brighton Railway selected No 23 to work the alternative service.

It was soon found that No 23, which had a superheater, would run the train quite easily from Rugby to Croydon or vice versa, without taking any water whereas *Titan* always found it necessary to pick up water from the Bushey troughs. Henceforth superheating was adopted for all main line passenger and large freight engines on the LNWR.

On their home ground No 23 and her sisters performed excellent work; many of the Brighton's crack trains, including the sumptuous all-Pullman *Southern Belle*, were worked almost exclusively by these engines with success for several years and I do not think any locomotives could have given less trouble.

The following dimensions applied to the superheated engines of this class: cylinders diameter 21 in., stroke 26 in. and fitted with 8 in. piston valves placed on top and driven by ordinary Stephenson link motion.

The wheel diameters were, bogie, 3 ft 6 in.; coupled, 6 ft 7½ in.; trailing 4 ft, on a total wheelbase of 31 ft 2 in. divided into 6 ft 3 in. plus 7 ft 8 in. plus 8 ft 9 in. plus 8 ft 6 in. Overhang was 2 ft 3 in. at the front and 4 ft at the back.

The boiler was in two rings, the larger of which was 4 ft 10 in. outside diameter; between tubeplates the length was 11 ft 5 in. and the centre line was 8 ft 4 in. above rail level. There were 165 small tubes of 1⅝ in. outside diameter, and 21 superheater flues of 4¾ in. dia., the heating surface amounting to 1,082 sq. ft to which the firebox added 120 sq. ft, making the total 1,202 sq. ft. The working pressure

was, originally, 160 p.s.i., but in later years was increased to 180 p.s.i., which put the tractive effort up from 19,615 lb to 22,100 lb.

The tanks and connecting pipes held 2,110 gallons of water, and the bunker 3 tons of coal. Grate area 23.75 sq. ft. In working order, the weight was 76 tons, distributed into 21 tons 5 cwt on the bogie, 19 tons 5 cwt on the driving axle, 18 tons 15 cwt on the coupled axle, and 16 tons 15 cwt on the trailing axle.

The non-superheated engines were Nos 27, 28, 29, 30, 75 and 76; they differed from the above in having a cylinder diameter of 19 in., flat valves between the cylinders, 315 small tubes of 1⅝ in. dia. of which the heating surface was 1,499 sq. ft, firebox heating surface 126 sq. ft, grate area 26 sq. ft and working 180 p.s.i. from the start. They weighed 73 tons in working order.

All these engines became Southern Railway property in 1923 and remained in service for some years afterwards, though relegated to secondary duties. They were gradually withdrawn until the last survivor, BR No 32091, was broken up in January 1953.

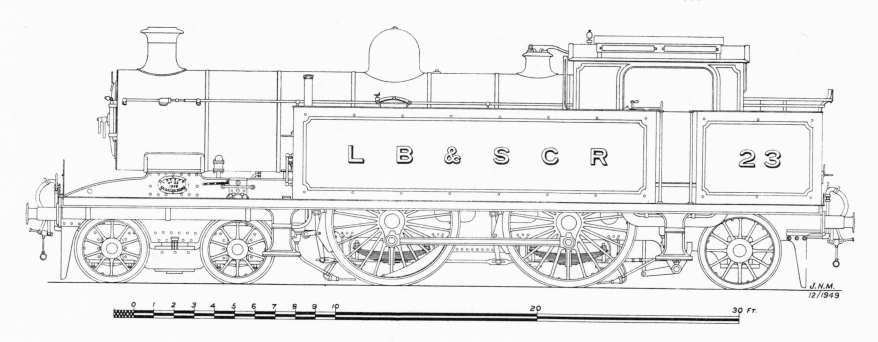

0 1 2 3 4 5 6 7 8 9 10   20   30 FT.

J.N.M.
12/1949

27

THE BRIGHTON 'TERRIERS'

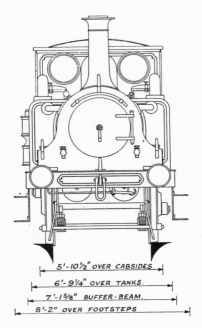

5'-10½" OVER CABSIDES.
6'-9¼" OVER TANKS.
7'-1⅝" BUFFER-BEAM.
8'-2" OVER FOOTSTEPS.

GENERAL SPECIFICATION

CYLINDERS			TUBES		
Diameter	...	13 in.	Number	...	121
Stroke	...	20 in.	Diameter	...	1¾ in.
BOILER					
Length, between			HEATING SURFACE		
tubeplates	7 ft 10 in.		Tubes	...	463 sq. ft
Maximum dia-			Firebox	...	55 sq. ft
meter	...	3 ft 5⅛ in.	Total	...	518 sq. ft
FIREBOX LENGTH					
Inside	...	3 ft 6⅞ in.	GRATE AREA		
Outside	...	4 ft 1 in.	Square feet	...	10

THESE astonishing little engines have a prominent place in my earliest recollections which go back to 1897. At that time, when I was still under six years of age, I had begun to differentiate clearly between the various classes of Brighton engines, most of which could be seen practically every day passing Wandsworth Common.

These small 0-6-0 tank engines, officially styled Class A but more usually referred to as " Terriers," " Pups " or " Rooters," worked many of the local trains that shuttled to and from Victoria and London Bridge via either Crystal Palace or Norwood Junction, and they were at once conspicuous by reason of their very small size, clearly apparent even to a child of my age.

They originated in 1872, between which date and 1880 no fewer than 50 were built; and they were certainly to be included among Stroudley's masterpieces. It is interesting to note that, in 1959, 13 of them are at work in the Southern Region of British Railways, one in its original condition and 12 reboilered, while a fourteenth, No 82, *Boxhill*, restored to her original state and painted in Stroudley's striking livery, is withdrawn for permanent preservation.

At first, in 1872, only six were built; but after thorough trials, the class was gradually increased to

50 by the addition of the following batches: six in 1874, 12 in 1875, six in 1877, six in 1878 and eight in 1880. In spite of their small size they were excellent workers with a truly astonishing versatility. They were popular with the enginemen and with passengers on the East and South London Railways.

There can be little doubt that their attractive yellow colour with its elaborate lining-out, and their usual spotless cleanliness, found great favour with the travelling public in a rather drab district. But very soon they were to be met with all over the Brighton Railway, and to see them working in rural Surrey and Sussex was to appreciate how well they harmonised with lovely scenery.

The original dimensions were: cylinders, 13 in. dia. by 20 in. stroke; wheels, 3 ft 11 in. dia. on a wheelbase of 12 ft equally divided; the overhang, including bufferbeams, was 4 ft 7¼ in. at the leading end and 6 ft 7¼ in. at the trailing end, the total length of the frames being 23 ft.

The boiler was made of 7/16 in. iron plate, the barrel being formed of three rings, the middle one of which was 3 ft 5⅛ in. outside dia.: the length of the barrel between tubeplates was 7 ft 10 in., and it was pitched 5 ft 8⅝ in. above rail level. There were 121 tubes of 1¾ in. dia., 8 ft 4¼ in. long. The outer casing of the

firebox was 4 ft 1 in. long, 3 ft 6⅞ in. wide and 3 ft. 10½ in. deep.

The total heating surface was only 518 sq. ft made up of 463 sq. ft for the tubes and 55 sq. ft for the firebox. The grate area was but 10 sq. ft, and the working pressure was 140 p.s.i. The capacity of the water tanks was 500 gallons, and that of the coal bunker about 18 cwt. The total length over buffers was 26 ft ½ in., and in full working order the weight was 24 tons 7 cwt. At 85 per cent. boiler pressure the tractive force was 7,650 lb.

The valves worked in a steamchest placed between the cylinders and were driven by Stephenson link motion having the weighshaft above; in full gear the valve travel was 3⅝ in. The ports were 1⅜ in. wide by 10½ in. long, and the cylinders were inclined 1 in 11.

Engine No 40, *Brighton*, was exhibited at the Paris Exhibition in 1878 and won a gold medal for excellence of design and workmanship. Subsequently she was stationed at Battersea and for many years was a familiar object in the South London suburban area, proudly displaying the legend " Gold Medal, Paris Exhibition, 1878 " painted above the name on her side tanks.

At one time there was a turn of duty which entailed the daily working of a main line train by one of these diminutive engines. A heavy afternoon train from the South Coast to London would stop at East Croydon to be divided. The express engine would then go forward to Victoria with the front portion of the train, leaving the rear portion to be taken to London Bridge by the East Croydon pilot.

The latter at that time was usually a New Cross "Terrier," often No 57, *Thames*, which would take this means of working home after her turn of pilot duties was finished. The time allowed for the 10¼ mile non-stop run from Croydon to London Bridge was, I believe, 17 minutes; but *Thames*, hauling four or five main line coaches, had no difficulty in keeping to schedule, and often attained a maximum speed exceeding 60 m.p.h. down the New Cross Bank.

It was a choice spectacle which richly entertained a select little band of schoolboys, myself among them, who were sometimes fortunate enough to be able to visit the lineside just south of Forest Hill station where *Thames* would be pretty well into her full stride.

But this was not the only turn on which a "Terrier" could be entertaining. Years later, around 1909, when my family lived at Edenbridge, I made close acquaintance with that popular type of "auto-train" consisting of a "Terrier" coupled to what was colloquially known as a "balloon," i.e. a fine, wide bogie vehicle of saloon type with a high elliptical roof. Of course, it completely dwarfed the engine; but the speed that this combination could reach was surprising.

One summer evening, I timed No 677 (old 77, *Wonersh*) and a "balloon" at 63 m.p.h. just south of Hilder's Lane tunnel, and I wondered if she would succeed in stopping at Edenbridge Town! But the engines seemed to revel in this sort of thing.

No 677 and her "balloon," at the period mentioned, was stationed at Tunbridge Wells, from which place she had a turn of duty that sent her out about 6.30 a.m. and brought her home about 10 p.m. During that time, she would cover something like 230 miles, visiting Oxted, East Grinstead, Three Bridges, Horsham and Haywards Heath in the process. In this way, she amassed a total weekly mileage of something like 1,400 miles.

To my certain knowledge, she worked this turn for three years at a stretch, and probably longer; these engines may have been small but they certainly had stamina, though the survivors now lead less strenuous lives.

It is worth mentioning that the wooden brake blocks shown in the drawing were fitted to all these engines, except the last eight which were provided with cast-iron blocks.

In late years, several of this class were sold to light railways, collieries and contractors, while two even found their way to a South American tramway. The survivors are used for locomotive shed pilot duties, shunting and such services as on the Hayling Island branch, where no heavier locomotives are permitted to run.

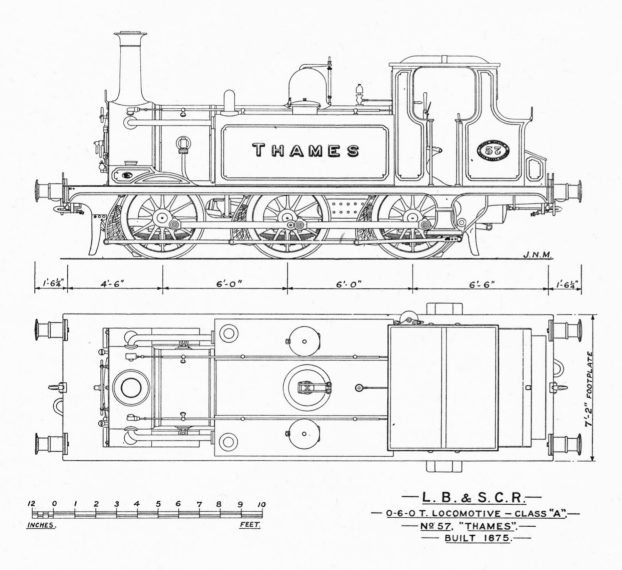

— L. B. & S. C. R. —
— 0-6-0 T. LOCOMOTIVE – CLASS "A". —
— Nº 57, "THAMES". —
— BUILT 1875. —

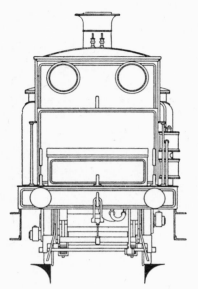

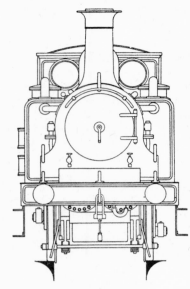

GENERAL SPECIFICATION			
CYLINDERS		**TUBES**	
Diameter ... ... 17 in.		Number 231	
Stroke ... ... 24 in.		Diameter ... ... 1½ in.	
BOILER		**HEATING SURFACE**	
Length, between		Tubes ... 952 sq. ft	
tubeplates 10 ft 2 in.		Firebox ... 87 sq. ft	
Maximum diameter 4 ft		Total ... 1,039 sq. ft	
FIREBOX LENGTH		**GRATE AREA**	
Inside ... 4 ft 7 in.		Square feet ... 15	
Outside ... 5 ft 2¼ in.			

STROUDLEY'S E1 Class 0-6-0 TANKS

IT was in March, 1871, that William Stoudley's appointment as locomotive superintendent of the London Brighton and South Coast Railway was confirmed, although he had actually occupied the post for more than 12 months, during which he had formulated his plans for achieving order out of comparative chaos. He decided that nine standard classes of engines, instead of 73, would meet the motive power requirements of the line.

He adopted a fairly rigid system of standardisation of details and set to work; it was not long before his plans began to make themselves apparent in the neat and efficient locomotives built to his designs. Among them were the 0-6-0 goods tank engines of the E1 class, the first two of which, No 97, *Honfleur* and 98, *Marseilles*, were put into service in November, 1874. Between that date and November, 1883, a further 70 engines of this class were built.

In nearly all their essential details these engines were interchangeable with the 0-4-2 passenger tanks of class D1, described in a previous chapter, the only differences, apart from the wheels, being the slightly longer frames and larger bunkers.

When the class was completed, the numbers were consecutive from 85 to 156, and the names were after

Continental towns, cities and places of interest, three of the Channel Islands and four Sussex villages. No 140, *Toulouse* and 142, *Toulon*, were the butt of certain young enthusiasts, though I do not think it was ever decided just what it was about the engines that was either too loose or too long! I sometimes think that the modern "locospotter" does not have half the fun that we used to get out of railway engines when I was a boy.

Be that as it may, the E1 class engines were great

favourites; they were to be seen anywhere on the LBSCR, and they were hard workers, though I cannot recall that I ever saw one being thrashed. They did their work in a stolid, businesslike way that was interesting to see. When I first knew them, they were anything from ten to 20 years old. At the time of writing, some 50 years later, there are still a few in active service in the Southern Region of British Railways.

When new, Nos 145 to 156 were fitted with the Westinghouse air brake and painted in passenger engine colours, Subsequently, when the earlier engines were equipped with the air break, some of them also were painted in the passenger style. Later, this practice was dropped and the entire class reverted to goods engine livery. It is worth noting that Nos 145 to 156 had cast iron brake blocks, whereas all the others had wooden blocks, as seen in the drawing.

On 14 April, 1899, No 139, *Lombardy* suffered a most unusual adventure. She was crossing over the main lines on her way from the locomotive depot to the marshalling yards at New Cross, when she came into oblique collision with a passenger train, hauled by D1-class engine No 226, *Westham*, travelling in the opposite direction. *Lombardy's* driver, as soon as he

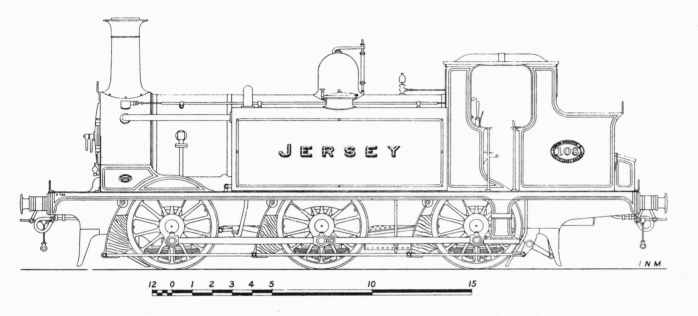

JERSEY 108

12 0 1 2 3 4 5 10 15

There were originally 160 tubes of $1\frac{3}{4}$ in. dia., the heating surface of which was 772 sq. ft; to this the firebox added 80 sq. ft to make a total of 852 sq. ft. Later, the tubing was altered to 231 tubes of $1\frac{1}{2}$ in. diameter, which gave 952 sq. ft of heating surface, and the firebox, which originally had been semicircular on top, was altered to a flat top, increasing its heating surface to 87 sq. ft; this made the total heating surface 1,039 sq. ft. The working pressure was 150 p.s.i. and the grate area was 15 sq. ft.

About 1895, R. J. Billinton replaced many of these boilers by new ones having the same dimensions; but the tubing was altered to 207 tubes of $1\frac{5}{8}$ in. dia. with a heating surface of 924.57 sq. ft, while the firebox heating surface was reduced to 82.06 sq. ft, making the total 1,006.63 sq. ft. The earlier examples of these new boilers had the dome mounted on the middle ring; but later ones reverted to the back-ring mounting, because it gave rather more satisfactory results.

In working order, the weight of an E1 class engine was 39 tons 10 cwt, with 13 tons 10 cwt on each of the leading and driving axles and 12 tons 10 cwt on the trailing axle. The capacity of the tanks was 900 gallons of water, and of the bunker 1 ton 15 cwt of coal.

Withdrawal of these engines began in 1908, but 62 of them survived to become Southern Railway property in 1923, while 39 of them passed into the hands of British Railways in 1948. Among those which became BR property were ten that had been converted into 0-6-2 type engines in 1927-8 and reclassed E1R. These ten engines had a pair of trailing wheels, 3 ft 1 in. dia. and provided with radial axleboxes, under the bunker, increasing the total wheel-base to 20 ft 9 in. A new and larger cab was fitted, and the coal capacity was increased to two tons by making the bunker longer and higher. When rebuilt in this form, the engines weighed 50 tons 5 cwt, and they were used chiefly for banking heavy trains up steep gradients such as that between the St Davids and Central stations at Exeter.

It is now some 75 years since the E1 class was first built, and though none of the few survivors is as old as that, it is remarkable that the class still operates. It is due, of course, to the availability of boilers, but there is little doubt that these old engines still possess their original frames, a tribute to the excellent workmanship.

saw that a collision was unavoidable, reversed his engine, but left the regulator open and then, with his fireman, jumped off the footplate. Immediately after the collision, which caused some damage to both engines, *Lombardy* began to move backwards and, before anyone could stop her, was away on the main line to the south !

Here was a risky situation—an unattended engine running away on the down main line ! Urgent warning of what was happening was sent from signalbox to signalbox, but there was nothing the signalmen could do about it; they could only stand and watch the engine go by. At the top of the Forest Hill bank, the gradient and lack of steam had begun to tell, and *Lombardy* was showing signs of becoming winded. A valiant porter at Forest Hill station, and another at Norwood Junction, made brave but unsuccessful attempts to grab hold of the engine as she passed. With the flattening of the gradient she had gathered a little speed and continued on her way as far as South Croydon. Here, the signalman was able to so set the road that *Lombardy* was turned into a siding, where she plunged into an embankment, trapped and unable

to cause any further excitement ! It is scarcely necessary to add that rarely have locomotives ever indulged in escapades of this description. The wonder is that, not only was *Lombardy* still on the track after the initial collision, but that she was able with no crew, to travel about 12 miles along a busy main line without meeting further disaster.

The principal dimensions of these engines were: cylinders, 17 in. dia., 24 in. stroke, 2 ft 2 in. apart, centre to centre, and inclined at an angle of 1 in $11\frac{1}{2}$. Ports, valves and valve gear were all exactly similar to those of the D1 class passenger engines but the reversing was effected by a lever instead of by wheel and screw.

The wheelbase was 15 ft 3 in. divided into 7 ft 6 in. and 7 ft 9 in.; the leading overhang was 6 ft $0\frac{1}{2}$ in. and the trailing 8 ft $1\frac{1}{4}$ in. The wheels were 4 ft 6 in. dia.; thinner flanges were provided on the driving wheels than on the others so as to ease the engine on curves, there being no other provision made for this.

The boiler was made in three rings, 3 ft 10 in., 3 ft 11 in. and 4 ft in diameter, the barrel length being 10 ft 2 in. and pitched 6 ft 11 in. above rail level.

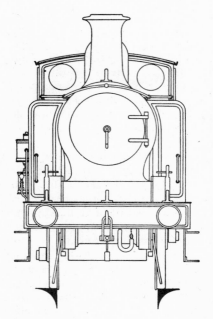

GENERAL SPECIFICATION

CYLINDERS			TUBES		
Diameter	...	18 in.	Number	...	242
Stroke	...	26 in.	Diameter	...	1¾ in.
BOILER			HEATING SURFACE		
Length, between			Tubes	...	1,106.44 sq. ft
tubeplates	10 ft 7¼ in		Firebox	...	93 sq ft
Maximum diameter 4 ft 3 in.			Total	...	1,199.44 sq. ft
FIREBOX LENGTH					
Inside	...	5 ft 1¾ in.	GRATE AREA		
Outside	...	5 ft 8¼ in.	Square feet	...	17.43

The Class E4 TANKS

THE 0-6-2 type of tank locomotive for local freight and passenger traffic was first introduced in England by W. Barton Wright, on the Lancashire and Yorkshire Railway, in 1879, and in the following year, F. W. Webb adopted the type for short-distance coal traffic on the London and North Western Railway.

Subsequently, few other railways took it up on an extensive scale; but in 1889 W. Stroudley designed a large engine, No 158, *West Brighton*, to work heavy goods traffic on the London, Brighton and South Coast Railway. When Stroudley died in December 1889, the construction of this engine had just been started at Brighton. However, Robt. J. Billinton, who succeeded Stroudley, issued a " cease work " order on it while he scrutinised the design and made some more or less minor alterations to it. The engine was completed in December 1891, and was designated " Class E Special "; it had 18¼ in. × 26 in. cylinders and 4 ft 6 in. coupled wheels.

For a year or two, Billinton watched the working of this engine and seems to have been so well satisfied that he decided to adopt the type as standard. He prepared a design of his own, closely following that of Stroudley, and between November 1894 and

November 1895, built 16 engines known as Class E3. Their cylinders were 18 in. by 26 in. and the coupled wheels were 4 ft 6 in. dia.; the boiler was pitched 7 ft 5⅜ in. above rail level.

At first, this class was put to working local goods trains, but was soon being frequently used on passenger trains with such success that Billinton decided that subsequent engines of the class should have 5 ft coupled wheels.

Thus, we come to Class E4, no fewer than 75 of which were built between December 1897 and September 1903. They were among the earliest engines that I ever knew, and there seemed to be a whole battalion of them in the London area then. They were precisely similar to Class E3, except for the larger coupled wheels and the fact that the height of the boiler was increased to 7 ft 8⅜ in., which

required the length of the chimney to be 3 in. shorter.

In appearance, they were neat and businesslike, but in working, they possessed certain peculiarities that were entirely their own; they rattled a good deal when running, and they never appeared to be able to reach anything that could be described as a high speed. The characteristic sprightliness of the little Stroudley D1 tank engines was missing.

For all that, the E4 class did an enormous amount of work, and they were to be found in numbers all over the Brighton Railway system, employed on all kinds of traffic short of express trains. They were numbered 463 to 520, 556 to 566 and 577 to 582. Of these, 463 to 486 were originally painted goods engine colours, though later several of them assumed the passenger engine livery; all the rest were in the passenger colours from the beginning, while Nos. 577 to 582 were given a much shorter chimney than the rest of the class had.

From No 518 onwards, the Salter safety-valves on the dome were discarded and replaced by a pair of lock-up valves in brass columns, mounted on the firebox manhole, and the whistle was removed to the front of the cab roof. No 565, *Littleton*, ran for some while in 1902 with oil-burning apparatus similar to that used on the Great Eastern Railway; but it was found to be too expensive and was discarded.

All the E4 class, with very few exceptions, were named after towns, villages and places of interest in Surrey and Sussex. When new, No 497 was named *Dennington*, but this was subsequently discovered to be an error and was altered to *Donnington*. No 472, *Fay Gate*, was a well-known engine in the London area, being stationed at New Cross for many years; although she was painted in the goods engine livery, she spent more than half her time on passenger work.

In November 1917, Nos 470, 481, 498, 504, 506, 516, 518, 562 to 565 and 580 were on loan to the Railway Operating Division and were sent to France for service behind the battle fronts. Each engine carried a small cast-iron plate, mounted on the back weather-board inside the cab and bearing the engine's number, together with the legend " L.B. & S.C.R. England."

At first, they were put to work in the extensive distribution centre at Audricq, but early in 1918 were moved nearer to the fighting line in the St Pol-Albert-

Arras area. After the end of the war, they worked local passenger trains on the Doullens-Arras direct line, and were returned to England, a few at a time, between March and September 1919.

The entire class became Southern Railway property at the time of the grouping of the railways in January 1923, while all except one, No 483—withdrawn in July 1944—passed into the hands of British Railways in January 1948

At the beginning of 1958, about half the class were still at work, though they are being withdrawn fairly rapidly and will soon be extinct It is of note, however, that they have averaged about 55 years, or more, of service apiece, sturdy, strong and stalwart to the end, in spite of their idiosyncrasies.

Their principal dimensions were: cylinders, 18 in. dia. by 26 in. stroke, inclined at 1 in 9½; the slide valves were inclined at 1 in 7¾ and were operated by Stephenson link motion, the valve travel in full gear being 4¼ in.

The diameter of the coupled wheels was 5 ft, and of the trailing wheels 4 ft. The total wheelbase was 21 ft 6 in., divided into 7 ft 9 in. plus 7 ft 6 in. plus 6 ft 3 in. At the front end, the overhang was 6 ft 1½ in.

and at the back it was 4 ft 7½ in., the length of the frames being 32 ft 4 in.

The boiler was made in three rings, the largest of which had a diameter of 4 ft 3 in.; the barrel was 10 ft 7¼ in. long, and its front end rested on cast steel brackets attached to the back of the cylinders. Pitched at 7 ft 8⅜ in. above rail level, it was higher than any other tank engine boiler in England at the time. The firebox casing was 5 ft 8¼ in. long, 4 ft 1 in. wide and, at the front, 5 ft 2 in. deep, sloping upwards to 4 ft 1¼ in. at the back. There were 242 brass tubes of 1¾ in. dia., the heating surface of which was 1,106.44 sq. ft; to this the firebox added 93 sq. ft, making the total 1,199.44 sq. ft. The grate area was 17.43 sq. ft.

The water capacity was 1,409 gallons, and the bunker carried 3 tons of coal. In working order, the engine weighed 51 tons distributed into: 13 tons on the leading axle, 14 tons on the driving axle, 11 tons on the rear coupled axle and 13 tons on the trailing axle. The total length over buffer heads was 35 ft 3 in.

It will be noted that, for the period, the dimensions were distinctly generous, but it is a pity that no particulars of port sizes and valve events are available, because I strongly suspect that, if this information

were to hand, it would contain the clue to the general sluggishness of the running of these engines. A very noticeable feature was that, at about 45 to 50 m.p.h., when the valve gear would be well notched up, the exhaust appeared to leave the chimney at the rate of one soft, woolly beat per revolution of the coupled wheels, and what happened to the other three beats was anybody's guess !

It is very easy, however, to conjecture on matters of this kind, and without the necessary technical information, no positive conclusions are possible. The plain facts are that the E4 class engines have had a very long life and have done an enormous amount of useful work.

After 1923, they were widely distributed over the Southern Railway; in very recent times, up to 1953, one of them was stationed at Reading South, where she was constantly employed on heavy shunting duties which she seemed to do quite well. At any rate, the local railwaymen usually spoke well of her; so much so, in fact, that when she eventually left Reading, she was replaced by another of her class, which remained for about 18 months and was used when the diesel shunters were out of commission.

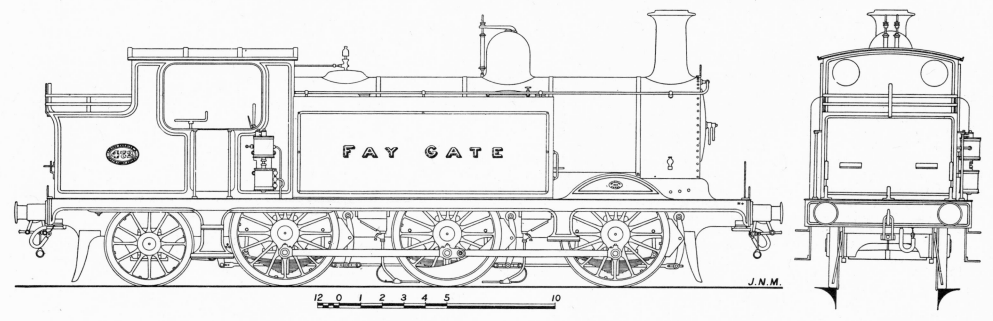

FAY GATE

J.N.M.

12 0 1 2 3 4 5   10

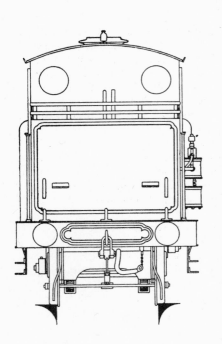

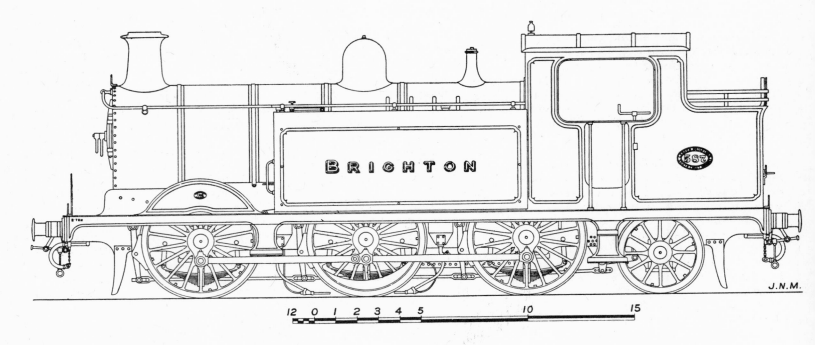

BILLINTON'S E5 CLASS 0-6-2T

IN October 1902, Brighton Works turned out the first of R. J. Billinton's last and, to all appearances, finest 0-6-2 tank locomotives. These new engines, of which 30 were built, were classed E5 and were rather a remarkable development of the E4 class; they were designed specially for secondary main line passenger traffic, on which they proved to be very successful. They were not only powerful; they were speedy and they rode very steadily.

In all this there was some element of mystery, because the principal dimensions of the two classes were very nearly alike; yet the E4s were comparatively sluggish and noisy while the E5s were just the reverse. As the frames, cylinders and valve gear were interchangeable between the two classes, the explanation of the difference in performance did not lie in that direction. But the E5s had larger tanks and

bunkers, boilers which were pitched higher, and larger coupled wheels; consequently they were somewhat heavier, which may well account for the steadiness of their running. The larger coupled wheels conduced to the higher speeds.

The E5s were built in three batches: six in 1902, Nos 567 to 572; ten in 1903, Nos 573 to 576 and 583 to 588, and 14 in 1904, Nos 589 to 594 and 399 to 406. With the exception of No 569 *Kensington*, they were named after places in Surrey, Sussex and the

GENERAL SPECIFICATION		
CYLINDERS		**TUBES**
Diameter ... ... 18 in.		Number 238
Stroke ... ... 26 in.		Diameter ... ... 1⅝ in.
BOILER		**HEATING SURFACE**
Length, between		Tubes ... 1,088 sq. ft
tubeplates 10 ft 7½ in.		Firebox ... 105 sq. ft
Maximum diameter 4 ft 3 in.		Total ... 1,193 sq. ft
FIREBOX LENGTH		**GRATE AREA**
Inside ... 5 ft 8 in.		Square feet ... 19.32
Outside ... 6 ft 2¼ in.		

A further selection of LOCOMOTIVES I HAVE KNOWN

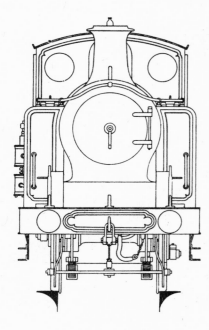

the afternoon. This was probably the longest single turn worked by the class; it covered something like 180 miles for the daily round. Up to the outbreak of war in 1914, all the engines were normally engaged in these duties and gave much satisfaction.

Sometimes, on a run that included a non-stop sprint of about 20 miles, such as from East Croydon to Horley, an E5 could be coaxed up to a speed of 65-70 m.p.h. with freedom and steadiness. On one occasion, I timed No 399 *Middleton* at 68 m.p.h. at the bottom of the New Cross bank, during a run up from East Croydon to London Bridge; her time for the 10¼ miles, including a long slow into the terminus, was exactly 15 minutes start to stop. She had a train of mixed stock weighing about 175 tons gross; but she got away from East Croydon in fine style, and then simply went for it. She ran perfectly sweetly and without the slightest sign of being thrashed.

Between 1906 and 1910 about a dozen E5s were running with the front parts of their coupling-rods removed, converting them for the time being into 2-4-2 engines. The reason for this was never divulged; there was a story that D. E. Marsh was contemplating the construction of some 2-4-2 tank engines and had decided to try it on the dog first !

My own recollection is that the converted E5s were much superior to Marsh's 4-4-2 tank engines of classes I1 and I2, and it may be that this caused him to forego any 2-4-2 engines of his own. After 1910, the converted E5s were quietly reconverted to their original 0-6-2 condition.

E5 cylinders were of the standard 18 in. dia., later reduced to 17½ in.; the stroke was 26 in., sloped at an angle of 1 in 9½. The steamchest was between the cylinders but inclined at 1 in 7¾. Stephenson link motion, similar to that of the earlier tank engines operated the valves.

In diameter the six coupled wheels were 5 ft 6 in. and the trailing wheels 4 ft. The wheelbase was 21 ft 6 in. divided into 7 ft 9 in. plus 7 ft 6 in. plus 6 ft 3 in. and the overhang was 6 ft 1½ in. at the front and 4 ft 7½ in. at the back, the length of the main frames being 32 ft 3 in. Over buffers the length of the engine was 36 ft.

The boiler was made in two rings of ½ in. plate, their diameters 4 ft 2 in. and 4 ft 3 in. outside. The centre-line was 8 ft above rail level and the barrel

length was 10 ft 7¼ in.; between tubeplates the distance was 10 ft 10¾ in.

There were 238 tubes of 1⅝ in. dia., with a heating surface of 1,088 sq. ft. The firebox casing was 6 ft 2¼ in. long and 4 ft 4 in. wide at the centre-line; the inner box was 5 ft 8 in. long, and the grate area was 19.32 sq. ft ; the heating surface of the firebox was 105 sq. ft, making the total 1,193.

A pair of direct-loaded safety-valves, enclosed in the characteristic " bathing drawers " casing, as on the B4 class engines, was mounted on the firebox, and set across the box instead of parallel to the boiler centre-line. They were adjusted for a pressure of 160 p.s.i.; but when the cylinder diameter was altered to 17½ in. the working pressure was increased to 175. The official tractive effort was 17,430 lb.

A neat little feature was the plain dome, 2 ft in diameter and 2 ft 2 in. high, placed exactly on the vertical centre-line through the driving wheels. The front edge of the cab was exactly on the centre-line through the trailing coupled wheels, and I assume that these two rather intriguing features were not merely accidental !

Nos 572, *Farncombe* and 573, *Nutbourne*, were built with three-ring boilers; the dome was placed on the middle ring. It is a moot point whether these two engines looked any better than the others; I think that the odds were about evenly divided.

The combined capacity of the two side tanks, bunker tank and their connecting pipes was 1,665 gallons, and the coal capacity was 3½ tons.

For a few months in 1903, Nos 573, *Nutbourne* and 574, *Copthorne* were fitted with James Holden's oil-burning apparatus.

In working order, an E5 weighed 60 tons, the leading axle carrying 15 tons, the driving axle carrying 16 tons 10 cwt, the rear coupled axle 14 tons 15 cwt, and the radial trailing axle 13 tons 15 cwt. The adhesion weight, therefore, was 46 tons 5 cwt, which accounted for the marked firm-footedness of these engines.

No 591 *Tillington* was the last LBSCR engine to run in Stroudley's yellow livery, which she retained until March 1917. The class became extinct in January 1956, when the last three survivors, BR Nos 32571, 32583 and 32593, were withdrawn for scrapping after nearly 55 years of service.

Isle of Wight. They were spread fairly evenly over the LBSCR system. From such places as New Cross, Battersea, Brighton, Portsmouth, Horsham, East-bourne and Tunbridge Wells, they worked semi-fast main line passenger trains, some of which were fairly tightly timed between stops. I can recall some of them. No 591, *Tillington*, a New Cross engine, for about nine years had the sole duty of working the night Continental Boat Train, the so-called Grande Vitesse, from London Bridge to Newhaven. No 585, *Crowborough*, a Battersea engine, worked for many years between Victoria and Tunbridge Wells. No 569, *Kensington*, of Eastbourne, pretty well monopolised a morning train from there to Victoria, stopping at Lewes, Horley, Redhill, East Croydon and Clapham Junction, returning on the 3.45 p.m. from Victoria to Tunbridge Wells, and running non-stop to Groombridge; later, she would work a stopping train from Tunbridge Wells to Eastbourne via Lewes, to be ready for the similar round next day.

No 405, *Fernhurst*, of Portsmouth often came up to London via Chichester, Horsham, Three Bridges, Redhill, East Croydon and Clapham Junction, returning to Portsmouth by the same route later in

MARSH'S 4-6-2 TANKS

THE old London Brighton and South Coast Railway was well suited to the use of tank locomotives, even for express passenger work; but this was not fully exploited until Mr D. E. Marsh brought out his 13 4-4-2 tank engines in 1907

The success of those engines prompted a further advance in express passenger tank engines for use on the heaviest express trains between London and Brighton; consequently, in 1910, an entirely new type of tank engine was put to work. It was officially designated class J, and the first was No 325, *Abergavenny*, completed at Brighton in December, 1910. She had the 4-6-2 wheel arrangement and was the first tank engine of her type to run in England; and a most impressive engine she was, with pleasing proportions and generally neat, clean outlines. In fact, for such a large engine her design was remarkable for its simplicity and trimness.

Her designer, however, retired in the same month that she was completed; but she was given an extended trial lasting nearly 18 months, during which she was painted grey picked out with black striping and white lines. She proved to be successful and

able to cope easily and economically with the fastest and heaviest trains between London, Eastbourne, Brighton and Portsmouth.

Meanwhile, a second engine, No 326, was being built. She was completed and put to work in February, 1912, and differed from *Abergavenny* in being fitted with outside Walschaerts valve gear instead of inside Stephenson gear, but was otherwise similar to her older sister.

Her name was *Bessborough*, which was rather in the nature of an anticlimax to many people who had taken it for granted that her name would be *Grosvenor*.

I have always understood that there was a good deal of difficulty in designing and assembling the Walschaerts gear for *Bessborough*, because it was quite a novelty for Brighton Works, nobody there having had any previous design or manufacturing experience with the gear. The problem was not made any easier by the cylinders being outside the frames and their steam chests inside. This was dictated by the desire to use cylinder castings similar to those of *Abergavenny*, so as to save expense; but *Bessborough* was duly finished and designated class J2, *Abergavenny* being reclassified as J1.

The two engines soon became popular, especially on such trains as the all-Pullman "Southern Belle" and the heavy 5.5 p.m., so-called "City Limited," the latter a fine corridor train conveying a large number of season-ticket holders from London Bridge to Brighton. On both trains speeds exceeding 75 m.p.h. were frequently noted, and occasionally something more than 80 m.p.h. was recorded behind *Bessborough*, which always seemed to be the speedier of the two locomotives.

The principal dimensions of these two engines were:

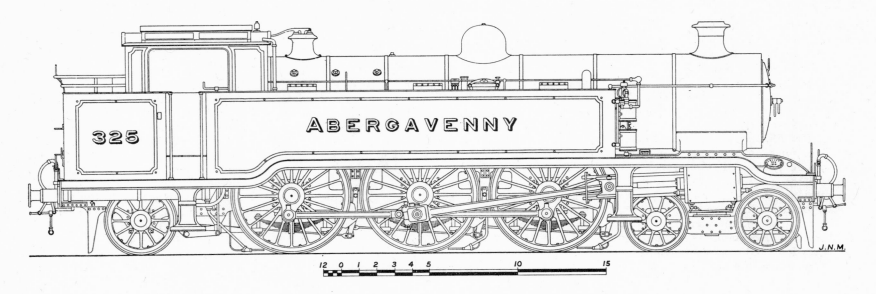

J.N.M.

cylinder diameter 21 in., stroke 26 in. and inclination 1 in 26. The wheel diameters were: bogie 3 ft 6 in., coupled 6 ft 7½ in. and trailing 4 ft, while the wheelbase was 35 ft 3 in. divided into 6 ft 3 in. plus 6 ft plus 7 ft 3 in. plus 7 ft 3 in. plus 8 ft 6 in. Overhang was 2 ft 6½ in. at the front end and 4 ft 6 in. at the back. The total length over buffers was 45 ft 6 in.

A good boiler was provided, made in two rings, the diameter of the larger (back) one being 5 ft 3 in. Between tubeplates, the barrel was 15 ft long and had its centre line 8 ft 8 in. above rail level. There were 110 tubes of 2¼ in. dia., giving 1,461.69 sq. ft of heating surface; to this, 21 superheater flues of 5½ in. dia. added 357 sq. ft. The firebox, which was 8 ft long and 3 ft 4⅞ in. wide outside, had a heating surface of 124.4 sq. ft, so that the total evaporative surface amounted to the respectable figure of 1,943.09 sq. ft. The working pressure was 170 p.s.i.

The side tanks and a well-tank under the bunker gave a total water capacity of 2,232 gallons, while the bunker would hold 3½ tons of coal. The weight in working order was 89 tons divided into 18 tons on the bogie, 17 tons 5 cwt on the first coupled axle, 19 tons 5 cwt on the driving axle, 16 tons on the third coupled axle and 16 tons 10 cwt on the trailing axle.

Apart from the valve gears, there were s ight

differences of detail to be noted in these two fine engines. When new, *Abergavenny* had superheater dampers and was equipped with brakes on the bogie wheels; after a short time, both these fitments were removed. Also, this engine had laminated springs for all her axleboxes. In 1913, the ventilator on the cab roof was removed and the Ramsbottom safety-valves were replaced by Ross "pops."

Bessborough never ran with either bogie brakes or superheater dampers, and her leading coupled and driving axles were carried on spiral springs. Later changes were the same as for *Abergavenny*. But I should add that the valances on *Bessborough* terminated, at each end, in nice shapely curves down to meet the bufferbeams and were not square-ended like those of her sister.

It will be noted that No 325 carried the same number and name as the Stroudley singlewheeler and this probably gave rise to the expectation that No 326 would be *Grosvenor*. Incidentally, these two 4-6-2 tank engines were originally intended to be numbered 36 and 37, respectively; but 37 would have clashed with the first Marsh Atlantic, so two other consecutive blank numbers in the official list were used instead.

I am aware that G. F. Burtt, the Brighton historian, states that both these engines had bogie brakes when new. I think this must be a mistake, because none of the official photographs of *Bessborough*, in her original condition, show such brakes, whereas those

of *Abergavenny* do. A possible explanation of Burtt's statement is that *Bessborough* was intended to have bogie brakes, and they probably showed on the original drawings, for which he, as senior draughtsman, was responsible; and even if they were put on the engine while she was being built, they were removed before she was put on the road. After all, it was in 1911 that bogie brakes began to be removed from the earlier Marsh Atlantics, so they are hardly likely to have appeared on any new engine built after that date.

To any railway enthusiast of that period, the sight of one or other of these two beautiful locomotives at the head of that sumptuous all-Pullman train, the Southern Belle, especially with the full nine-car formation, was unforgettable. It was a glorious vision of dignified neatness and scrupulous cleanliness from one end to the other. And it matched perfectly with the beautiful and then entirely unspoiled Sussex countryside through which it ran. Another vivid recollection to me, is of that train, with the proud, sedate, but lively *Abergavenny* in charge, dead on time, tearing through East Croydon station in the evening sunshine, receding rapidly into the distance round the north curve, followed by a faint cloud of dust and always a few whirling scraps of paper. It was a never-failing thrill!

These two engines were withdrawn in 1951.

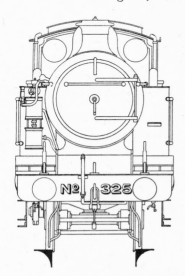

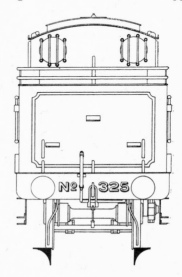

GENERAL SPECIFICATION			
CYLINDERS		**TUBES**	
Diameter ... ... 21 in.		Number ... 110 & 21	
Stroke ... ... 26 in.		Diameter 2¼ in. & 5½ in.	
BOILER			
Length, between		**HEATING SURFACE**	
tubeplates ... 15 ft		Tubes ... 1,818.69 sq. ft	
Maximum dia-		Firebox ... 124.4 sq. ft	
meter ... 5 ft 3 in.		Total ... 1943.09 sq. ft	
FIREBOX LENGTH			
Inside ... 7 ft 5½ in.		**GRATE AREA**	
Outside ... ... 8 ft		Square feet ... 25.16	

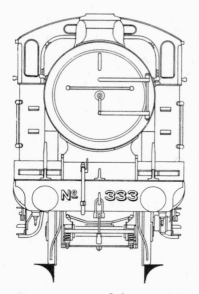

GENERAL SPECIFICATION

CYLINDERS				TUBES		
Diameter	...	...	22 in.	Number	...	152 & 21
Stroke	...	...	28 in.	Diameter	$2\frac{1}{4}$ & $5\frac{1}{2}$ in.	
BOILER						
Length, between				HEATING SURFACE		
tubeplates	14 ft	$7\frac{3}{4}$ in.		Tubes	...	1,664.47 sq. ft
Maximum dia-				Firebox	...	152.08 sq. ft
meter	...	5 ft	$5\frac{1}{2}$ in.	Total	...	1,816.55 sq. ft
FIREBOX LENGTH						
Inside	...	7 ft	$10\frac{1}{4}$ in.	GRATE AREA		
Outside	...	8 ft	6 in.	Square feet	...	26.68

THE BRIGHTON 4-6-4 TANKS

FOLLOWERS of these articles, no doubt, will have realised that the old London, Brighton and South Coast Railway was a consistent user of tank engines, some of which had been specially designed for express passenger work; but since the longest possible non-stop run on the line was only about 87 miles, there was nothing incongruous in this liking for suitably-designed tank engines.

In 1912, there were some of us who, having bestowed our faith and affections upon the two splendid 4-6-2 tank engines *Abergavenny* and *Bessborough*, would have regarded with incredulity anybody who suggested that we had not seen the "last word" in tank engines. When, in the latter part of 1913, a rumour began to circulate to the effect that Brighton was building "an enormous tank engine," we frankly disbelieved it. Why was such an engine needed? Surely, the two 4-6-2 tank engines were large enough?

The rumour, however, persisted and soon became varied to the extent of suggesting that not one, but *two* very large 4-6-4 tank engines were under construction. This news created some excitement which culminated in April, 1914, when engine No 327, *Charles C. Macrae*, came out, the first of class L. Here, in truth, was one of the finest tank locomotives ever seen; even in her preliminary grey paint, she

commanded—and received—respect and admiration. The usual Brighton neatness and trimness were to be noted, and in spite of her great size, the general external proportions could hardly have been matched, let alone surpassed.

On trial, this engine suffered a series of mishaps which prompted some more or less minor alterations to the general arrangement. The capacity of the side tanks was reduced by half, and the loss was made up by the fitting of a belly-tank under the boiler. It was also found necessary to make some adjustments to the suspension gear, to improve the riding qualities. All this suggested that in this engine, as built and with her side tanks full of water, the centre of gravity was inadvisably high. After modification, there was no further trouble.

This technical hitch, as it were, delayed the arrival of the second engine, No 328, which was not turned out until September, 1914, after being modified similarly to No 327. Meanwhile, in the previous month, the first world war had broken out, and several years had yet to pass before these two engines could settle down to normal duties. But, by this time we had learnt that they had been designed and built because the LBSCR directors were contemplating the introduction of a substantial cut in the standard 60-minute timing between

London and Brighton for the principal expresses. That cut was never made; and now, 37 years after the substitution of electricity for steam power, 60 minutes is still the standard public timing, though I believe the working timetable does—or did—call for a time of 58 minutes, by certain non-stop trains, for the 51 miles.

The two magnificent class L locomotives had the following dimensions: cylinder diameter 22 in.; stroke 28 in.; piston valves, 10 in. dia., arranged behind the frames and driven by rocking shafts, one on each side of the engine. Each rocking shaft carried a pair of pendulum links, one of which was pivoted to the valve spindle, the other to the upper end of the combination lever of the Walschaerts valve gear. The lap was $1\frac{5}{16}$ in., lead $\frac{3}{16}$ in., and there was an exhaust clearance of $\frac{1}{16}$ in., according to the official drawings, though another source has recorded this clearance as 1/64 in. which, to my mind, does not make sense. The inclination of cylinders and valves was 1 in 24, while the width of the steam ports was $1\frac{1}{2}$ in. and of the exhaust ports 3 in. The exhaust ways were located exactly halfway along the length of the valve chamber and directly below the blastpipe, providing a good, straight passage for the exhaust steam.

The boiler was made in two rings, the diameters

of which were 5 ft 4¼ in. and 5 ft 5½ in., respectively. Between tubeplates, the barrel was 15 ft 1⅛ in. long and its centre line was 8 ft 11½ in. above rail level; it contained 123 tubes of 2¼ in. dia. and 21 superheater flues of 5½ in. dia., of which the combined heating surface was 1,534.92 sq. ft. The superheating surface was 383 sq. ft.

The firebox was of Belpaire type, 8 ft 6 in. long outside and 7 ft 10¼ in. inside; its heating surface was 152.08 sq. ft, so that the total, including the super-heater, was 2,070 sq. ft. The grate area was 26.68 sq ft and the working pressure ·170 p.s.i. The water capacity was 2,713 gallons and the bunker space was for 3½ tons of coal.

The wheel diameters were: bogie 3 ft 6 in., coupled 6 ft 9 in.; the total wheelbase was 40 ft, divided into 6 ft 9 in., plus 5 ft 10½ in., plus 7 ft 4½ in., plus 7 ft 4½ in., plus 5 ft 10½ in., plus 6 ft 9 in. Overhang at the front was 3 ft 0½ in. and at the back 3 ft 9 in. The length over bufferheads was 50 ft 4¾ in. In working trim the weight was 98 tons 5 cwt, with 19 tons 5 cwt on the leading bogie, 18 tons 10 cwt on the first coupled axle, 19 tons each on the second and third coupled axles and 22 tons 10 cwt on the rear bogie. The widths were

8 ft 4 in. across the tanks, cab sides and bunker, 8 ft 10 in. across the running plate and 8 ft 11 in. over the cylinder covers.

From all these dimensions it is clear that the designer, Lt-Col L. B. Billinton, was evidently set upon out-Marshing Marsh ! But it also seems that, during the war years 1914-1918, opportunity was taken to overhaul the design in certain particulars, because five more of these beautiful engines were added to the class, No 329 in October 1921, followed by 330 and 331 in December 1921, 332 in February and 333 in April 1922, and these five differed from their two older sisters in the following details: the front tubeplate was recessed 6 in. into the boiler barrel, the length of which became 14 ft 7¾ in. There were 152 tubes of 2¼ in., the heating surface of which was 1,103.12 sq. ft. In all other respects the boilers were as before, except for the altered heating surfaces, which totalled 1,816.55 sq. ft.

The apparent side tanks were dummies, water being carried in a large tank built under the boiler, between the frames, and another under the bunker, as usual. The total water capacity was 2,686 gallons.

Two of these engines, 329 and 333, were named. At the request of the Stephenson Locomotive Society,

No. 329 became *Stephenson* in November 1921. Circumstances were quite different in the case of No 333; she had been chosen as the LBSCR War Memorial engine and it had almost been decided that her name should be *Victorious*. At the last minute, however, some inspired individual had the idea that, in addition to being a war memorial, No 333 was the last tank engine that would ever be built for the old LBSCR; therefore, it would be more appropriate to associate her somehow with love's last reward, *Remembrance*. And that is what she was christened, with due ceremony and the dedication of special plaques commemorating 532 LBSCR employees who were killed in the war.

I got to know Col Billinton fairly well after 1923, and he told me that when this L class was being designed he visualised an engine capable of running the *Southern Belle*, and other crack trains, each way between London and Brighton in 45 min. or less. It is a thousand pities that the " substantial cut " in the 60-minute timing was never made !

After the electrification of the Brighton line in 1933, these engines were converted into 4-6-0 tender engines. All are now scrapped, but they made locomotive history.

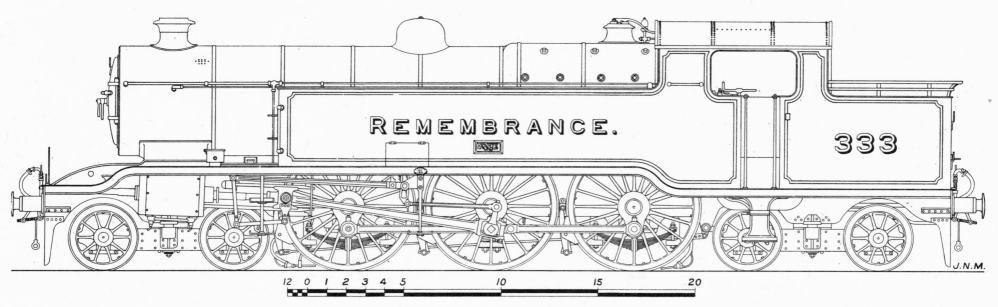

No 999 SIR ALEXANDER

GENERAL SPECIFICATION			
CYLINDERS		**TUBES**	
Diameter ... ... 18 in.		Number 246	
Stroke ... ... 24 in.		Diameter ... ... $1\frac{5}{8}$ in.	
BOILER		**HEATING SURFACE**	
Length between		Tubes... ... 1,127 sq. ft.	
tubeplates ... 10 ft 6 in.		Firebox ... 122 sq. ft.	
Maximum diameter 4 ft 2 in.		Total ... ... 1,249 sq. ft.	
FIREBOX LENGTH			
Inside ... ... —		**GRATE AREA**	
Outside ... 6 ft 0 in.		Square feet 18	

IN the beginning of this century the Great Western Railway still owned several 2-2-2 type express passenger locomotives which were used on the lighter fast passenger trains. The engines were of three different classes: the Sir Watkin class, the Cobham class and the Queen class.

The last-named were the largest, and No 999, *Sir Alexander*, was one of them. This engine was rather a pet of mine, partly because I saw her so infrequently and partly because her appearance was so different from that of most of the others. In any case my first sight of her left an indelible impression on my mind.

One summer's day in 1901 I was in a train bound for Reading from Paddington. We passed the Westbourne Park engine sheds—a place which never failed to attract my attention—and as usual quite a lot of engines were to be seen. But standing slightly apart from the rest was *Sir Alexander*—beautifully clean and literally glistening in the brilliant sunshine.

At once I noticed that she had a boiler with a high, raised round-top firebox and with a very tall dome set far forward on the barrel. I know now that she carried that boiler for the last four years of her existence—from May 1900, until October 1904; also, only two of her 20 sisters ever had such a boiler.

This class of very efficient singlewheelers originated with No 55, *Queen*, in 1873; in 1875, 20 more, with slight alterations and numbered 999, 1000 and 1116 to 1133, were built. Between October 1903, and May 1914, they were gradually withdrawn and scrapped. In their original condition all except No 55 had domeless boilers, but in my time all these boilers had been replaced by a variety of more modern types, and hardly two engines looked exactly alike.

The dimensions of No 999 were: Cylinders, diameter 18 in., stroke 24 in.; boiler, length 10 ft 6 in., diameter 4 ft 2 in. maximum; 246 tubes, $1\frac{5}{8}$ in. dia.; firebox casing 6 ft long; heating surface, 1,127 sq. ft for tubes, 122 sq. ft for firebox; pressure 140 lb.; grate area, 18 sq. ft; wheels, leading and trailing, 4 ft $1\frac{1}{2}$ in., driving 7 ft $1\frac{1}{2}$ in.; weight in working order, 37 tons, of which 15 tons 6 cwt rested on the driving wheels.

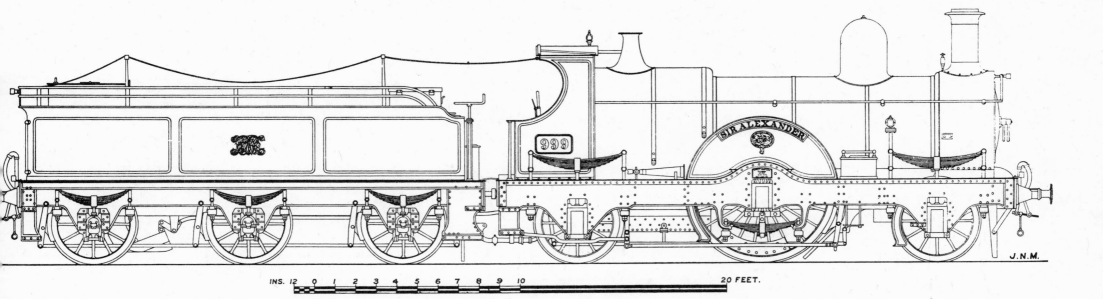

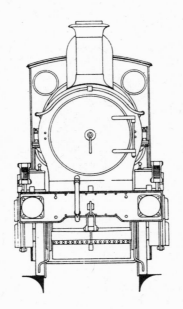

The wheelbase was 17 ft 6 in., divided into 8 ft 6 in. plus 9 ft. The tractive effort at 85 per cent boiler pressure was 11,016 lb.

Sir Alexander was stationed at Wolverhampton and worked expresses from there to Oxford, though she often came through to London. Like the other engines of her type, she was a fast runner though she could be easily hindered by inclement weather and strong winds. Generally, however, these engines gave satisfactory service until outclassed by larger and more powerful types.

It is worth mentioning that the nameplates of *Sir Alexander* were unique in having letters of the well-known GWR style, but sunk into a plain brass plate and filled in with black wax. In other words these plates were the reverse of the normal pattern.

One of them has been preserved by the Stephenson Locomotive Society and hangs in the meeting room at the society's headquarters. There was nothing unusual about the numberplates.

When I knew No 999, she was fitted with the later Swindon pattern of 3,000-gallon tender weighing 36 tons 15 cwt in working order. It was, I believe, the third and last type of tender to be attached to her, but it suited her very well and definitely placed her in the " express passenger " category.

She remained, until the end of her days, on the sort of work for which she had been designed. After all, an engine of this type was unsuitable for anything else and would almost certainly be withdrawn from traffic as soon as the normal weight of trains became more than she could manage.

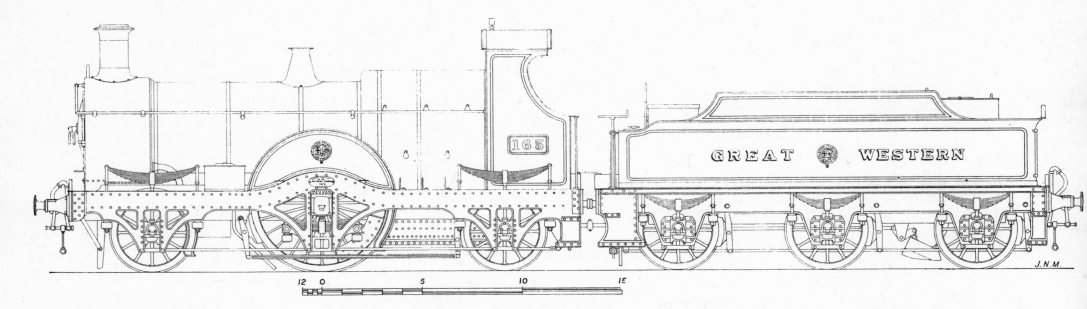

THE LAST 2-2-2 IN REGULAR SERVICE

THIS is an engine I came to know very well somewhere around 1908. She was then stationed at Oxford, whence she often worked fast trains to London until about 1910 when she was put on to purely secondary duties.

She spent her last years working stopping trains on the Fairford branch, generally doing quite well with them in spite of the fact that she was scarcely an ideal type of engine for such a job.

She was one of a class of ten engines built at Swindon in 1878-9 to replace ten very similar engines that had been built by Sharp Stewart and Co. of Glasgow, in 1862. The new engines, like the old ones they superseded, were numbered 157 to 166 and originally they all had domeless boilers.

In course of time reboilering was needed, and when I made my first acquaintance with this class, in the early 1900s, hardly two of the engines were exactly alike in appearance. No 160 had a large boiler with a Belpaire firebox and a big brass dome; her cab was almost the full width of the running plate and had a high rounded roof.

Nos 159, 163 and 165 had domeless boilers with Belpaire fireboxes, as seen in the drawing; but although the height of their cabs was increased to clear the fireboxes, the width was not altered. Nos 161, 162 and 164 had small boilers with flush, round-topped fireboxes and the dome on the back ring. No 166 had a similar boiler, but with the dome on the front ring.

No 157, however, was the most distinctive of them all; her boiler was of the Wolverhampton pattern similar to that of No 999. It had the characteristic round-topped, raised firebox, and the tall brass dome was placed at the forward end of the barrel close to the smokebox. No 157 carried this boiler until she was withdrawn.

Until the early 1900s, these engines were employed chiefly on expresses between London and Birmingham, a route on which they were well known and very popular. No 162, *Cobham*, the only named engine of the class, was in charge of Driver David Hughes for many years on this service, and had a wonderful reputation for punctuality. It is said that many stationmasters, and some of the farmers near the line, would set their clocks when Hughes and *Cobham* passed by.

It was in their last years that I got to know several of these engines; by that time, they had been taken off the Birmingham expresses, and were working semi-fast trains between Paddington, Oxford, Swindon and Bristol. Occasionally, one would be seen on the Berks and Hants line working to or from Winchester via Newbury.

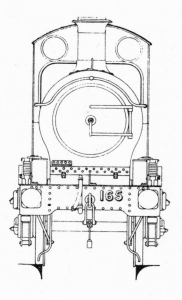

GENERAL SPECIFICATION

CYLINDERS			TUBES		
Diameter	...	... 18 in.	Number	...	... 244
Stroke	...	... 24 in.	Diameter	...	... 1⅝ in.
BOILER			HEATING SURFACE		
Length between			Tubes...		1,174.25 sq. ft.
tubeplates ...		11 ft 0 in.	Firebox	...	115.6 sq. ft.
Maximum diameter	4 ft 5 in.		Total	...	1,289.85 sq. ft.
FIREBOX LENGTH			GRATE AREA		
Inside...	...	—	Square feet	...	... 18.37
Outside	...	5 ft 1 1⁄16 in.			

No 165, rebuilt as shown in the drawing, was then stationed at Oxford and sometimes came up to London. The last time I saw her at Paddington was one morning in the summer of 1910, when she arrived on a two-coach special which, I was told, was conveying a party of Oxford dons to some convention or conference. She returned home on the 12.30 p.m. to Oxford, piloted by a 4-4-0 of the Atbara class, and so far as I know, she never came to London again.

The normal duties of No 165 were the stopping trains between Oxford and Reading, or Banbury; but she very often worked on the Fairford branch, and actually finished her days on that line. She was withdrawn for scrap, the last survivor of her class, in December 1912; incidentally, she was the last 2-2-2 type engine to be in regular service in England.

Her dimensions were: cylinders 18 in. dia., 24 in. stroke; leading and trailing wheels 4 ft dia.; driving wheels 7 ft dia.; wheelbase 17 ft 8 in., divided into 8 ft 6 in. plus 9 ft 2 in.; the overhang was 4 ft at the front and 3 ft 9 in. at the back.

The domeless boiler with raised Belpaire firebox shown on the drawing was not a new one; it had been put on to a sister engine, No 159, in June 1900 and was transferred to No 165 in July 1906 after No 159 had been scrapped. The diameter of the barrel was 4 ft 5 in. and its length was 11 ft. There were 244 tubes of 1⅝ in. dia.; the firebox was 5 ft 1 1⁄16 in. long and 3 ft 3⅛ in. wide, its height 6 ft 2 in.

The heating surface of the tubes was 1,174.25 sq. ft, and that of the firebox 115.6 sq. ft, making the total 1,289.85 sq. ft. The grate area was 18.37 sq. ft and the working pressure was 165 lb., believed to have been increased at a later date to 180 lb. The engine weight in working order was 38 tons, approximately, but I have not been able to discover the precise details as no official diagram seems to have been issued for an engine of this class rebuilt with the domeless Belpaire boiler.

The original tenders for these engines were of the Armstrong sandwich-frame pattern with 3,000 gallons capacity; but in my time all the engines, except No 157, had been fitted with standard Dean tenders, which did not match up with the engines so well. No 157 retained her original tender until she was withdrawn in June 1903.

The only other engine of this class to be rebuilt with a domeless Belpaire boiler was No 163; in this form, at first, she looked exactly like No 165 but later on she was provided with a very tall, slender-looking safety-valve casing which gave her a distinctive though decidedly curious appearance. I never knew the reason for that particular casing, and I certainly never saw another like it on the GWR. If Swindon was merely trying it out as an experiment in aesthetics I can only say that it was not particularly successful !

DEAN'S 3232 CLASS

THE Great Western Railway, like several other railways before 1890, relied very largely upon the 2-4-0 locomotive for standard-gauge express passenger work. It had a number of different classes of 2-4-0, most of them notable for the excellent work that was obtained from them; they were well distributed all over the GWR system and were frequently to be seen on top-link express trains which they shared with the more famous single-wheelers.

The basis of the usual design was a set of 20 engines, the 806 class, built by Joseph Armstrong at Swindon in 1873. William Dean in 1881-2 built another 20, the 2201 class, a somewhat modernised version of the Armstrong engines. All the engines had 17 in. × 24 in. cylinders and 6 ft 6½ in. coupled wheels. .

Finally, between September 1892, and July 1893, Dean brought out a further 20, the 3232 class, which were the last new engines of the 2-4-0 type to be built for the GWR. They were great favourites of mine, more massive and considerably more powerful than their predecessors; they were put straight away to working express trains between London and South Wales and Weymouth, and on that backwater of the GWR, the line between Bristol and the north via Shrewsbury. In their early years they were seldom or ever to be seen on the West of England main line; but later they took to working semi-fast passenger trains between Bristol and Exeter, Swindon and Weymouth and Paddington and Swindon.

It is on record that, on one occasion, No 3240, working the Night Mail from Shrewsbury to Bristol, attained 93 m.p.h. somewhere between Craven Arms and Hereford in an all-out effort to make up time lost in the early stages of the run. Such a speed

[Drawing unfinished]

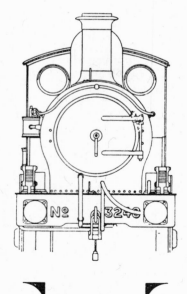

as this was, of course, very exceptional in those days; but I see no reason to doubt it. My personal experiences and observations showed the 3232 class to be very speedy engines, even with heavy trains; but I never noted anything much in excess of 70 m.p.h. with them, and that only rarely. One thing was very noticeable: these beautiful engines performed their allotted tasks without anything like the raucous, noisy fuss which was so characteristic of their more famous 2-4-0 counterparts, the LNWR Jumbos.

It is now necessary to give the dimensions of the 3232 class, because I want to tell you about a mysterious occurrence involving two of the 806 class, Nos 812 and 817, and confirmed by photographs which I have.

The 3232 class had cylinders 17½ in. dia. × 24 in. stroke. Leading wheels were originally 4 ft 1 in. dia., and driving and coupled 6 ft 7 in. dia.; but thicker tyres were adopted soon afterwards, making the diameters 4 ft 1½ in. and 6 ft 8½ in. The wheelbase was 16 ft 6 in., divided into 8 ft plus 8 ft 6 in., while the overhangs were 4 ft 7 in. at front and 4 ft 4 in. at back.

Different varieties of boiler were used; the one in the drawing had the barrel 11 ft long and made in two rings, 4 ft 1½ in. and 4 ft 3 in. diameter. The outer firebox was 5 ft 4 in. long, and the inner one 4 ft 8 in. There were 245 tubes of 1¾ in. dia., and the heating surface was 1,264.92 sq. ft for the tubes and 98.6 sq. ft for the firebox, a total of 1,363.52 sq. ft.

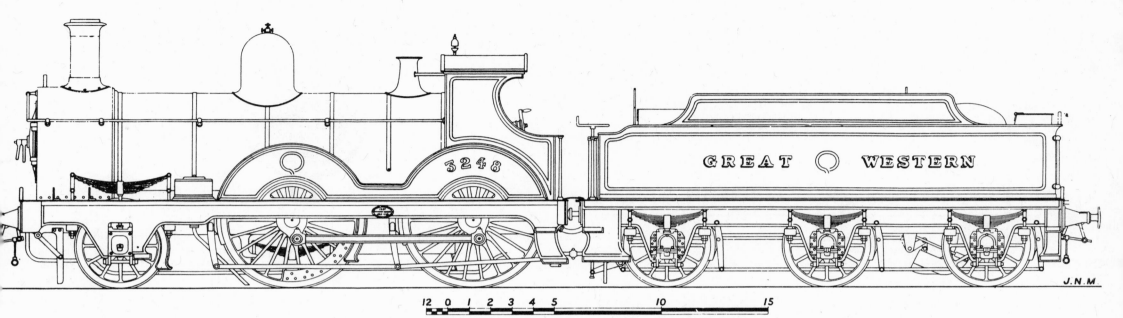

The pitch of the centre-line was 7 ft 1½ in. from rail level; the grate area was 17.17 sq. ft; and the working pressure was 150 p.s.i. All the original boilers were similar to these, except that the dome position was on the front ring.

In working order, the engine weight was 39 tons 8 cwt with 12 tons on the leading axle, 14 tons 16 cwt on the driving axle, and 12 tons 12 cwt on the trailing one. The official figure for the tractive effort was 11,641 lb. About 1912, Nos 3235, 3245 and 3247 were fitted with the automatic train control apparatus; but none of the others seem ever to have had it, and 3235 was deprived of it in 1922.

Now we come to the mystery; but first I must state that the wheelbase of the 806 and 2201 classes was 8 ft 3 in. plus 8 ft 6 in., totalling 16 ft 9 in. and the leading overhang was 4 ft 4 in.; at the same time I must point out that the four-coupled wheels of the 806 and 2201 classes had only 18 spokes compared with the 22 spokes of the 3232 class.

With all this in mind, you will have some idea of the surprise which was caused when, in the summer of 1907, No 817 appeared as a 3232 class engine. There could be no doubt about it; she had the shorter wheelbase, longer front overhang, larger cab and 22-spoked coupled wheels. In other words, she had been rebuilt with new frames, new wheels, new boiler and new superstructure; *ergo*, she was a brand new engine, exactly similar to a class that was, at least, rapidly becoming obsolescent!

Surprise was repeated and to some extent intensified in May 1917, when No 812 was turned out "rebuilt" in exactly the same way, except that she had acquired a Belpaire firebox which, by that time, had been fitted to several engines of the 3232 class. So far as I have been able to discover, 812 and 817 were the only two engines transformed in this way.

What lay behind this mysterious occurrence? The mystery is heightened by the fact that there is no official record that it ever took place; yet photographs exist to prove it. The official records for the dates which I have given show that both engines received new boilers; but there is no mention of any other alterations. I suppose that we shall never know the full explanation, unless these notes happen to catch the eye of someone who was at Swindon and can remember the circumstances.

The tenders were of two sizes; most of them were the standard 3,000-gallon type seen in the drawing, though some of the engines had the shorter 2,500-gallon tender, probably depending upon the sizes of turntables in the districts in which the engines were stationed.

No 3248 was an engine that I knew very well in my younger days; she was often to be seen on the Reading-Newbury line, working trains to and from Trowbridge, and was always in spic and span condition. But I knew many more of the class and can just remember them when they worked South Wales expresses, as they continued to do right down to about 1907, in spite of the introduction of larger and more powerful express passenger types.

The first to be scrapped was 3243, in August 1918. General withdrawal did not begin until 1925; it proceeded gradually until the last two survivors were, rather oddly, 3232 and 3251, the first and the last to be built. The first was withdrawn in August, 1929, and the last in April 1930.

Nos 3239, 3241, 3242, 3248, 3249 and 3250 were fitted with the Westinghouse air brake, in addition to the usual vacuum brake, so that they could work trains of Westinghouse-fitted stock that came through occasionally from other railways. The apparatus was transferred to more powerful engines about 20 years later.

A QUAINT LITTLE 2-4-0

GENERAL SPECIFICATION

CYLINDERS
Diameter ... ... 17 in.
Stroke ... ... 24 in.

BOILER
Length, between
tubeplates 10 ft 10 in.
Maximum dia-
meter ... 4 ft 3 in.

FIREBOX LENGTH
Inside ... 4 ft 8$\frac{1}{16}$ in.
Outside ... 5 ft 4 in.

TUBES
Number 243
Diameter ... ... 1$\frac{5}{8}$ in.

HEATING SURFACE
Tubes ... 1,147.87 sq. ft
Firebox ... 99.4 sq. ft
Total ... 1,247.27 sq. ft

GRATE AREA
Square feet ... 15.62

THIS drawing shows GWR engine No 3230, which in 1920, was very well known to me.

At that date she was stationed at Didcot and worked almost exclusively on the Didcot, Newbury and Southampton line. She was then 30 years old and, as befits an engine of her small size and venerable age, she was working out her last days on light passenger duties that required no great haste or exertion. She was one of a set of six, numbered 3226 to 3231, which were of more than usual interest to locomotive historians.

The basic design dated from 1863, when Joseph Armstrong started the construction of 20 engines, known as the 111 class and completed in 1867—all at Wolverhampton.

In 1889, nearly 23 years later, the need for some further engines of this type arose, and William Dean simply took the original Armstrong design, gave it fluted instead of plain coupling rods, added a cab over the footplate, closed in the former open splashers and provided the then standard Wolverhampton boiler; he then ordered six engines to embody his modifications, and so the 3226 class came into being. They were the last tender engines to be built at Wolverhampton.

At first all six engines, like the 111 class, were in the Northern Division; but later they drifted Londonwards, and, in course of time, I made the acquaintance of all six. This would have been about 1911.

By 1919 four had been scrapped, leaving only Nos 3230 and 3231 in service. The latter was then

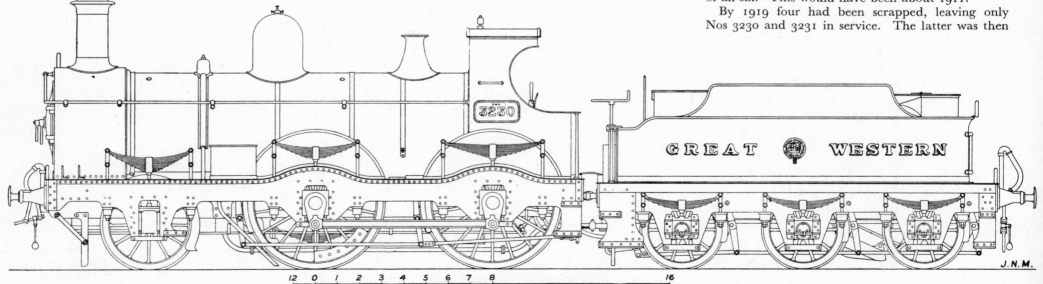

in the Shrewsbury area and could rarely, if ever, be seen south of Birmingham. She outlasted her sister by five months, being withdrawn in September 1922.

When stationed at Didcot 3230 at first was engaged in working stopping passenger trains between there and Reading or Oxford. But soon she settled down to the Didcot-Newbury-Winchester trains, confining her activities to the western side of the Didcot-Newbury-Reading triangle.

She was a quaint little object and I had a great affection for her. One of her drivers, with whom I was on speaking terms, was a fine old chap who also seemed to be very fond of her; but the young fireman obviously regarded her with a kind of amused tolerance, looking forward to the time when he would, as he thought, fire something better. Of course, he may be driving the Bristolian today!

The general dimensions of the 3226 class engines were: cylinders, 17 in. dia. and 24 in. stroke; leading wheels, 4 ft 1½ in. dia., coupled wheels, 6 ft 2 in. dia. The total wheelbase, according to the official diagrams, was 15 ft 6 in., divided into 7 ft 5½ in. plus 8 ft ½ in.; overhangs, 4 ft 6 in. in front and 4 ft at the back.

The boiler particulars that follow are based on probability, because there does not appear to have been an official diagram made for an engine of this class as fitted with a boiler of the type shown in my drawing.

The only certain information I can give is that 3230 acquired the boiler in April 1915, and it was of Swindon design and build. I surmise, therefore, that it was one of a batch of about 30 built between 1904 and 1909 for use on some of the smaller and older types of engines, in which case the following particulars would apply:

The barrel was made in two rings, the larger (back) one of which was 4 ft 3 in. dia. and had the dome mounted on it; the length of the barrel was 10 ft 10 in., and its pitch was 6 ft 10 in. There were 243 tubes of 1⅝ in. dia. and the working pressure was 150 p.s.i.

The firebox was 4 ft 8 1/16 in. long, 3 ft 8 in. wide and 5 ft 7¾ in. high, and the grate area was 15.62 sq. ft. The tube heating surface was 1,147.87 sq. ft, and that of the firebox was 99.4 sq. ft, making the total 1,247.27 sq. ft. An added point of interest is that top-feed was fitted, as shown; this was not usual on these boilers.

The normal tenders for these engines were of 2,500 gallon type; but, for some reason or other, 3230 had one of the very small 2,000-gallon tenders. The weight of this engine was about 36 tons, of which some 24½ tons rested on the coupled wheels. The tender, full, weighed 24 tons.

Other engines of this class that I often saw prior to 1915 were 3226, 3228 and 3231. The first of these was often to be seen at Didcot, though I believe she

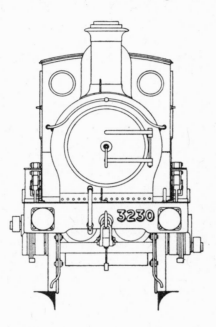

was actually stationed at Swindon. At that time she carried a boiler of similar type to the one on 3230—although the chimney appeared to be slightly longer and had no smoke deflector. Her tender was larger and longer, being of the 2,500-gallon type.

No 3228, when I first met her in 1910, was really the gem of the series; her boiler was of the Wolverhampton pattern, having a raised round-top firebox, and fitted with an extended smokebox on which was mounted a short chimney with a smoke deflector. Her boiler barrel appeared to be made in two rings, with a tall dome set at the back end of the front ring.

Her tender was an old one of the Gooch slotted, sandwich-frame type, possibly from an old goods

engine that had been scrapped some years before. It had not then had the coal rails replaced by a raised coalplate.

A year or two later, about 1912, I met 3228 again, and was not a little amused to see that her appearance was much altered, for she now had a boiler with a Belpaire firebox and with the dome on the back ring. She still had her old tender, but the coal rails had gone and a raised coalplate had been put on instead.

No 3231 was often to be seen at Birmingham Snow Hill Station, when I was temporarily stationed there in 1920. She had a Wolverhampton boiler similar to the one that 3228 formerly carried. Her tender was of the Dean 2,500-gallon type at that time. Nos 3227 and 3229, so far as I can recall, were similar to 3230 in general appearance, except for larger tenders.

These fascinating little engines may have seemed small, but they were quite powerful for their size; with 150 p.s.i. pressure in the boiler, the official tractive effort figure was 11,950 lb. I never saw one on a really heavy train, but, except when working goods trains, they generally gave the impression of being in a hurry, which was always rather amusing to watch.

Outside coupling rods, at one time so commonly seen on the GWR, were a never-ending source of interest to me—and this, together with the almost infinite variety of detail changes to be noted, probably accounted for my fondness for so many of the older GWR locomotives.

At any rate, by that time I had become a confirmed enthusiast for the creations of Dean and Churchward. But of all the GWR engines, 3230 is one of my outstanding memories.

Her small tender was of interest, in that it was one of those designed by William Dean for the Duke-class 4-4-0s in 1895. Its small size was necessary because in Devon and Cornwall the existing turntables were not long enough to take engines fitted with the larger sizes of tender.

The same restrictions applied in later years to other localities, especially in Wales and on some cross-country connecting routes nearer London. The result was that this small type of tender, with its 11 ft equally-divided wheelbase, was attached to certain engines of the Armstrong and Dean 0-6-0 types, Dukes, Bulldogs and some 2-4-0s.

GENERAL SPECIFICATION

CYLINDERS			**TUBES**	
Diameter	... ... 17 in.		Number 245	
Stroke	... ... 24 in.		Diameter ... ... 1¾ in.	
BOILER				
Length, between			**HEATING SURFACE**	
tubeplates	... 11 ft		Tubes ... 1,264.93 sq. ft	
Maximum dia-			Firebox ... 101.17 sq. ft	
meter	... 4 ft 3 in.		Total ... 1,366.1 sq. ft	
FIREBOX LENGTH				
Inside	... 4 ft 8⅟₁₆ in.		**GRATE AREA**	
Outside	... 5 ft 4 in.		Square feet ... 17.33	

2-4-0 ISIS No 73

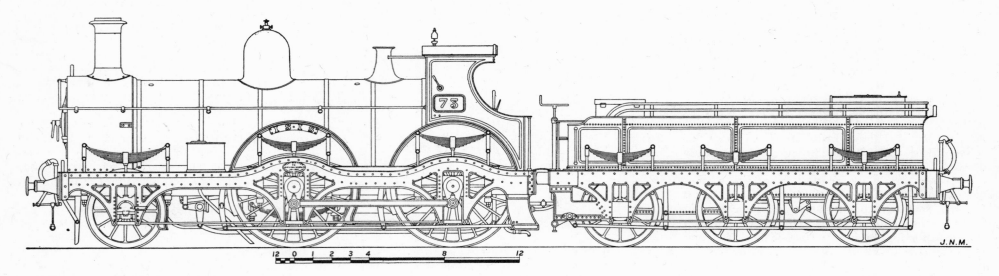

O F all the hundreds of locomotives that I have known, this one is remembered with a very special affection; for in September, 1904, when I was a boy of 12, she was the engine on which I had my first footplate ride.

I had spent part of my summer holidays with my grandparents, as usual, at their country cottage at Bucklebury, Berks, and was returning home to London with my grandfather. While we were waiting for the train at Midgham station, I noticed that my grandfather had a quiet conversation with the station-master; but not until the train arrived was I made aware of anything unusual. Then the stationmaster laid a hand on my shoulder and, with a: " This way, young man," hurried me towards the engine and helped me up into the cab, where the driver had obviously been warned to expect me.

I remained on the engine until we got to Reading, a 10-mile trip during which we stopped at the two intermediate stations, Aldermaston and Theale. From each of these, the driver allowed me to start the engine by pushing the regulator handle over, a job which, I recall, required all my strength. But I think my most vivid recollection is the terrific heat in the cab; it was like no heat I had ever experienced, especially when the fireman was firing.

Isis and her seven sisters, *Avon, Dart, Dee, Exe, Stour, Teign* and *Wye*, became favourites of mine; they were beautiful engines to look at, and they were very frequent visitors to Paddington. I knew them all, though *Dee* and *Wye* were to be seen much less often than the others. They were numbered 69 to 76, and they were extremely interesting historically; they were built by Beyer Peacock and Co., as 2-2-2 type single-wheeled express engines, 69 to 72 in 1855, and 73 to 76 in 1856. Not only were they the first standard-gauge passenger engines to be built for the GWR, but they were the first locomotives to be constructed by the famous firm of Beyer Peacock and Co. They were renewed between 1872 and 1875, at Wolverhampton, and it seems that certain usable parts of the original engines were incorporated in the renewals. By 1895 their usefulness as single-wheelers was becoming dubious, owing to their light weight; so

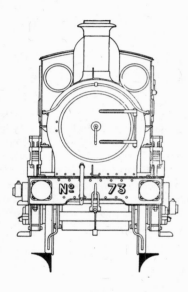

they were all sent to Swindon where they were completely reconstructed as 2-4-0 express engines. This is the form in which I knew them.

The old Wolverhampton frames were used again, but were lengthened, and in some the former boilers were retained for a few years. New cylinders, wheels and valve gear were provided and the result was a class of eight excellent engines which did good work for about another 20 years.

An added distinction, unusual for GWR standard-gauge 2-4-0 engines, was the provision of names, which led to the engines becoming known as the "River" class. No 74 was intended to be *Thames*,

but the six-letter nameplate would not fit nicely between the two upper ends of the spring hangers, so *Stour* was substituted.

On January 16, 1907, *Dart* (No 70) was in collision with a Dean 0-6-0, No 2448, at Thingley Junction, and both engines were so badly damaged that they had to be scrapped. In March, 1907, No 69, *Avon*, was scrapped for some reason which, so far as I have been able to discover, was never divulged. The other six engines remained at work for several years afterwards, No 71, *Dee* and 72, *Exe*, being withdrawn in June, 1913; No 76, *Wye*, in May, 1914; No 75, *Teign*, in June, 1915, and Nos 73 and 74, *Isis* and *Stour*, in October and December 1918.

The drawing shows *Isis* as she was when I rode on her; not long before, she had been to Swindon to have her old boiler replaced by the one shown. In this condition the dimensions were: cylinders, 17 in. dia., 24 in. stroke; wheel diameters, leading, 4 ft 1½ in., coupled 6 ft 8 in.; wheelbase, 17 ft 6 in., divided into 9 ft plus 8 ft 6 in.; overhang at the front 3 ft 6 in., at the back 4 ft 3 in.

The boiler was in two rings, the back one 4 ft 3 in. dia.; the length of the barrel was 11 ft and its pitch 6 ft 11 in. above rail level. The firebox was 5 ft 4 in. long outside; inside it measured 4 ft 8 1/16 in. long, 3 ft 8 in. wide and 5 ft 7¾ in. high. The grate area was 17.33 sq. ft.

There were 245 tubes of 1¾ in. dia. giving 1,264.93 sq. ft of heating surface, to which the firebox added 101.17 sq. ft, so the total heating surface was 1,366.10 sq. ft. The working pressure was 150 p.s.i., and the tractive effort 12,084 lb.

The type of tender shown in my drawing was, at first, common to all eight engines of the River class; its capacity was for about 2,250 gallons of water and 4½ tons of coal. Later, the coal rails on all except one of these tenders were replaced by raised coal-plates. The exception was No 74, *Stour*, the old tender of which was replaced by a standard Dean 2,500-gallon type.

The old form of tender was carried on six 4 ft wheels; its wheelbase was 13 ft, divided into 6 ft 2 in. plus 6 ft 10 in. The leading and trailing overhangs respectively were 3 ft 9 in. and 3 ft 4½ in. The rear buffer beam was a massive baulk of oak, 7 ft 2 in. long, 1 ft 6½ in. deep and 6 in. thick, with a ¾ in.

steel flitchplate bolted to its back face. In working trim, the weight of the tender was, I believe, 29 tons.

The weight of the engine was 12 tons on the leading wheels, 14 tons 16 cwt on the driving wheels and 12 tons 12 cwt on the trailing wheels, totalling 39 tons 8 cwt.

In my time, most of these engines were stationed at Swindon and Trowbridge, the only exception that I can recall being No 76, *Wye*, which was at Worcester and rarely seen on the London side of Oxford. Later, No 75, *Teign*, went to Reading whence she worked secondary trains between London and Didcot, or from Reading to Winchester via Newbury. *Isis* and *Stour* spent their last years at Banbury and worked chiefly on local goods trains. The last one I ever saw was, oddly enough, the *Isis*, on a goods train near Haddenham in August 1918.

About the end of 1913, *Teign* acquired a short chimney, 2 ft 8 in. high, which gave her a rather pleasing sturdy look, but I understand that it made no difference to her steaming; she retained it until she was withdrawn. Like her sisters, this engine was a swift runner when she had the chance. For some time she monopolised a turn on an up semi-fast train from Reading in mid-morning, returning in the afternoon on a 42-minute non-stop to Reading.

When reconstructed in 1895 these beautiful engines were the last to be supplied with the old Gooch type of slotted sandwich frames, a relic of the former broad-gauge era. That type of frame was extremely strong and rigid, and it was used in GWR Swindon designs for about 50 years. It was a characteristic feature of nearly all the broad-gauge engines, but on the standard gauge it shared its popularity with double plate-frames, as well as with single inside frames.

There was the usual amount of bright polished metalwork about these engines in their early years: copper-topped chimney; brass dome, safety-valve casing, whistles (two) and beading for splashers and cab, while the outer heads of the spring-hanger bolts were flat and polished, on both engine and tender. The coal rails on the tender, at one time, were kept bright; but this was probably owing to the enterprise and energy of the cleaners. But no matter how they were decorated, these were beautifully shaped engines and remarkably graceful in movement.

LORNA DOONE

LORNA DOONE was one of a class of 80 express passenger engines which to me, when a boy, were almost sacred. They stood apart from *all* other engines, and they achieved the summit of beauty in locomotive design.

I will not argue on this matter; my opinion was formed just 62 years ago and has remained unaltered ever since—against the test of time and an ever-growing appreciation of the finer details of locomotive anatomy. I should add that this applies to the engines when they were in the condition illustrated in my drawing.

Later, these engines were subjected to various changes of detail, none of which improved the appearance; some very definitely ruined it. However, this famous class originated with No 3031, *Achilles*, in March 1894 and finished with No 3080, *Windsor Castle*, exactly five years later. Meanwhile, 30 earlier engines built as 2-2-2s in 1891-2 were converted to 4-2-2s and added to the other 50 to make up the total of 80. But William Dean excelled himself with their design, producing something unique and of compelling aspect.

Swindon, their birthplace, was justifiably proud of them, and when the town became a borough in 1898, a representation of No 3029, *White Horse*, was incorporated in its coat-of-arms. Further, No 3012, *Great Western*, is the subject of an excellent mural pleasingly built up in coloued tiles on the left-hand wall of the entrance to the Great Western Hotel at Swindon.

The appearance of these beautiful engines has often been the subject of considerable discussion. The general concensus of opinion is that they were the loveliest locomotive design ever conceived; but there are dissentients from that opinion.

During my college days, I had the interesting experience of discussing this design with a student of aesthetics; he started the discussion by declaring that a locomotive was not, and never could be an object of beauty, and I strongly refuted this—naturally !

To support my argument, I produced a bundle of photographs of many types of locomotives, and handing it to my friend, without comment, told him to pick out any that he thought could be regarded as beautiful. He knew nothing about locomotives; I knew very little about aesthetics.

With a smile, he took my bundle and studied its contents for quite a long while, occasionally asking the reasons for the existence and the positions of certain details. Then, picking out a fine photograph of one of these Dean singlewheelers, he said he was prepared to revise his opinion because whoever had prepared that design *must* have possessed a rare knowledge of aesthetics.

He pointed out that engine and tender, from one end to the other, made up one harmonious whole; every detail was the right size, the right shape and in the right position, while the glorious sweep of the framing over the driving axlebox was exactly correct and could never be bettered. In short, the whole scheme was as perfect as circumstances allowed. I had known all this instinctively, beforehand, but was glad to have it confirmed !

The class has made a strong appeal to model makers—many models have been made. Some are even now in course of construction—in all sizes from 4 mm. to $\frac{3}{4}$ in. scale. Not the least attractive feature was the wonderful series of names these engines carried: *Amazon, Courier, Dragon, Westward Ho, The Queen, Lord of the Isles, Lorna Doone, Majestic*, to mention only a few. The full list embodied romance, mythology, splendour and regality in plenty.

All this was backed up by the generally good work these engines did. The run by No 3065, *Duke of Connaught*, on 9 May 1904, when she covered the $118\frac{1}{2}$ miles from Pylle Hill to Paddington in 99 min. 46 sec. with a 120-ton Ocean Mails special remains a classic. Yet the archives at Paddington show that this was not her fastest run, but is better known because it

GENERAL SPECIFICATION		
CYLINDERS	**TUBES**	
Diameter ... ... 19 in.	Number 266	
Stroke ... ... 24 in	Diameter ... ... $1\frac{1}{4}$ in.	
BOILER		
Length, between	**HEATING SURFACE**	
tubeplates 11 ft 6 in.	Tubes ... 1,434.27 sq. ft	
Maximum dia-	Firebox ... 127.06 sq. ft	
meter ... 4 ft 3 in.	Total ... 1,561.33 sq. ft	
FIREBOX LENGTH		
Inside ... 5 ft 8 in.	**GRATE AREA**	
Outside ... 6 ft 4 in.	Square feet ... 20.8	

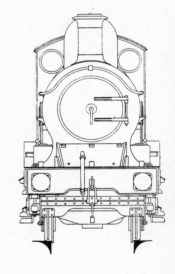

was her contribution to the astounding Record of Records run from Plymouth to London on that day.

In ordinary work not so much haste was required, and the engines performed their duties in good style for nearly a quarter of a century in spite of their being of an obsolescent type. The class became extinct in December 1915, with the withdrawal of No 3050, *Royal Sovereign*, and No 3074, *Princess Helena*.

To the man-in-the-street the main feature of these remarkable locomotives was their truly arresting appearance, with its beautiful proportions, green and Indian red livery, black and orange lining and the lavish display of polished brass, copper and steel. Yet this was not overdone. It was just right; any more would have ruined it the way that the very fine model of No 3048, *Majestic*, at Paddington Station has been spoilt by over-decoration—a pity, because with the exception of the coal-plates on the tender, which belong to a later period, this model is well-nigh perfect.

From the technical angle I always regard these engines as the beginning of that exceptional combination of dimensions and ratios that was so persistently developed at Swindon during the next 60 years. Their chief trouble was, of course, wheel slip when starting, and I can recall some really painful exhibitions of that kind. Yet, on rare occasions, I have seen an engine of this class start a train of 10 corridor coaches without any slipping at all. I think a lot depended on how they were handled. There is a story that only two engines of the class were ever seen at Gloucester, simply because the two drivers concerned were the only men who would undertake to get one of these single-wheelers up the Sapperton bank.

The two engines were No 3031, *Achilles*, and No 3048, *Majestic*; I have an old, faded photograph of the latter in Gloucester station, but have never seen another. It is worth noting that No 3080, *Windsor Castle*, differed from all the others in being reversed by a lever instead of by the normal screw gear, and I wonder if this had anything to do with the fact that the work of this engine was never outstanding.

Some of the leading dimensions of these engines were: cylinders, 19 in. dia. by 24 in. stroke; the steamchest was underneath the cylinders, with the valves upside down and direct-driven by a beautifully-designed Stephenson link motion; the width of the steam ports was 2 in., while that of the exhaust ports was 3¼ in., the common length being 14 in. The wheel diameters were: bogie, 4 ft 1½ in. driving, 7 ft 9 in.; trailing, 4 ft 7½ in., and tender 4 ft 1½ in. The wheelbase of the engine was divided into 7 ft plus 7 ft 6 in. plus 9 ft, totalling 23 ft 6 in.; the overhang was 3 ft at the front and 4 ft 6 in. at the back. The tender wheelbase was 15 ft equally divided and the overhang 4 ft at the front and 3 ft 6 in. at the back.

The boiler was made in two rings, 4 ft 2⅛ in. and 4 ft 3 in. dia.; the barrel was 11 ft 6 in. long and pitched 7 ft 7½ in. above rail level. It had a firebox of the raised round-top pattern, the outer casing of which was 6 ft 4 in. long by 4 ft wide; the inner casing was 5 ft 8 in. long by 3 ft 4 in. wide and was 6 ft 2 in. high. The steam space was augmented by the provision of a very large dome, in which the regulator was housed, mounted on the back ring of the barrel.

There were 266 tubes of 1¾ in. dia. and 11 ft 9¼ in. long; their heating surface amounted to 1,434.27 sq. ft, while the firebox added 127.06 sq. ft to make up the respectable total of 1,561.33 sq. ft. The grate area was 20.8 sq. ft, and the working pressure was 160 p.s.i., at 85 per cent. of which the tractive effort was 12,670 lb.

The tenders for the entire class were of the standard 3,000-gallon pattern, the coal-rails of which were originally kept bright. In 1906, however, a start was made in replacing the coal-rails with raised coal-plates, a disfigurement that rapidly became standard for all types of GWR tenders.

Lorna Doone, one of my special pets in this lovely class, was never rebuilt. She was withdrawn, to my sorrow, in November 1912.

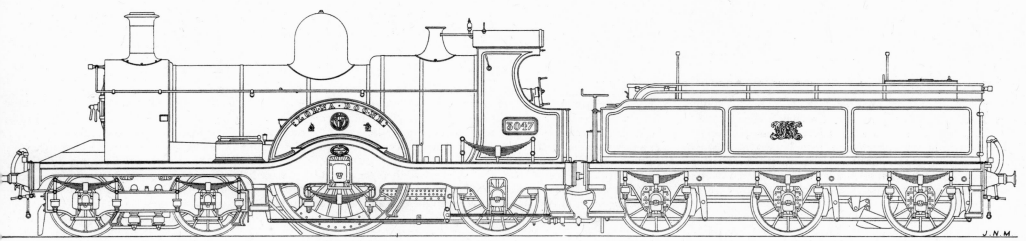

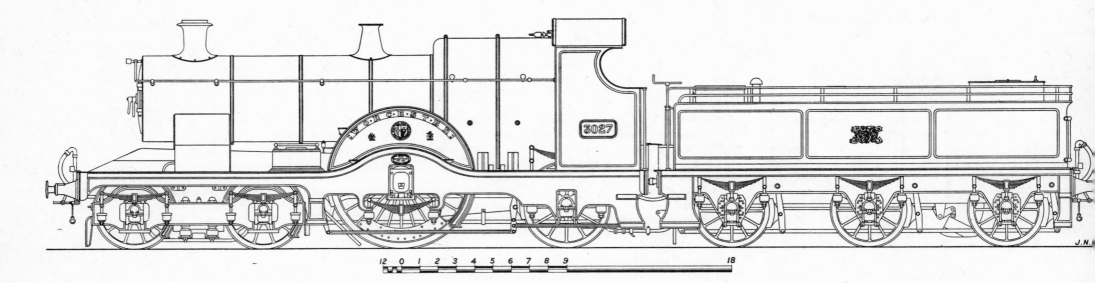

GENERAL SPECIFICATION

CYLINDERS				TUBES			
Diameter	...	...	19 in.	Number	...	...	277
Stroke	...	...	24 in.	Diameter	...	...	$1\frac{7}{8}$ in.

BOILER			
Length, between			
tubeplates	...		11 ft
Maximum dia-			
meter	...		4 ft 6 in.

HEATING SURFACE

Tubes	...	1,538.06 sq. ft
Firebox	...	124.96 sq. ft
Total	...	1,663.02 sq. ft

FIREBOX LENGTH			
Inside	...		6 ft $4\frac{1}{18}$ in.
Outside	...	...	7 ft

GRATE AREA

Square feet	...	21.45

The first rebuild of
THE DEAN BOGIE
SINGLEWHEELERS

IN the previous chapter I wrote about William Dean's magnificent bogie singlewheelers as they were when I first knew them. In the opinion of most people, they were then at their best, at least so far as their appearance was concerned; moreover, it was a time when those engines were employed in the top-link express passenger services and doing good work.

Part of the Swindon Works routine, however, was always to keep locomotives of all types well up-to-date by detail modification, rebuildings where necessary, and other processes apart from general repairs. Naturally, the Dean bogie singles became involved in this important programme, and in due time, these engines were subjected to three different styles of rebuilding. The present article deals with and illustrates the first. In the next one I have described the third, and last, style; the second was not of much consequence and, in any case, was applied to only three engines of the class.

Engine No 3027, *Worcester*, was the first to be rebuilt, and she was put into traffic in August 1900.

To put it plainly, she was a violent shock to enthusiasts of that period. I felt angry because the transformation seemed to be a hideous desecration of the loveliest engines then known to me. Later, when other engines of the class were similarly rebuilt, the idea dawned that they still possessed some degree of elegance, common to all singlewheelers, and they certainly continued to do excellent work.

In the Swindon Engine Diagram book, six diagrams, lettered A to F, were allocated to these 4-2-2s, and this first rebuild appeared on Diagram C. It applied to 13 engines: 3004 *Black Prince*, 3013 *Great Britain*, 3016 *Lightning*, 3018 *Racer*, 3027 *Worcester*, 3033 *Albatross*, 3039 *Dreadnought*, 3048 *Majestic*, 3052 *Sir Walter Raleigh*, 3058 *Grierson*, 3067 *Duchess of Tick*, 3070 *Earl of Warwick* and 3079 *Thunderbolt*. There were no others, though I believe the original intention was to rebuild 24; for some reason, the order was altered.

For a few years, these "Diagram C" engines were engaged on express passenger trains between London and Newton Abbot, Birmingham and Worcester. Some of them were later sent to work between Shrewsbury and Bristol via Hereford, a comparatively mountainous road on which singlewheelers might have been expected to show up badly; but they didn't. Their sojourn on that line was not of long duration, and eventually these rebuilds were confined to the Oxford, Worcester, Bristol, Exeter and Newton Abbot routes, and some of the engines were stationed at all five places as well as in London. It is worth noting, too, that the line from Bristol to Exeter includes the formidable climb up the Whiteball bank, but this seemed to be no stumbling-block for single-wheelers, provided they were able to take their time and were not forced.

The "Diagram C" rebuilding was simply the replacement of the original boiler with a domeless Standard No 2 boiler having a large, high Belpaire firebox. The cab had to be altered by being made higher and much wider; otherwise, little alteration was made to the engine, except that a new bogie, with a deep frame, was later substituted for the old one. This new bogie was Churchward's modification of the Dean design, the chief difference being that the weight was supported by two outside bearers, each side, instead of by vertical tie-rods.

The tenders of most of the rebuilt engines were, at first, unaltered; but in due course, the coal rails were removed and replaced by raised coal-plates, or fenders, above the coping. The old style of painting the engines and tenders was retained until about 1906, when a new style was generally introduced for all GWR engines.

Some mitigation of the severe and austere appearance of these rebuilds took place on most of the engines, when the plain, but shapely cast iron chimney was replaced by a built-up one of larger diameter and provided with a copper cap. This welcome change was introduced on engines 3013, *Great Britain* and 3033, *Albatross*, both of which became "Diagram C" engines in November, 1906; thereafter, some of the earlier rebuilds had their chimneys changed.

I have seen it stated that a few of these rebuilds were fitted with tapered boilers; but this was impossible without putting the centre line up to an inordinate height in order to clear the driving wheels. I am certain that no GWR singlewheeler of either 2-2-2 or 4-2-2 type ever carried a tapered boiler, though many were fitted with domeless boilers.

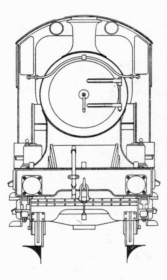

The dimensions of the "Diagram C" engines were: cylinders, 19 in. dia. and 24 in. stroke; port widths, steam 2 in., exhaust 3¼ in., with a length of 14 in. for each.

The boiler barrel was 11 ft long and made in two rings 4 ft 5 in. and 4 ft 6 in. dia., respectively; the centre line was 8 ft 6 in. above rail level. The firebox, outside, was 7 ft long, the widths being 5 ft on the centre line and 4 ft between frames; inside, the length was 6 ft 4 1/16 in. and the widths 4 ft 4⅛ in. and 3 ft 4⅛ in., the depth below centre line being 5 ft 11 1/16 in. at the front and 4 ft 11 1/16 in. at the back. There were 277 tubes of 1⅞ in. dia., the heating surface of which was 1,538.06 sq. ft; the firebox heating surface was 124.96 sq. ft, making the total 1,663.02 sq. ft. The working pressure was 180 p.s.i. and the grate area was 21.45 sq. ft.

The wheel diameters were: bogie and tender, 4 ft 1½ in.; driving, 7 ft 9 in. and trailing 4 ft 7½ in. The wheelbase was 7 ft plus 7 ft 6 in. plus 9 ft. totalling 29 ft 6 in., and the overhangs were 2 ft 1 in. in front and 4 ft 3 in. at the back. In working order, the weight distribution was: 18 tons 16 cwt equally divided between the two bogie axles, 18 tons 2 cwt on the driving axle, and 14 tons 2 cwt on the trailing axle, making a total of 51 tons. The tractive force was 14,250 lb.

A 3,000-gallon tender, capable of carrying five tons of coal, was provided and was of similar pattern to the tenders designed for the 4-4-0 Atbara class. At a later date, however, the rebuilt singlewheelers were provided with slightly modified versions of their original tenders; but all the tenders were of the same size and had a wheelbase of 15 ft, equally divided, and overhangs of 4 ft in front and 3 ft 6 in. at the back; they made the total length of engine and tender, over buffers, 57 ft 7¾ in.

The dates of these "Diagram C" engines in order of numbers, were: 3004, April, 1906; 3013, November 1906; 3016, December, 1906; 3018, November, 1906; 3027, August, 1900; 3033, November, 1906; 3039, April, 1906; 3048, April, 1906; 3052, March, 1906; 3058, November, 1906; 3067, March, 1906; 3070, September, 1905, and 3079, March, 1906. These dates are from the official records, but in one or two instances, e.g. 3033, the engines were put into service a month or so later. It will be noted that five years elapsed between 3027 and the next one, 3070.

Eight of these engines, Nos 3013, 3018, 3027, 3039, 3048, 3052, 3067 and 3070, were rebuilt to "Diagram F" in 1910-11, but further reference to them will be found in the next chapter, as "Diagram F" was a more interesting and more significant reconstruction.

The last "Diagram C" engine in service was 3058, *Grierson*; she was withdrawn in February, 1912, after more than five years' express passenger work between London and her home-town, Bristol. She was originally built in April, 1895, and was named *Ulysses*. For some unexplained reason, her name was changed when she was only three weeks old.

WHEN describing the first style of rebuilding Dean's 4-2-2 engines, in the previous chapter, I mentioned that, later on, two other styles were applied. I also stated that, in the official Diagram Book, six diagrams were issued for this class; the first rebuild was on "Diagram C," the second on "Diagram D," and the third on "Diagram F."

Before I deal with the last mentioned of these diagrams, a brief reference to "Diagram D" may be of interest, though it was not of great importance or significance. It applied to three engines: 3015, *Kennet*, 3049, *Nelson* and 3050, *Royal Sovereign*. The domeless boiler was similar in appearance to that on "Diagram C," but it retained the old form of smokebox, made higher owing to the boiler centre line being raised from 7 ft 7½ in. to 8 ft 2 in. The cab roof was much flatter than that on "Diagram C," and the cab sides were of a somewhat different shape; the cab itself was almost as wide as the footplating, and its front edges, instead of being straight from top to bottom, curved forwards gently at the lower end to meet the footplating as in the original engines. *Nelson* and *Royal Sovereign* eventually came on to "Diagram F"; so we shall meet them again later in this chapter.

In 1908, the singlewheeler, which had been so popular on several British railways, had become almost obsolete, and on the GWR eight of the Dean engines were withdrawn in that year; but G. J. Churchward paused before deciding to withdraw any more. His great programme of locomotive standardisation and development was then in full swing, and he was able to give almost undivided attention to the modernisation of the best of the earlier types then existing. He asked the various district locomotive superintendents to submit reports as to the general condition of the older locomotives. As a result, it was found that many of the Dean singlewheelers were really in too good a condition to scrap, so a scheme was prepared for converting a number of them into 4-4-0 express engines which would have a better adhesion than was possible with only a single pair of driving wheels.

Further investigation, however, revealed that the cost of this scheme, per engine, was uneconomical. On the other hand, the boilers of the existing singlewheelers were wearing out. As there was still a

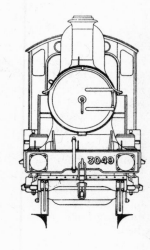

GENERAL SPECIFICATION			
CYLINDERS		**TUBES**	
Diameter ... ... 19 in.		Number 233	
Stroke ... ... 24 in.		Diameter ... ... 1⅝ in.	
BOILER			
Length, between		**HEATING SURFACE**	
tubeplates 11 ft 6 in.		Tubes ... 1,170.34 sq. ft	
Maximum dia-		Firebox ... 115.11 sq. ft	
meter ... 4 ft 3 in.		Total ... 1,285.45 sq. ft	
FIREBOX LENGTH			
Inside ... 5 ft 6 11/16 in.		**GRATE AREA**	
Outside ... 6 ft 4 in.		Square feet ... 18.12	

The third rebuilding of
DEAN'S 4-2-2s

great deal of work that the engines could do without trouble, a new design of boiler was prepared and an order issued that when the singlewheelers came into shops for heavy repairs, the best of them were to be given the new boilers and returned to traffic. The result was "Diagram F."

The first engine to be rebuilt in this style was 3070, *Earl of Warwick*, which was already a "Diagram C" engine, and she became "Diagram F" in June, 1910. It will be seen that the new boiler was, from the appearance point of view, a remarkable combination of the old and the new. It was quite pleasing to look at, but the long chimney imparted rather an old-fashioned aspect very different from the impression of stately boldness and sturdiness given by these engines before they were rebuilt. However, the experiment was successful and 23 more engines were similarly rebuilt. They were: 3006, *Courier*, in September 1910; 3009, *Flying Dutchman* (September,

1911); 3013, *Great Britain* (October, 1910); 3018, *Glenside* (formerly *Racer*) (December, 1911); 3027, *Worcester* (March, 1911); 3032, *Agamemnon* (March, 1911); 3039, *Dreadnought* (March, 1911); 3043, *Hercules* (April, 1911); 3045, *Hirondelle* (September, 1911); 3048, *Majestic* (July, 1910); 3049, *Nelson* (August, 1910); 3050, *Royal Sovereign* (February, 1914); 3052, *Sir Walter Raleigh* (March, 1911); 3055, *Lambert* (August, 1911); 3056, *Wilkinson* (September, 1910); 3060, *John G. Griffiths* (June, 1911); 3062, *Albert Edward* (August, 1911); 3065, *Duke of Connaught* (December, 1910); 3066, *Duchess of Albany* (June, 1911); 3067, *Duchess of Teck* (September, 1910); 3071, *Emlyn* (November, 1910); 3074, *Princess Helena* (November, 1911) and 3080, *Windsor Castle* (July, 1910).

As was to be expected, the life of these "Diagram F" engines was not a long one, but they managed to put in a considerable amount of useful work on the less important express passenger traffic while they

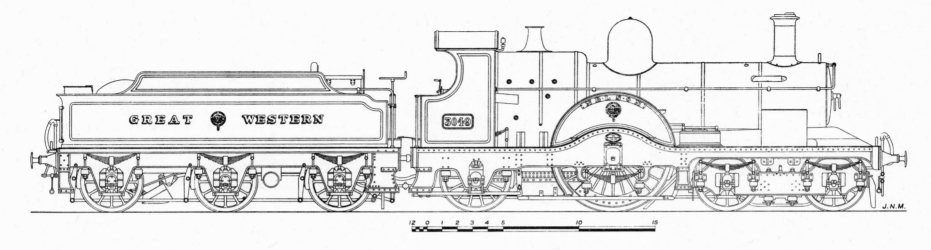

lasted. They were withdrawn from service between June, 1913 and December, 1915. The last two in traffic were 3050 and 3074.

Although I knew all these engines well, the one I knew best was 3027, *Worcester*; she was, appropriately enough, stationed at Worcester and, to the end of her days, worked the regular daily non-stop express to London and back. I especially recall her old driver. He was a gentle spoken, ascetic type of man whom I called Cesar Franck, because of his extraordinary resemblance to the celebrated Belgian organist and composer. This was all the more striking because he told me that his hobby was organ playing, and he had access to the fine organ in Worcester cathedral. He had spent practically the whole of his footplate life on singlewheelers; as a youngster, he had fired them, and as a driver he had known no other type. He was devoted to his *Worcester*, and would not have exchanged her for any other. He retired in June, 1914, and his engine was withdrawn the following month. I have an idea that the coincidence was not entirely due to chance.

Another engine I particularly remember was 3032, *Agamemnon*. I did not see her until she had become " Diagram F," and I had feared that she would spoil the record in my notebook, in which I had set down the names and numbers of all except one of the 80. After being rebuilt, 3032 was stationed at Oxford, and then, for months on end, she regularly worked an early morning fast train from there to London and returned on the 11.15 a.m. to Oxford via Maidenhead, High Wycombe and Princes Risborough.

Knowing that route as I do, I should say it was not an ideal one for singlewheelers; but 3032 was not the only one to have worked that turn, for some of the little Armstrong 7 ft singles had a regular turn on that line, and I possess a photograph of one of them running into Bourne End station. So the Dean bogie singles were merely following the tracks of their older and smaller predecessors, in spite of the nasty gradients and curves.

The dimensions of the " Diagram F " engines were very similar to the originals, but I am giving them in full, for ready reference. The cylinders were 19 in. dia., 24 in. stroke and had the steam chest underneath. The width of the steam ports was 2 in. and of the exhaust ports 3¼ in.; both were 16 in. long.

The boiler was in two rings, 4 ft 2 in. and 4 ft 3 in. dia. outside, and was 11 ft 6 in. long. Its centre line was 7 ft 10 in. above rail level. There were 233 tubes of 1⅝ in. dia., and the working pressure was 180 p.s.i.

The firebox was of the Belpaire type, the outer casing of which was 6 ft 4 in. long and 4 ft wide. The inner box was 6 ft 6 15/16 in. long, 3 ft 4 in. and 3 ft 3 in. wide, 6 ft 0½ in. high and had a grate area of 18.12 sq. ft. The heating surface totalled 1,285.45 sq. ft, that of the tubes being 1,170.34 sq. ft, and of the firebox 115.11 sq. ft.

Wheel diameters were: bogie and tender, 4 ft 1½ in.; driving, 7 ft 9 in., and trailing, 4 ft 7½ in. The tractive effort, at 85 per cent boiler pressure, was 14,250 lb.

In working order, the weight distribution was: 18 tons 2 cwt equally divided between the two bogie axles; 19 tons 11 cwt on the driving axle and 12 tons 4 cwt on the trailing axle, totalling 49 tons 17 cwt. The tender, which was of the 3,000 gallon type that I have described before, weighed 36 tons 15 cwt; so the total weight of engine and tender, all found, was 86 tons 12 cwt. Over bufferheads, the total length was 57 ft 7¾ in.

The style of finish was the standard lined green-and-black livery, with green dome, brass safety valve casing, and copper cap on the chimney. Brass moulding decorated the splashers of bogie and driving wheels and the mudguards, while engine and tender were fully lined and adorned with transfers of the GWR coat-of-arms. The front uprights of the cab sides were beaded with ¾ in. split brass tube.

Although these rebuilt engines did good work on express trains for a few years, they never had the opportunity to indulge in such exploits as had made them famous in their original condition. With the withdrawal of Nos 3050 and 3074 in December, 1915, the singlewheeler disappeared for ever from the GWR which, until then, had been a most consistent user of the type since its inception in 1837, and had produced the most celebrated examples.

THE ARMSTRONG CLASS

THE Armstrong class, GWR, consisted of four beautiful 4-4-0 express passenger locomotives, the first standard gauge engines of their type to run on the Great Western Railway and the only 7 ft 4-4-0 engines ever to run on the GWR standard gauge. In a way, they were derived from four 7 ft 2-4-0 engines built some years previously for the broad gauge, and numbered 7, 8, 14 and 16, respectively.

Numbers 7 and 8 had been built as experimental tandem compounds, in 1886, but were extremely troublesome and erratic when running, and they did little useful work. Numbers 14 and 16, however, were built in 1888, as two-cylinder simple 2-4-0s with the Gooch sandwich frames, arranged on the convertible plan and with the wheels outside the frames to adapt them for running on the broad gauge; these were good engines.

In 1892, when the broad gauge was finally abandoned, all four of these engines were withdrawn and retained pending a decision as to their future. The two compounds were definitely failures and would probably have been reconstructed as simple engines in any case; the other two were possibly scheduled

for conversion to standard gauge as soon as might be convenient. But they were all large engines for 2-4-0s, and owing to the fact that Dean's large 7 ft 8 in. 2-2-2s had given trouble which led, in 1893, to their being withdrawn for conversion into 4-2-2s, a somewhat similar process was decided upon for the four big 2-4-0s.

When at length, it came to the point, the reconstruction of the 2-4-0s was of so drastic a nature that an entirely new design was prepared utilising only the 7 ft coupled wheels of the 2-4-0s. The result was four handsome 4-4-0s built in 1894 and

known as the Armstrong class; they were numbered and named: No 7, *Armstrong*; No 8, *Gooch*; No 14, *Charles Saunders*, and No 16, *Brunel*. Surely, no lovelier 4-4-0s were ever seen! Swindon had then only recently completed the design for Dean's noble 4-2-2s, and it was but a natural step for that design to be taken as the basis of the Armstrong class. Therefore, except for the wheels, frames and a slightly lower boiler centre line, these 4-4-0s were interchangeable with the famous single-wheelers.

A comparison of the two types in traffic was interesting, as it revealed a state of affairs which, to put it flatly, was unexpected; for, in spite of the greater adhesion given by four-coupled wheels, the Armstrongs were distinctly less lively than the single-wheelers, and the reason has never been fully explained. In fact, it would take some finding, because the boilers, cylinders and valve gear were the same for both classes. It was one of those quaint little mysteries which have cropped up, from time to time, in locomotive history. All the same, the Armstrongs were not entirely unsatisfactory, within their capacity, and they outlasted the single-wheelers by about 15 years.

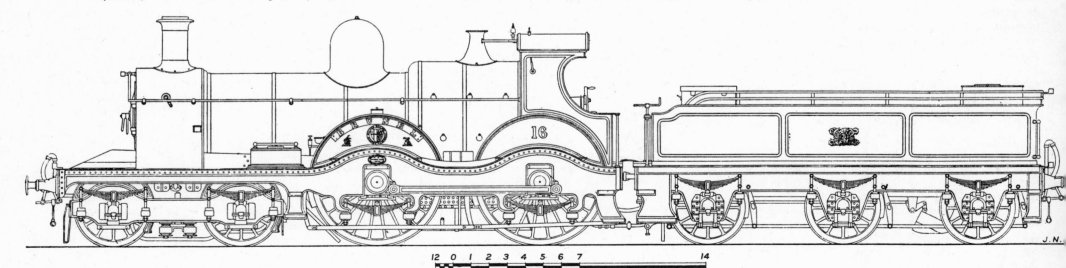

```
┌────────────────────────────────────────────────────────────────┐
│                     GENERAL SPECIFICATION                       │
│                                                                  │
│   CYLINDERS                          TUBES                       │
│       Diameter    ...    ... 20 in.      Number    ...    ...  266 │
│       Stroke      ...    ... 26 in.      Diameter  ...    ... 1¾ in.│
│                                                                  │
│   BOILER                             HEATING SURFACE             │
│       Length  between                    Tubes...    1,434.27 sq. ft.│
│          tubeplates ...   11 ft 6 in.    Firebox  ...  127.06 sq. ft.│
│       Maximum diameter 4 ft 3 in.        Total ...   1,561.33 sq. ft.│
│                                                                  │
│   FIREBOX LENGTH                     GRATE AREA                  │
│       Inside...    ...    ...  —         Square feet  ...    ...  20.8│
│       Outside     ...   6 ft 4 in.                               │
└────────────────────────────────────────────────────────────────┘
```

All four engines, at different times, were re-boilered with various sorts of domeless boilers, and they never looked so well as they did when in the condition depicted in my drawing; that is, with the original boiler fitted with a slightly extended smoke-box. They were in this condition when I first knew them, and judging from photographs, the slight extension of the smokebox considerably enhanced the appearance; all subsequent alterations did exactly the opposite !

The cylinders originally were 20 in. dia. with a stroke of 26 in., but in 1903 the diameter was reduced to 19 in. The admission ports were 14 in. long and 2 in. wide, those for exhaust being 14 in. long and 3¼ in. wide, and the Stephenson valve gear was exactly the same as that for the bogie singles.

An adequate boiler was provided; its diameters were 4 ft 2⅛ in. and 4 ft 3 in.; the barrel length was 11 ft 6 in. and the centre line stood 7 ft 4¾ in. from rail level. There were 266 tubes of 1¾ in. dia. and the working pressure was 160 p.s.i. To permit of sufficient steam space in the boiler, the top of the firebox was raised 7 in. above the top line of the barrel; the casing was 6 ft 4 in. long and 4 ft wide, and the grate area was 20.8 sq. ft. The heating surface of the tubes was 1,434.27 sq. ft, and of the firebox 127.06 sq. ft, making a respectable total of 1,561.33 sq. ft.

Wheel diameters were: bogie and tender, 4 ft 1½ in.; coupled, 7 ft 1½ in. The engine wheelbase was 23 ft 6 in. divided into 7 ft plus 7 ft 6 in. plus 9 ft. Overhang at the front was 3 ft, and at the back

4 ft 6 in., while the total length of engine and tender, over buffers, was 57 ft 10¼ in.

The tender was of the standard Dean 3,000-gallon type with a wheelbase of 15 ft, equally divided, and overhangs of 4 ft at the front and 3 ft 6 in. at the back; its full weight was 30 tons 15 cwt. The engine

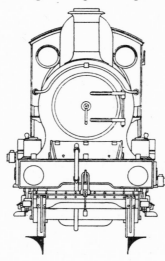

in working order, weighed 50 tons 16 cwt, divided into 19 tons 6 cwt on the bogie, 15 tons 18 cwt on the driving axle and 15 tons 12 cwt on the trailing axle. Originally, the tractive force was 16,640 lb., but was reduced when 19 in. cylinders were fitted in 1903.

Until about 1909, all four of these engines were in the Southern Division, working mainly between London and Bristol, but seldom on top-link turns; semi-fast passenger work was their usual duty, though they were sometimes used for fast freight and fish trains. By 1911, they had all been transferred to the Northern Division for working fast passenger trains from Wolverhampton to Chester and Birkenhead, and they were seldom seen in London again.

In April 1915, No 16 was altered by being fitted with 6 ft 8½ in. coupled wheels in place of her former 7-footers. At the same time, she was given a No 2 standard boiler, a brass-bound nameplate and renumbered 4169. As a result, she was assimilated into the Flower class, since the alterations made her almost exactly similar to the engines of that class. Number 14 was similarly treated in May 1917, and followed by Nos 7 and 8 in February 1923; these three engines retained their old nameplates, but were renumbered 4170, 4171 and 4172, respectively. They were withdrawn from service between August 1928, and July 1930; but the class had virtually disappeared when the Flowerising was completed in February 1923; for it was then that their unique features were removed.

My own interest in these engines was due, not only to the extraordinary beauty of their original appearance, but also to the fact that they were unique, there being no other engines like them anywhere in the world. This last remark, however, could apply to most GWR locomotives at any time in the history of Swindon productions.

After the abolition of the Great Western Railway's 7 ft gauge, in 1892, the need for a powerful, but flexible standard gauge express passenger type of engine, for working over the mountainous gradients west of Newton Abbot, became a matter of some urgency, because the average weight of trains to be hauled from Newton Abbot to Penzance had become greater than the existing types of engines could cope with satisfactorily.

William Dean, therefore, designed his celebrated Duke class of 4-4-0 engines, the first two of which were put into service in May, 1895. Between then and August, 1899, 58 more of the class were built, including one, No 3312, *Bulldog*, which, although she had the standard Duke chassis, etc., had a boiler and mountings that were altogether different from the others. This engine, new in October, 1898, was subsequently rebuilt with a Standard No 2 domeless boiler and transferred, together with 19 other Dukes, similarly rebuilt, to what eventually became the Bulldog class.

This meant that the Duke class was reduced to 40 engines, and although they were, in time, rebuilt with a variety of boilers, they remained Dukes and were never transferred to the Bulldog class. For their time, they were sturdy, powerful engines and so successful that, although the majority, for many years, worked in the Devon and Cornwall area, the rest were to be found all over the Southern Division of the GWR. I cannot recall any period between 1899 and 1951 when no Dukes were to be seen in the London district; and I do not think any other class of engine anywhere could have worked harder or better for more than 50 years.

During that time, these engines were constantly subjected to detail changes to keep them up-to-date as far as possible without adding to their weight; for there was always a need for a passenger engine type of almost Bulldog power, but capable of being used on sections of the GWR system for which the Bulldogs were too heavy. This became apparent after the grouping of the railways in 1923, when many of the Dukes were sent to work on what had been the Cambrian Railways, where the Bulldogs were never seen.

In time, all the Dukes acquired Belpaire boilers, the dimensions of which were similar to those of the original boilers with round-top fireboxes. Most of the

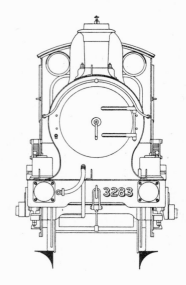

GENERAL SPECIFICATION			
CYLINDERS		**TUBES**	
Diameter ... ... 18 in.		Number ... 134 & 12	
Stroke ... ... 26 in.		Diameter ... 1⅝ & 5¼ in.	
BOILER			
Length, between		**HEATING SURFACE**	
tubeplates ... 11 ft		Tubes 826.64 & 182.51 sq. ft	
Maximum dia-		Firebox ... 114.42 sq. ft	
meter ... 4 ft 5 in.		Total ... 1,123.57 sq. ft	
FIREBOX LENGTH			
Inside ... 5 ft 1 15/16 in.		**GRATE AREA**	
Outside ... 5 ft 10 in.		Square feet ... 17.2	

THE DUKES (or DEVONS)
and Engine No 3283 *Comet* in particular

engines, when reboilered, were fitted with the large, wide, high-arched type of cab; but a few retained the original narrow cab, and of these No 3283, *Comet*, was one. This cab, however, was increased in height to clear the Belpaire firebox, and the result was that it looked narrower than ever.

For about the last 30 years of her existence, *Comet* was stationed at Didcot and was well known in the London - Oxford - Newbury - Reading - Southampton area. At first, she was employed on passenger trains; but during the war period she was relegated to freight

traffic and worked on it until she was withdrawn for scrap in December, 1950. I knew her well, and she was rather a pet of quite a number of people.

I remember one afternoon at Reading in 1948. I saw *Comet* approaching on a heavy goods bound for Southall, or Acton. When she was near enough, I was much amused to notice that some humorist had been at work on the nameplate by neatly chalking the letters " IN " at one end, " AX " at the other and whitening the rest so that the plate displayed the word INCOMETAX ! This may have been the work of the same individual who, a year or two before, had done some titivation to a decrepit and badly run-down goods engine, whose tender displayed a neatly chalked notice reading: " For sale, or would exchange for a Spitfire in going order," which caused laughter among a number of passengers waiting on Maidenhead station.

In their original condition, the Dukes, in those days known as either the Pendennis Castle class, or the Devons, were smartly turned out and embellished with the usual polished brass and copper work. In their last years, all this had been sadly changed: for a while, the engines were painted in the plain, unlined green-and-black livery, with little or no embellishment; later, even this gave way to a funereal black all over, except for red bufferbeams.

Most of the engines had the handsome built-up type of chimney replaced by the tapered cast iron chimney seen in my drawing. I have depicted *Comet* as she was when she was first stationed at Didcot, because she was, perhaps, best known in that condition; but she was really little better than a travesty of her former handsome self. At a later date, the beading on the splashers of the driving and coupled wheels was removed—the final blow in the devastation she suffered ! But she was still a game little engine, and managed to retain something of the attraction which she and her sisters had always possessed.

The dimensions of these engines, in the later years, were: wheel diameters, bogie, 3 ft 8 in.; coupled, 5 ft 8 in.; the wheelbase was 22 ft 3 in., divided into 6 ft 6 in. plus 7 ft 3 in. plus 8 ft. 6 in., and the overhangs were 2 ft 9 in. in front and 4 ft 3 in. at the back.

The cylinders were 18 in. dia., 26 in. stroke and, after 1915, were fitted with piston valves operated by Stephenson link motion. The steam ports, which were round the periphery of the piston-valve liner, had a length of $25\frac{1}{8}$ in. and a width of $1\frac{3}{4}$ in.; the exhaust ports were $10\frac{3}{8}$ in. long and $3\frac{7}{8}$ in. wide. The diameter of the valves was 8 in., their lap $1\frac{1}{2}$ in. and the lead in full gear was $\frac{1}{4}$ in., while the travel was $5\frac{3}{8}$ in.

The boiler rings were 4 ft 4 in. and 4 ft 5 in. dia.; the barrel was 11 ft long and pitched 7 ft 2 in. above rail level. About 1925, however, five of the engines were fitted with cylinders of a new type having raised steam pipe flanges, which necessitated the boiler height being raised to 7 ft 5 in.

There were considerable variations in the tubing, according to the number of superheater flues, when fitted. *Comet* had 134 tubes of $1\frac{5}{8}$ in. dia., and 12 superheater flues of $5\frac{1}{8}$ in. dia.; their heating surfaces, respectively, were 826.64 and 182.51 sq. ft, to which the firebox added 114.42 sq ft to make the total heating surface 1,123.57 sq. ft. The working pressure

was 180 p.s.i., but at one time was as much as 200 p.s.i. The grate area was 17.2 sq. ft, and the tractive effort, with 180 lb. pressure, was 18,955 lb.

The weight of these engines was also subject to variation according to the type of boiler fitted, but all the reboilered engines appeared to have been slightly lighter than they were in their original condition; this was probably intentional, to give the engines the widest possible scope. *Comet*, and other engines like her, would seem to have weighed 45 tons 15 cwt, with 17 tons 3 cwt on the bogie, 15 tons 14 cwt on the driving axle and 12 tons 18 cwt on the trailing axle.

Standard tenders of all sizes from 2,000 to 3,500 gallons capacity were, at different times, attached to these engines. *Comet* had a 2,500-gallon tender, as shown in the drawing. Its wheelbaase was 13 ft, equally divided, the overhangs being 4 ft at the front and 3 ft 6 in. at the back; its loaded weight was 34 tons 5 cwt.

Withdrawal of this class began in 1936 and took place gradually until 1951 when the last two, Nos 3284 and 3289, went to the scrap-heap in May and July, 1951, respectively. The average age of these engines when the class became extinct, after a long and honourable career, was approximately 54 years. A more striking tribute to their quality is scarcely possible.

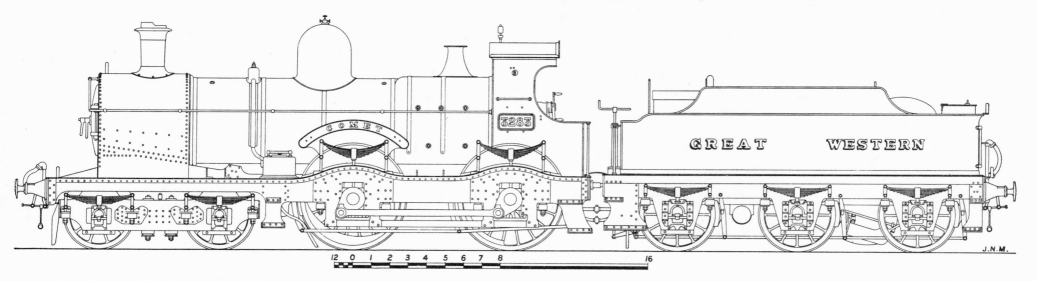

WILLIAM DEAN'S

BULLDOGS

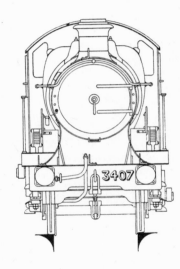

THIS engine was one of a class of no fewer than 156 sturdy and lively, double-framed 4-4-0 engines universally known as the "Bulldogs." In the course of years I came to know all of them; several were special "pets" of mine, and of these *Madras* was perhaps the prime favourite, largely because of purely personal associations and memories.

The pioneer engine was No. 3312, *Bulldog*, which was completed at Swindon in 1898 to the designs of William Dean. While she was generally in accordance with standard GWR practice of the period, she was something of an oddity. She had a boiler with a Belpaire firebox with a large and somewhat squat brass dome at the rear end of the barrel; the smokebox was of the old type, but extended, and was surmounted by a rather short copper-capped chimney. The whole effect was quite attractive.

The engine gave no particular trouble in service, so far as I ever knew, yet no more engines exactly like her were built. In 1906, *Bulldog* was reboilered with a domeless boiler and generally brought into line with later engines of her type.

After 1902 G. J. Churchward continued to build engines of this class and to make various detail modifications until he had brought these engines to their final form, as seen in my drawing.

Even then there were certain differences to be noted. The earliest engines had frames which were curved over the driving and coupled outside bearings while later examples had the straight-topped framing

GENERAL SPECIFICATION		
CYLINDERS		**TUBES**
Diameter ... ... 18 in.		Number ... ... 218 & 6
Stroke ... ... 26 in.		Diameter ... $1\frac{5}{8}$ in. & $5\frac{1}{8}$ in.
BOILER		
Length, between		**HEATING SURFACE**
tubeplates ... 11 ft		Tubes ... 1,144.94 sq. ft
Maximum dia-		Firebox ... 121.8 sq. ft
meter ... 5 ft $0\frac{1}{2}$ in.		Total ... 1,266.74 sq. ft
FIREBOX LENGTH		
Inside ... 6 ft $2\frac{11}{16}$ in.		**GRATE AREA**
Outside ... ... 7 ft		Square feet ... 20.35

on two levels (see drawing). The last examples, built in 1909, had much deeper frames down to the level of the bottom of the hornblocks between the driving and coupled wheels.

Sturdy and stocky, the " Bulldogs " were ready for anything. They were fairly evenly distributed over most of the Great Western Railway system, and there was hardly a main-line locomotive shed that did not have its quota of them. They worked fast and semi-fast passenger trains, perishable-freight trains and, when they were in a somewhat run-down

to be negotiated; but the engines acquitted themselves magnificently, their comparatively small wheels and prodigious pulling power being exactly what was required.

With it all, they were remarkably free runners, capable of being urged up to speeds in excess of 80 m.p.h. without difficulty; but this was scarcely surprising, since their cylinders and valve gear were practically identical with those of the famous racers, the Cities.

In their later years, the Bulldogs, although down-

saw her so frequently and for so many years. She remained in service until the end of 1949, when she was withdrawn and scrapped. The last two survivors of this once-numerous class were withdrawn in November 1951, and the Western Region, to me, has never seemed the same since.

In the condition depicted these engines had the following dimensions: cylinders, 18 in. dia., 26 in. stroke; wheels, bogie 3 ft 8 in., coupled 5 ft 8 in.; wheelbase, 6 ft 6 in. plus 7 ft 3 in. plus 8 ft 6 in., totalling 22 ft 3 in. ; overhang, 2 ft 9 in. at the front,

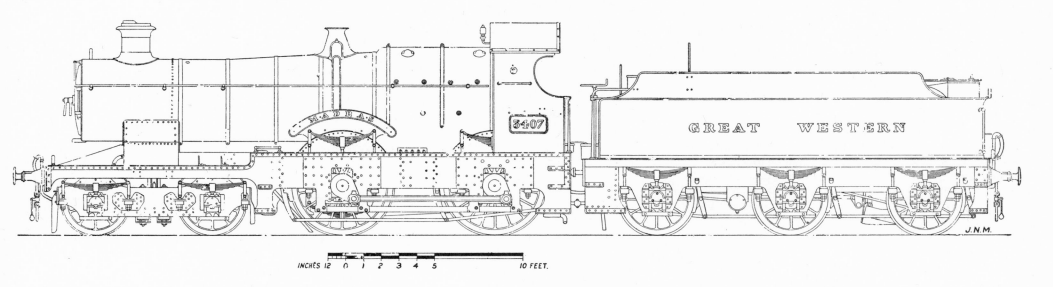

INCHES 12   0   1   2   3   4   5   10 FEET.

condition after long spells of main-line duty, they put in a lot of time on local passenger and freight traffic before going to the shops for overhaul.

West of Newton Abbot, from 1899 until about 1909, quite an army of Bulldogs was used on top-link express passenger trains, including the world-renowned " Cornish Riviera Express "; I also recall that several of the class were allocated to the best trains—often very heavy—between London and South Wales, while another route which saw Bulldogs employed as the principal express engines was from Bristol to Shrewsbury via Hereford and Craven Arms. In all these cases, the reason lay in the heavy gradients

graded to less important status, still found plenty of work to do in assisting heavy express trains up and down the hills of Devon and Cornwall, and many of them were employed in this way until the end of their days, being kept in first-class condition by the locomotive works and the running-shed staff at Newton Abbot. But they were favourites everywhere, their stirling qualities producing a remarkable enthusiasm in the men who drove them.

For many years *Madras* was stationed at Reading, whence she worked fast trains to London, Didcot, Swindon, Westbury, or farther afield. She became almost part of the landscape in that area where I

4 ft 3 in. at the back. The boiler was pitched 7 ft 9 in. from rail level and had a tapered barrel 4 ft 5⅛ in. dia. in front and 5 ft 0½ in. at the back.

There were 218 tubes of 1⅝ in. dia. and six super-heater flues 5⅛ in. dia. containing 36 elements 1 in. diameter. The heating surface of the tubes was 1,144.94 sq. ft; of the superheater, 91.11 sq. ft, and of the firebox 121.8 sq. ft. The working pressure was 200 p.s.i.

The tenders varied in size from 2,500 to 3,500 gallons capacity. The one I have depicted is one of the last Churchward 3,000-gallon tenders, which is the type that *Madras* had when I last saw her.

4-4-0 ATBARAS

THE GWR Atbara class of 4-4-0 express passenger engines were rather remarkable in more ways than one, and I remember them well, from the time when they were still being built in 1901 until the last were withdrawn from service in April 1931.

It will be noted that their life, so to speak, was a comparatively short one, but may be said to have been, on the whole, a merry one; for they must be given credit for two things; first, they marked the culmination of William Dean's efforts, begun in 1894, to produce a thoroughly satisfactory express passenger engine with which to supersede his splendid single-wheelers, and secondly, they laid the solid foundation on which G. J. Churchward originated his policy of subsequent locomotive developments. Therefore, from the historical point of view, the Atbaras ended and began, respectively, two important epochs in Swindon lore.

There were 40 engines in the class, the first 20 being completed between April and September 1900, the second 20 between June and October 1901, and they quickly established themselves as swift and powerful machines. To the eye, they presented an austere and angular aspect, markedly different from former GWR practice, and it took some years to get used to. But their reputation for power and speed more than made up for their looks. My drawing depicts the original condition in all its stark severity.

These engines had only a few years as top-link express passenger engines; they were superseded by the Cities in 1903, the Counties in 1904 and by 4-6-0s in 1906. Yet, oddly enough, in 1908, Swindon turned out another 20 4-4-0s which, except for tapered boilers and very deep frames, were practically identical with the Atbaras; these were the Flowers, into which class most of the Atbaras and Badmintons were assimilated by being rebuilt with tapered boilers. It was an altogether curious and surprising business; but the 4-4-0s were extremely useful in replacing older engines on ordinary passenger work.

For the next quarter of a century, these 4-4-0s were to be found all over the GWR except west of Newton Abbot; at first they were used on every variety of passenger trains, except the crack expresses.

GENERAL SPECIFICATION

CYLINDERS			TUBES		
Diameter	...	... 18 in.	Number	...	... 277
Stroke	...	... 26 in.	Diameter	...	... 1⅝ in.
BOILER					
Length between			**HEATING SURFACE**		
tubeplates ...		11 ft 0 in.	Tubes...	1,540.18 sq. ft.	
Maximum			Firebox	...	124.1 sq. ft.
diameter	...	4 ft 6¼ in.	Total ...	1,664.28 sq. ft.	
FIREBOX LENGTH					
Inside...	...	6 ft 3¹¹⁄₁₆ in.	**GRATE AREA**		
Outside	...	7 ft 0 in.	Square feet	...	... 21.28

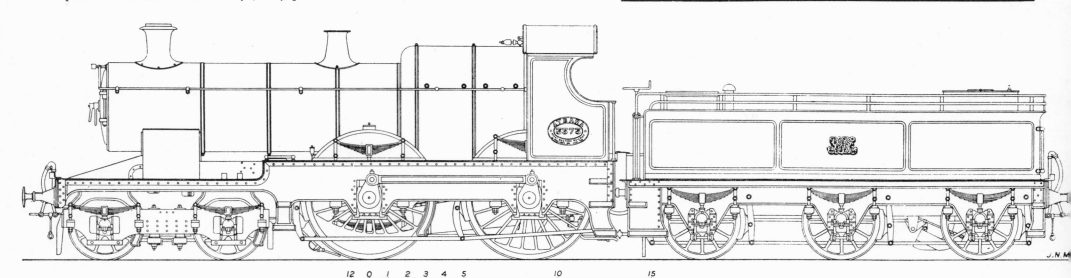

On this sort of work they seldom had an opportunity to display that wonderful capacity for speed which everybody knew they possessed. As time went on they were relegated more and more to freight work, until, in the late 1920s, they were mostly employed in this way—some of them even on ordinary local pick-up goods trains. This, however, was owing to the fact that, by that time, the engines had become entirely redundant, and had to be put on any kind of work in order to make up their mileage.

A curious feature of the Atbaras, even in their original condition, was the extraordinary variations of details. For example, the wheel balance-weights, which were massive in most of the engines, seemed quite unable to settle down to anything like standard positions; some were in the lower quadrant, others in the upper quadrant, while some of the engines had weights in *both* quadrants! This must have been an expensive business since, in most cases, the balance-weights were cast integral with the wheels.

Then the frames of the first 20 engines had a different shape, at the rear end, from those of the second lot; and this difference was worse confounded in later years, when strengthening plates were added. There were scarcely two arrangements of these strengtheners that were alike, and in one or two cases they were not even similar on the two sides of one engine!

The large oval plate displaying the name, number, works number and date of engine was, at first, applied to Nos 3373 to 3395; but beginning with No 3396, *Brisbane*, a standard numberplate was fixed to the cabside, and the name was put on to a plate that spanned the whole of the periphery of the driving-wheel splasher. At a later date, the second lot of engines and two of the first lot acquired the standard type of nameplate mounted on a backplate fitted to the driving-wheel splasher.

The original dimensions of the Atbaras were: cylinder, 18 in. dia., stroke 26 in. and incline 1 in 10. The valve gear was Stephenson's, and reversal was effected by steam power. The steamchest was underneath the cylinders, and the valves were of flat type in 24 of the engines, the other 16 having 6 in. piston valves. For the flat valves, the steam ports were 16 in. long and $1\frac{3}{4}$ in. wide; the width of the exhaust port was 3 in. The lap was $1\frac{1}{8}$ in., lead $\frac{1}{4}$ in. at the front, $\frac{3}{16}$ in. at the back, and the valve travel in full gear was $4\frac{5}{8}$ in.

For the piston valve engines the ports were $25\frac{1}{8}$ in.

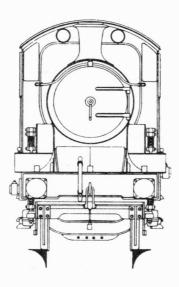

long and $1\frac{1}{4}$ in. wide, the exhaust port being $10\frac{3}{8}$ in. long and $3\frac{7}{8}$ in. wide; the lap and lead were the same as for the flat valves, but the valve travel was increased to, I think, $5\frac{1}{4}$ in., though I have not discovered any definite official statement of this last figure.

The boiler barrel was 11 ft long and made in two rings, the diameters of which were 4 ft $5\frac{1}{8}$ in. and 4 ft $6\frac{1}{4}$ in., respectively. There were 277 tubes, 11 ft $3\frac{13}{16}$ in. long, between tubeplates, and $1\frac{7}{8}$ in.

dia.; their heating surface was 1,540.18 sq. ft. Centre line height above rail level was 8 ft $3\frac{1}{4}$ in.

A large Belpaire firebox was provided, its outer casing being 7 ft long. The inner box was of copper, 6 ft $3\frac{11}{16}$ in. long and 4 ft $3\frac{7}{8}$ in. wide at the boiler centre line. Its heating surface was 124.1 sq. ft, making the total heating surface 1,664.28 sq. ft. The grate area was 21.28 sq. ft and the working pressure was 195 p.s.i.

Wheel diameters were: bogie, 3 ft 8 in. and coupled 6 ft $8\frac{1}{2}$ in., on a wheelbase of 22 ft 6 in. divided into 6 ft 6 in. plus 7 ft 6 in. plus 8 ft 6 in. Overhang was 2 ft 6 in. at the front and 4 ft 6 in. at the back. The engine weighed 51 tons 12 cwt, divided into 18 tons on the bogie, 17 tons 8 cwt on the driving wheels and 16 tons 4 cwt on the trailing wheels.

The normal tender was of 3,000 gallons capacity, but 3,500 and 4,000 gallon tenders were noted on some of the engines; all, however, were equipped with water pick-up apparatus, as by this time water troughs were installed at several places on the GWR main line.

No 3405, *Mauritius*, when only 12 months old in September 1902, was rebuilt with a No 4 tapered boiler, to become the prototype of the famous City class of 1903. In 1907-8, nine more Atbaras were similarly rebuilt. The rest of the class, in later years, were all rebuilt with No 2 superheated boilers, and became similar to the Flower class of 1908, into which they were assimilated.

In 1901-2, some of these engines made fast runs on Ocean Mails specials from Plymouth to London, creating a few records which, however, were beaten in 1903-4 by engines of the City class. But it was the Atbaras that originally set up the standard of high-speed performance that subsequently made the GWR famous. They were extraordinarily free-running engines which always gave the impression of being difficult to hold in check. Does not their appearance somehow suggest this, in spite of its austerity?

The history of this famous class of swift and powerful 4-4-0 express passenger engines is somewhat involved, and tends to cause considerable trouble to modern historians, who are apt to confuse the City class with its immediate predecessor, the Atbara.

The confusion is understandable by reason of the fact that the prototype of the City class was an Atbara, No 3405, *Mauritius*, which had been re-boilered with a standard No 4 boiler in September 1902. The reason for the reboilering was that, although the Atbaras were giving considerable satisfaction on the express passenger services operated by the GWR at that time, Churchwood felt that some extra reserve of boiler power would be an advantage on the heaviest West of England expresses. *Mauritius* with her larger boiler left no doubt about the matter, and an order was placed for ten engines to be built exactly similar.

These were the Cities proper, the first being completed in March 1903, the other nine following in May. They were numbered 3433 to 3442 and named: (*City of*) *Bath, Birmingham, Bristol, Chester, Gloucester, Hereford, London, Truro, Winchester* and *Exeter*; they were the first examples of what later became the well known Swindon practice of class names for engines. An interesting point is that the last name in the City list comes well out of alphabetical order, and the story is that the last engine was intended to be *City of York*; someone objected to this on the grounds that York was not in the GWR territory, so the name *City of Exeter* was chosen instead.

The Cities were an immediate success and quickly established a reputation for power and speed. A number of record runs was made by them in 1903 and 1904, the best being the scintillating performance put up by No 3440, *City of Truro*, when hauling an Ocean Mails special from Plymouth to Bristol on 9 May 1904. During this run, and for the first time in the history of transport, a speed of 100 m.p.h. was reached, if not exceeded, and was timed by two individuals on the train, quite independently.

One was a Post Office official, the other was Mr Charles Rous-Marten, the well-known authority and writer on locomotive performances. The first published his story in a Bristol newspaper within a few days of the event, but Rous-Marten's log was not divulged until 20 years later, on the grounds that it might have caused alarm to the travelling public!

The postal worker gave 100 m.p.h. as the maximum speed when descending the Wellington bank but his story was discredited; Rous-Marten's log, when it was eventually made public, claimed 102.3 m.p.h. at the same place!

Whatever may the the rights or wrongs of Rous-Marten's figure—it was the subject of considerable controversy in the early 1930s—there seems little room for doubt that the maximum speed was at least 100 m.p.h., and this was the first time that such a speed had been officially recorded. On the strength of this, early in 1931, when *City of Truro* was withdrawn from service, she was not scrapped but sent to the Railway Museum at York for preservation.

Meanwhile, the 4-4-0 express engines of the Badminton class, which were the immediate predecessors of the Atbara, became due for heavy repairs, and the opportunity was taken, between November 1903 and January 1907, to rebuild 16 of them by fitting No 4 boilers; this process made the engines similar to the Cities.

Between February 1907 and March 1910, one more Badminton and nine more Atbaras were similarly treated, by which time the City class consisted vir-

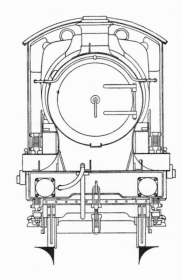

tually of 37 engines, i.e. 17 rebuilt Badmintons, 10 rebuilt Atbaras and the 10 Cities proper.

By 1910, however, these engines had become redundant, because Churchward's 4-6-0 engines of the Saint and Star classes had taken control of all the best and fastest trains, and it is not easy to understand why so many Badmintons and Atbaras were

THE CITY CLASS 4-4-0

GENERAL SPECIFICATION

CYLINDERS			**TUBES**		
Diameter	... ...	18 in.	Number	...	210 & 14
Stroke	... ...	26 in.	Diameter	...	1⅝ & 5⅛ in.
BOILER					
Length, between			**HEATING SURFACE**		
tubeplates	...	11 ft	Tubes 1,228.02 & 215.8 sq. ft		
Maximum dia-			Firebox ... 128.3 sq. ft		
meter	...	5 ft 6 in.	Total ... 1,572.12 sq. ft		
FIREBOX LENGTH					
Inside	...	5 ft 9 in.	**GRATE AREA**		
Outside	... ...	7 ft	Square feet ... 20.56		

fitted with No 4 boilers. However, within the next three years, the rebuilt Badmintons had their No 4 boilers replaced by the smaller and lighter No 2 tapered boiler, and these engines were then assimilated into the Flower class.

The 10 rebuilt Atbaras, and the 10 Cities proper remained unaltered and put in many years of useful work on secondary express passenger trains. Very occasionally, one would be called upon to take over a top-link turn, and she seldom failed to show something of her old form by putting up a commendably speedy performance. The class was withdrawn from service gradually, over a period of some three and a half years from October 1927, until May 1931.

The principal dimensions of the Cities were: cylinders 18 in. by 26 in.; bogie wheels, 3 ft 8 in. dia.; coupled wheels 6 ft 8½ in. dia.; wheelbase 22 ft 6 in. divided into 6 ft 6 in. plus 7 ft 6 in. plus 8 ft 6 in.; the overhang was 2 ft 6 in. at the front and 4 ft 6 in. at the back.

The boiler was made in three rings, the front one of which was cylindrical, 4 ft 10¾ in. dia. outside; the other two rings formed a cone tapering uniformly to a maximum of 5 ft 6 in. dia. where it joined the firebox; the length of the barrel was 11 ft, and its bottom line was horizontal throughout its length. In the days before superheating was introduced, there were 350 tubes of 1⅝ in. dia., giving a heating surface of 1,689.82 sq. ft; the firebox added 128.3 sq. ft, making the total 1,818.12 sq. ft. The grate area was 20.56 sq. ft, and the working pressure 200 p.s.i. The centre line of the boiler was 8 ft 6½ in. from rail level.

In working order, the engine weighed 55 tons 6 cwt, of which the bogie carried 19 tons 4 cwt, the driving wheels 18 tons 10 cwt, and the trailing wheels 17 tons 12 cwt.

Superheating was introduced in 1910, and it modified the tubing of the boilers. At first, there were 84 elements, later altered to 112. With the later pattern, the tubing and heating surfaces were: 210 of 1⅝ in. dia., 1,228.02 sq. ft and 14 of 5⅛ in. dia., 215.8 sq. ft, making the total tube heating surface 1,443.82 sq. ft. The pressure remained at 200 p.s.i.

Most of the engines were supplied with the standard 3,000 gallon tender with 15 ft wheelbase, though a few had the 2,500 gallon tender with a 14 ft wheelbase. The tender wheels were 4 ft 1½ in. dia. With the 3,000 gallon tender the total weight was 92 tons 1 cwt. The official tractive effort was given as 17,790 lb.

Of all the Cities, No 3440, *City of Truro* is the best known, not only for her great exploit in 1904, but also because she was one of the major exhibits in the Railway Museum at York from March 1931 until December 1956. With the dawn of 1957, this engine was also given the unique distinction of being brought out of the museum and returned to active service in the Western Region of British Railways, primarily for running enthusiasts' excursions.

For this purpose, the engine was given a thorough overhaul at Swindon and repainted in the old GWR livery of 1903. As a result she looks very fine, though the double lining seems a little odd, even to GWR enthusiasts; but it is right, because some engines, including one or two of the Cities, were painted in that style about 1902-1905. It did not become general, however; and that may be the reason why it is not shown on the official paint chart.

Since March 1957, *City of Truro* has run several special trips. She indulged in some high speed on occasions, the maximum, so far, being 84 m.p.h.— not too bad for a 55-year-old just fresh from a 25-year sojourn in a museum!

When not engaged on this sort of duty, she was stationed at Didcot and worked a placid daily return passenger turn to Southampton and back via Newbury. I saw her on this turn many times during the year 1957, and must congratulate the Didcot people who were responsible for keeping her clean; they turned her out in first-class condition, as befits the heroine of *the* railway event of all time. She was later stationed at Swindon.

My drawing depicts the engine as she is now, which is not quite as she was in 1904; but she is better thus than not at all.

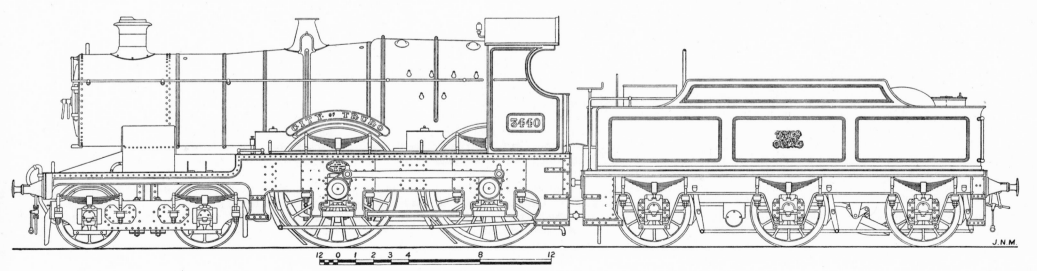

A comedian among railway engines

4-4-0 EARL CAWDOR

OF 1903

GENERAL SPECIFICATION		
CYLINDERS	**TUBES**	
Diameter ... ... 18 in.	Number 359	
Stroke ... ... 26 in.	Diameter ... ... 1⅛ in.	
BOILER		
Length, between	**HEATING SURFACE**	
tubeplates 11 ft 6 in.	Tubes ... 1,803.27 sq. ft	
Maximum dia-	Firebox ... 130.75 sq. ft	
meter ... 5 ft 5 in.	Total ... 1,934.02 sq. ft	
FIREBOX LENGTH		
Inside ... 5 ft 6 11/16 in.	**GRATE AREA**	
Outside ... 6 ft 4 in.	Square feet ... 17.85	

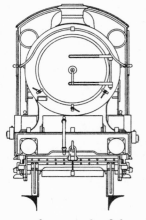

In the late 1890s and early 1900s, Swindon produced a few locomotives which were rather out of the ordinary, one or two of them becoming the prototypes of later classes, while the rest may be regarded as being somewhat freakish. Among the latter, engine No 3297, *Earl Cawdor*, must be included when rebuilt as shown in my drawing.

Originally built in May, 1896, *Earl Cawdor* was the sixth of William Dean's stately Badminton class of 6 ft 8 in. 4-4-0 express passenger engines, 20 of which were completed by the following January. At the outset, this class was made the guinea-pig for a series of interesting experiments with boilers, *Earl Cawdor* being one of the engines concerned. In the early months of 1903, after five years' work, she went to Swindon for a major overhaul and the opportunity was taken to fit a new boiler which, in those days, was very much of an outsize, at least in appearance.

I remember that, when a photograph of the rebuilt engine appeared in *The Locomotive Magazine* on 10 October 1903, a small group of schoolboys—myself included—dissolved into fits of laughter! That absurd dome—which, incidentally, was a remarkable anticipation of the "tin hat" that became such a familiar item of the military sartorial outfit, 40 years later—perched on the huge boiler; that tremendous smokebox surmounted by a squat chimney, and that great cab with its elongated roof and large, double side-windows, together with the general effect of obesity and bloatedness, were too much for us. We could not look at that photograph without merriment; but we were young, not one of us having entered his teens, and it meant that our sense of the ridiculous was apt to overflow at the least provocation.

It so happened, however, that the mirth-provoking photograph was a real godsend to me, because a few weeks before, while returning home from a holiday in Berkshire, I had seen *Earl Cawdor*. I was in a semi-fast train travelling on the Relief Line, and as we were approaching Slough, *Earl Cawdor*, at the head of an express on the Main Line, overtook us and whistled lustily. At that moment, I had two of the greatest surprises of my life; the first was the engine herself, about which I had known nothing whatever before, and the second was the sound of that whistle.

The standard GWR whistle of that period was a high-pitched, but not altogether unpleasant squealer; *Earl Cawdor's* had a much lower tone of a mellow quality similar to that of the LBSCR engines so familiar to my friends and me at Wandsworth Common. I tried to describe all this to my friends when I got home, without much impression, I am afraid; but when *The Locomotive Magazine* photograph appeared, my reputation was saved!

Then another surprise came our way. At the preparatory school I was then attending, one of the masters was interested in railway engines; he studied *The Locomotive Magazine* photograph and listened attentively to what I had to say about the great engine I had seen.

He then arranged to take some of us one Saturday afternoon to Paddington Station, hoping that *Earl Cawdor* might put in an appearance. We got there in time to see the arrival of the express but the engine, this time, was a singlewheeler. Our guide was not perturbed; he said he had read a notice announcing the imminent arrival of an Ocean Mails special train from Plymouth, and he thought *Earl Cawdor* might be on it. I believe now that he had made enquiries as to the trains the engine was working.

Sure enough, when the mail train came in, the great engine *was* on it; and as she slowly glided down Platform 8 and drew up to a standstill, after a 248-mile run from Plymouth, the effect on us was remarkable. First sight of the engine caused a stir of excitement; but when she stood before us in all her mighty bulk and gleaming new paint, we forgot to laugh and could only stare in awe and wonder.

Our guide had a chat with the driver, who did not seem to think much of the engine; he said she ought to be able to pull a house down, but she wanted far more coaxing than any other engine he had driven. We asked him to blow the whistle, and he said he would when the "back-out" signal was given. In due course, the signal came and was acknowledged by a blast from the whistle, and we all heard, for the first time (except me) the new, but afterwards familiar GWR mellow tone.

Two years later, my parents moved from Wandsworth Common to a new home in North Kensington, and it put me in close touch with the GWR. For a while, I frequently saw *Earl Cawdor*, but she had then been taken off express work and was being used on secondary duties. Her favourite turn then was an up semi-fast passenger train from Swindon, arriving at Paddington about 11.00 a.m. and returning on the 3.15 p.m. milk empties from Addison Road (now Kensington, Olympia). In those days, there was a very considerable milk traffic from Wiltshire and Berkshire to London, and a train made up entirely of milk vans and a passenger brake van for the guard was a commonplace sight on the GWR. My last sight of *Earl Cawdor* with her outsize boiler, however, was one Sunday afternoon in the summer of 1906, when I happened to be at Westbourne Park station waiting for a Metropolitan train. On this occasion, the great engine was more amusing than ever; she was piloting an Armstrong double-framed 0-6-0 on the 4.55 p.m. all stations to Swindon, and was running with her coupling-rods removed. Her outside cranks had got well out of phase, and when combined with those of the 0-6-0, turning at a much faster rate, the effect was highly diverting. Towards the end of 1906, the big boiler was replaced by one of Churchward's

standard types of more normal dimensions and the engine returned to express passenger work.

A few years afterwards, from a relative who was at Swindon Works, I heard something of the " inside " story of *Earl Cawdor*. During Churchward's intensive experiments with boilers, his chief draughtsman, F. G. Wright, was concerned with them of course; and he had the idea that a locomotive boiler should be regarded more as a thermal-storage vessel. He expounded this idea so persuasively that Churchward eventually gave him *carte blanche* to try it out. The result was *Earl Cawdor's* bulky storer of thermal units and, of course, it failed.

Churchward's opinion was that the function of a boiler is to produce steam and not to emulate the purposes of a foot-warmer! Events over the years have more than proved the soundness of this. Wright thought that with a greater storage of heat in a boiler, a more constant pressure would be maintained; but in practice, it did not work out like that, and whatever success that large boiler may have had as a heat-conserver, it seems to have found some difficulty in producing steam, while putting a severe burden upon the engine's frames.

The barrel was 11 ft 6 in. long, made in two rings, the diameters being 5 ft 3⅝ in. and 5 ft 5 in.; the centre line was 8 ft 8 in. above rail level. The outside diameter of the smokebox was 6 ft 3 in., and the height from rail level to the top of the chimney was 13 ft 1½ in. There were 359 tubes of 1⅝ in. dia., and

the heating surface totalled 1,934.02 sq. ft, made up of 1,803.27 sq. ft for the tubes and 130.75 sq. ft for the firebox. The grate area was 17.85 sq. ft, and the working pressure was 210 p.s.i., at 85 per cent of which the tractive effort was 18,680 lb.

The engine wheelbase was 23 ft 3 in., divided into 7 ft plus 7 ft 3 in. plus 9 ft; the overhangs were 2 ft 6 in. in front and 4 ft 3 in. at the back. The tender wheelbase was 15 ft equally divided, and the total length of engine and tender was 57 ft 4¾ in.

In working order, the engine weighed 56 tons 14 cwt, distributed into 21 tons 4 cwt on the bogie, 19 tons on the driving axle and 16 tons 10 cwt on the trailing axle. The tender, with 3,000 gallons of water and 5 tons of coal, weighed 32 tons 10 cwt.

I never regretted this queer experiment. At the time, I had not the slightest notion of what were the purely technical reasons for it; but during the 3½ years that it lasted, it provided a good deal of fun to at least one small company of schoolboys who thought it the most amusingly grotesque effect ever seen on a British locomotive. But then, none of us had seen a Great Eastern " Humpty Dumpty," or even a Great Northern Atlantic, or the Great Eastern Decapod 0-10-0 tank engine!

About 1906, there was a 2½ in. gauge, electrically-operated model railway at Madame Tussaud's. The engine was a 4-4-0 which, while not to scale, was obviously inspired by the rebuilt *Earl Cawdor*. I have never seen another anywhere, rather to my surprise.

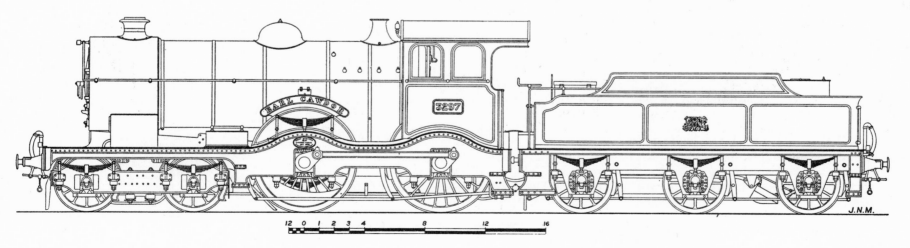

THE SAINTS

IN February 1902, while William Dean was still in charge of the locomotive department of the Great Western Railway, a large, two-cylinder 4-6-0 express passenger engine was put into traffic.

This engine, No 100, was a dramatic change from the hitherto normal trend of Swindon policy in locomotive design, and there can be no doubt that Dean's chief assistant, G. J. Churchward, was more than a little responsible for her. Locomotive enthusiasts everywhere were profoundly shocked by her seemingly uncouth appearance.

She marked the beginning of that steady and persistent development that Churchward carried out during the following ten years, to culminate in the truly outstanding Courts of 1911-13. These Courts, of which there were 25, were actually a superheated modification of the 20 even more celebrated Saints, built in August and September 1907, and of which more anon.

To go back to the beginning, for a moment, Dean retired at the end of 1902 and was succeeded by Churchward, who immediately began what amounted to a revolution in GWR locomotive policy. At that time, another large 4-6-0 engine, No 98, was already under construction; she was completed in March 1903, and while she was generally similar to No 100, she possessed some important modifications.

The boiler had a tapered barrel, whereas No 100's was cylindrical; but probably the most important change was in the arrangement of cylinders and valve gear. For No 100, the cylinders were 18 in. dia. with

a stroke of 30 in., and they had double-ported piston valves of 6½ in. dia., which was subsequently altered to 7 in. and later to 7½ in.; they were indirectly driven by Stephenson link motion, and the valve travel was, I believe, 5 in.

For No 98, however, the cylinders were altogether different; they were 18 in. by 30 in., as before, but they were each cast with half the smokebox saddle, and were bolted together as well as to the main frames which, at the front, were set inwards. The piston valves were of single-ported type and were no less than 10 in. dia.; they were directly driven by Stephenson link-motion, once more, but with launch-type links, and the travel was increased to 5⅞ in. The boiler pressure of both these engines was 200 p.s.i.

In December 1903, a third engine of this type was produced, similar to No 98, except that the boiler pressure was increased to 225 p.s.i., which remained the standard henceforth. This engine was the ever-popular favourite, No 171, *Albion*, and in October 1904, she was temporarily converted to the 4-4-2 type, so as to be tested as fairly as possible against the French compound 4-4-2, No 102, *La France*, which the GWR had purchased the previous year for special trials.

Between February and September 1905, a further 19 engines, Nos 172 to 190, were built, all generally similar to *Albion*, but 13 of them were temporarily given the 4-4-2 wheel arrangement while the other six were 4-6-0s. In May 1906, these were followed by ten 4-6-0s, Nos 2901-2910, subsequently named

after various ladies of history, fiction and fact. No 2901 had cylinders 18¼ in. dia., but in the rest the diameter was 18⅜ in.; in all, the valve travel was increased to 6¼ in., which now became the standard for the whole class, excepting No 100.

In August and September 1907, came the 20 ever-memorable Saints, named after patron and other saints of history, and numbered 2911 to 2930. Finally, between October 1911 and April 1913, the Courts appeared, numbered 2931 to 2955 and named after famous English mansions and country houses in the home and western counties; they were simply super-heated Saints.

The Saints and Courts marked the climax of Churchward's steady development of the two-cylinder 4-6-0, and they incorporated some further modifications of design. The cylinder diameter was now 18½ in.; the valve gear was operated by turn crank and screw instead of by the former large and heavy

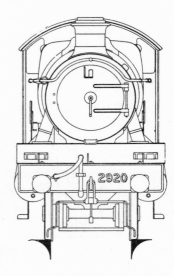

lever, while a pleasing change that very much enhanced the appearance of the engines was the introduction of the curved down-drop between the higher and lower levels of the running-plates.

So successful and so popular did these last 45 engines become that, excepting No 100, the earlier engines all had their cylinders, valve gears and boilers brought into line with the later ones, so as to form one uniform class. This process was retarded by war conditions between 1914 and 1919, but it was completed by the end of 1922, and the entire class was superheated.

I had a great affection for the Saints; they were powerful and speedy, and No 2913, *Saint Andrew*, in 1913, when hauling a Birmingham-Paddington two-hour train of 11 corridor coaches, gave me my first experience of travelling at 90 m.p.h.

The 30 in. piston stroke, necessitating a 15 in. crank throw, fully visible throughout its rotation, irresistibly suggested high-stepping thoroughbred horses; it was most attractive to watch. These fine engines inspired the confidence of the men who had to work them, and I have never known a class that was more popular with drivers and firemen.

The dimensions were bold, original and, to not a few locomotive engineers, even terrifying; to enginemen, they were "just right; you know *exactly* what she will do"—as one driver once said to me. In those days, of course, the maintenance was also "just right," as it had to be, and coal was of tip-top quality.

Churchward had set himself the task of producing a high-speed express engine that would give a drawbar pull of two tons at 70 m.p.h., continuously, on level track; he achieved it in the Saints, by giving the greatest possible thought and care to the design and layout of cylinders, ports and valve gear.

His basic boiler design was already finally established, subsequent changes being of detail rather than of fundamental design; but the "machinery" was now, in the Saints, brought to its triumphant finality for the two-cylinder passenger and mixed-traffic engines, and it has remained unchanged ever since. Neither of Churchward's successors, Collett and Hawksworth, found any necessity for making any alterations, in later years. Some American features were deliberately introduced, as Churchward admitted, "to beat the Americans at their own game."

The heads of the 10 in. piston valves were placed over the ends of the cylinder bores, so that the steam passages for admission had practically no length. The steam lap was $1\frac{5}{8}$ in., exhaust lap nil, and there was no exhaust clearance. A special feature was the short length of the eccentric rods, 3 ft 10 in., purposely planned to give a big variation of lead.

At 25 per cent cut-off, the lead was $\frac{1}{8}$ in.; in midgear, it was $\frac{5}{8}$ in., and on this basis the full-gear lead was negative to the extent of about $\frac{3}{16}$ in. (the official figure is — 0.15 in.).

The usual position of the reversing gear, when running, was notched up to between 20 and 25 per cent cut-off, and in these conditions there appeared to be no holding the engines; moreover, they were very economical in fuel consumption with loads up to 400 tons.

The bogie wheels were 3 ft 2 in. dia. and the coupled wheels 6 ft $8\frac{1}{2}$ in. dia. Wheelbase was 27 ft 1 in., divided into 7 ft plus 5 ft 4 in. plus 7 ft plus 7 ft 9 in., and the overhangs were: front 2 ft 6 in., and back 6 ft 6 in.

The boiler was a Swindon Standard No 1 with a coned barrel 4 ft $10\frac{3}{4}$ in. dia. at the front and 5 ft 6 in. at the back, pitched 8 ft 6 in. from rail level, the length being 14 ft 10 in. There were 176 tubes, 2 in. dia. and 14 superheater flues $5\frac{1}{8}$ in. dia.; the elements were 1 in. dia. The heating surface of the tubes was 1,686.6 sq. ft, and of the firebox 154.78 sq. ft. The firebox casing was 5 ft 9 in. wide at the boiler centre line, and 9 ft long. The engine weight was 68 tons 6 cwt, of which 41 tons 18 cwt rested on the coupled wheels. The 3,000 gal. tender shown in the drawing weighed 43 tons 3 cwt in working order, making the total 111 tons 9 cwt.

The working pressure was 225 p.s.i., and the tractive effort at 85 per cent of the boiler pressure was 20,530 lb.

Saint David was the last survivor of this celebrated class and was withdrawn in September 1953.

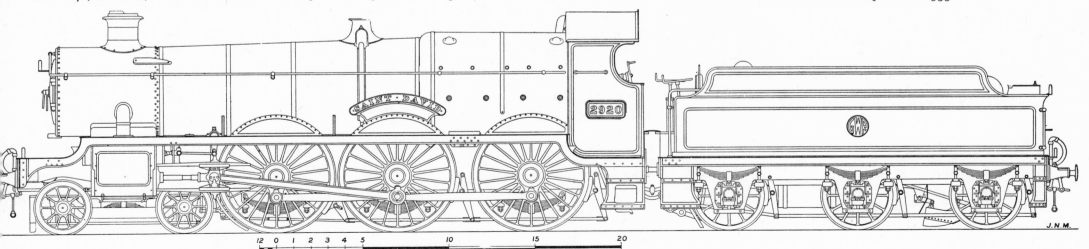

CHURCHWARD'S STAR CLASS

GENERAL SPECIFICATION

CYLINDERS			TUBES		
Diameter	... 15 in.	(four)	Number	...	176 & 14
Stroke	... 26 in.	(four)	Diameter	...	2 in. & 5⅛ in.
BOILER					
Length, between			HEATING SURFACE		
tubeplates	15 ft 2⁷⁄₁₆ in.		Tubes	...	1,686.6 sq. ft
Maximum dia-			Firebox	...	154.78 sq. ft
meter	...	5 ft 6 in.	Total	...	1,841.38 sq. ft
FIREBOX LENGTH					
Inside	...	8 ft 1⁵⁄₁₆ in.	GRATE AREA		
Outside	... ...	9 ft	Square feet	...	27.07

IN 1903 the Great Western Railway bought a 4-cylinder compound 4-4-2 engine that became No 102 *La France*; she was an exact mechanical duplicate of the very celebrated engines of the same type then putting up some wonderful performances on the C. F. du Nord in France, and Churchward was much impressed by her design, construction and performance.

The provision of a divided drive between two axles especially appealed to him, and in 1905, when he decided to put in hand a design for a 4-cylinder express passenger engine, he adopted the divided drive, but he could not tolerate the idea of compounding a locomotive for service on the GWR, as a standard.

The proposed 4-cylinder engine was put in hand at the Swindon factory, and was completed in April 1906. This was No 40, and she created wide interest both inside and outside the locomotive profession, for she was virtually a new type of steam locomotive; nothing quite like her had been seen before.

The novelty lay in the provision of four simple-expansion cylinders with the drive divided between two axles and the operation of the four valves by only two sets of valve gear, necessitating a 180-deg. setting for each pair of cranks on each side of the engine.

One pair, of course, was set at 90 deg. to the opposite pair, and in this way an almost perfect balance of reciprocating and rotating masses was automatically achieved.

The valve gear itself was a novelty for English locomotives, though No 40 was the only GWR locomotive ever to have it. It was directly derived from the Stevart gear, which R. M. Deeley had adopted on his 999-class 4-4-0 2-cylinder engines on the Midland Railway.

Its chief feature was that the oscillation of each expansion link was derived from the reciprocation of the main crosshead on the opposite side of the engine. But, whereas in the original gear as designed by Stevart for use on small 2-cylinder marine and stationary engines, and by Deeley on his locomotives, the two valve rods were of unequal lengths, Churchward modified the arrangement so that not only were there less parts, but the two valve rods were of equal length and the two sets of gear alike mirror-wise.

At Swindon this gear was unofficially called the " Scissors " gear because of its vague similarity to a pair of scissors. It worked very well and remained in No 40 until 1929, when she was rebuilt as a Castle.

This fine engine, on trial, was so successful that an order was passed to the Swindon factory for ten more, to be generally similar to No 40 but with the 4-6-0 wheel arrangement and—to avoid the complication of the " Scissors " valve gear—a specially-designed arrangement of the Walschaerts gear, the two sets of which were to be operated by two large eccentrics mounted on the leading coupled axle between the two cranks.

From that day in 1907 all the four-cylinder express locomotives built for the GWR had this arrangement of valve gear; it was never altered.

The valves of the two outside cylinders were operated by means of two horizontal cranked levers which were more ingenious than might appear at first sight. Each lever was pivoted at about, *not* exactly, the middle, the vertical pivot being carried by a bracket

attached to the main frame. The inner arm of the lever was knuckle-jointed to the inside valve rod which projected rearwards from the inside valve chest; the outer arm was similarly jointed to the outside valve rod which projected forwards from the outside valve chest.

So far, the arrangement is similar to that in any other four-cylinder engines employing two sets of valve gear for operating four valves. But Churchward realised that, due to the effect of the angularity of the connecting-rods, a straight lever causes dissimilar timings of the port openings in the two adjacent valve chests; so, to avoid this undesirable state of affairs, he cranked his lever so that the rearward angle between the two arms was 167 deg., ensuring that the timings of the port openings were similar and simultaneous in each direction of valve movement. Clever, wasn't it?

In this way the masterpiece Churchward Star class came into being. The first engine was No 4001, *Dog Star*, a never-to-be-forgotten favourite of mine. She was followed by No 4002 to 4010, named respectively, *Evening Star, Lode Star, Morning Star, Polar Star, Red Star, Rising Star, Royal Star, Shooting Star* and *Western Star*.

To this set of choice names must be added *North Star*, which No 40 was christened in September 1906; she was re-numbered 4000 in 1912. She had proved her worth. Her ten immediate successors very soon did the same with 3 tons pull at 70 m.p.h.—and, into the bargain, fully demonstrated the superiority of

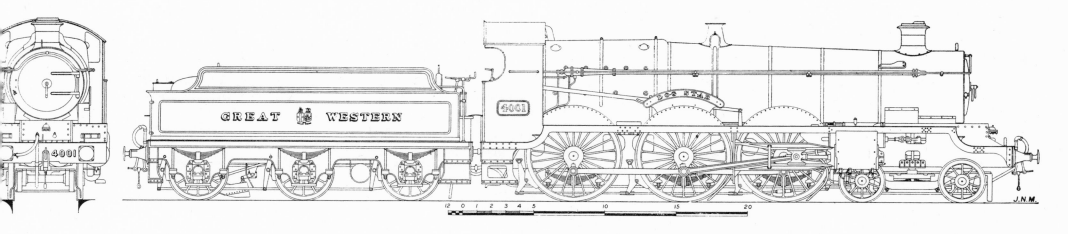

six-coupled wheels. *North Star* was converted into a 4-6-0 in 1909.

These splendid engines created quite a sensation 50 years ago; their performances placed them far ahead of any other comparable locomotives of the period, and for the next 20 years locomotive engineers seemed to be wondering how it was done.

Moreover, the consumption of coal and water in the Stars was little more, if any, than that of the French compounds, two more of which—larger than *La France*—had been purchased by the GWR in 1905, but were soon ousted from the West of England main line by the Stars.

In 1908 ten more Star-class engines, Nos 4011 to 4020, were built and named after Knights. In these the former swing-link bogie was replaced by one having side-control springs and outside bearers as in the French engines, while No 4011 was equipped with a superheater, after some experiments in this direction had been made with No 4010.

In 1909, Nos 4021 to 4030 appeared and were named after Kings of England; they were followed by Nos 4031 to 4040, the Queens, in 1910-11; Nos 4041 to 4045, the Princes, in 1913; Nos 4046 to 4060, the Princesses, in 1914, and Nos 4061 to 4072, the Abbeys, in 1922-3. All are now withdrawn.

No 4041 was fitted with 15 in. instead of 14¼ in. cylinders, which caused some eyebrows to be lifted by locomotive men who seriously doubted Churchward's sanity in expecting the boiler to steam four 15 in. cylinders. No 4041 was so successful, however,

that Nos 4046 to 4072 were built with 15 in. cylinders and the entire class was eventually fitted with them. Also, from 1913 onwards, superheaters became standard equipment.

Between 1925 and 1940, 16 of these engines were reconstructed as Castles, but the rest remained virtually unaltered except for minor details. And it is interesting to note that, though they changed their sheds during their last years, they were always employed on the best main-line express passenger work in their districts.

They were very free-running engines and, for their size, extremely powerful. The following dimensions became standard for the whole class: cylinders 15 in. dia., 26 in. stroke, with piston valves 8 in. dia. Wheel diameters, bogie 3 ft 2 in., coupled 6 ft 8½ in. The wheelbase was 27 ft 3 in. divided into 7 ft plus 5 ft 6 in. plus 7 ft plus 7 ft 9 in.

The Walschaerts valve gear gave a valve travel of 7¼ in.; the valve lap was 1⅝ in. and the lead was ⅛ in. On the exhaust side there was no lap or clearance, the valves being line-on-line with the ports. Steam ports were 1¾ in. wide, the exhaust 4 in.

A standard No 1 boiler was included, pitched 8 ft 6 in. above the rails. All its other particulars were as given on page 81. The front overhang of the engine was 3 ft 6 in., the back 6 ft 6 in.

The tenders varied: 3,000, 3,500 and 4,000 gallon types were all in use on these engines. My drawing shows a Collett rebuild of a Churchward 3,500 gallon tender as attached to *Dog Star* during her last years.

The re-building consisted mainly of the ugly modifications to the spring hangers. It is also worth noting that this tender was fully lined whereas the engine had no lining.

Incidentally, the Stars were originally fitted with equalisers between the springs of the six coupled wheels. In later years, springs were made more flexible and the equalisers were abandoned.

No 4003 *Lode Star* is preserved at Swindon as a memento of an epoch-making class. For there can be little doubt that, in 1907, these very remarkable locomotives were at least 20 years ahead of their contemporaries, and set a standard of performance that took a long while to catch up on. Some of their work on West-of-England expresses, from Paddington to Newton Abbot and Plymouth, would not disgrace some of the engines designed and built 40 years later for the same sort of work. Churchward was one of those men who, if he had reason to think that he was not getting the results he ought to get, spared no pains to search for the cause and, if possible, eradicate it. He seemed to know by instinct just where the root of any trouble lay, and would not rest until he had tried every possible remedy. He was a hard taskmaster, and his methods sometimes aroused the anger of his associates; but it was not often that he was unable to prove his point by practical demonstration, once he had found the proof, and in this way he succeeded in overcoming objections and opposition, at the same time winning the respect of his subordinates.

Few locomotive designs have created so much interest, or led to so much discussion, as the Great Western Castles have done. These engines built up a reputation for power and speed that placed them second to none of their size, and they have held it ever since.

The design, by C. B. Collett, was prepared in 1922, and the first engine, No 4073 *Caerphilly Castle*, was completed in August, 1923. She was not quite what had been intended because Collett's original conception for this enlarged Star class had been a 4-6-0 incorporating a Star chassis, slightly strengthened, and a standard No 7 boiler.

The then chief engineer, however, turned down this design on the grounds that it would have been too heavy to run over many routes on the GWR main line. Regretfully, therefore, a new boiler had to be designed for the new engines; it became Standard No 8, and was a veritable triumph of compromise.

In size, it came about midway between the Standard No 1 and Standard No 7 boilers, having a larger barrel than the former but the same size of firebox as the latter.

Between August 1923 and August 1950, 155 of these fine engines were built, including 30 for British Railways. Add 15 of the Star class and one Pacific (*The Great Bear*) all rebuilt as Castles, and the total for the class was 171—it is worth noting that their building was spread over exactly 27 years.

The last one built for the old Great Western Railway company was No 7007, originally *Ogmore Castle*, built July 1946, and rechristened *Great Western* in January 1948. She is the subject of my drawing, which shows her as running for a few months, in 1948, until the unfamiliar legend on the tender was replaced by the British Railways emblem—though the old Great Western crest is retained on this engine's second coupled wheel splasher. She was actually the last express passenger engine built for the GWR.

The Castles, being among the best known and most popular of modern steam locomotives, require little description from me; their performances, too, have been constantly described in railway and engineering periodicals ever since the first engines of the class were introduced.

I had my first sight of one when 4073 *Caerphilly Castle* stood end-to-end with the LNER Pacific, 4472, at the British Empire Exhibition at Wembley, in 1924; I have been an arden admirer of both engines ever since, but the Castle won my heart—and she retains it ! In view of the inside story of their design, these engines are probably the most remarkable steam locomotives ever built.

In technical details certain alterations and improvements have been made from time to time as necessary, so as to keep the engines well abreast of traffic requirements. But never could the Castles be regarded as big engines, which makes their success all the more creditable. The following dimensions apply to the latest developments in this class.

Cylinders (four) 16 in. dia., 26 in. stroke and fitted with 8 in. piston valves operated by the Churchward-Walschaerts valve gear. As in all GWR four-cylinder engines, the inside cylinders are placed well forward and drive the leading coupled axle, while the outside cylinders are set back and drive the second coupled axle. The wheel diameters are: bogie, 3 ft 2 in. and coupled 6 ft $8\frac{1}{2}$ in.; the wheelbase is 7 ft plus 5 ft 6 in. plus 7 ft plus 7 ft 9 in., totalling 27 ft 3 in.

The boiler is pitched 8 ft $8\frac{1}{2}$ in. above rail level; the barrel is 14 ft 10 in. long and its outside diameter is 5 ft $1\frac{11}{16}$ in. at the front, widening to 5 ft 9 in. at the back. There are 170 tubes of 2 in. dia., giving 1,799.5 sq. ft of heating surface, to which the firebox

No 7007
One of the famous
CASTLE
CLASS

GENERAL SPECIFICATION

CYLINDERS			TUBES		
Diameter	...	16 in. (four)	Number	...	138 & 28
Stroke	...	26 in. (four)	Diameter	...	2 in. & $5\frac{1}{8}$ in.
BOILER					
Length, between			HEATING SURFACE		
tubeplates		15 ft $2\frac{15}{16}$ in.	Tubes 1,670.1 & 393.2 sq. ft		
Maximum dia-			Firebox	...	163.32 sq. ft
meter	...	5 ft 9 in.	Total	...	2,226.62 sq. ft
FIREBOX LENGTH					
Inside	...	9 ft $2\frac{7}{16}$ in.	GRATE AREA		
Outside	... ...	10 ft	Square feet	...	29.36

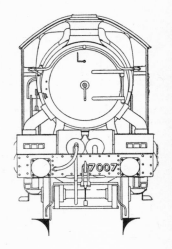

adds 163.5 sq. ft, making the total evaporative heating surface 1,963 sq. ft.

Superheater flues of 5⅛ in. dia. number 21, housing 84 elements of 1 in. dia.; these add 302 sq. ft of superheating surface. However, at the time of writing, a variation of this boiler, incorporating a 112-element superheater, is coming into use; it reduces the number of 2 in. tubes to 138, with 1,670.1 sq. ft of heating surface, the firebox to 163.32 sq. ft, and it increases the 5⅛ in. flues to 28 and the superheating surface to 393.2 sq. ft. The grate area for both types of boilers is 29.36 sq. ft.

The valve travel and events are similar to those of the Stars, and the Castles repeat the main performance characteristics of the Stars, but have a greater reserve of power. They are noticeably free from slipping when starting on a dry rail, while their ability to accelerate rapidly has often provoked comment.

The Castles have been subjected to various trials and tests in which they have always shown up well.

As early as 1924 No 4074 *Caldicot Castle* was put through some systematic trials between Swindon and Plymouth, on trains to which the dynamometer car was attached; she produced results the like of which had not been seen before.

The exchange trials between No 4079 *Pendennis Castle* and the LNER Pacific No 4474, in 1925, are well known, while in 1926 No 5000 *Launceston Castle*

on loan to the LMSR for trials between Euston and Carlisle, astonished everyone concerned with her performances.

There can be little doubt that the results of all these tests had a very considerable influence upon locomotive design outside the GWR. At last locomotive engineers had begun to realise and appreciate what was the significance of the revolutionary ideas of G. J. Churchward and his successors.

Gresley made some basic changes in the detail design of his LNER Pacifics, Maunsell was openly copying Swindon practice in some of his designs for the Southern, and when in 1932 the LMSR company wanted a new chief mechanical engineer, they chose Stanier, a Swindon man, pupil of Churchward and chief assistant to the designer of the Castles.

The advantages derived from long-travel valves had been known for some 70 years before Churchward began his systematic study of valves and valve events. But it was Churchward who seems to have been the first to realise that a long valve-travel alone was not enough.

Other factors, such as the sizes of steam pipes, ports and passages, and the internal streamlining of exhaust ways, all play an important part in obtaining maximum efficiency from an engine. The Castles incorporated all these features in addition to a boiler that produced the necessary steam to meet almost any requirement and still leave some in reserve.

In working trim, a Castle weighed 80 tons 18 cwt, 20 tons 17 cwt resting on the bogie, 19 tons 15 cwt on the leading coupled axle, while the middle coupled and trailing axles carried 19 tons 18 cwt each. It will be noted that the weight on the three coupled axles was almost exactly equally distributed. The weight of the 4,000-gallon tender was 46 tons 14 cwt, so the total weight of engine and tender was 147 tons 12 cwt.

The speed of the Castles is well known; it was demonstrated in no uncertain fashion by several of the class in pre-war days when taking it in turns to work the Cheltenham Flyer on its 67-minute schedule for the 77¼ mile non-stop sprint from Swindon to London. *Tregenna Castle's* time of 56 min. 47 sec. made on 6 June 1932 still stands as *the* record, though it was but a few seconds better than a number of other runs made on this train.

On the latter-day high-speed train, the Bristolian, 100 m.p.h. has been exceeded on a number of occasions with Castles.

Great Western was the name of the first express passenger engine built at Swindon in April 1846; it was, therefore, the most suitable name to bestow upon the last express passenger engine built for the old Great Western Railway, at the same place, in July 1946, just over a 100 years later. No 7007 carried it with distinction. She was one of the best of a fine class.

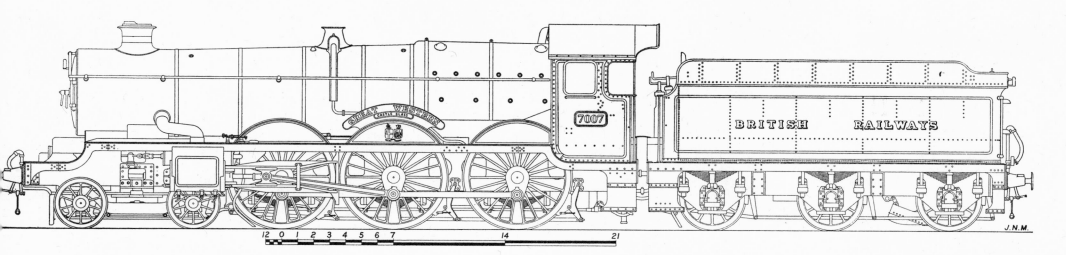

12 0 1 2 3 4 5 6 7   14   21   J.N.M.

73

BRITAIN'S FIRST PACIFIC
No 111 THE GREAT BEAR

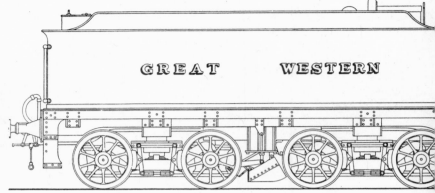

GENERAL SPECIFICATION

CYLINDERS			TUBES		
Diameter	...	... 15 in.	Number	...	141 & 21
Stroke	...	... 26 in.	Diameter	2½ in. & 4¾ in.	
BOILER			HEATING SURFACE		
Length between			Tubes...	3,242.67 sq. ft.	
tubeplates ...		22 ft 7 in.	Firebox	... 158.14 sq. ft.	
Maximum diameter 6 ft 0 in.			Total ...	3,400.81 sq. ft.	
FIREBOX LENGTH					
Outside	...	—	GRATE AREA		
Inside...	...	8 ft 0 in.	Square feet	...	... 41.79

JANUARY 1908, was an important month in British locomotive history; it marked the completion of the first 4-6-2 express passenger engine for a British line. This engine, GWR No 111, *The Great Bear*, was only the third example of its type in Europe—though this seems to have been overlooked by most of its critics.

After the success which the 4-6-2, or Pacific type of locomotive has had in England and on the Continent, it is more than interesting to look back on the introduction and working of England's first—and for 14 years, only—example of the type. I witnessed the coming of *The Great Bear*, with the very considerable stir that she made; I watched her working for many years. I will admit that I was one of the many who fell for her; for there has never been a more impressive locomotive.

Why was she built? Various reasons have been given. I will tell you the story which I had from a director of the Great Western Railway.

In the early years of G. J. Churchward's reign at Swindon, his unorthodox and expensive designs and policies caused some uneasiness among the directors. Fortunately one of them was Sir Aubrey Brocklebank, who by training and reputation was an engineer.

Alone among his colleagues, he understood and appreciated Churchward's revolutionary notions, and in time he succeeded in establishing peace and mutual confidence between the locomotive department at Swindon and the board room at Paddington.

It then occurred to one of the directors that, if the GWR Company was being supplied with the finest and most efficient engines in the country, what a splendid thing it would be if the GWR could claim that it had the *largest* engine. It would act as a spur to the intensive advertising campaign which was being launched. And so the directors consulted Churchward, and he told them flatly that if they wanted such an engine they could have it; but it would cost a tidy sum and they would never be able to use it. Nevertheless the directors voted in favour of having Britain's largest locomotive, and Churchward was instructed to build it, as cheaply as possible.

The design incorporated a bogie, coupled wheels, cylinder castings and motion of standard type, similar to those of the Star class four-cylinder 4-6-0s. The frames and boiler were, of course, special, and the trailing axle was mounted in radial axleboxes. The tender was designed and partly built as a six-wheeler; but before it was completed it was altered

to be carried on two bogies, which, except for their shortened wheelbase, were the same as the standard engine bogie, without the side bearers.

The change involved an alteration to the position of the water scoop, which had to be between the two bogies instead of just behind the rear bogie centre. Permanent evidence of this change could always be seen, when the engine was on shed, in a large patch-plate covering the original position of the scoop in the bottom of the water tank.

When *The Great Bear* was completed, she was brought from Swindon to Paddington for the directors to see, and they expressed themselves thoroughly satisfied. They had by far the largest passenger locomotive in Britain, and they were well content; it was an unrivalled advertisement.

During the trip from Swindon, the leading footsteps, just below the smokebox, displayed a disconcerting tendency to scrape the edges of station platforms; and so they were removed. Then, for a few weeks, the engine was engaged on trial runs.

To the traffic department she was an everlasting worry; she suffered many teething troubles, and she always appeared to be subject to the activities of a large company of what were later called gremlins.

74

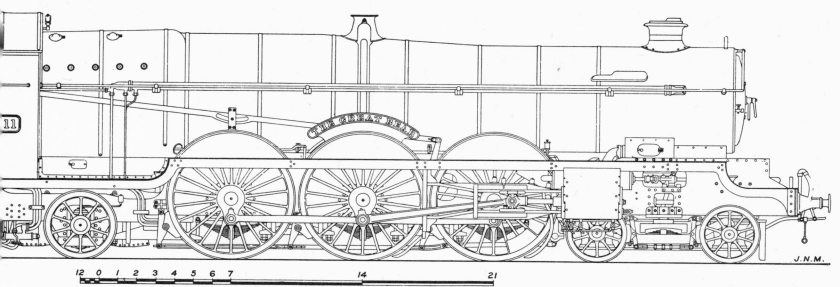

34 ft 6 in. divided into 7 ft plus 5 ft 6 in. plus 7 ft plus 7 ft plus 8 ft. Overhang was 3 ft 6 in. at the front and 6 ft at the back. The footplating was 8 ft 8 in. across at the front end and 9 ft at the back.

The boiler was truly a whopper, made in three rings, the front one 5 ft 6 in. dia. and the back one 6 ft, outside; the middle one tapered between the other two. The length of the barrel, between tube-plates, was 22 ft 7 in. and its centre-line was 9 ft above rail level; the working pressure was the usual 225 p.s.i. The firebox was a combination of Belpaire and wide types, 8 ft long and 6 ft 6 in. wide; its grate area was 41.79 sq. ft.

There were 141 tubes of $2\frac{1}{8}$ in., 21 of $4\frac{3}{4}$ in., 84 superheater tubes of $1\frac{3}{8}$ in. and, in the firebox, four water tubes of $3\frac{3}{8}$ in.; a total heating surface of 3,400.81 sq. ft, including 158.14 sq. ft for the firebox. The chimney cap was brass, not copper.

In working order, the weights were 97 ton for the engine, 45 tons 15 cwt for the 3,500-gallon tender, totalling 142 tons 15 cwt. Sixty tons were available for adhesion. The total length over buffers was 71 ft $2\frac{1}{4}$ in.

Originally the cab roof was longer than I have shown it; it was shortened after an unfortunate fireman got the long pricker so tightly jammed between the rear firebars, and cab roof that it took three men to release it!

With all her faults and foibles, and in spite of the gremlins, *The Great Bear* was a most lovable engine. Many regretted the day in January 1924 when she was taken out of service to be converted into a 4-6-0 of the Castle class and renamed *Viscount Churchill*; for, in her time, as Britain's first Pacific, she had made locomotive history and she ought to have been preserved.

She was a holy terror for slipping. Her bulk and weight precluded her from running with safety anywhere but on the Paddington-Bristol main line. On one occasion she got as far as Newton Abbot via Bristol, and on another she worked through to Wolverhampton; but never again! She developed an annoying habit of jumping off the track at the approaches to Paddington departure platforms, in backing on to a train, and this led to her being barred from using Platform 1.

On a train, she was restricted to a maximum speed of 65 m.p.h., with the result that her performances could never be outstanding, especially on such trains as the Bristol two-hour expresses which she occasionally worked. But when the gremlins chose to take time off, she could work without trouble, and for a long while she was fairly regularly employed on the 6.30 p.m. Paddington-Bristol semi-fast train, returning on a heavy early-morning freight.

There was one incident which was not calculated to enhance *The Great Bear's* already rather shaky reputation. The original tender tank filler was in the dome immediately above the top of the pipe leading up from the water scoop, and was closed by a hinged flap. One day, those mischievous gremlins got really busy and arranged that somebody should leave the flap unfastened after the tender had been filled at the running shed before a journey.

At the first water troughs the fireman dutifully let down the scoop. Very little water went into the tank; instead, a mighty cataract burst through the unfastened flap, poured over the back of the tender, brought down the vestibule connection of the leading coach and, before anyone could realise what was going on, flooded the coach to a depth of more than a foot! Compensation for aggrieved passengers cost a considerable sum, and it was some time before the locomotive design staff at Swindon regained the confidence of the higher-ups.

The Great Bear had four cylinders, 15 in. dia., 26 in. stroke, piston valves 8 in. dia., with a maximum travel of $7\frac{1}{4}$ in. Two sets of Walschaerts were between the frames, connected directly to the inside valve spindles and transmitting motion to the outside valves by horizontal rockers. The lap was $1\frac{5}{8}$ in. and the lead $\frac{1}{8}$ in., while the port length was $31\frac{1}{2}$ in. and the effective widths $1\frac{1}{4}$ in. for admission and $3\frac{5}{8}$ in. for exhaust.

Wheel diameters were: bogie 3 ft 2 in.; coupled, 6 ft $8\frac{1}{2}$ in., and trailing 3 ft 8 in.; the wheelbase was

GENERAL SPECIFICATION

CYLINDERS			TUBES		
Diameter	...	... 17 in.	Number	...	... 246
Stroke	...	... 24 in.	Diameter	...	... 1⅝ in.
BOILER			HEATING SURFACE		
Length between			Tubes...	...	1,127 sq. ft.
tubeplates ...		11 ft 0 in.	Firebox	...	122 sq. ft.
Maximum diameter 4 ft 2 in.			Total ...	...	1,249 sq. ft.
FIREBOX LENGTH					
Inside	...	... —	GRATE AREA		
Outside	...	... —	Square feet	...	—

No 143
A REALLY QUAINT SPECIMEN

YES, there really *was* an engine like this ! In fact, at one time there were as many as seven and they belonged to a set of 13 engines which had a very interesting history; the tale, however, is far too long to be repeated here in full detail. No 143 was the one that I knew best, so I shall devote this chapter to her, primarily.

I first met her at Chester in the summer of 1918, and at once noticed that her appearance was quite unlike that of two of her sisters, Nos 141 and 146, who were often to be seen at Chester at that time. I also noticed that whenever these three engines came to Chester, they approached from the direction of Crewe, not from Birkenhead or Shrewsbury, and they never went to the Great Western running-sheds.

To me, this seemed rather odd, until I discovered that, due to the fact that there was a war on, the engines were on loan to the London and North Western Railway.

The main attraction of No 143 was her delightfully absurd appearance; but, for me, the unusual, even grotesque, often had a strong fascination. In the case of No 143, the effect was due to the fact that she had acquired a Wolverhampton boiler with a tall

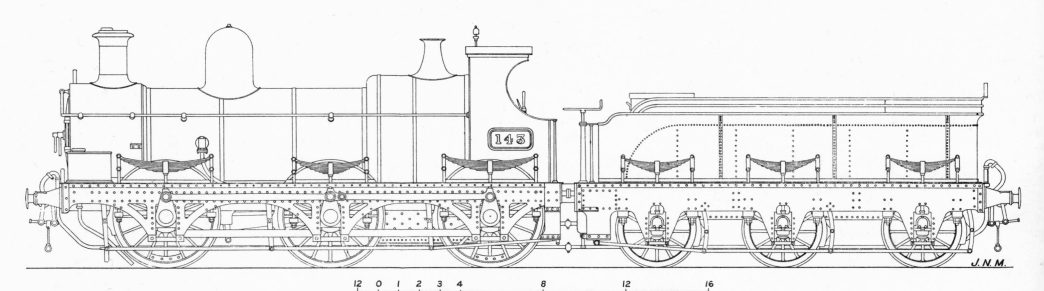

dome, set far forward on the barrel, and with a rather prominent raised firebox casing; the whole lot was set very low in the frames, which were of the slotted, sandwich type having outside bearings.

Just to add the final touch, so to speak, a short chimney with a rather heavily-moulded copper cap had been fitted, while the tender was a secondhand one from a different class of engine !

I always took great delight in oddities of this sort, so long as they were not downright silly, though I must admit that it was sometimes difficult to decide just what was silly and what was not.

No 143, in spite of her age, was a hard worker, due to the prevailing conditions at the time. She usually brought in fairly heavy mixed-goods trains to Chester from Crewe and then spent much time in shunting and marshalling in the Chester yards. The return to Crewe would usually be with part of a South Wales coal train brought in from the south by a massive 2-8-0 engine from Cardiff.

She seemed to have plenty of power and could get away without much bother at the head of a 45-wagon coal train, though I was told at the time that the official limit for such a train, behind an engine of this class, was 33 wagons. In wartime, however, I noticed that official instructions were subject to variations of interpretation that may not be official.

No 143 was built at Swindon in 1886, and it will be noted that the outside frames were of the Gooch slotted type, first introduced by Daniel Gooch as far back as 1838, and known as sandwich-frames because of the mode of their construction. Each frame was formed of two slotted plates held together by cast-iron (originally oak, or teak) blocks placed between them.

The inside frames were of the ordinary plate variety, stayed by the front and back bufferbeams and by flat stays—at convenient places along their length—to the outside frames. This form of construction resulted in a very strong and rigid foundation for the whole engine; and it would make a nice little exercise for model makers, especially if the 222 rivets in each outside frame are correctly represented !

The coupled wheels were 5 ft 2 in. dia.; the wheelbase was apparently subject to some variations in spacing, as well as in total length, in the various batches built. As far as I could discover from official data, the total wheelbase was 15 ft 9 in. divided into 8 ft plus 7 ft 9 in. The overhang was 5 ft at the front and 3 ft 5 in. at the back. The tender wheelbase was 15 ft divided into 6 ft 2 in. plus 6 ft 10 in., with overhangs of 4 ft at the front and 3 ft at the back.

The boiler was pitched 6 ft 8 in. above rail level ; the barrel was 11 ft long and made in three rings, the largest of which was 4 ft 2 in. dia.; and a raised round-top firebox was fitted. There were 246 tubes of $1\frac{5}{8}$ in. dia., the heating surface of which was 1,127 sq. ft; the firebox heating surface was 122 sq. ft, making the total 1,249 sq. ft.

The cylinders were 17 in. dia. and 24 in. stroke, and the working pressure was 140 p.s.i., at 80 per cent. of which the tractive effort was about 14,260 lb.

No 143 was running in this condition from November 1907 until she was withdrawn for scrap in August 1919. Officially, she was a " renewal "

of a former engine of similar design and carrying the same number. It would appear, however, that nothing whatever of the older engine was used in the renewal which, therefore, was a brand new engine when built.

It should be recorded that when No 143 had been rebuilt in November 1907 into the form depicted in the drawing, she had a longer chimney ; the short one that I have shown dated from about 1916, when many engines of different classes were being fitted with shorter chimneys. The reason is said to have been that the reduction in the chimney length improved the steaming of the boilers.

No 146 was the last survivor of this very interesting class; in 1915 she was fitted with a boiler similar to 143's, but she acquired one of a different type in 1917, and another, having a Belpaire firebox, in 1920. She ran with this one until she was withdrawn in April 1925. I believe she was the last sandwich-framed 0-6-0 to run on the GWR.

I commend the curious No 143 to anyone who would care to build a model that is a little out of the ordinary, at least in appearance. The slotted sandwich frames are the only feature which would require rather more than the usual time and patience to reproduce. Their marking-out would require care, and I must add that the radius of the curves of the lower edge was 3 ft $7\frac{1}{2}$ in. and the minimum depth between hornplates was 12 in.

None of the other details should present any special difficulty, since, in spite of their peculiar appearance, they were all fairly straightforward.

The performance of these engines certainly gave the lie to their " old crock " appearance. On goods trains they could develop quite an astonishing amount of power, while their use on passenger trains showed them to be capable of running at fairly high speeds when called upon to do so.

The only one of this class that I ever saw in the London area was No 132; one day, early in 1916, I was surprised to see her at Reading, on a passenger train bound for Didcot where I believe she was stationed at that time. Except for this solitary stray, the entire class spent the whole of its existence in the Northern Division, and never came further south than Birmingham.

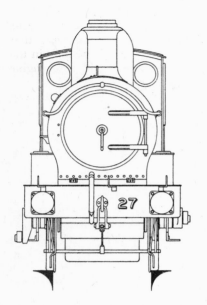

27

GENERAL SPECIFICATION		
CYLINDERS		
Diameter ... ... 17 in.	**TUBES**	
Stroke ... ... 24 in.	Number 249	
	Diameter ... ... $1\frac{3}{4}$ in.	
BOILER		
Length, between	**HEATING SURFACE**	
tubeplates ... 11 ft	Tubes ... 1,285.58 sq. ft	
Maximum dia-	Firebox ... 107.72 sq. ft	
meter ... 4 ft. 5 in.	Total ... 1,393.3 sq. ft	
w		
FIREBOX LENGTH		
Inside ... 4 ft 8 $\frac{1}{16}$ in.	**GRATE AREA**	
Outside ... 5 ft 4 in.	Square feet ... 17.33	

0-6-0 GOODS ENGINE No 27

"OLD 27," as I called her, was one of a class that consisted of no fewer than 310 engines built at Swindon between 1866 and 1876. They were to be found all over the GWR system, and I knew very many of them.

With such a large number of engines in one class, it is hardly a matter for surprise that Swindon really went to town in providing a most extensive series of variations on a theme; for the number of different types of boiler to be noted in use on these engines, all at one time, beggars description, though it was quite characteristic and, at the period, only to be expected.

Officially, the class was known as the Standard Goods, or 388 Class, but when I knew them they had become the Old Standard Goods, to prevent confusion with the Dean's Standard Goods, or 2301 Class. Joseph Armstrong was responsible for the original design, and all 310 engines were constructed during his term of office. Thereafter, both William Dean and G. J. Churchward carried out the various re-boilerings and general modernisation which kept the engines in traffic for upwards of 50 years.

In fact, the last of them to be withdrawn was No 1195, which was new in April, 1876 and scrapped in October, 1934, aged 58½ years. Yet she was not

the oldest; according to my records, the palm must be awarded to No 392, built November 1866, and withdrawn in October 1928, aged 62.

The mileage travelled by most of the class amounted to well over a million an engine; the greatest appears to have been run by No 422, built in July 1867, for when she was withdrawn in January 1929, aged 61½ years, she had totalled 1,394,729 miles. I am not claiming that as a record, but it is quite a respectable distance. And by no means all of it was run on goods trains, because the engines were often used for passenger traffic.

This class of fine old engine was a very great favourite of mine, and the only reason why I have chosen "Old 27" as the subject of my drawing is that, like the old 2-4-0 No 3230, she was stationed at Didcot in 1919, working out her last years in my particular part of the country. At the same time, she was one of the few which, unlike most, had boilers with flush, round-top fireboxes instead of Belpaires.

Her dome and safety-valve cover were brass, and her chimney cap was copper, to all of which the enterprising cleaners had tried to restore the original polish; but I regret the engine was never very clean.

Perhaps the choicest of my many recollections is of a Saturday in the summer of 1907, when the up Cornish Riviera Express failed to pass Wormwood Scrubbs at its proper time. I was with a friend at whose house I was supposed to be having tea; but we decided to forgo the tea and wait for the express. When, in due course, it arrived it was headed by two Armstrong Goods engines, 424 and 1202; my friend and myself considered this sufficient reward for missing our tea that day ! The train was more than an hour late.

On another occasion, when I was going to Reading, on the way to a holiday at my grandparents' country home, I travelled by the 4.5 p.m. Trowbridge train, at the head of which was Armstrong Goods engine 1207. The 36 miles to Reading were run in 42 minutes, with the old engine hauling the eight-coach train at a steady 60 m.p.h. for most of the way after passing Southall.

"Old 27" may possibly have indulged in exploits of a like kind during her life; but when I knew her she was usually working pick-up goods trains on the Didcot, Newbury and Southampton line, though I have seen her shunting at either Goring or Pangbourne, on the Didcot-Reading line. She did not last very long in that district, however, as she was withdrawn in June, 1920, aged 44½ years.

About 20 of the engines were sold to the Government for war service overseas in 1916 and 1917. " Old 27 " was among them, but for some reason was returned to the GWR almost at once. Eight of them were lost at sea by enemy torpedo, but the rest saw service in Iraq and Serbia; six of these eventually came home, but were in such a bad state that they were broken up, while the others finished their days in the Middle East, where they worked on the Ottoman (Aidin) Railway until the early 1930s.

The main dimensions of the engines were: cylinders 17 in. dia. by 24 in. stroke; wheel diameter 5 ft 2 in.; wheelbase 15 ft 8 in., divided into 7 ft 4 in. plus 8 ft 4 in. The leading overhang was 4 ft 10 in. and the rear one 2 ft 10 in., the length of the frames being 23 ft 4 in.

There were slight variations to be noted in the shape of the outside frames; in some, the plates were deepened by a small amount just above the spring-hanger pads, as seen in my drawing, while in others this deepening was absent. The number and positions of the galaxy of rivets in the frames were also subject to slight modifications.

The boiler on No 27 was of the usual two-ring type,

having diameters of 4 ft 4 in. and 4 ft 5 in., a barrel length of 11 ft, and a very large dome mounted on the back ring; the centre-line was 6 ft 11¼ in. above rail level. There were 249 tubes of 1¾ in. dia.; the grate area was 17.33 sq. ft and the working pressure was 140 p.s.i.

A firebox casing of round-top type, flush with the boiler barrel, was fitted; its length was 5 ft 4 in. and its width, at the centre line, was 4 ft 7⅛ in. The inner firebox was 4 ft 8 1/16 in. long, 3 ft 8 in. wide and 6 ft 0½ in. high. The total heating surface was 1,393.3 sq. ft, to which the tubes contributed 1,285.58 sq. ft, and the firebox 107.72 sq. ft; the grate area was 17.33 sq. ft. The tractive effort was 13,313 lb.

Although the engines were, of course, intended primarily for goods traffic, they were, as I have already mentioned, often used on passenger trains. This was particularly noticeable in some districts around Chester and in the West Midlands. I remember that when I spent a fortnight at Chester in the summer of 1918, No 700 was an especially busy engine.

She was stationed at Shrewsbury, and would arrive on a goods train at Chester about 11 o'clock in the morning. After disposing of this train in the goods yard, she would go to the running shed for coal and

servicing, to be ready for working a passenger train to Birkenhead, about 1.15 p.m. She would be back in Chester, on a passenger train, at about 4.30 p.m.; be making another trip to Birkenhead at 6.10 p.m.; and be back in Chester about 7.45 p.m., with another visit to the running shed.

Believe it or not, the return to Shrewsbury was made on the 9.35 p.m. *express* train, complete with dining-car, bound for such places as Birmingham, Leamington, Banbury, Oxford, Didcot, Reading and London. This programme was performed daily, Mondays to Saturdays, during the fortnight I was at Chester, and I thought it a fairly stiff one for a 46-year-old goods engine.

A marked steadiness at speed was a very noticeable feature of the running, confirmed by drivers to whom I had commented about it. No driver would agree that the engines " ran hard " on the road; but all agreed that they rode easily and steadily, and would run up to 60 m.p.h. without any coaxing whatever.

The sight of a Standard Goods at speed was fascinating and mildly amusing, with those outside rods whirling round and looking as if they might fly off at any moment. But I never heard of such a mishap occurring; on the contrary, the engines worked well and gave excellent service for upwards of 50 years.

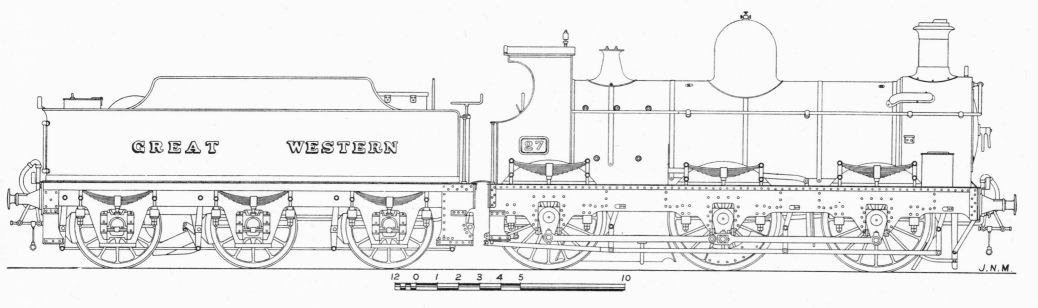

THESE engines, of which there were no fewer than 260, must be included among the classics. Not that there was anything exciting or remarkably outstanding in their design; but their subsequent history and, particularly, their war record render them deserving of a niche to themselves in the annals of locomotive history.

It is, indeed, good to know that the British Transport Commission has acquired No 2516 for permanent preservation; in addition to being a memento of a class that had a wonderful history, she is an example of the typical, plain, simple and straightforward 0-6-0 goods engine that has served the railways of Britain so well for more than 120 years.

To me, the GWR 2301-class 0-6-0s—or Dean Goods, as they have become universally known—were always extremely attractive, chiefly because of their extraordinary versatility; for I have seen them on literally every class of locomotive work from express passenger trains to shunting in locomotive running-shed yards; and that is no exaggeration.

In two great wars, a large number of these engines were sent to work behind various battle fronts, where they performed yeoman service. Because of their simplicity, power and lightness, they could be sent

THE DEAN GOODS

out on the flimsiest of track and handled successfully by the least experienced of enginemen for hauling heavy trains of military supplies to the most unlikely places. On this work they won for themselves opinions that they were " anybody's engine " and the " backbone of the Railway Operating Division."

The wars over, and just after the nationalisation of British railways had been accomplished, came the crowning glory of the Dean Goods. Their numbers had been woefully diminished by war casualties, and

the few which were still in service were obviously nearing the end of their usefulness. But the problem arose as to what should replace them.

Eventually, a then new LMR Class 2 MT 2-6-0 engine, No 46419, was sent to the Western Region for trial on Dean Goods' duties. For some time this engine ran in direct competition with a Dean Goods on certain routes. At first, the drivers reported that the 2-6-0 was no better than a Dean; then they went so far as to complain that the 2-6-0 could not time

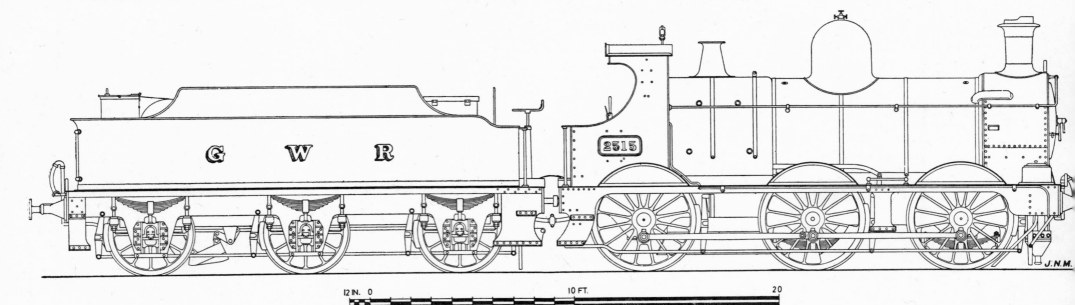

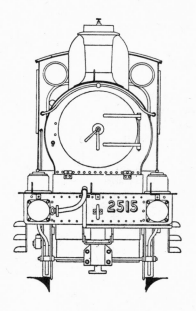

GENERAL SPECIFICATION

CYLINDERS			TUBES		
Diameter	...	... 17½ in.	Number	...	219 & 2
Stroke	...	... 24 in.	Diameter	...	1⅝ & 5⅛ in.
BOILER			HEATING SURFACE		
Length between			Tubes	...	1,012.8 sq. ft
tubeplates		10 ft 3 in.	Firebox	...	102.5 sq. ft
Maximum dia-			Total	...	1,115.3 sq. ft
meter	...	4 ft 5 in.			
FIREBOX LENGTH			GRATE AREA		
Inside	...	... 4 ft 8 1/16 in.	Square feet	...	15.3
Outside	...	5 ft 4 in.			

the trains. Swindon sent out some inspectors and the dynamometer car to make a strict investigation into the matter, and they confirmed the drivers' reports.

The next step was to take that 2-6-0 into the works at Swindon and put her on the testing plant, where she was given a thorough test.

There happened to be in the erecting shop a Dean Goods, No 2579, which had just been given a complete overhaul and refit; before she was returned to her home station, she, too, was given the same test. The whole of the information obtained from these tests has been published in the *Journal of the Institution of Locomotive Engineers* for September-October 1950 and it shows that the Dean engine was *the better of the two* !

This result surprised the Swindon technical staff and dumbfounded the Railway Executive's mechanical engineers, while the fact that an 1899 0-6-0 had proved to be superior to a 1948 2-6-0 caused some merriment in the locomotive profession generally.

There can be little doubt that as a result of analysing the information obtained during these tests, the Swindon people made an important discovery; but what it was has not yet been clearly stated. Un-

questionably, however, it has been the basis of the improved draughting arrangements that have since been successfully applied to different types of locomotives in the Eastern, London Midland and Western Regions.

The original design for the Dean Goods, or " Standard Goods " as they were semi-officially described, dated from 1883, when the first examples were built. Engines 2301 to 2320 originally had domeless boilers, with flush smoke boxes and fireboxes. All the later engines, numbered 2321 to 2360 and 2381 to 2580, had domed boilers.

My drawing shows No 2515 in the final condition, with a modern domed boiler having a Belpaire firebox, and may be taken as representative of the majority of the survivors of this class as they were after about 1930, though this particular boiler and the cast-iron tapered chimney first appeared on these engines some ten years previously.

The following dimensions apply to the class in the form which is seen in the drawing: cylinders, dia. 17½ in., stroke 24 in.; wheels, dia. 5 ft 2 in.; wheelbase 15 ft 6 in., divided into 7 ft 3 in. plus 8 ft 3 in.; leading overhang 4 ft 9 in.; trailing overhang 4 ft; length of engine frames 24 ft 3 in.

The boiler was 4 ft 5 in. dia. outside the larger (back) ring, and its length was 10 ft 3 in.; the pitch of the centre line was 7 ft 3 in. There were 219 tubes of 1⅝ in. dia. and two of 5⅛ in. dia., the heating surface of which was 1,012.8 sq. ft. The firebox

added 102.5 sq. ft, making the total heating surface 1,115.3 sq. ft. The grate area was 15.3 sq. ft, and the working pressure was usually 160 p.s.i., though it was higher in some cases.

A well-designed Stephenson link-motion operated the slide valves; its inclination was 13 in 87, a distinctly unusual slope. Valve travel, in full gear, was 4½ in., and in mid-gear it was 3⅞ in. The valves, which were 11⅜ in. long and 17 in. wide, were provided with 1 1/16 in. steam lap and ⅛ in. exhaust lap; they worked on port faces in which the ports were 15 in. long, 1¾ in. wide for admission and 4 in. wide for exhaust. The port bars were 1 in. wide.

Although drawings of this gear, showing the valves and port faces, have been published (*Railway Engineer*, 1889), I can find no mention of the lead. I think, however, it was about ½ in. in full gear, though it might have varied in different lots of these engines.

I must interpolate here that all the 260 engines of this class were built with 17 in. cylinders; in the majority, however, this was subsequently enlarged to 17½ in., which is the figure I have quoted above.

In 1954, all except two of this class, Nos 2516 and 2538, had been broken up, after long, honourable and, in the case of those commandeered for service in two wars, unusually strenuous service.

In 1952, I was approached by Mr A. J. Maxwell, of Newton Abbot, to see if anything could be done to save one of these historic engines from destruction. I tested out this idea on fellow-enthusiasts and found it extremely popular; so, with such backing, I put it forward in the right quarter. For many months afterwards, I could get no definite information, but eventually I was told that a Dean Goods would be preserved; No 2516, withdrawn in 1954, is the one concerned.

I must add a few words about the tenders; many and various types have been attached to Dean Goods engines at different times. My drawing shows the standard Dean-cum-Churchward 3,000 gal. type as attached to some of the engines which worked a considerable amount of passenger traffic, especially in Wales; but the more usual tender was the 2,500 gal. type.

About 50 of this celebrated class survived to become the property of British Railways in 1948, and the last one, No 2538, was withdrawn in May, 1957.

THE GWR 'ABERDARES'

FROM about 1895 the Great Western Railway seemed to concentrate upon the development of a highly individualistic style of locomotive design, to such an extent that almost any one of its locomotives could be instantly and certainly identified anywhere; but of all the many types and classes of engines designed at Swindon, the Aberdares could be claimed, without fear of contradiction, to be unique, for there were no other goods engines in the world that even remotely resembled them.

This was all the more remarkable when the design was built up very largely of standard parts and was perfectly plain, simple and straightforward, merely a striking inside-cylindered 2-6-0 with double frames and outside cranks. To me all this was extremely interesting, particularly in later years when I had acquired some knowledge of the intricacies of locomotive design. I was never fortunate enough to travel either on or behind any of the Aberdares; but I saw most of them during the course of many years and was always fascinated by them.

The class had its direct origin in a solitary engine, No 33, which grew, so to speak, out of a number of experimental engines built at Swindon between 1896 and 1900, during an attempt to evolve a really satisfactory type for hauling the very heavy South Wales coal trains through the Severn Tunnel without

assistance. The tunnel is straight, but the track through it is in the form of a flat V with a gradient of 1 in 90 down from the western end to a point about midway, and then 1 in 100 up to the eastern end and some distance beyond.

While the tunnel is slightly more than 4½ miles long, the graded length of track, including the approaches at each end, is about six miles; and so the engines required for working coal trains of 900 to 1,000 tons weight over that road had to be powerful.

No 33 was built in August 1900, and was somewhat smaller and lighter than any of the experimental engines that had preceded her; she was undoubtedly neater in external appearance. In broad terms, she was a 2-6-0 version of the *Atbara*, except for her pony truck and very small coupled wheels; but she succeeded where her predecessors had failed, with the result that in 1901-2, 40 further engines like her, numbered 2621 to 2660, were put into traffic. They were subject to sundry experiments in boiler design, though the boilers were all of the Standard No 2 size some with cylindrical barrels like No 33, and others with tapered barrels.

September of 1902 brought a change to the larger,

Standard No 4, boiler which was fitted to engines 2661 to 2680, built between September and December 1902. Of these, the boiler on No 2661 was unique in being supplied with a cylindrical barrel. It was the only No 4 of this kind ever made. All the others had tapered barrels, which eventually became standard for the whole class.

In July and August 1903, Nos 2611 to 2620 were added to the class, which then numbered 71 engines, including No 33; no more were built until 1906, when nine more arrived in a curious order: 2607 and 2608 in January; 2601, 2603 and 2605 in February; 2604 and 2610 in April; 2606 in May and 2609 in December. Finally, 2602 came out in January 1907, and completed the class. The reason for this apparently haphazard order of construction was that 2601 to 2610 were replacements of ten extremely ugly and ungainly engines, known as the Krugers, one of them a 4-6-0 and the other nine 2-6-0s, which had been built for trial purposes between December, 1899, and June, 1903. The last ten Aberdares were built in the order in which the Krugers were scrapped.

No 33 was rebuilt with a No 4 boiler in January 1903, and in December 1912, she was renumbered 2600 to bring her into line numerically with the

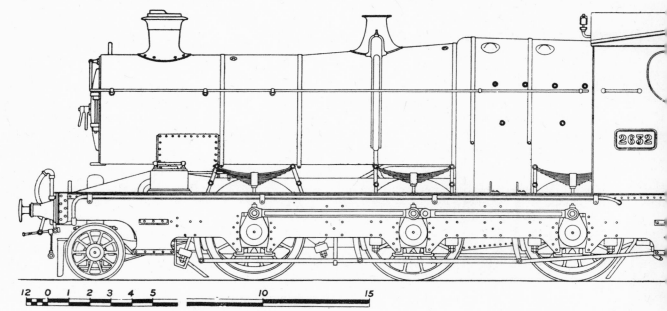

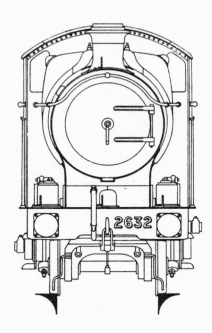

Wales coal traffic which they worked through to London and, via Hereford and Shrewsbury, as far north as Chester. But after about 20 years, Churchward's 2800 mineral engines succeeded the Aberdares which then became more widely distributed over the GWR system. Some of them, including 2632, came to be stationed in London and I recall seeing them on the heavy and important goods trains to Birmingham, the North, and to Wales and the West.

As a class, the Aberdares displayed a remarkable variety of chimneys; at first they all had the Dean plain cast-iron chimney of the Atbara type. This was the regular pattern for about eight years. In 1908 for some reason that was never explained, a special chimney was introduced, with a rather steeply tapered barrel below a parallel-sided copper cap. This pattern seemed to be the perfect match for the general ungainliness of the engine! But about three years later, the Aberdares had a variant which was very similar except that the copper cap was tapered to match the barrel, as shown in my drawing of No 2632. Later still, during the 1914-18 war years, both these special chimneys began to be replaced by the modern tapered cast-iron one; in the meantime, City-class copper-capped chimneys appeared on some of the engines.

Aberdare cylinders had a diameter of 18 in., and a stroke of 26 in.; the diameter of the pony wheels was 2 ft 8 in., and of the coupled 4 ft 7½ in.; the

rest of the class, of which she had been a representative since 1903.

It is scarcely surprising that these cumbrous, even clumsy, but curiously fascinating and highly successful locomotives were worked extremely hard. At first they were almost exclusively employed on the South

wheelbase was 22 ft 6 in. divided into 7 ft 6 in. plus 7 ft 6 in. plus 7 ft 6 in.; and the overhang was 1 ft 9 in. at the front, and 5 ft 3 in. at the back.

The boiler barrel was 11 ft long and was made in two rings, the front one of which was 4 ft 10¾ in. dia., while the back one tapered from 5 ft 6 in. to 5 ft 0¼ in. The centre-line was 8 ft 3 in. above rail level.

There were 235 tubes of 1⅝ in. dia. and 14 of 5⅛ in., giving 1,349.64 sq. ft of heating surface. The crater firebox was 7 ft long and the inner one 6 ft 2½ in., and the heating surface was 128.72 sq. ft, making the total evaporative surface 1,478.36 sq. ft. Grate area was 20.56 sq. ft and pressure 200 p.s.i.

In working order the weight of the engine was 56 tons 15 cwt, with 7 tons 2 cwt on the pony truck, 15 tons 4 cwt on the leading coupled axle, 17 tons 10 cwt on the driving, and 16 tons 19 cwt on the trailing. With the GWR standard 3,000-gallon tender seen in the drawing, the total weight was 93 tons 10 cwt; but after 1929, more than half the class was fitted with Great Central 4,000-gallon tenders from scrapped ROD 2-8-0 engines, putting the total weight up to 104 tons 9 cwt.

The class was equipped with steam reversing gear which, in spite of its refusal to maintain a constant point of cut-off, was never altered.

These ungainly, cumbrous, but affectionately remembered engines became extinct in October, 1949, with the withdrawal of No 2667.

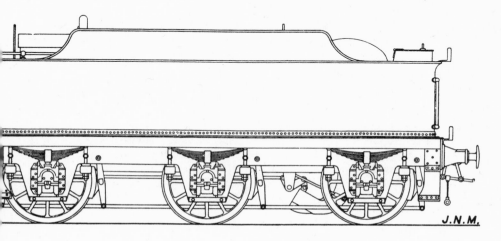

J.N.M.

GENERAL SPECIFICATION			
CYLINDERS		**TUBES**	
Diameter ... ... 18 in.		Number ... 235 & 14	
Stroke ... ... 26 in.		Diameter 1⅝ in. & 5⅛ in.	
BOILER		**HEATING SURFACE**	
Length between		Tubes... 1,349.64 sq. ft.	
tubeplates ... 11 ft 0 in.		Firebox ... 128.72 sq. ft.	
Maximum diameter 5 ft 6 in.		Total ... 1,478.36 sq. ft.	
FIREBOX LENGTH			
Inside ... 6 ft 2½ in.		**GRATE AREA**	
Outside ... 7 ft 0 in.		Square feet 20.56	

1334 CLASS 2-4-0 ENGINES

GENERAL SPECIFICATION

CYLINDERS			TUBES		
Diameter	...	17 in.	Number	...	213 & 2
Stroke	...	24 in.	Diameter	1⅝ in. & 5⅛ in.	
BOILER			HEATING SURFACE		
Length between			Tubes...	1,004.2 sq. ft	
tubeplates ...	10 ft 6 in.		Firebox	...	81.8 sq. ft
Maximum diameter	4 ft 3 in.		Total ...	1,086 sq. ft	
FIREBOX LENGTH			GRATE AREA		
Inside...	...	—	Square feet	...	16.76
Outside	...	5 ft 6 in.			

Thatcham only. The engine on this train usually displayed the express passenger headcode; in 1937-8, this train was probably the only one on which a 2-4-0 engine could be seen running regularly on an express passenger train, in Britain, or elsewhere.

In fact, by that time the 1334 class, together with the LNER 2-4-0 engines of the E4 class, had become the last active examples of the once-popular and very numerous 2-4-0 type locomotive; for this reason alone, they deserve more than purely local interest. A Johnson 2-4-0 had survived as a de-

Among a large and decidedly varied assortment of locomotives which were absorbed into Great Western Railway ownership at the time of the grouping of the British Railways in 1923, were three sturdy little 2-4-0s that had belonged to the Midland and South Western Junction Railway.

The MSWJR was a small cross-country line from Cheltenham to Andover Junction and then exercised running powers over the LSWR from Andover via Stockbridge, Romsey and Redbridge to Southampton. At the time of the grouping it owned 29 locomotives comprising: ten 4-4-0, ten 0-6-0, one 2-6-0, three 2-4-0, two 4-4-4T, two 0-6-0T and one 0-4-4T, all of which became GWR property. Swindon reboilered most of them and sent them back to their native haunts; but, within a few years, all except the three 2-4-0 engines were withdrawn.

It seems that the GWR decided that it could find plenty of work for the 2-4-0s to do on its own territory. They were thoroughly refurbished, given the distinction of becoming officially the " 1334 class," and then one was sent to Didcot and the other two to Reading, from which places they were constantly employed until July, 1951.

They were most attractive engines, three little sisters—triplets—which managed to endear themselves to many people in the Didcot-Newbury-Reading area for more than 25 years, during which time, the work they did had to be seen to be believed. The Reading duo worked local trains between there and Devizes, via Newbury; the Didcot engine

worked, at first, from there to Oxford, or Reading and then, for several years, settled down to regular running to and from Southampton via Newbury.

Apart from their energy, the chief attraction of these engines was their extreme simplicity and neatness. They were not so very young, either, for they were built by Dübs and Co., Glasgow, in 1894; so they were nearly 30 years old when the GWR acquired them. But they could pull and they could run, which probably accounted for their long survival, after all the rest of their MSWJ compatriots had gone to the scrap-heap.

When the war broke out in 1939, I fully expected that the days of the 1334 class would be numbered. But no, the engines were put to working local goods trains, so as to release other and more powerful engines for heavier duties. For the next twelve years, the 1334 class remained almost exclusively on goods traffic, and were seldom seen again on passenger trains.

However, somebody discovered that an engine of this class was very suitable for the Lambourn Valley line, with the result that the afternoon train up that line was worked regularly by one of these engines for some years. At first, this turn was operated from Didcot, but later, Reading took it over. It was the last passenger turn run regularly by one of these engines, all three of which took it in turns.

In the late 1930s one or other of the two Reading engines was always to be seen on the 8.16 a.m. fast train from Newbury to Reading, stopping at

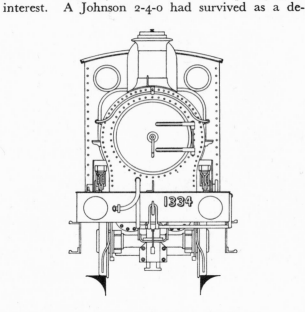

partmental engine in the Midland Region until 1950, used for nothing but very occasional official inspection tours, whereas the E4s and 1334 class were in very active service. All three of the 1334 class were withdrawn together for scrapping in January, 1952, at the ripe old age of 58 years.

When they were first reboilered at Swindon, in 1923, all three engines presented the appearance shown in my drawing, except that the coalplates on the tender were about double the height that I have shown. This was subsequently reduced because,

I understand, there was sometimes a tendency for the tender to be overloaded with coal. In later years, 1335 and 1336 were fitted with the tapered cast-iron chimney; at the same time, 1336 was fitted with a superheater and her chimney was consequently further forward on the smokebox.

No 1334 was never altered; in addition, she could always be distinguished from her two sisters because, for some reason, her driving-wheel splashers boasted a polished brass beading which she retained until the end of her days. It was ever a peculiarity of Swindon practice to have *one* engine in a class possessing some minor differences from all the others.

Until the early 1940s, these engines were painted

apparatus, which was not always to be found on engines intended for secondary duties; it suggested that the 1334 class were, at the outset, regarded as being suitable for main-line work.

The principal dimensions of these fascinating engines were: cylinder diameter 17 in., stroke 24 in.; wheel diameters, leading, 3 ft 6 in.; driving and coupled, 5 ft 6 in.; tender, 4 ft; wheelbase, 7 ft 7 in. plus 8 ft; tender 12 ft, equally divided; total (engine and tender) 36 ft 0¼ in.

The boiler was of the usual two-ring type with outside diameters of 4 ft 2 in. and 4 ft 3 in., barrel length being 10 ft 6 in.; its centre-line was 7 ft above rail level. The firebox casing was 5 ft 6 in. long, 4 ft

trim was 28 tons 8 cwt. The engine weight was 35 tons 5 cwt divided into 11 tons 11 cwt on the leading axle, 12 tons 7 cwt on the driving axle and 11 tons 7 cwt on the trailing axle.

The height from rail level to the extreme top of the chimney was 12 ft $5\frac{1}{16}$ in., and to the top of the cab roof 11 ft $5\frac{5}{8}$ in. The tractive effort was 14,740 lb., and the total length of engine and tender, over buffers, was 48 ft 0¼ in.

I must add that the overhangs of the engine were 4 ft 11 in. at the front and 3 ft 6 in. at the back; for the tender they were 3 ft $7\frac{3}{4}$ in. and 3 ft 5 in., respectively.

It should be noted that, on Nos 1334 and 1335,

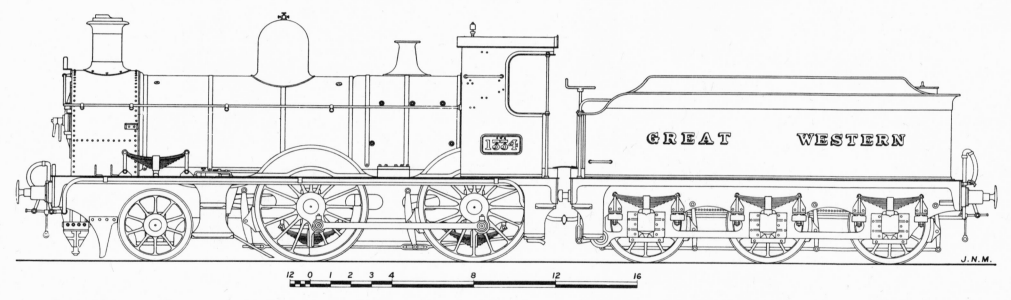

GREAT   WESTERN

1334

J.N.M.

12 0 1 2 3 4   8   12   16

in the plain unlined green-and-black livery, the only relief being the legend "Great Western" on the tender. Later, this gave way to a sombre black all over, and the tenders were lettered "GWR," in golden-yellow letters shaded in dark red, just to break the monotony of the funereal livery.

A noticeable feature, common to all three engines, was the unusual thinness of the tyres of the wheels, the reason for which has never been forthcoming. Another point worth mentioning is that these engines were equipped with the automatic train control

1 in. wide, outside, and the grate area was 16.76 sq. ft.

The superheated boiler on No 1336 had two tubes of $5\frac{1}{8}$ in. dia. and 213 of $1\frac{5}{8}$ in. dia. Their heating surface was 1,004.2 sq. ft; that of the firebox was 81.8 sq. ft, making the total h.s. 1,086 sq. ft. The working pressure was 165 p.s.i. The boilers of Nos 1334 and 1335 were similar to the above, except that they had 221 tubes and no superheaters; the heating surface was 1,090 sq. ft.

The capacity of the tender was for 2,600 gallons of water and 4 tons of coal; its weight in working

the grab-handles on the cab-sides were placed as shown on the drawing; on No 1336, they were situated on the same horizontal centre-line as the main handrails on the boiler barrel—yet one more instance of that slight difference in one engine of a class !

Variations of minor details like these are traps which model makers are constantly falling into. It is never perfectly safe to work to line drawings alone; at least one photograph of the engine being modelled is essential if the details are to be correct.

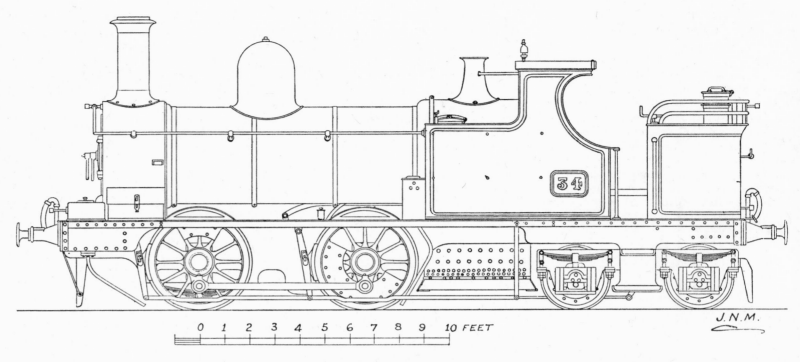

J.N.M.

0 1 2 3 4 5 6 7 8 9 10 FEET

WILLIAM DEAN'S
0-4-4 TANK No 34

GENERAL SPECIFICATION

CYLINDERS				TUBES			
Diameter	...	...	16 in.	Number	...	...	237
Stroke	...	...	24 in.	Diameter	...	...	1¾ in.
BOILER							
Length between				HEATING SURFACE			
tubeplates	...	10 ft 3 in.		Tubes...		1,142.2 sq. ft.	
Maximum				Firebox	...	93 sq. ft.	
diameter	...	3 ft 10 in.		Total ...		1,235.2 sq. ft.	
FIREBOX LENGTH							
Inside...	...	...	—	GRATE AREA			
Outside	...		—	Square feet	...	...	14.8

I HAVE always been fascinated by locomotives that were, so to speak, rather out of the common. I am not referring to freaks, too many of which have sullied the pages of locomotive history, but there have been some which were non-standard, though perfectly orthodox, usually built for some special purpose, and I have known a number of these.

One such was the Great Western Railway 0-4-4 tank engine No 34 depicted in the picture and my drawing. Actually, there were two of these engines, the other being No 35; but I never saw her. I must admit that I can only just claim to have known No 34. As a boy, I had read about her, seen her photograph in *The Locomotive Magazine* and I also possessed a postcard of her, and from this information I worked up quite an affection for this delightful little engine.

Then, one day in 1907, I was on Swindon station and had the intense satisfaction of seeing her arrive on a short train from the easterly direction. She was obviously just out of the works after an overhaul

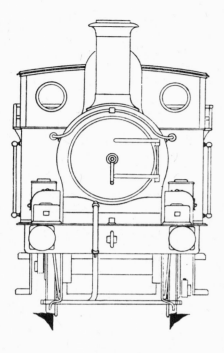

and repaint, and was probably being run-in on local work before being returned to her proper home in Cornwall, though there may be some doubt about this in view of the fact that the engine was sold by the GWR to the War Office in November 1908 for use on the Military Training Railways at Bordon.

She remained military property for about twenty years afterwards, during which I caught sight of her at Bordon on two or three occasions. But I was never fortunate enough to photograph her myself; in those days, visitors with cameras were not warmly welcomed by the authorities!

These two most intriguing little engines, Nos 34 and 35, were designed by William Dean and built at Swindon in 1890, specially for working on the Cornish branch lines from Gwinear Road to Helston and from St Erith to St Ives; I wish I had known those branches in those days! The general dimensions of the engines were distinctly diminutive, but I am convinced that a model for $3\frac{1}{2}$ in., 5 in. or $7\frac{1}{4}$ in. gauge, or even larger, would be powerful enough, and handy enough, for most purposes.

The cylinders were 16 in. dia. × 24 in. stroke; the coupled wheels were only 4 ft $1\frac{1}{2}$ in. dia.; the bogie wheels, which were of Mansell pattern were 2 ft 8 in.; the wheelbase was 6 ft 8 in. plus 8 ft 6 in. plus 5 ft; the overhang at the front was 5 ft 6 in., and at the back 1 ft 8 in.; the total length over buffers was 31 ft $0\frac{5}{8}$ in.

The boiler was 3 ft 10 in. dia. and 10 ft 3 in. long; it was pitched 6 ft $6\frac{1}{2}$ in. above rail level and contained 237 tubes of $1\frac{3}{4}$ in. dia. The heating surface was 1,142.2 sq. ft, to which the raised round-top firebox added 93 sq. ft, making the total 1,235.2 sq. ft—quite an amount for so small an engine. The grate area was 14.8 sq. ft, and the working pressure was 150 lb. p.s.i. In working order, the engine weighed 40 tons 6 cwt, 25 tons of which were equally divided between the coupled wheels for adhesion. The tractive effort was 16,756 lb.

Nobody seems able to say what became of No 35, except that she was withdrawn in 1910. One account says that she, too, went to Bordon, but I never saw her there. It is enough for me that I *did* know her sister No 34.

THE DANCERS

Great Western Railway Metro Tanks

In 1869 the Great Western Railway built the first of what afterwards became quite an army of 2-4-0 side-tank locomotives for suburban work and general branch line traffic. The building of these engines went on until 1899, by which time the type numbered 140 engines, all built at Swindon.

During the 30 years of the building programme, the earlier engines were subjected to continuous modifications and improvements in order to keep them up to date and more or less in line with the latest-built examples, since the basic design was modified from time to time as construction progressed.

After 1899 no new engines of this type were built; but the modernisation programme was continued right up to 1928, so that the engines were, as far as possible, always in line with current practice.

However, these engines could always be divided into two distinct classes, one smaller than the other. But the whole lot were officially styled Metro tanks.

The basic design was by Joseph Armstrong, and the later variants were due to William Dean. But after 1899 G. J. Churchward became responsible for slight modifications which kept this class well abreast of requirements and put the engines into the form in which I knew them.

They were great favourites with everybody concerned.

I first became familiar with them in 1905 when I rode behind one of them daily to and from school. At that time the majority of the large London contingent were without cabs, only a plain low weatherboard being provided to protect the enginemen from the elements. This was due to the fact that these engines worked the through Great Western trains from Hammersmith and Southall to Aldgate, via the underground line from Bishop's Road (Paddington). Odd as it may seem, the men disliked cabs on engines used on those services, and preferred to chance the weather when the engines were working the above-ground suburban services. But all the same, the cabless engines, were usually referred to as the " get-wets " !

After the electrification of the Hammersmith and City line, in 1905, most of the 2-4-0 tank engines were transferred to the main line for suburban work and acquired the scanty, open-back half-cab as a result. Five of them, however, remained cabless for working goods trains from Acton to Farringdon yards, through the tunnels of the Metropolitan line.

These smart little engines were not only surprisingly

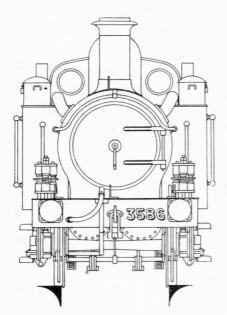

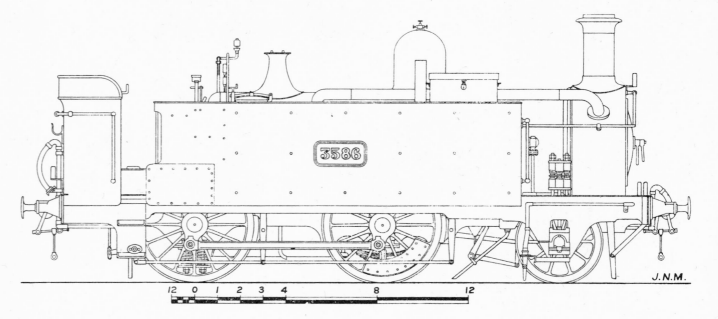

88

powerful; they had an extraordinary capacity for speed. When running really fast, they did not look safe, for they indulged in a sort of merry dance on their springs, which was quite alarming to watch. But they came to no harm.

I once enjoyed an amusing and quite exciting experience with 2-4-0 tank engine No 3586, one of the cabless five. I was travelling from Reading to Ealing Broadway one Sunday, in a train that was booked to stop at Slough and West Drayton only. No 3586 with seven non-corridor eight-wheelers and travelling on the relief line, started off from Reading not more than ten seconds before an express, headed by 4-6-0 No 4001 *Dog Star*, started on the up main.

About half a mile from the start *Dog Star* caught us up and was steadily overhauling us; our driver evidently saw what was afoot and made up his mind that he would show *Dog Star* that four-cylinder 4-6-0 express passenger engines were not the only ones that could run fast.

Fortunately, both trains had all signals clear, and for rather more than 15 miles there ensued quite an exciting race in which many passengers in both trains were soon taking a lively, and even vociferous interest. One train would draw slightly ahead, only to be caught up by the other, and several times during this really hectic sprinting, our game little 3586 managed to hold her own against her big rival.

Just after we had safely negotiated the relief line curves through Taplow station, I did some timing and found that our little tank was hurtling her train along at 68 m.p.h.!

By now *Dog Star* was drawing ahead gradually, but remorselessly, to win the race, while we had to prepare for stopping at Slough. But I am convinced that if the stop could have been omitted No 3586 would have kept well up with the other train for several more miles.

This episode, of course, was exceptional, but it shows what these little engines *could* do. When, in ordinary circumstances, they worked such trains as the 5.45 p.m. from Paddington to Aylesbury, booked to run the $24\frac{1}{2}$ miles to Maidenhead non-stop in 31 minutes, they could be relied upon to reach and sustain a steady 60 m.p.h. for several miles towards the end of the non-stop trip. But at such speeds, conditions on the footplate must have been somewhat lively for the men, as a result of the "dancing" I have mentioned! I imagine, too, that the distribution of the weight on the axles would have given some curious figures, if it could have been ascertained, while the dance was in progress.

But, no matter! Almost to the last months of their existence these Metro tanks of the GWR remained among the best and most successful suburban engines I have ever known.

Although the majority were in the London district in my early days, there were always many of them to be found at Birmingham, Gloucester, Cheltenham, Bristol, Exeter and other provincial centres, at all of which they were popular.

Another fascinating feature, which applied to both classes, was the extraordinary variation of details to be seen. For example, there were four distinct shapes of cab all in use at the same time; and if we add the rather special cab on No 3596 and the huge affair No 3593—rebuilt as a 2-4-2T—boasted, we have no fewer than six different cabs from which to take our choice, so to speak, in the pre-1914 era.

The position of the toolbox was another item which appeared to be very reluctant to become stabilised; it was always on top of the tank, but it could be seen either in front of or behind the condenser exhaust pipe, or in some cases it would be close to the cab.

What was more intriguing to the lay observer, however, was that if the toolbox was in one position on the left of the engine, it did not necessarily follow that the one on the right would be in the corresponding position on that side!

The dimensions of the larger engines of this type, as represented by No 3586 in my drawing, were: Cylinder diameter, 16 in.; stroke 24 in.; ports, $13\frac{1}{2}$ in. × $1\frac{3}{8}$ in. (steam) and $3\frac{1}{4}$ in. (exhaust). The condensing apparatus was fitted to only those engines which worked over the Metropolitan line to Aldgate.

The boiler barrel was 10 ft 6 in. long, in two rings with outside diameters of 4 ft $2\frac{1}{8}$ in. and 4 ft 3 in. There were 245 tubes of $1\frac{3}{4}$ in. dia., giving a heating surface of 1,208.81 sq. ft; the heating surface of the firebox was 97.6 sq. ft, making the total 1,306.41 sq. ft. The grate area was 16.44 sq. ft. The inside firebox was 4 ft $5\frac{1}{16}$ in. long, 3 ft $4\frac{1}{8}$ in. wide and 5 ft $7\frac{3}{4}$ in. high, and the working pressure was 150 p.s.i.

The tank capacity was 1,100 gallons and the bunker would hold 2 tons 18 cwt of coal. The wheel diameters were, leading, 3 ft 8 in., coupled 5 ft 2 in., and the official tractive effort figure was 12,635 lb. The wheelbase was 16 ft divided into 7 ft 9 in. and 8 ft 3 in.; there was an overhang of 4 ft at the front and 5 ft $9\frac{3}{4}$ in. at the back. Over buffer-heads, the length was 29 ft $3\frac{3}{4}$ in., and in working order the weight was 12 tons 6 cwt on the leading axle, 15 tons 13 cwt on the driving axle and 15 tons 14 cwt on the trailing axle, totalling 43 tons 13 cwt.

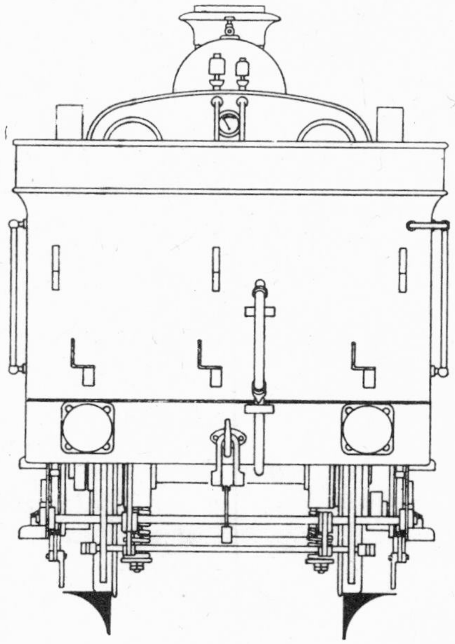

GENERAL SPECIFICATION

CYLINDERS		TUBES	
Diameter ...	16 in.	Number ...	245
Stroke ...	24 in.	Diameter ...	$1\frac{3}{4}$ in.
BOILER		HEATING SURFACE	
Length, between tubeplates ...	10 ft 6 in.	Tubes...	1,208.81 sq. ft.
Maximum diameter	4 ft 3 in.	Firebox ...	97.6 sq. ft.
		Total ...	1,306.41 sq. ft.
FIREBOX LENGTH		GRATE AREA	
Inside...	4 ft $5\frac{1}{16}$ in.	Square feet ...	16.44
Outside ...	—		

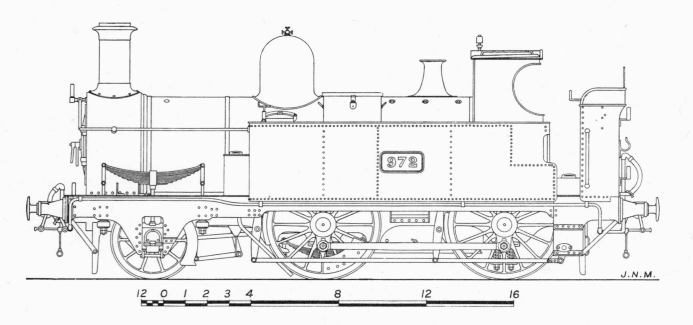

12 0 1 2 3 4   8   12   16

J.N.M.

THE
'SMALL METRO'
TANKS

Tese small, but always smart little engines were possibly the liveliest suburban tank locomotives that ever worked local passenger services in the London area; for they were not only remarkably powerful, but they could run at really astonishing speed when they had the chance.

As a result, they were popular, and even as late as 1905, their drivers preferred them to the newer and more modern engines that were intended to supersede them. They frequently worked fast outer-suburban trains, in spite of their limited capacity for coal and water. Several times I noted them on non-stop trains of six or seven bogie coaches between London and Reading, covering the 36 miles in the allotted 42 or 43 minutes without any difficulty whatever, easily attaining speeds in excess of 60 m.p.h. in order to keep time.

Their more normal duties, however, were on trains stopping at all stations, for which they seemed eminently suited. On this sort of work, their usual trains were close-coupled sets each of nine four-wheeled coaches. At every station the process of starting was characteristic; there would be some

ten or a dozen short, sharp exhaust beats and then the driver would shut the regulator while he notched up the reversing gear to the running position, after which the regulator would be reopened and the train was away with a fine show of acceleration. This performance occurred with unfailing precision, the only noticeable differences being that, in the rush hours when those nine four-wheelers were packed to overflowing, the initial exhaust beats would be rather louder and, occasionally, there would be a slip or two.

One train that I particularly remember, about 1908, must have tested the engine—usually one of these diminutive Metros—to the absolute limit. It left Paddington at 1.4 p.m. on Saturdays only, and consisted of never less than 12, and often more, of the smaller clerestory, non-corridor bogie coaches. It was really two trains in one and the first stop was Maidenhead, $24\frac{1}{4}$ miles in 32 minutes booked time.

Many times I saw this train leave Paddington; there was never any trouble or undue fuss. But, on one particular Saturday, I saw it pass through Slough at quite 60 m.p.h., in just under 23 minutes,

with 14 coaches, the engine, Metro No 976, apparently working absolutely flat out. At Maidenhead, after taking a much needed drink, she would go forward with some six or seven coaches, all stations to Aylesbury via High Wycombe, leaving the rest of the train for another engine to take on to Reading and possibly Didcot.

Not long afterwards this turn was taken over by the much larger 4-4-2 County tanks, but I doubt if they did any better with it than the little Metros had done. I was often puzzled as to how the Metros were able to generate so much liveliness and versatility; their dimensions gave no clue, for I have known many a larger engine to be in difficulties on the sort of work that the little Metros simply played with.

These small engines must not be confused with the " 3581 " class which were similar, but larger, and built in 1899. The smaller engines dated from 1871, though a batch of 20 comparable engines had been built in 1869 and were subsequently modernised to make them uniform with the Metros. Between 1871 and 1894, 78 of the latter were built and many were rebuilt, in later years, with bigger tanks and bunkers,

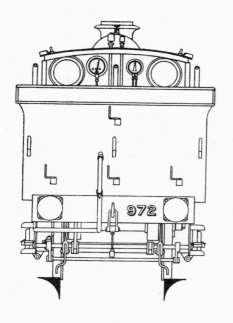

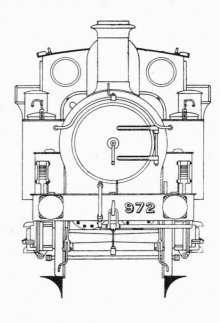

GENERAL SPECIFICATION

CYLINDERS			TUBES		
Diameter	...	... 16 in.	Number	...	... 221
Stroke	...	... 24 in.	Diameter	...	... 1⅝ in.

BOILER			HEATING SURFACE	
Length between			Tubes...	1,008.01 sq. ft.
tubeplates	...	10 ft 6 in.	Firebox	... 91.53 sq. ft.
Maximum diameter	4 ft 3 in.		Total	... 1,099.54 sq. ft.

FIREBOX LENGTH			GRATE AREA	
Inside...	...	—	Square feet	... ... 14.61
Outside	...	5 ft 1 in.		

so that they became practically identical with the larger Metros. For working purposes, both classes were lumped together and known simply as the Metros, irrespective of size. At first, most of the engines were devoid of protective cover for the enginemen; but those in provincial districts were provided with the familiar GWR open-back cab.

Subsequently, this amenity spread to many more engines of this class, and I recall that these cabs, if they could be so called, exhibited a bewildering variety of shapes and sizes, though they were all of the same general type. In the early 1920s, the foot-plate covering was improved by having a windscreen fitted above the coaling plate of the bunker and the cab roof extended backwards to meet it.

The small Metros had the following dimensions: cylinders, 16 in. dia., 24 in. stroke, set horizontally with the steam chest between them; steam port length, 13½ in.; width 1⅜ in. for admission, 3¼ in. for exhaust. The valve gear was Stephenson's with the weighshaft below and with the expansion links suspended in the middle on the line of drive. The lap was 1 1/16 in. on the admission side and ⅛ in. on

the exhaust side, and the lead in full gear was, I believe, ¼ in., while the valve travel was 4½ in. It is possible that here lies the secret of the liveliness of these engines.

Most of the class, when I knew them best, had been fitted the later type of boiler having a Belpaire firebox, as depicted in my drawing of No 972. Its length was 10 ft 6 in. and its two rings were 4 ft 2¼ in. and 4 ft 3 in. dia. respectively; the centre line was 6 ft 4 in. from rail level. The firebox shell was 5 ft 1 in. long and 4 ft wide, and the grate area was 14.61 sq. ft. There were 221 tubes of 1⅝ in. dia., the heating surface of which was 1,008.01 sq. ft, to which the firebox added 91.53 sq. ft to make the total heating surface 1,099.54 sq. ft. The working pressure was 165 p.s.i. The tank capacity was for 820 gallons of water, and the bunker carried 1 ton 12 cwt of coal. Fully loaded, the weight was 38 tons 15 cwt divided into 10 tons 19 cwt on the leading axle, 14 tons 12 cwt on the driving axle and 13 tons 4 cwt on the trailing axle. The tractive effort was 13,900 lb.

Wheel diameters were, leading 3 ft 8 in., driving

and trailing 5 ft 2 in. The wheelbase was 16 ft divided into 7 ft 9 in. and 8 ft 3 in.

In my schooldays, when I rode every day behind one of these fascinating little engines to and from Hammersmith, they were always kept clean and in first-class trim. They were extremely pretty, with their copper chimney caps, brass domes and safety valve casings highly polished, and their paintwork nicely lined out. In later years, this decorative finery was all painted over; but that did not diminish their sprightliness. The last was withdrawn in 1949.

In their last years, many of this class were adapted for auto-train working on branch lines, and examples were to be seen in practically every district on the GWR from Birkenhead in the north to Plymouth in the south. This kind of work added much to their popularity, even though the opportunities for indulging in fast running were drastically curtailed. All the same, one of these engines on a Reading-Maidenhead auto-train, one afternoon in August 1939, treated me to a lively 65 m.p.h. sprint during the run. They always seemed to have difficulty in keeping speed *down*!

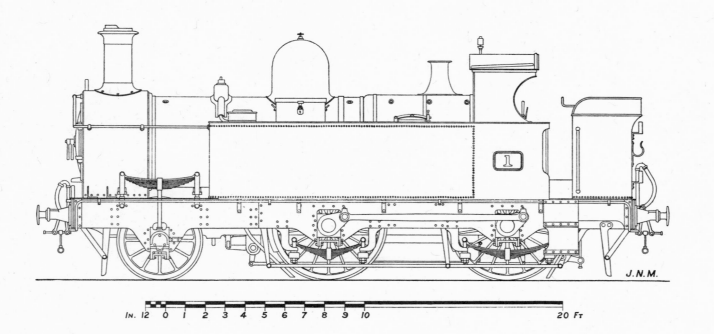

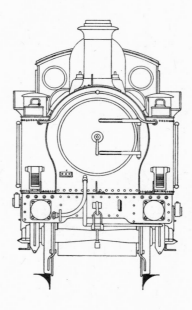

GREAT WESTERN RAILWAY No 1

IN May 1880 Swindon Works of the old Great Western Railway completed a large experimental tank engine which was given the number " 1."

This engine had the 4-4-0 wheel arrangement, double frames with outside cranks, and inside cylinders. I have always understood that, in spite of all efforts, the engine got no farther than the works yards; the reason was that the bogie, at the leading end, would persist in riding on the ballast rather than on the rails !

I am perfectly prepared to believe this story, because I am sure that no weirder contraption than that bogie was ever put under a locomotive. It was the experimental feature of No 1 and it proved to be a fiasco, so the engine was taken back into the factory to be altered. A description of the bogie, together with a drawing of No 1 in her original

condition, appeared in an article by E. W. Twining, published in *The Locomotive* for January 1940.

After alteration, No 1 was a 2-4-0 tank engine of somewhat massive proportions, but she was a success. All the same, no more engines of her class were built and she remained a solitary oddity until

she was withdrawn and scrapped in July 1924. At first, she was sent to South Devon to work around Exeter and Newton Abbot. Some years later, she was transferred to South Wales, and worked chiefly between Carmarthen and Tenby.

In 1906, she was reboilered with a new and larger boiler having a Belpaire firebox. At the same time, the cab width, which had been 7 ft 8 in. up to then, was reduced to 6 ft, and a few other minor alterations were made.

The engine was sent to Chester and there she remained for the rest of her days, employed in working fast passenger trains to and from Birkenhead or Shrewsbury and Wolverhampton.

In 1918, I made my first acquaintance with No 1 and fell in love with her at once ! She was a fine, sturdy, very well-proportioned engine with, as I soon discovered, a remarkable capacity for fast running. I got to know one of her drivers, Frank Dodd, who was full of praise for her and he certainly knew how to manage her, judging by some runs that I had with him.

The engine's only apparent fault was lack of water capacity, which prevented her being used on longer journeys. My only regret is that I had not met her 20 years before, when her dome, safety-valve casing, cab window frames and beading were polished brass; the chimney cap polished copper, and the tanks, bunker, cab sides, boiler bands and frames would have been nicely lined out. All this finery had gone when I knew the engine, but she was still most attractive, and I have always thought that a large-scale steam model of her would be about ideal on some of the smaller continuous tracks.

The main dimensions of No 1 were: cylinders, 17 in. dia. by 26 in. stroke; diameter of the leading wheels was 4 ft 1 in. and of the driving and coupled wheels 5 ft 8 in.; the wheelbase was 8 ft 6 in. plus 9 ft and the overhangs were 4 ft 4 in. in front and 6 ft 3¾ in. at the back; the total length over the buffers was 31 ft 9¾ in.

The boiler was pitched 7 ft 2 in. above rail level

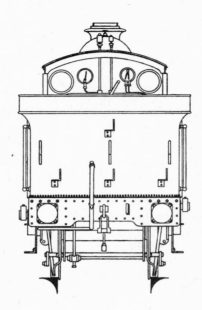

and its length was 11 ft. It was formed of two rings, arranged telescopically, their diameters being 4 ft 4 in. and 4 ft 5 in. respectively. There were 243 tubes of 1⅝ in. dia., 11 ft 3 11/16 in. long; the firebox was 5 ft 10 in. long by 4 ft wide, outside, and the grate area was 17.2 sq. ft.

The heating surface was made up of 1,168.88 sq. ft for the tubes and 113.86 sq. ft for the firebox, totalling 1,282.74 sq. ft. The working pressure was 180 p.s.i.

The tank capacity was for 850 gallons of water—a surprisingly small amount for so large an engine, but I suspect this was deliberately done in order to keep the weight down.

In working order, this fine engine weighed 46 tons 18 cwt, of which 33 tons 6 cwt were available for adhesion. The tractive effort at 80 per cent of the boiler pressure amounted to 16,900 lb.

All these particulars apply to No 1 in her final form as shown in my drawings. I was sorry when she was scrapped, but she had been just over 44 years in service and had run more than 1¼ million miles.

She had earned her keep and the cost of her alterations many times over !

GENERAL SPECIFICATION

CYLINDERS		
Diameter	... ...	17 in.
Stroke	...	26 in.
BOILER		
Length between tubeplates	...	11 ft 0 in.
Maximum diameter		4 ft 5 in.
FIREBOX LENGTH		
Inside	...	—
Outside	...	5 ft 10 in.
TUBES		
Number	... ...	243
Diameter	... ...	1⅝ in.
HEATING SURFACE		
Tubes...	1,168.88 sq. ft.	
Firebox	... 113.86 sq. ft.	
Total ...	1,282.74 sq. ft.	
GRATE AREA		
Square feet ...	...	17.2

GREAT WESTERN RAILWAY

SADDLE TANK

No 1925

THE GWR saddle tank No 1925 was one of my favourite engines. The first of the class, No 850, was completed to the designs of Mr Joseph Armstrong at Wolverhampton as far back as 1874!

I should, perhaps, make it clear that the Wolverhampton factory was then under the control of Joseph Armstrong's brother, George, who was responsible for the construction, but not all the designs, of the locomotives and boilers built there; it remained so until 1897.

The construction of the 850 class was continued until 1895, by which time no fewer than 168 of them had been built. They were 0-6-0 saddle tank engines for shunting and local goods traffic, but they were often to be seen on passenger trains around the larger towns and on country branches in almost any locality on the GWR.

At one time some 20 or 30 of them were stationed in London and were used mainly for empty coach working into and out of Paddington, work which they continued to do until superseded by later engines of more modern design.

About 1908 a start was made on rebuilding the 850 class into pannier tank engines—everything else being left practically unaltered; by 1935 about 100 of the engines had been modified in this way. All except a very few of the rest had been scrapped, and by 1940 only two were left in the original saddle tank condition.

These two engines were Nos 1925 and 2007, which were then stationed at Didcot and took turns in working the Newbury-Lambourn branch; they had been employed on this work for some years.

About the end of 1940 both these engines were among several that were " commandeered " by the War Department, and they were sent to Bordon Camp, in Hampshire. But after some months it seemed that they were not wanted, and were returned to the GWR at Reading. But here, too, it seems, there was no work for them so 1925 was sent to Slough and 2007 to Worcester. This was in the early part of 1942, and it brought No 1925 right under my nose !

I trust that I may be forgiven if from now on I use masculine pronouns when referring to this engine, for I cannot think of any locomotive for which the almost universal " she " is less appropriate !

He was at Slough for some three or four months, during which he seemed to be regarded as the

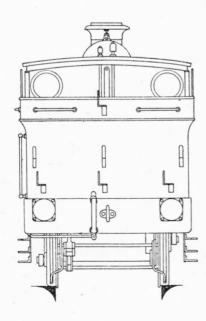

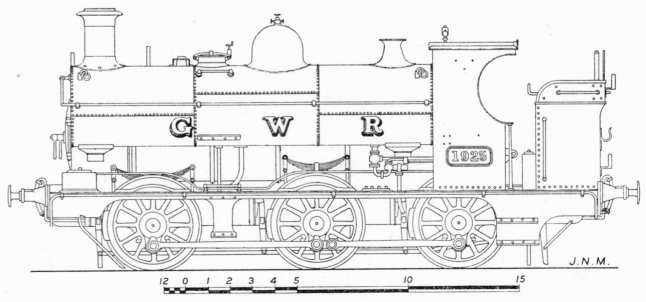

12 0 1 2 3 4 5   10   15

J.N.M.

94

Taplow shunter. For five days a week he was to be seen at Taplow on shunting duties which often entailed long spells of sitting in a siding doing nothing.

I called him " Old Podgy " because he looked like it; he was built in 1884, and by 1942 he had become somewhat decrepit and suffered rather badly from the effects of old age. However, it would appear that the Taplow duties quickly became irksome, for one day I went over there only to find him gone; I was informed that he had left Slough and had been moved to Southall, where he apparently found things more to his liking because he spent eight years there.

For a while this meant that I lost touch with " Old Podgy." But when my office was removed from Maidenhead to London in April 1946, and I began the daily journey to and from Paddington, scarcely a day passed without at least a sight of the old engine somewhere between West Drayton and West Ealing. He had become something of a local institution in that part of the London Division, and was employed on shunting and local goods work exclusively.

A rather amusing thing was that he would be one way round one day and the opposite way about the next, suggesting that, at one point of the full turn of duty, he took a triangular route somewhere.

Then, one morning towards the end of 1946, 1 saw my old friend standing, minus his leading buffer-beam, in a siding at Southall Loco Depot. But a day or two later he had gone, and I thought I had seen the last of him. About three weeks later, however, he turned up again, complete with a new front bufferbeam, and settled down to his usual duties once more; he was so occupied until about the middle of July 1947, when he disappeared again.

This time weeks went by without a sight of him, and I feared the worst. Then a wonderful thing happened. On October 20, as my morning train was passing West Ealing sidings, my old friend came into view, back on his usual job, but resplendent in new paint and with the time-honoured initials GWR prominently displayed on his saddle tank, as in my drawing. I believe that this engine was the only standard GWR saddle tank to display those initials in that style.

The normal daily routine was renewed and proceeded exactly as before, even to the about-turn performance; it continued until about the end of 1947, or beginning of 1948, when the engine was absent for some ten days.

I learnt that he had been " borrowed " in order to take part in a scene in the film " The Chiltern Hundreds," and so he became a film star. After that, he came back to work for some months before being removed to Reading for service as the Signal Department's shunter. Finally, he was withdrawn from service, in April 1951, and broken up soon afterwards, the last unrebuilt example of his class.

During the years that this engine was working from Southall, 1 had opportunities of getting at close quarters with him, for the purpose of obtaining dimensions and particulars for my drawing. The wheels were most interesting in being rather massive iron castings with H-section spokes, and they had no balance-weights; their diameter, with new tyres, was 4 ft 1½ in. The wheelbase was 13 ft 8 in., divided into 7 ft 4 in. plus 6 ft 4 in., and the overhangs were 4 ft 7 in. at the front and 6 ft 3 in. at the back.

The boiler was pitched 6 ft 1 in. from rail level; the barrel was made in two rings, the larger of which was 4 ft 3 in. dia., and the length was 10 ft 6 in. The dome was on the back ring, and the firebox casing, which was flush with the barrel, was 5 ft 1 in. long.

There were 245 tubes of 1⅝ in. dia., the heating surface of which was 1,122.61 sq. ft; to this the firebox added 95.27 sq. ft, making the total heating surface 1,217.88 sq. ft. The working pressure was 150 p.s.i.

A curious and, to my mind, distinctly risky detail was that the leading guard-irons were formed of small downward extensions of the front brake hangers; I should have thought that if the engine had collided with any low obstruction, the result would have been badly damaged, if not entirely demolished, brake rigging !

Yet all these engines had that extraordinary arrangement, and I have never heard of any trouble resulting from it. This particular form of guard-iron certainly had the merit of simplicity, and to some extent, perhaps, it was an obvious design; but I have grave doubts as to its efficiency.

After his departure from Southall to Reading, I missed my old friend rather badly; moreover, I guessed that he was really making his way to Swindon, never to return.

Looking back on it now, it is remarkable how this one engine, out of a class of 168, should have remained virtually in his original state for so long, while the others of the class had either been broken up years before, or rebuilt as pannier tanks.

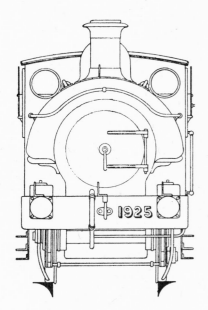

GENERAL SPECIFICATION

CYLINDERS				TUBES			
Diameter	...	...	—	Number	...	...	245
Stroke	...	...	—	Diameter	...	...	1⅝ in.
BOILER							
Length between				HEATING SURFACE			
tubeplates	...	10 ft 6 in.		Tubes...		1,122.61 sq. ft.	
Maximum diameter	4 ft 3 in.			Firebox	...	95.27 sq. ft.	
				Total ...		1,217.88 sq. ft.	
FIREBOX LENGTH							
Inside		—		GRATE AREA			
Outside	...	5 ft 1 in.		Square feet	...	...	—

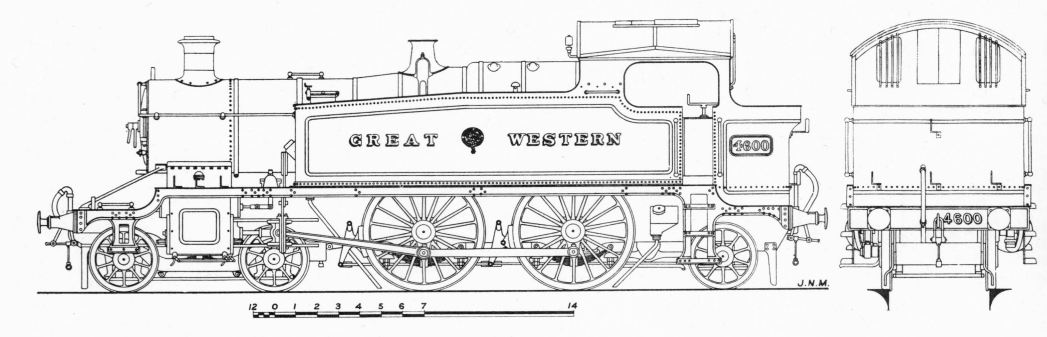

GWR LIGHT SUBURBAN ENGINE No 4600

THIS was an attractive little tank engine with an interesting history. She was a one-off job, solitary and, in a way, unfortunate; not that she was quite a failure, but she was redundant as soon as she went into service, and in the following circumstances:

In 1904, G. J. Churchward introduced the 4400 class of small 2-6-2 tank engines with 4 ft 1 in. coupled wheels for working local traffic on light branch lines over the formidable gradients in Devon and Cornwall. These engines were followed in 1906 by the 4500 class which were very similar to the 44s but had 4 ft 7½ in. coupled wheels. Both classes were extremely successful on the sort of work they were designed to do, and Churchward seemed content to let matters rest at that for some years, so far as local and branch traffic was concerned. He built a considerable number of the 45s and distributed them fairly widely over the GWR system.

In 1913, however, the success of the 45s made him obsessed with the idea that a light 4-4-2 tank with 5 ft 8 in. coupled wheels should have some scope in districts where there were no very severe gradients, and where the larger wheels would enable it to run at higher speeds than were possible with the 45s.

For once, Churchward's judgment misfired; he built No 4600 out of standard parts and with most of her details, except the coupled wheels, similar to those of the 45s. She was completed in December 1913 and sent to work in South Wales, where she remained only a very short time. She was then transferred to Tyseley and spent the rest of her existence working local trains around Leamington, Stratford-on-Avon and Birmingham.

I frequently saw her during 1920-1, when I was a resident in Birmingham; for I often went over to Leamington and usually did not have to wait very long before No 4600 put in an appearance. Generally, she was popular and quite a pet of many of her regular patrons; but experience of her work showed that she had nothing on a 45 in power or speed. No more of her kind were built; they could not have competed on equal terms with the 45s, and the " Light Suburban 4-4-2 tank engine " idea was quietly forgotten at Swindon !

My own experiences with 4600 were not numerous, but they showed that she was powerful and speedy enough with her normal train of four or five bogie coaches.

Her principal dimensions were: cylinders, 17 in. dia., 24 in. stroke and fitted with 10 in. piston valves actuated by the normal Churchward-Stephenson link motion giving a valve travel of 6¼ in. in full gear.

Wheel diameters were: bogie and trailing, 3 ft 2 in.; coupled, 5 ft 8 in. The wheelbase was 28 ft divided into four 7 ft lengths. The trailing axle was mounted in radial axleboxes. Overhang at the leading end was 2 ft 2¾ in., and at the back 3 ft 1 in.; the total length over buffers was 36 ft 11¾ in.

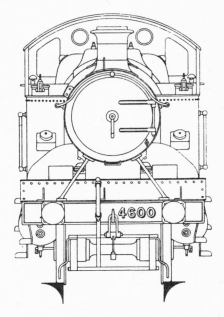

GENERAL SPECIFICATION

CYLINDERS			TUBES		
Diameter	...	... 17 in.	Number	... ...	255
Stroke	...	... 24 in.	Diameter	... ...	1⅝ in.
BOILER					
Length between			HEATING SURFACE		
tubeplates	...	10 ft 6 in.	Tubes...	1,178.01 sq. ft.	
Maximum			Firebox	... 93.85 sq. ft.	
diameter	...	4 ft 9½ in.	Total ...	1,271.86 sq. ft.	
FIREBOX LENGTH					
Inside	...	5 ft 0³⁄₁₆ in.	GRATE AREA		
Outside	...	5 ft 10 in.	Square feet ...	... 16.6	

A Churchward dream that came to nothing

The original boiler was a No 5 standard, but without a superheater; the barrel was 10 ft 6 in. long, made in two rings of which the forward one was 4 ft 2 in. dia. outside, while the rear one tapered from 4 ft 3 in. to 4 ft 9½ in. The distance between the tubeplates was 10 ft 10⁵⁄₁₆ in., and the centre-line was pitched 8 ft 0¾ in. above rail level. There were 255 tubes of 1⅝ in. dia., their heating surface amounting to 1,178.01 sq. ft.

The firebox outer shell was 5 ft 10 in. long with a width of 5 ft at the boiler centre-line; the inner box was 5 ft 0³⁄₁₆ in. long and 4 ft wide at the centre-line, and its heating surface was 93.85 sq. ft, making the total 1,271.86 sq. ft. The grate area was 16.6 sq. ft and the working pressure was 200 p.s.i. The capacity of the tanks was 1,100 gallons, and of the coal bunker 3 tons.

In working order, this engine weighed 60 tons 12 cwt divided into 18 tons 12 cwt on the bogie, 16 tons on the driving axle, 14 tons 15 cwt on the intermediate axle and 11 tons 5 cwt. on the trailing axle. The official figure for the tractive effort was 18,360 lb.

The position of the leading sandboxes was note-

worthy and, so far as I can recall, unique. They were built into the front end of the side tanks, the fillers being located about halfway up, where they projected at an angle of about 45 deg. The one on the left-hand side of the engine can be readily seen in the drawing.

As was only to be expected, this engine's life was not a very long one. When, after nearly 12 years of steady, regular, but not very distinguished service, really heavy repairs became necessary, she was withdrawn and broken up in August 1925.

The chief fault was that only about half the total weight, 30 tons 15 cwt. out of 60 tons 12 cwt, was available for adhesion; it compared unfavourably with the 37 tons 15 cwt out of 61 tons for a 45, and was not enough, especially when the water supply became depleted—as it did rather quickly—and lightened the weight.

On ordinary suburban trains, especially during the peak hours in the morning and evening, 4600 could be something of a nuisance in having to spend time so frequently in topping-up the tanks in order to keep the adhesion weight somewhere near its maximum. Otherwise, she would lose still more time in slipping when starting from the many stations.

With regard to the ratio of adhesion weight to total weight, the 45s and even the 2-4-0 Metro tanks were much superior, and it was reflected in their marked ability to start away from a standstill without slipping. But all the same, both these classes were rapidly superseded, in the Birmingham area, by the larger and heavier 2-6-2 tank engines of the 4100 and 5100 classes, and in the London area by the 61s.

These later and larger engines monopolised the suburban traffic in both districts after 1930, and the wisdom of dropping the "Light Suburban" 4-4-2 design after experiences with 4600 is abundantly clear.

However, 4600 had not cost much to build and she was certainly not an expensive engine to operate. She must have earned her keep and probably a good deal more besides. But it does seem rather curious that, with some six years of experience of the excellent work obtained from the small 2-6-2 tank engines to guide him, Churchward should have contemplated, let alone built, a small 4-4-2 tank engine that clearly had no chance of achieving a similar success, even if confined to a road as flat as a billiard-table.

My own last sight of 4600 was from a Paddington-Birmingham express, in the summer of 1923. As we passed through Hatton station, I saw her, as I had often seen her before, standing there on a train bound for Stratford-on-Avon. I little thought then that I should never see her again; but so it transpired.

Practically unknown outside her normal terrain, she served a most historic district, regularly, for about seven years. And I like to think that this unquestionably attractive little engine contributed a modest quota to that local history; for I have found that she is still affectionately remembered there more than 35 years after she was scrapped.

```
          GENERAL  SPECIFICATION

CYLINDERS                        TUBES
    Diameter  ...    ... 17¼ in.     Number   ...    ...    186
    Stroke    ...    ... 24 in.      Diameter ...    ...  1⅞ in.

BOILER
    Length, between              HEATING SURFACE
      tubeplates  10 ft 3½ in.       Tubes   ...    981 sq. ft
    Maximum dia-                     Firebox ...    87.3 sq. ft
      meter   ... 3 ft 11 3/16 in.   Total   ...  1,068.3 sq. ft

FIREBOX LENGTH
    Inside    ...    4 ft 6 in.   GRATE AREA
    Outside   ...    ...    5 ft      Square feet   ...     15
```

ALTHOUGH I had known the historic *Cornwall* for many years from published descriptions and photographs, it was not until 1925, at the Railway Centenary festivities on the Stockton and Darlington Railway, that I saw her.

When I began this book I had no intention of including any museum pieces; but, for several reasons, the *Cornwall* must be regarded as an exception. For one thing, the engine was still on the active list when I first knew anything about her; another reason is that I have received more than one request to give her a place in these records, and lastly, her unique interest is justification enough for me to deal with her.

In November 1959, she passed her 112th birthday! There is much more of the original engine left in *Cornwall* than there is in many other locomotives claimed to be old. But I must briefly review her history which is her chief claim to fame.

About 1845 there began a considerable controversy about the much vaunted superiority of the Great Western broad-gauge engines, compared with anything then existing on the standard gauge. There can be little doubt that the GWR locomotives of that period were speedier and more powerful than any others; but the ensuing " battle of the gauges " ended in victory for the standard gauge, on the grounds that it was less costly and required less space.

Meanwhile, designers for the standard gauge, being disinclined to accept it as a fact that their engines

could not be as powerful and speedy as the GWR engines, produced several replies to the implied challenge. *Cornwall* was one of these and is now our only direct link with that historic episode. She was designed by Francis Trevithick, in collaboration with Thomas Crampton, and was completed at Crewe Works in November 1847.

To obtain the necessary speed, large driving-wheels, 8 ft 6 in. dia., were provided, and to keep the centre of gravity as low as possible, the original boiler was slung below the driving axle. There is some doubt as to whether the engine, in this condition, ran on six wheels or eight; drawings exist showing both arrangements, but the illustration of her in the catalogue of the Crystal Palace Exhibition, 1851, shows her as an eight-wheeler.

In this form the engine was more or less successful, so far as the attainment of high speed was concerned.

During a special run a maximum speed of 117 m.p.h. was said to have been reached, but this was never accepted as correct and, years later, was to be disproved. The extraordinary boiler, however, gave a great deal of trouble and in 1858, was replaced by one of orthodox type mounted above the driving axle.

Thereafter the engine remained in normal service and for more than 40 years, was chiefly employed on express passenger trains between Liverpool and Manchester, and occasionally between Crewe and London. She retired from ordinary main line work in 1905, and for a few years was used for working the chief engineer's inspection saloon. My drawing shows her as she was then, with the 3 ft 9 in. chimney. Her present one is 6 in. shorter. Finally she was transferred to the locomotive department and became the chief mechanical engineer's special locomotive for running his private coach when he visited the various locomotive depots on the LNWR, and she was thus employed for nearly 20 years.

Cornwall's last trip to London, under her own steam, was a notable event, in more ways than one. It was on Tuesday, July 20, 1920, that the CME, Mr C. J. Bowen-Cooke, travelled from Crewe to St Just, near Falmouth, hoping to recuperate from a serious illness. His private coach was hauled from Crewe to Euston by *Cornwall*, and news of the famous old engine's arrival in London that morning spread quickly. Later in the day, the London *Evening News* published a brief account of her, under the heading " Grandpa Puff-Puff."

Of course, *Cornwall* had to return to Crewe and some brilliant genius arranged that she should be sent back as pilot to the 1.15 p.m. Scotch Express, then being regularly hauled by the four-cylinder, 4-6-0 Claughton class engine No 1914, *Patriot*. What a combination ! Two engines, the difference in whose ages was 68 years, at the head of one of the most important trains of the day; no wonder there was an unusual crowd at Euston to see them depart. A photograph of them starting is reproduced in O. S. Nock's book, *The Premier Line*.

Now I must relate the story of the turntable. I do not think it has been published before. *Cornwall* had to be turned and as time was short, she could not be sent to the Camden depot; so the operation was carried out at Euston, where the turntable, then due for repairs, was in an extremely rocky condition. As the engine ran slowly on to the table, it tilted to form a step about 3 in. deep between the rails on the ground and those on the table. But nothing untoward happened, and after some careful balancing manoeuvres, it was successfully turned.

To get the engine off the table was a different matter. The driver, in view of the engine's age and the condition of the turntable, gave her just enough steam to move her. The table, of course, tilted once

more but the engine's leading wheels surmounted the step all right. The shock, however, destroyed all the way that she had. She came to a stop with her leading wheels on *terra firma* track, her trailing wheels at a lower level on the table track and her driving wheels just short of the step, and practically suspended in mid-air. Giving her more steam was useless as she could not muster enough adhesion to move one way or the other. She had to be rescued by another engine taking her in tow. I think this episode must be unique.

In steam, *Cornwall* ran in the grand procession of locomotives of all ages, over the Stockton and Darlington Railway, during the Railway Centenary celebrations in July 1925. She was exhibited during the Liverpool and Manchester Railway centenary in September 1930, and she was brought to Euston as an exhibit in the London and Birmingham Railway centenary exhibition held there in September, 1938. On this occasion, I had an opportunity to examine her thoroughly and check her dimensions, since no drawings of her, in her present form existed.

The dimensions are: cylinders, $17\frac{1}{4}$ in. dia., 24 in. stroke, with vertical steamchests, the valves being operated through rocking shafts by Stephenson link-motion having launch-type links.

The wheel diameters are, leading and trailing 3 ft 6 in.; driving 8 ft 6 in.—now the largest loco-

motive wheels in the world. The wheelbase is 14 ft $10\frac{1}{4}$ in. divided into 7 ft 6 in. and 7 ft $4\frac{1}{4}$ in., and the overhangs are, leading 4 ft 4 in. and trailing 2 ft $10\frac{1}{4}$ in.

The boiler is pitched 6 ft $9\frac{7}{8}$ in. above rail level and is made in two rings, the outside diameter of the larger being 3 ft $11\frac{3}{16}$ in. There are 186 tubes of $1\frac{7}{8}$ in. dia., the heating surface of which is 981 sq. ft; the firebox heating surface is 87.3 sq. ft, and the grate area is 15 sq. ft. This boiler dates from 1897 and is now in such poor fettle that it cannot be steamed. The working pressure was 140 p.s.i.

The engine weighs 29 tons 18 cwt in working trim, the leading axle carrying 10 tons 11 cwt, the driving axle 12 tons 11 cwt and the trailing axle 6 tons 16 cwt. The tractive effort is 8,700 lb.

The tender carries 1,800 gallons of water, $4\frac{1}{2}$ tons of coal and fully loaded, weighs 25 tons. Its wheels are 3 ft 9 in. dia., and the wheelbase is 6 ft 6 in. plus 6 ft, with overhangs of 3 ft 3 in. in front and 2 ft 3 in. at the back.

I have not the least doubt that the driving wheels, the wonderful " paddle-box " splashers, considerable portions of the frames, and the circular connecting rods, 6 ft 3 in. long, with their broad, forked little-ends, are the originals. The nameplate still carries the date November 1847—" Grandpa Puff-Puff," indeed !

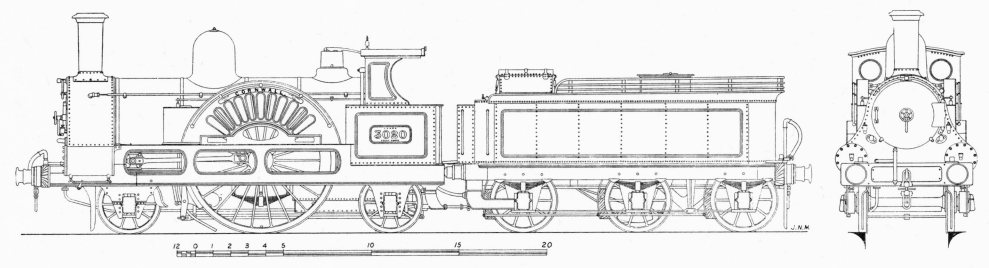

I CAN just remember some of the very celebrated little 2-2-2 engines of the LNWR, right at the end of their long career; at that time, most of the survivors were working placid branch-line turns, such as Bletchley-Oxford and Bletchley-Cambridge, or local passenger traffic around Crewe, Birmingham and Rugby. But a few, including No 1, *Saracen*, were still being used as pilots on main line expresses, work to which most of them were put after having been rebuilt by F. W. Webb in 1896. My drawing shows *Saracen* in the rebuilt condition.

There were people who claimed that these rather odd-looking engines were the prettiest locomotives ever built. I would not go so far as that; I found them too amusing to watch. They were capable of running at very high speed, and when they were seen in those conditions the impression they gave of an excited chicken streaking across a farmyard was irresistible. The smokebox and long chimney set well ahead of the leading axle, the outside cylinders, the long connecting-rod whirling round and round with the great single driving-wheel, all contributed to the chickenesque effect !

For all that, they were fascinating little engines with a charm that was all their own; but I would hesitate a long time before I called them pretty. Originally, there were 60 of them, designed by John Ramsbottom and all built at Crewe between November 1859, and July 1865. In those days, they had very small boilers and no cabs, which may be said to have made them more like pullets than chickens; for, even by the standards of that time, they were not large. But throughout their long existence, they retained their remarkable capacity for speed, with light trains.

The first one to be built was No 184, which, for some obscure reason now lost in the mists of antiquity, was named *Problem*, and generally gave her name to the class. Later it became customary to refer to the class as the " Lady of the Lakes " (or should it be " Ladies of the Lakes ? "), or as simply the "Ramsbottom Singles"; none of these appellations was really satisfactory. After Webb's modernisation in 1896, little more than the purely basic design of Ramsbottom's remained; almost everything else was unadulterated Webb.

But Webb had been associated with the engines right from the beginning. As a young and progressive chief draughtsman, not very long out of his pupilage, he had prepared the original drawings in 1858. About 20 years later, when he had succeeded Ramsbottom as locomotive superintendent of the LNWR, he modified the external details of the engines, from time to time, to keep them up-to-date as far as possible. In 1895, 37 years after *Problem* had been built, he had not the heart to scrap them, as he might well have been justified in doing because of their age; instead, he completely overhauled the original design, and then rebuilt the entire class to conform with the modifications which he had made. In this way, he produced a class of 60 delightful singlewheelers which managed to add upwards of 20 years to their already venerable age.

When the last survivor eventually went to the scrap-heap, in 1907, the average age amounted to about 55 years; so the engines had earned not only more than their keep, but a very considerable revenue as well. Until their last years they worked hard, and were always kept in first-class order, mechanically and externally.

THE LADIES OF THE LAKE

[*Drawing unfinished*]

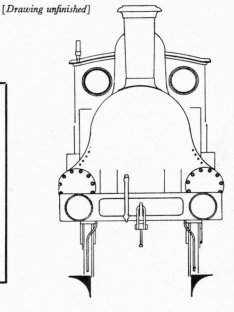

2-2-2

GENERAL SPECIFICATION			
CYLINDERS		**TUBES**	
Diameter ... ... 16 in.		Number 193	
Stroke ... ... 24 in.		Diameter ... ... 1⅞ in.	
BOILER			
Length, between		**HEATING SURFACE**	
tubeplates 9 ft 9⅞ in.		Tubes ... 980 sq. ft.	
Maximum dia-		Firebox ... 94.6 sq. ft.	
meter ... 4 ft 2 in.		Total ... 1,074.6 sq. ft.	
FIREBOX LENGTH			
Inside ... 4 ft 10⅜ in.		**GRATE AREA**	
Outside ... 5 ft 5 in.		Square feet ... 17.1	

After the 1896 rebuilding their cylinders were 16 in. dia. and 24 in. stroke, with ports 1½ in. and 3¼ in. wide and 13½ in. long. The valves, which were operated by Stephenson link motion, had 1 in. lap and 5/32 in. lead; in full gear the valve travel was 3¾ in., not a very large amount, perhaps, but enough in proportion to the size of the cylinders, apparently.

Leading and trailing wheels were 3 ft 9 in. dia. and the driving wheels 7 ft 9 in. The wheelbase was 15 ft 5 in. divided into 7 ft 7 in. plus 7 ft 10 in., while the leading overhang was 4 ft and the trailing 2 ft 6 in., the main frames of 1 in. steel having a length of 21 ft 11 in.

The boiler was of entirely new and special design; its length was 9 ft 9⅞ in., in three rings 4 ft, 4 ft 1 in. and 4 ft 2 in. diameter. The diameter outside the clothing plates was 4 ft 6¼ in. There were 193 tubes of 1⅞ in. dia., 10 ft 1 in. long between tubeplates, giving a heating surface of 980 sq. ft. The firebox casing was 5 ft 5 in. long and 4 ft 0½ in. wide and the inner box 4 ft 10⅜ in. long and 3 ft 6 in. wide; the heating surface was 94.6 sq. ft, making the total 1,074.6 sq. ft. Grate area was 17.1 sq. ft, and working pressure 150 p.s.i.

In working order, the engine weighed only 31 tons 7 cwt, the leading axle carrying 10 tons, the driving axle 14 tons 5 cwt, and the trailing axle 7 tons 2 cwt. This light weight makes the ability of the engines to hold the road at high speed all the more astonishing, especially as they were by no means steady riders. I recall engines of the class, usually piloting 2-4-0 Jumbos, on up expresses passing Harlesden at about 70 m.p.h., the singlewheeler rolling in what seemed to be a highly dangerous fashion. Yet they never came to any harm.

At slower speeds, the 2-2-2s had a readily apparent boxing motion, and this must have made things rather lively in the cab up to about 45 m.p.h.; at higher speeds, the unpleasant effect would probably diminish, but it would reach its maximum when the timing of the revolutions of the driving wheels coincided with the natural period of horizontal oscillation of the engine.

After the 1896 rebuilding the tenders were of the standard 1,800-gallon type, weighing 25 tons each all found, so that the total weight of engine and tender, in full working order, was only 56 tons 7 cwt. remarkably light for an express passenger engine and tender in 1906.

The last survivor was No 1434, *Eunomia*, a Bletchley engine used principally for working local trains to either Cambridge or Oxford; she occasionally came to London on stopping trains. She was withdrawn from service in 1907. Others that I remember were: No 1, *Saracen*; No 33, *Erebus*; No 44, *Harlequin*; No 77, *Mersey*; No 184, *Problem*; No 279, *Stephenson*; No 610, *Princess Royal*; No 622, *Prince Alfred*; No 806, *Waverley* and No 1429, *Alfred Paget*. Nos 184 and 610 seem to have been used as main line pilots until they were withdrawn; all the others I have mentioned were mostly on local work, or on slow main line passenger trains. Rather strangely, and unlike other old and historic LNWR locomotive classes, none of them was ever transferred to the engineering departments for working inspection trains and the like. Perhaps, in the end, they had worn themselves out too much to be of any use on such duties; for I do not think that any other locomotives ever worked harder for such a long period.

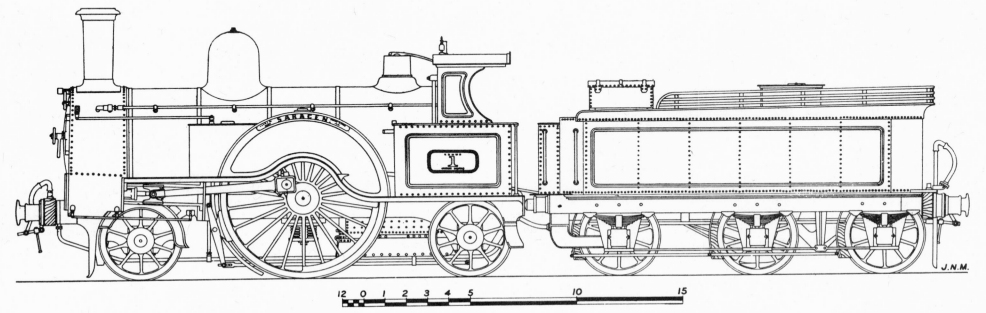

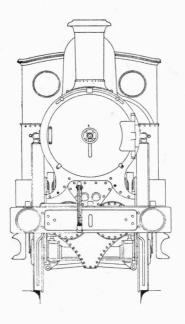

GENERAL SPECIFICATION

CYLINDERS			TUBES		
Diameter	...	... 17 in.	Number	...	... 198
Stroke	...	... 24 in.	Diameter	...	... 1⅝ in.
BOILER					
Length, between			**HEATING SURFACE**		
tubeplates		9 ft 10 in.	Tubes	...	980 sq. ft
Maximum dia-			Firebox	...	103 sq. ft
meter	...	4 ft 3 in.	Total	...	1,083 sq. ft
FIREBOX LENGTH					
Inside	...	4 ft 10⅝ in.	**GRATE AREA**		
Outside	...	5 ft 5 in.	Square feet	...	17.1

THE 'JUMBOS'

WE now come to one of the most famous classes of locomotives in the history of railways—the London and North Western Railway's 2-4-0 express passenger engines of the "Precedent" class. Because of their extraordinary capacity for hard work these engines were known far and wide as "Jumbos"; but there was nothing even remotely to suggest elephants about their appearance! Rather the reverse, in fact, because they were light, slender-looking, lively little racers which might be more properly likened to greyhounds.

The general design dates from the years 1866 to 1871, when John Ramsbottom built 76 engines of this type, but with 6 ft 6 in. driving wheels, 17 in. by 24 in. cylinders and a rather small boiler pressed to 120 p.s.i. In 1872 F. W. Webb built another 20, but slightly modified them by making the driving wheels 6 ft 7½ in. dia. and adding his well-known type of cab. The Webb chimney also made its first appearance on these engines, and the boiler pressure was raised to 140 lb. From then until 1882 Webb built a further 70 of these modified engines and generally modernised the earlier ones, so that the class now totalled 166.

Finally, between 1891 and 1895, Webb completely renewed the whole class by the simple process of scrapping the earlier engines and building new ones incorporating certain usable parts, including the original nameplates and numberplates. The diameter of the driving wheels was now 6 ft 9 in. and the new steel boilers carried 150 lb. pressure. It is in this form that my drawing shows No 790 *Hardwicke*, the most famous of a famous class; I knew her well.

My reason for stressing the fame of these engines is that so many of them made railway history, especially during the "races" from London to Scotland in 1888 and 1895. It was *Hardwicke* which, during the night of 22-23 August 1895, put up a performance the like of which had never been done before and remained unequalled for several years afterwards; for on this occasion she became the first steam locomotive to run more than 140 miles at an average speed of close on 70 m.p.h., start to stop.

And this was not on a flat road, either; the run was made from Crewe to Carlisle, 141½ miles, in 126 minutes and involved lifting the train, albeit a light one of 70½ tons, up the Grayrigg and Shap inclines to a height of 915 ft at the summit and then hurtling like a hawk down the remaining 31½ mile descent into Carlisle. I have always marvelled that *Hardwicke* was able to hold the road at the terrific speed she must have made, which an unconfirmed report puts at 96 m.p.h.!

But the official point-to-point speeds show clearly that some very high maximum speeds must have been reached; for the sake of interest, here they are: Crewe to Preston, 66.7 m.p.h.; Preston to Carnforth, 66.9 m.p.h.; Carnforth to Oxenholme, 67 m.p.h.; Oxenholme to Tebay, 61.1 m.p.h.; Tebay to Shap Summit, 55 m.p.h., and Summit to Carlisle, 74.2 m.p.h. The overall average was, thus, 67.2 m.p.h. Some racing! And this in 1895.

Another outstanding achievement by one of these engines goes to the credit of No 955, *Charles Dickens*, which monopolised the 8.30 a.m. express from Manchester to London and returned on the 4.30 p.m.

from Euston daily from February 1882 until March 1902; in 20 years 73 days this engine covered 2,000,000 miles on this turn alone, and thereby set up a record that has never been beaten. After 1902, however, *Charles Dickens* was relegated to lighter duties but managed to add approximately 500,000 miles to her record mileage before being scrapped—by mistake, so it is said—in 1912.

I could write a lot more about exploits by individual engines of this remarkable class of stalwart little racers, but space forbids. Suffice it to say that when the time came for *Hardwicke* to be withdrawn from service, in 1931, she was not scrapped but was transferred to the collection of railway relics and now rests in the Works at Crewe, painted in the original LNWR style. She looks small and fragile beside modern locomotive monsters, but she, like the rest of her clan, must be remembered as one of the liveliest locomotives I have ever known. What was the secret of this liveliness? I think the general simplicity, the triangular steam-chest, the Allan straight-link valve gear and the limited cut-off all had much to do with it.

The principal dimensions of these engines, after 1895, were: cylinders, 17 in. dia. by 24 in. stroke;

the port length was 14 in. and the widths were $1\frac{1}{2}$ in. for admission, $3\frac{1}{4}$ in. for exhaust.

With new tyres the wheel diameters were: leading, 3 ft 9 in.; driving and coupled, 6 ft 9 in. The wheelbase was 15 ft 8 in. divided into 7 ft 5 in. plus 8 ft 3 in., while the overhang was 4 ft at the front and 4 ft 1 in. at the back.

The boiler was made in three rings of $\frac{1}{2}$ in. steel plate, the maximum diameter being 4 ft 3 in., length 9 ft 10 in., and the pitch of the centre-line above rail level 7 ft $5\frac{1}{2}$ in.

One hundred and ninety-eight flue tubes of $1\frac{7}{8}$ in. diameter gave 980 sq. ft of heating surface; the firebox added 103 sq. ft, making the total 1,083 sq. ft. The grate area was 17.1 sq. ft, and the working pressure 150 p.s.i.

In working order, the weight was 32 tons 15 cwt, distributed into 10 tons 5 cwt on the leading axle, 11 tons 10 cwt on the driving axle, and 11 tons on the trailing axle.

The tender was of the standard 1,800-gallon type weighing, when full, 25 tons. It will be noted, therefore, that the total weight of engine and tender, all found, was only 57 tons 15 cwt. This makes the safe,

steady running of these wonderful little engines—especially at 92 m.p.h., which appears to be the maximum speed officially recorded with them—all the more remarkable. Many times I have seen them pass through Harrow station, in the Up direction, at well over 80 m.p.h.; the effect was ever to marvel at the manner in which they held the road at such a speed. They swayed visibly; but there was never any appearance of violent oscillation, their riding always seeming to be perfectly easy and comfortable.

A very curious fact came to light when engine No 2191, *Snowdon*, was broken up in the early 1930s; it was discovered that this engine still had $\frac{7}{8}$ in. frames dating from 1874, whereas all the others, when "renewed" in 1891-5, received new $1\frac{1}{8}$ in. frames! This is but one of those rare mysteries that occur, for which nobody can give an explanation.

Finally, I would add that there was a class of 90 similar engines, known as the "Whitworth" class, or "Small Jumbos," which were exactly the same as the "Precedents" except that the diameter of the coupled wheels was 6 ft 3 in. and everything above footplate level was 3 in. lower.

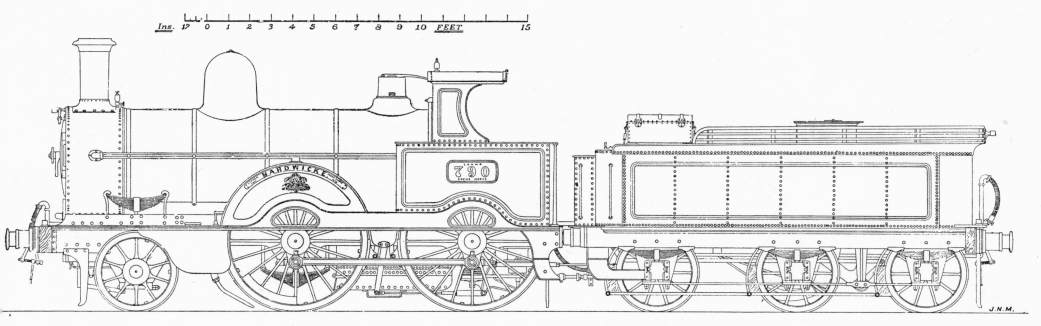

F. W. WEBB'S JUBILEE
4-cylinder 4-4-o compounds

IT was not until my later schooldays—1906 to 1910—that I got to know the London and North Western Railway really well.

By that time, F. W. Webb's notorious three-cylinder compounds had been dispensed with, and his successor, George Whale, had begun the process of converting the four-cylinder 4-4-o compounds into the two-cylinder 4-4-o simple engines of the Renown class. This process, however, did not take place at the furious speed with which Whale scrapped the three-cylinder compounds; and so, even as late as 1920, several of the four-cylinder compound express passenger and many of the goods engines were still running in their original condition; I got to know them fairly well.

There were two classes of passenger engines, both very much alike; they originated in 1897 with the Jubilee class, followed in 1901 by the similar, but slightly larger Alfred the Great class.

From the point of view of appearance, I preferred the Jubilees; the later and larger Alfreds were not so attractive to my artistic eye! The performances of both classes were never really outstanding, though No 1939 *Temeraire*, the subject of my drawing, gave me one of the biggest and most thrilling surprises that I have ever experienced on the railway.

It happened one very cold, snowy day in December 1912 on my return to London from a visit to Bletchley. (If I remember rightly, the train was due to leave Bletchley about 6.30 p.m. and run non-stop to Euston.) Probably owing to worse weather farther north, the train was 25 minutes late at Bletchley; but I was rather astonished and pleased to note that the engine was a Jubilee four-cylinder compound—1939 *Temeraire* —in her original condition. The train was a light one of five corridor coaches.

The start from Bletchley was not very energetic, the maximum speed being no more than 40 m.p.h. anywhere on the 16-mile gentle rise to Tring. Once over the top at the latter place, however, a great change occurred, as if *Temeraire* had suddenly woke up to the fact that we were almost half an hour late.

In the dark, we got up to what seemed to be a terrific pace, and I was so surprised that I timed the train from the rail joints, to obtain, for the second time in my life, a reading of 80 m.p.h. Thinking that I had made a mistake, I tried again, but got the same

result; so I came to the conclusion that engines were changed at Bletchley !

But when we arrived at Euston, I discovered that *Temeraire* was still at the head of the train, and *alone*; moreover, the arrival was only 19 minutes late, so she had wiped out some six or seven minutes of the arrears—a most exceptional feat for an engine of that class.

To this day, I wonder how on earth it was done; and there are some among my locomotive acquaintances who refuse to believe it, even now. However, Webb compound performance was always unpredictable, and I can only add that out of a number of runs I had behind Webb four-cylinder compounds, *Temeraire's* effort was the only one on which a speed exceeding 60 m.p.h. was timed.

A study of the working drawings can produce evidence to explain why the usual performance of the engines was sluggish; there is nothing to show why,

very occasionally, some quite brilliant running would be made.

The first engine of this class was turned out as a four-cylinder simple with cylinders 15 in. dia. and 26 in. stroke. The boiler proved to be incapable of supplying enough steam for four cylinders, so after a few weeks of rather abortive tests, the engine was converted into a compound like the others of the class.

The principal dimensions of these engines were: cylinders, h.p. (outside) 15 in. dia.; l.p. (inside) 19½ in. dia. The stroke of all four was 24 in., and they were all in line under the smoke box. The h.p.

GENERAL SPECIFICATION

CYLINDERS			TUBES		
Diameter ...	h.p.	15 in.	Number ...	...	225
	l.p.	19½ in.	Diameter ...	...	1⅞ in.
Stroke ...	...	24 in.			
BOILER					
Length, between			**HEATING SURFACE**		
tubeplates	10 ft	11⅞ in.	Tubes ...	1,241.3 sq. ft	
Maximum dia-			Firebox ...	159.1 sq. ft	
meter ...	4 ft	4 in.	Total ...	1,400.4 sq. ft	
FIREBOX LENGTH					
Inside ...	6 ft	3 in.	**GRATE AREA**		
Outside ...	6 ft	10 in.	Square feet	...	20.5

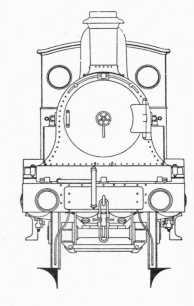

cylinders had piston valves, 6 in. dia., whereas the l.p. were provided with flat valves; they were operated by Joy's valve gear, of which there were two sets.

The inside and outside cranks on each side of the engine were set at 180 deg., the off-side pair being 90 deg. in advance of the near-side pair. The valve gears were directly connected to the l.p. valves, while rocking shafts—one on each side of the engine and situated in front of the cylinder block—transmitted motion to the h.p. valves.

This arrangement meant that notching up the valve gear automatically shortened the stroke of all four valves, which, in a four-cylinder compound engine, is a distinct disadvantage, and undoubtedly accounted for the general sluggishness of running for which these engines were notorious.

The bogie wheels were 3 ft 9 in. dia., and the coupled wheels 7 ft 1 in. A total wheel base of 23 ft 2 in. was divided into 6 ft 3 in. plus 7 ft 3 in. plus 9 ft 8 in., while the overhang was 2 ft 6 in. at the front and 4 ft 3 in. at the back.

The bogie was something of an oddity in not being strictly a *bogie*; it was really a double radial truck, since its massive main bearing, which took the whole of the 19 tons 6 cwt load of the front end of the

engine, was arranged to slide in a curved channel on a radius of 10 ft 9 in. A powerful spiral spring controlled the lateral movement of the truck; in other respects the truck was similar to an ordinary bogie.

The boiler was a good one, and was similar to that used by Webb on his three-cylinder compound engines of the Teutonic class. It was made in three rings of $\frac{1}{2}$ in. plate, the outside diameters being, respectively, 4 ft 2 in., 4 ft 3 in. and 4 ft 4 in. The pitch was 7 ft $10\frac{1}{2}$ in. above rail level.

There were 225 tubes of $1\frac{7}{8}$ in. dia., giving a heating surface of 1,241.3 sq. ft, to which the fire-box added 159.1 sq. ft to make a total of 1,400.4 sq. ft. The length of the barrel was 10 ft $11\frac{7}{8}$ in. and the grate area was 20.5 sq. ft.

In working order, the engine weighed 53 tons 18 cwt, the two truck axles carrying 9 tons 18 cwt each, the driving axle 17 tons 8 cwt and the trailing axle 16 tons 14 cwt. The width of the footplate was 8 ft 2 in. and the maximum width over the outside cylinder covers was 8 ft $3\frac{1}{2}$ in.

The tenders used on these engines were of two different patterns, one having the wheelbase equally divided, as on *Temeraire*, the other having unequal divisions as on *Hardwicke* in the previous chapter but

one. The former was used on about half the Jubilees and all of the Alfreds. The water capacity of both was 2,500 gallons, and about four tons of coal could be carried.

The wheelbase of *Temeraire's* tender was 13 ft, equally divided, while the overhangs were 3 ft $3\frac{1}{2}$ in. at the front and 3 ft 6 in. at the back.

The framing was the usual LNWR wooden type, used for the last time on Webb's 4-6-0, four-cylinder compound mixed-traffic engines, the notorious Bill Baileys, which immediately followed the 4-4-0s. The wheels were 3 ft 9 in. dia.

From the historical point of view, these four-cylinder compounds were of considerable interest. Today, we can appreciate what their failings were, if only because we have the advantage of possessing the knowledge gained by the French, who specialised in designing and operating such engines.

But I am going to suggest that the very occasional brilliant run which a Webb four-cylinder compound could put up, as in the case of *Temeraire's* astonishing performance, *might* have been due to the driver setting the valve gear at, or near full gear and driving entirely off the regulator, up hill and down dale. That is the only explanation I can offer.

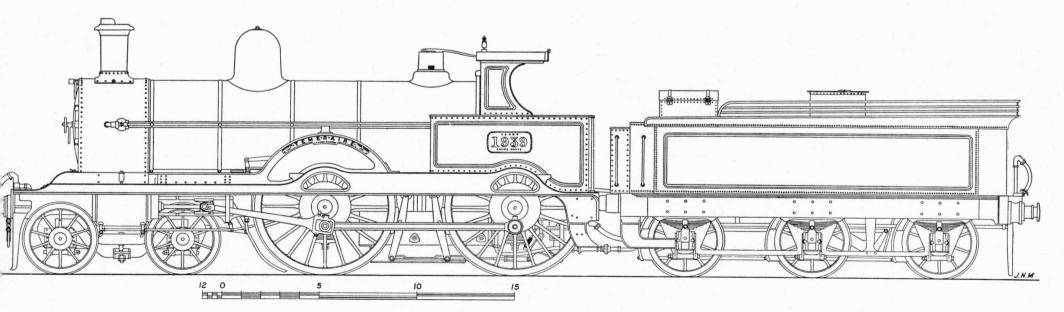

Express Passenger Engine
No 1 CLIVE

No 1 *Clive* was one of the memorable Precursor class designed by George Whale for the LNWR and introduced in 1904. She was one of several No 1s that I knew; but my interest in her was very strongly personal, and for reasons that I will mention later, if only because of one of the most astonishing coincidences that could ever have happened to anyone.

The Precursors were of interest because not only were they intended to provide the LNWR with some express passenger engines to replace the notorious Webb three-cylinder compounds that Whale was scrapping at such a furious rate, but the design had to be simple and quite straightforward, and the engines had to be quickly and cheaply built and at the same time powerful and more in keeping with the then modern ideas.

To achieve these very desirable and urgently-needed ends, Whale produced what was virtually an enlargement and modernisation of Webb's redoubtable 2-4-0 Precedent class described on page 88. The new engines, externally, were neat, bold and very

nicely proportioned, and I have no hesitation in placing them among England's most handsome 4-4-0s.

From the technical point of view, they were typical of their period in being plain, two-cylinder simple engines with inside cylinders and good boilers, but no superheaters. The cylinders were 19 in. dia., 26 in. stroke and had the valves on top, operated by Joy's valve gear. Particulars of valve setting, port

sizes and so forth, have never been available; but they must have been very good, because the engines brought about what amounted to a revolution in the general standard of LNWR locomotive performance. All the same, the exhaust beats gave out that characteristically uneven tattoo that was the mark of the Joy gear—two dashes and a couple of dots per revolution of the driving wheels !

What mattered most was that the first engine of the class, No 513, *Precursor*, completed in March 1904, had not been in existence a week before she had shown quite clearly that, at last, the LNWR possessed a good express engine—so good, in fact, that the company's directors had no hesitation in giving their consent to Whale's request that large numbers of similar engines should be built as quickly as possible. Crewe works got going to such effect that, between June 1904 and May 1906, no fewer than 110 of these fine engines had been built. Twenty more, bringing the total to 130, were added between June and August 1907; No 1, *Clive*, was the first of this final batch.

There can be little doubt that the boiler design,

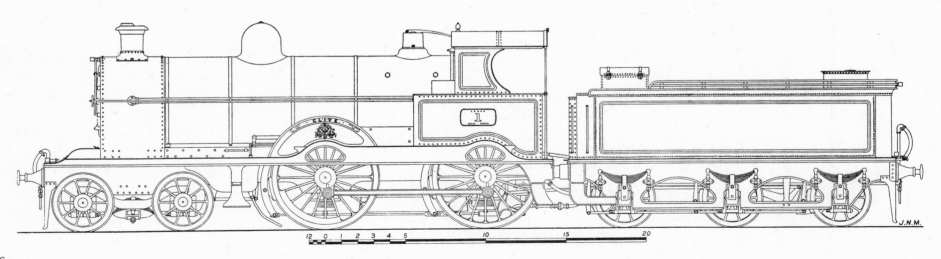

next to the extraordinary simplicity of the whole engine, contributed much to the success of the Precursors. The barrel contained 309 tubes of $1\frac{7}{8}$ in. dia., and was made in three rings, the diameters of which were 4 ft $11\frac{1}{2}$ in., 5 ft $0\frac{3}{4}$ in. and 5 ft 2 in. The pitch was 8 ft 5 in. from rail level.

The firebox, outside, was 7 ft 4 in. long and 4 ft 1 in. wide, at grate level, while its depth below the boiler centre line was 6 ft 3 in. The grate area was 22.4 sq. ft. The heating surface of the firebox was 161.3 sq. ft, and that of the tubes was no less than 1,848.4 sq. ft, making the total 2,009.7 sq. ft—a remarkable figure for a 4-4-0 engine of *any* period, let alone 1904! The working pressure of the boiler was 175 p.s.i., the usual pressure for LNWR express locomotives for many years.

The tubes were not so crowded as might have been supposed, because the boiler barrel was quite large, and the firebox very high; in fact, the distance between the tops of the two casings was about 1 ft 4 in. Nevertheless, the water range and steam space were decidedly limited, though I believe that there was never a recorded case of a Precursor being short of steam.

The wheelbase was 6 ft 3 in. plus 8 ft $10\frac{1}{2}$ in. plus 10 ft, totalling 25 ft $1\frac{1}{2}$ in., while the overhang at the front was 2 ft 6 in., and at the back 4 ft 3 in. As with the Webb four-cylinder compound 4-4-0s, the leading truck was not a bogie but a four-wheeled

radial truck with wheels 3 ft 9 in. dia. The coupled wheels were 6 ft 9 in. dia.

In working order, the engine weighed 59 tons 15 cwt, with 21 tons 15 cwt resting on the leading truck and 19 tons on each of the coupled axles.

The tender was a novelty for the LNWR in that its framing was of steel, thereby breaking away from the former Crewe practice of making tender frames of timber. Its capacity was 3,600 gallons of water and $6\frac{3}{4}$ tons of coal.

As might be expected, and in fact was definitely intended, the Precursors were powerful and speedy. They immediately found favour with the men who had to handle them. There was no difficulty in timing trains of 300 or more tons weight on 55 m.p.h. schedules, even between Crewe and Carlisle; and a very noticeable feature of Precursor work was that, even with heavy trains, good speed could be maintained on up-grades, so there was no need for furious pace on the down-grades.

Engine No 1, *Clive*, was, of course, named after Clive of India. I had a younger brother who, because of family associations, was also named after him. During the 1914-18 war my brother served as an officer in France. And this brings me to the curious coincidence I mentioned.

One afternoon in 1916, my office telephone rang, and on picking up the receiver I was surprised to hear my brother's voice on the line. He asked me

to advise the family that he was unexpectedly in London for a few days and would be home later that evening; and he mentioned that he had just been appointed adjutant to his regiment.

About an hour afterwards, going home on the Bakerloo Tube, I did a thing I had never done before and do not remember doing since. I overran my station and found myself at Queen's Park instead of Kilburn Park.

Now, Queen's Park station is alongside what used to be the LNW main line, and during not more than a three-minute wait for a train back to Kilburn Park, an up express came by—a very long train headed by two Precursors. Imagine my feelings when I noticed that those two engines were No 1, *Clive*, piloting No 675, *Adjutant*!

I had known both these engines for some years, and I knew them for several years afterwards; but that evening at Queen's Park was the only occasion when I saw them together, or even in the same place at the same time.

As I am writing these notes, one of *Clive's* nameplates is in front of me. It is quite a massive piece of brass, $\frac{3}{16}$ in. thick, $2\frac{1}{2}$ in. wide, approximately 4 ft 6 in. long and curved on a radius of about 3 ft 6 in. The name, in the characteristic LNWR capitals, the company's initials, the Crewe Works title and the engine's date are all sunk into the surface of the plate and filled in with black wax. I have never weighed it, but I think it must weigh some 25 to 30 lb. A curious little detail, which was common to all LNWR nameplates, is the full stop which appears after the name.

This nameplate is, of course, one of the two which the engine carried for upwards of 30 years, and it shows little sign of maltreatment. Its general condition is quite good. I acquired it about 20 years ago, and I keep it as a memento, not only of a curious experience, but also of a very lovable locomotive.

A detail worth mentioning is that all the nameplates of the Precursors were the same length, no matter whether the actual name was a short one like *Arab* (No 2576), or a long one like *Richard Trevithick* (No 1650). I believe that this was the first instance of the adoption of a standard length of nameplate, and it remained the usual practice at Crewe ever afterwards.

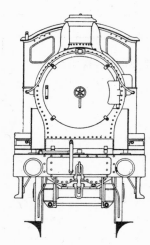

GENERAL SPECIFICATION			
CYLINDERS			
Diameter	...	...	19 in.
Stroke	...	...	26 in.
BOILER			
Length, between tubeplates			11 ft $9\frac{3}{4}$ in.
Maximum diameter	...		5 ft 2 in.
FIREBOX LENGTH			
Inside	...		6 ft $5\frac{3}{4}$ in.
Outside	...		7 ft 4 in.
TUBES			
Number	...	...	309
Diameter	...	...	$1\frac{7}{8}$ in.
HEATING SURFACE			
Tubes	...	1,848.4 sq. ft
Firebox	...	161.3 sq. ft
Total	...	2,009.7 sq. ft
GRATE AREA			
Square feet	...	...	22.4

THIS class is another that must be placed among the classics of English locomotives; they were not large engines, even for their day, but the work they did on the fastest and best LNWR expresses of that time would have put many a larger engine in considerable difficulty.

The Georges, as they were universally known, were virtually a superheated version of the Precursors and, from the outset, they were supremely successful in traffic, as well as being among the most popular of English locomotives.

It is not strictly accurate to regard the Georges as being merely superheated Precursors; they were really a new design by C. J. Bowen-Cooke, based on his predecessor's masterpieces, and there were certainly a number of components and details that were common to the two classes. For example, the frames; the double radial truck at the leading end, but with reduced wheel diameter; the boiler, except for the tubing, and the cab were all the same as those of the Precursors. The boiler mountings were also similar, but the smokebox on the Georges was 1 ft longer, while the alteration made in the driving-splashers is obvious.

It would appear that, at first, Bowen-Cooke was undecided whether he would adopt the use of superheated steam as a standard feature for his express engines, because the first 20 of his new class were divided into two sets of ten, one set being superheated, the other not.

No 2663, *George the Fifth*, was the first of the superheated set, and No 2664, *Queen Mary*, headed the ten engines which, for the time being, were to use saturated steam; both engines were completed, and testing of them inaugurated, in April 1910. In the meantime, nine more engines of both sets were building.

Outwardly, there was no apparent difference between the two sets, since the general dimensions and particulars were common to the whole lot. In fact, the only actual differences lay in the boilers and the cylinder sizes.

In all, 90 Georges were built, for in addition to the ten already mentioned, 40 were built in 1911, 20 in 1913 and a further 20 in 1916. To these must be added the ten Queen Marys which were eventually converted to Georges, and 31 Precursors which, in the 1920s, were similarly converted by being fitted with superheaters, extended smokeboxes and piston-valve cylinders.

All this came about simply because, in the early months of their existence, the Georges, in traffic, showed themselves to be considerably superior, not only to the Precursors but to the Queen Marys as well. Obviously, the use of superheated steam more than outweighed the troubles that its very high temperature caused in the lubrication system.

The superheater adopted was the Schmidt apparatus, and Ing.-Doktor Schmidt himself paid an extended visit to Crewe to give advice as to details and to supervise the installation of the apparatus in *George the Fifth* while the engine was being built. In spite of this, however, there was a good deal of trouble from carbonisation of the piston-valves and ports, as well as from burning of the elements at the return-bends.

The former trouble was eventually overcome by the discovery of a more heat-resisting oil, but the latter difficulty tended to persist until the elements were shortened by about 10 in.

After these troubles had been overcome, the Georges stood up well to the very hard work they had to do for upwards of ten years. It must be admitted, however, that the engines were scarcely robust enough to cope with the extremely strenuous conditions for more than a limited period.

Perhaps they were not intended to; but the fact remains that in the early 1920s they had begun to acquire an unenviable reputation for very rough

GEORGE THE FIFTH Class

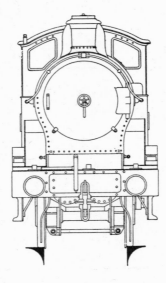

GENERAL SPECIFICATION	
CYLINDERS	**TUBES**
Diameter ... ... 20½ in.	Number ... 168 & 24
Stroke ... ... 26 in.	Diameter ... 1⅞ & 5 in.
BOILER	
Length, between tubeplates 11 ft 9¾ in.	**HEATING SURFACE**
Maximum dia-meter ... 5 ft 2 in.	Tubes ... 1,384.5 sq. ft
	Firebox ... 161.7 sq. ft
	Total ... 1,546.2 sq. ft
FIREBOX LENGTH	
Inside ... 6 ft 5¾ in.	**GRATE AREA**
Outside ... 7 ft 4 in.	Square feet ... 22.4

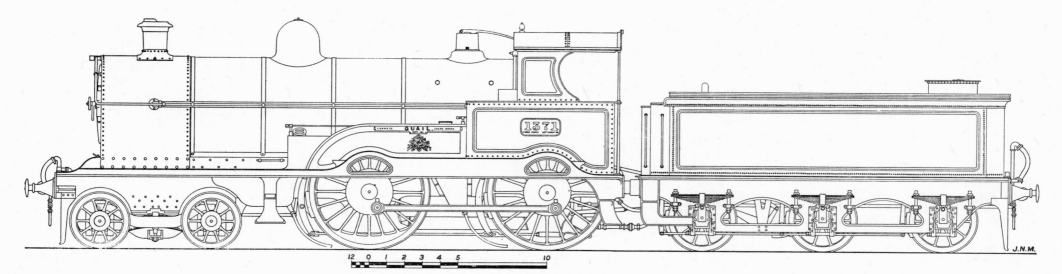

riding, and it was noticeable that their mileage between heavy repairs was diminishing. All the same, when a George was in good trim, the prime feature of her performance was a most astonishing power output for an engine of such moderate dimensions.

Two classic instances timed, respectively, by Mr Cecil J. Allen and Mr R. E. Charlewood, must suffice to support my statement. No 1595, *Wild Duck*, with a 410 ton train, slipped so badly after starting from Euston that she stalled on the Camden bank, just outside. By the time help was obtained, in the form of a pusher in the rear, the train restarted 11 min. late. *Wild Duck* then got going with, literally, such fury that she not only regained the whole of the lost 11 min., but she clipped half a minute off the schedule as well, and arrived at Crewe 25 sec. early, having covered the 158.1 miles from Euston in 170 min. 35 sec., *including* the Camden stall.

The second instance was, perhaps, even better, because the load behind the engine, No 1294, *F. S. P. Wolferstan*, was no less than 435 tons. There was a bad relaying check in force near Roade, 59 miles from Euston; but by the time she got to it, 1294 had just under 5 min. in hand. The result was that she arrived at Rugby only 24 sec. late, whereas if she had run exactly to schedule before Roade, the lateness at Rugby might well have been 6 min.

Work like this, however, was really typical of the Georges when in good form, and fortunately, many records have been kept of it. There must have been few people who would have expected it after studying the engines' dimensions, which were: cylinders, originally, 20 in., but later $20\frac{1}{2}$ in. dia. by 26 in. stroke; the 8 in. piston valves, operated by Joy valve gear, had a lap of $1\frac{1}{4}$ in., an exhaust clearance of $\frac{1}{16}$ in. and a full-gear travel of $5\frac{7}{16}$ in. The ports were 1 in. wide.

The diameter of the leading truck wheels was 3 ft 3 in. and of the coupled wheels 6 ft 9 in.; the wheelbase was 25 ft $1\frac{1}{2}$ in. divided into 6 ft 3 in. plus 8 ft $10\frac{1}{2}$ in. plus 10 ft, and the overhangs were, leading, 2 ft 6 in. and, trailing, 4 ft 3 in. A central stay, arranged longitudinally, was provided to incorporate a main bearing for the driving axle, in addition to the normal two bearings in the main frames. The main cranks were of the built-up type with balanced webs.

The boiler was made in three rings, 4 ft $11\frac{1}{2}$ in., 5 ft $0\frac{3}{4}$ in. and 5 ft 2 in. dia., respectively. The barrel length was 11 ft $9\frac{3}{4}$ in. and its centre line was 8 ft 5 in. from rail level. There were 168 tubes of $1\frac{7}{8}$ in. dia. and 24 superheater flues of 5 in. dia. The firebox casing was 7 ft 4 in. long, 4 ft 1 in. wide and 6 ft 3 in. deep. The grate area was 22.4 sq. ft.

The tube heating surface was 1,384.5 sq. ft, to which the firebox added 161.7 sq. ft; the superheater surface was 302.5 sq. ft. The working pressure was the usual 175 p.s.i.

In working order, the weight on the leading truck was 21 tons 12 cwt, on the driving wheels 19 tons 2 cwt, and on the trailing wheels 19 tons 3 cwt, totalling 59 tons 17 cwt. The tender capacity was for 3,600 gallons of water and $6\frac{3}{4}$ tons of coal; its wheelbase was 13 ft 6 in., equally divided. There were actually three different types of tenders, all of the same size and capacity, in use on the Georges; one had a single flared coping surmounted by two coal rails; the second had an additional raised solid portion on top of the coping, while the third had the single coping and only one coal rail.

As is usual with a numerous class of engines, there were variations of minor details to be noted. In the earlier engines, the leading sandbox was below the running plate ahead of the driving wheels; in the later engines, it was above the running plate, butting against the splasher. The dust guard behind the leading footsteps was absent from most of the later engines, and was, I believe, eventually removed from all of them.

No 1371, *Quail*, was a particular pet of mine, as I enjoyed a number of runs behind her in my Birmingham days. She was a good runner, usually to the accompaniment of a remarkably syncopated exhaust!

THE old London and North Western Railway was a curious concern, particularly with regard to its locomotives; for something like 40 years, its principal express passenger traffic was handled by locomotives that were either of dubious quality, like the Webb three-cylinder compounds, or absolutely first-class, though by prevailing standards, very small. The good engines always had to be worked extremely hard in order to keep time with the heavy trains, even though, for many years, the timetables called for no higher average speed than 40 m.p.h., more often much less.

In the early 1900s, however, the company had begun to realise that, on other railways, not only were train loads increasing, but the speeds were becoming higher, and it was time the LNWR followed suit. The old 40 m.p.h. ruling was scrapped and much higher speeds called for, which put the locomotive department in a quandary. There was nothing to compare with the 4-4-2 and 4-6-0 types which were being introduced by other lines, and nearly all the principal trains of the LNWR had, perforce, to be double-headed.

To study the problem on a practical basis, C. J. Bowen-Cooke, the CME, arranged some interesting trials with engines from other railways. First, a Great Northern Atlantic was tried, followed by the great Caledonian 4-6-0 *Cardean*, and a Brighton superheated 4-4-2 tank engine, No 23; these trials took place in the summer of 1909. Twelve months later a Great Western Star, No 4005, *Royal Star*, was borrowed for a fortnight and ran regularly between Euston and Crewe.

Finally, in January, 1913, Crewe Works turned out a really big engine, No 2222, *Sir Gilbert Claughton*; how well I remember her, and how impressive she was! A friend who was a keen LNWR enthusiast, got to know that this engine would be running a special train at 8.30 a.m. from Euston to Crewe on a certain morning; so he and I arranged to meet at Euston at 8.15 a.m. and, sure enough, there was the engine at the head of the special.

She was fitted up with indicator shelters and had not then been properly painted; yet we could see that she was a fine engine, grand, massive and of pleasing outline. With it all she was a typical Crewe product, except for the outside Walschaerts valve gear. All the familiar LNWR features were readily recognisable. This was remarkable and, to us, satisfactory in an engine which was so much larger than any other hitherto produced by Crewe.

The train was a long and heavy one of 14 coaches, including the dynamometer car, and there was every indication that the performance of the engine would be carefully watched during the run to Crewe. My friend and I were surprised to notice that when the train started, the usual assistance from the shunting engine at the back was not given; *Sir Gilbert Claughton* was "lifting" that heavy load unaided, and she got away well. For some minutes afterwards we could hear her climbing the 1 in 77 of the Camden bank; the exhaust was heavy and ponderous, arousing all the echoes of the neighbourhood, but the engine was clearly mastering that load. We both felt that we had witnessed an epoch-making event.

It was some time before this engine came to London again, for she was transferred, under official observation and test, to the difficult Crewe-Carlisle line, where her powers were more particularly needed. Meanwhile, nine more engines of the class came out, completed in June 1913; and then there was quite an orgy of trials and tests with them.

There was, at first, some trouble with steaming, probably owing to the firemen not having properly

CLAUGHTONS

acquired the knack of firing that long, narrow Belpaire firebox with its partly sloping grate. When this difficulty had been overcome, the Claughtons settled down to some magnificent and truly outstanding work for several years.

The technical and semi-technical periodicals of the period published and discussed a great deal of information about Claughton performance which, at the time, was some of the finest ever obtained from steam locomotives.

However, it did not last. Within ten years, the engines began to show signs of distress, and repairs were frequent and costly. Defects in the design became apparent, and the blaze of glory with which the Claughtons made their debut faded; they could no longer stand up to the exacting and heavy tasks alone, and double-heading of the chief expresses

GENERAL SPECIFICATION			
CYLINDERS		**TUBES**	
Diameter	16 in. (four)	Number	149 & 24
Stroke	26 in. (four)	Diameter	1⅝ & 5¼ in.
BOILER			
Length, between		**HEATING SURFACE**	
tubeplates	14 ft 5⅞ in.	Tubes	1,087.9 & 486.3 sq. ft
Maximum dia-		Firebox	171.2 sq. ft
meter	5 ft 2 in.	Total	1,745.4 sq. ft
FIREBOX LENGTH			
Inside	8 ft 9 in.	**GRATE AREA**	
Outside	9 ft 6 in.	Square feet	30.5

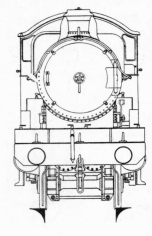

became, once more, the rule. Conditions brought about by the 1914-18 war aggravated matters to such an extent that soon after the grouping of the railways in January, 1923, the Claughtons began to give way to the Midland three-cylinder 4-4-0 compounds and Lancashire and Yorkshire four-cylinder 4-6-0s, which were considered to be more competent and reliable. To those of us who had known the Claughtons from their inception, it was all rather tragic and melancholy.

In spite of all this, however, my last run behind a Claughton, which took place as late as July, 1929, showed plainly that, with an engine in good condition and in the hands of a determined crew, she could still be made to show something of her old form.

The engine was LMS No 5989 (old LNW No 1133), hauling a 15-coach train, unassisted. She left Rugby $4\frac{1}{2}$ minutes late, but arrived at Euston only half a minute late, her maximum speed being 88 m.p.h. near Kings Langley. It was quite a meritorious performance with such a heavy train, especially as the engine was steadily gaining time as far as Willesden. But I am convinced that she required—and received—most expert handling from her driver and fireman.

The dimensions of the Claughtons were interesting when compared with those of other 4-6-0 express

locomotives of their period. Once more, the Webb double radial truck was provided for supporting the leading end of the engine. Above its transverse centre line, all four cylinders, 16 in. dia. by 26 in. stroke, were arranged in line; they drove the leading coupled axle. They were provided with 8 in. piston valves, the four of which were operated by two sets of Walschaerts valve gear, the movement being transmitted to the inside valves by means of straight, horizontal rocking shafts.

The ports were located exactly above the ends of the cylinder bores; the exhaust passages and blastpipe were situated at the rear end of the cylinders, which meant that the exhaust steam from the forward ports had a somewhat tortuous path to traverse. It is clear that, in the whole layout of cylinders, valves, ports, passages and cranks, lay the chief weakness of the design. Add to this a full gear valve travel of only $4\frac{1}{2}$ in. and a boiler pressure of only 175 p.s.i. and the reason for erratic performances stands revealed.

The wheel diameters were: leading truck, 3 ft 3 in.; coupled, 6 ft 9 in., and the wheelbase was 6 ft 3 in. plus 7 ft 6 in. plus 7 ft 5 in. plus 7 ft 10 in., totalling 29 ft. The leading overhang was 2 ft 6 in. and the trailing 7 ft $2\frac{1}{4}$ in.

A fairly good boiler was provided, 14 ft $5\frac{7}{8}$ in.

long, made in three rings, 4 ft $11\frac{1}{2}$ in., 5 ft $1\frac{1}{4}$ in. and 5 ft 2 in., respectively, in diameter and pitched 8 ft 9 in. above rail level. There were 149 tubes of $1\frac{7}{8}$ in. dia., 24 tubes of $5\frac{1}{4}$ in. dia. and 24 sets of superheater tubes of $1\frac{3}{16}$ in. dia., the respective heating surfaces of which were 1,087.9 sq. ft, 486.3 sq. ft and 413.6 sq. ft. The Belpaire firebox, the external length of which was 9 ft 6 in., added 171.2 sq. ft to make a grand total heating surface of 2,159 sq. ft. The grate area was 30.5 sq. ft.

In working order, the engine weight was 77 tons 15 cwt distributed into: 18 tons 15 cwt on the leading truck, 19 tons 15 cwt on each of the leading and intermediate coupled axles, and 19 tons 10 cwt on the trailing axle.

The tender had a 13 ft 6 in. wheelbase, equally divided, and carried 3,000 gallons of water and 7 tons of coal.

The last 40 Claughtons were built in 1920 and brought the total number of engines to 130. They differed from the earlier lots in having the cylinder diameter reduced to $15\frac{3}{4}$ in.; also, they had Ross pop safety valves instead of the Ramsbottom type, and were painted without lining. No 1914, *Patriot*, the war memorial engine, was one of these, as was No 2499, *Patience*, which was one of my particular favourites—hence my drawing of her.

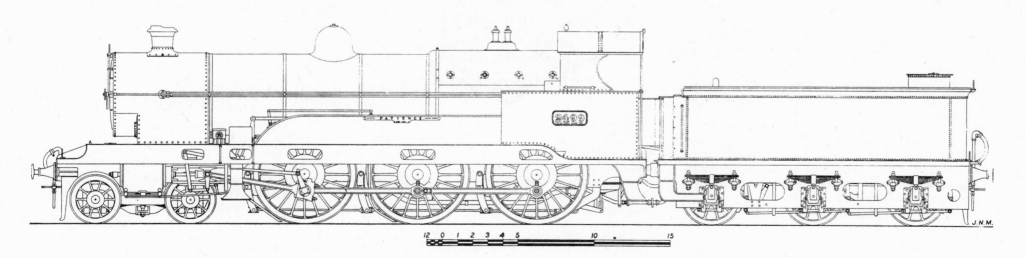

THE 'CAULIFLOWERS' or 'CRESTED GOODS'

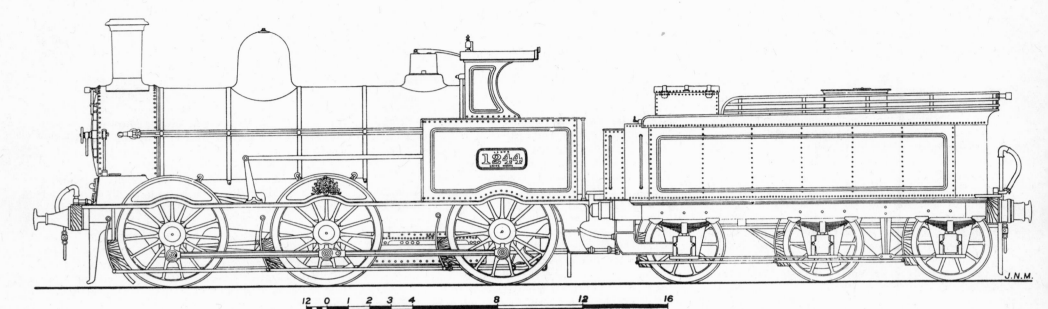

I SUPPOSE a whole book could be written about the fascinating subject of nicknames for locomotives; for there were many such names, some fanciful others apt and clever, a few merely silly, but all more or less amusing, and there were quite interesting reasons for most of them.

Perhaps one of the most startling of these popular nicknames was " Cauliflowers," applied to F. W. Webb's 0-6-0 express goods engines for the old London and North Western Railway. Officially, the engines were styled " 18 in. Goods," but they were also popularly known as the " Crested Goods." The two nicknames derived from the fact that the LNWR crest decorated their driving wheel splashers, and when seen from a distance it had some slight resemblance to a full-grown cauliflower; it had nothing to do with horticulture.

The " 18 in. Goods " class first came out in 1880, in circumstances that were of some interest. In May 1879, David Joy visited Crewe Works to discuss and explain the Joy radial valve gear with

F. W. Webb. At that time, Webb, who was then a member of the Council of the Institution of Mechanical Engineers, had just begun to design a new class of 0-6-0 goods engine to replace his predecessor's celebrated DX class. He was so attracted by the design and especially the simplicity of Joy's gear that he decided to incorporate it in his new engines. He also invited Joy to read a paper on the gear at the Institute's summer meeting at Barrow in August 1880.

By that time, the first of the " Cauliflowers " had been built and it was exhibited at the meeting. Subsequently, several different classes of LNW locomotives were provided with the Joy gear.

The first ten " Cauliflowers " were built between 1880 and 1883; they had cast iron wheels with H-section spokes and a diameter of 5 ft 1½ in. From 1887 until 1902, no fewer than 300 more of the class were built. They were similar to the earlier ones, except that the wheels were of cast steel, 5 ft 2 in. dia. and with nicely proportioned oval spokes, to the advantage of the engines' appearance.

Although designed as express goods engines, the " Cauliflowers " were often used on fast passenger trains, with which they sometimes indulged in quite astonishing speeds. There used to be a story, current among LNWR fans 50 years ago, describing a run made by " Cauliflower " No 34 piloting the 6 ft 6 in. 2-4-0 No 2179, *Avon*, on an express from Carlisle to Carnforth. The 62¾ miles, including the 30-odd miles of steady climbing to Shap summit, were covered in exactly 66 minutes, start to stop; during the descent from Shap to Carnforth, speed rose to 84 m.p.h. which, for a 5 ft 2 in. 0-6-0, was not bad going ! The load was stated to have been about 220 tons, so the engines were not unduly taxed; but it says something for the quality of their riding that the drivers allowed them to get up to such a pace.

I was never fortunate enough to be in an express train behind a " Cauliflower "; but on semi-fast outer-suburban trains, I have timed engines of this class at 65-70 m.p.h. This was often done on trains running non-stop from Watford to Euston, as might be expected from engines for which the boilers, wheels, cylinders and valve gear were interchangeable with those of the Watford Tanks.

I can remember the time, around 1908, when many of the " Cauliflowers " were stationed in the London area and used on all kinds of goods traffic as well as on suburban passenger trains and occasionally as pilots on secondary express passenger trains. At a later period, some of them were put to empty coach working between Euston and the carriage sidings at Willesden. It did not seem to matter what sort of work they were called upon to do; they always did it well—sometimes astonishingly well.

I remember one afternoon at Euston, when a train from Northampton arrived with a " Cauliflower " piloting a 4-4-0 of the Renown class; it was about 20 minutes late. I noticed that the " Cauliflower " seemed to be rather hot and was blowing fairly hard at the safety valves, while the Renown was absolutely silent and, to all appearances, lifeless and cold. Sensing trouble, I went up to the " Cauliflower " and found the fireman alone on the footplate; his driver was talking to the crew of the other engine. I asked what was the trouble. Pointing to the Renown, the fireman replied, with more than a sprinkling of unprintable adjectives: " We've had to haul *that* and the train all the way from Bletchley. He's dropped his brick arch and lost some of his firebars and can't get any steam."

I asked why in the world they had not left such a cripple behind at Bletchley, and got the reply: " He's supposed to work the 6.30 back from here to Bletchley, but he'll be (adjective) lucky if he does it. I expect we'll have to carry him again ! "

That was no answer to my question, but I let it go. What I had hoped the fireman would say was that the " Cauliflower " would have done better hauling only the train without having a crippled engine to drag along too; but he made no such remark, and I felt a little disappointed.

As their official designation implied, the standard cylinder diameter for this class was 18 in.; but according to an official list in my possession, Nos 715, 879 and 1641 had 17½ in. cylinders, while for Nos

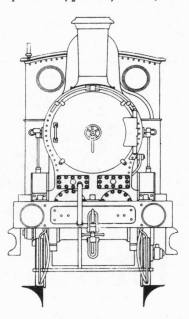

39, 168, 454, 548, 726, 930, 1146, 1175, 1235, 1268, 1269 and 2319, the diameter was only 17 in. In all, the stroke was 24 in. It is also interesting to note in the same list, that Nos 100, 143, 174, 441, 449, 450, 451, 453, 455, 755, 774, 776, 800, 801, 812, 1010, 1130, 1298, 1798, 2070, 2227 and 2502, at one time, had piston valves, but appear to have reverted to flat valves at a later date. I have never seen this mentioned anywhere before.

The official wheel diameter was 5 ft, but it was actually 5 ft 2½ in. with new tyres. The wheelbase was 15 ft 6 in. divided into 7 ft 3 in. plus 8 ft 3 in. Overhang at the front was 4 ft 3 in., and at the back 4 ft 1 in.

The boiler was made in three rings of ½ in. steel plate, 4 ft 1 in., 4 ft 2 in., and 4 ft 3 in. dia., respectively. The barrel was 9 ft 10 in. long and pitched 7 ft 5½ in. above rail level. There were 198 tubes of $1\frac{7}{8}$ in. dia., giving 980 sq. ft of heating surface out of a total of 1,083.5 sq. ft, the balance being made up by the firebox. In working order, the engine weighed 35 tons 4 cwt, 11 tons 14 cwt being on the leading axle, 12 tons on the driving axle and 11 tons 10 cwt on the trailing axle—a very nice balance. The tender was of the standard 1,800-gallon type weighing 25 tons.

An interesting point is that the " Cauliflowers," unlike the Watford Tanks, mostly retained their light, plain, black-painted coupling rods throughout their existence; all the Watford Tanks had rather heavy bright steel fluted coupling rods.

GENERAL SPECIFICATION

CYLINDERS			TUBES		
Diameter	...	... 18 in.	Number	...	... 198
Stroke	...	... 24 in.	Diameter	...	... $1\frac{7}{8}$ in.
BOILER			HEATING SURFACE		
Length between			Tubes	...	980 sq. ft.
tubeplates ...	9 ft. 10 in.		Firebox	...	103.5 sq. ft.
Maximum diameter 4 ft. 3 in.			Total ...	...	1,083.5 sq. ft.
FIREBOX LENGTH					
Inside...	...	... —	GRATE AREA		
Outside	...	... —	Square feet ...	...	—

It was in the historic year, 1897, that F. W. Webb designed and introduced his second series of 0-6-2 tank engines on the London and North Western Railway. Unlike the first series, the new engines were intended primarily for working suburban passenger traffic, more especially the intensive service between Euston and Watford; hence, the engines became widely known as the Watford tanks.

There could scarcely have been a simpler design, or a better engine for the job; moreover, the engines were neat and trim, always kept in good condition and soon became very popular. Basically, the design was simply a tank engine version of the numerous and successful 18 in. 0-6-0 tender engines, the so-called Cauliflowers; so the first cost of the tank engines was kept down to an absolute minimum. Boilers, cylinders, coupled wheels and Joy valve-gear were all interchangeable between the two classes, so no new patterns were required.

The Watford tanks, of which 80 were built between 1897 and 1902, soon showed themselves to be powerful and remarkably speedy, frequently exceeding 60 m.p.h. when the opportunity occurred. Considering that the dimensions of these engines were so similar to those of the LBSCR E4 class engines, the difference in the performance was surprising; and what Webb did that Billinton didn't can be the subject of considerable conjecture and discussion. More than once, I timed a Watford tank at 65 m.p.h., and other observers, who were more closely and regularly associated with the engines than I was, frequently noted similar speeds. I think the maximum speed I ever noted behind a Brighton E4 was 52 m.p.h.—quite a contrast!

My first acquaintance with the Watford tanks was made long before I knew anything about the London and North Western Railway, other than its title; it was at Wandsworth Common, on the LBSCR, somewhere around 1899. The reason was that, in those days and right up to 1914, the LNWR operated a service of some half-a-dozen trains each way, daily, between Willesden Junction and East Croydon. The route was via the West London and West London Extension Railways to Clapham Junction, and thence over the LBSCR through Wandsworth Common, Balham and Crystal Palace to Croydon. The engines used were usually Webb's small 4 ft 6 in. 2-4-2 tanks,

GENERAL SPECIFICATION			
CYLINDERS		**TUBES**	
Diameter ... ... 18 in.		Number 198	
Stroke ... ... 24 in.		Diameter ... ... $1\frac{7}{8}$ in.	
BOILER			
Length, between		**HEATING SURFACE**	
tubeplates 9 ft 10 in.		Tubes ... 980 sq. ft	
Maximum dia-		Firebox ... 103 sq. ft	
meter ... 4 ft 3 in.		Total ... 1,083 sq. ft	
FIREBOX LENGTH			
Inside ... 4 ft $10\frac{5}{8}$ in.		**GRATE AREA**	
Outside ... 5 ft 5 in.		Square feet ... 17.1	

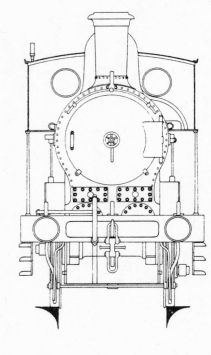

WEBB'S WATFORD TANKS

0-6-2 coal tanks and occasionally a Watford tank; together, these three classes were the first LNWR engines that I knew, though not many years later, I got to know several more.

After my parents had moved house from Wandsworth Common to North Kensington, in 1904, I was able to make frequent visits to the London terminal stations north of the Thames. Paddington, Euston, Kings Cross and St Pancras all had their little companies of interested spectators, not all of them schoolboys; and there was the added attraction that the stations were " open " with prominent vantage points easily accessible. Euston was a prime favourite of many enthusiasts, and there, in those days, the

Watford tanks handled a major share of the suburban traffic; they always seemed to be extremely busy.

However, London did not hold the monopoly of these engines; they were to be seen in numbers working suburban traffic in the Birmingham area, in company with F. W. Webb's equally well-known 5 ft 6 in. 2-4-2 tank engines—a class that was rarely, if ever, seen in the London district. In 1920, when I was transferred to Birmingham on business, the Watford tanks and the 2-4-2 engines were still the principal suburban engines to be seen there; and they were certainly doing good work, for the morning and evening rush-hour trains at New Street were heavy and quite sharply timed.

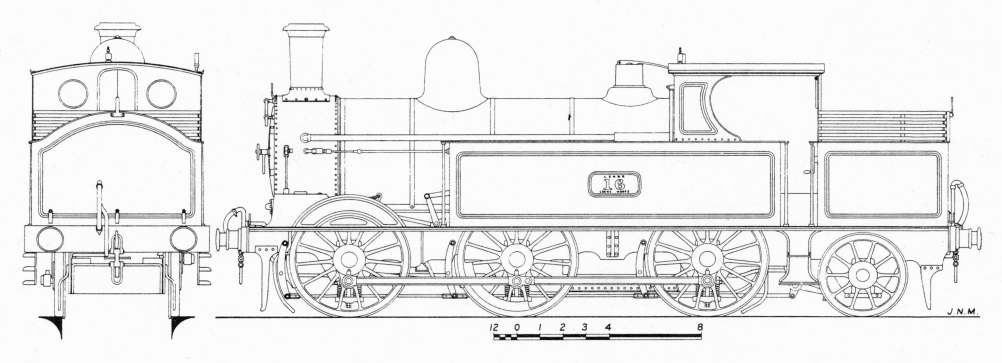

These engines had the following dimensions: cylinders 18 in. dia. by 24 in. stroke, with the steam-chests above; the length of the ports was 14 in., and the widths were 1½ in. for admission and 3¼ in. for exhaust. The slide valves were operated by Joy's valve gear.

The wheelbase was 22 ft 3 in. divided into 7 ft 3 in. plus 8 ft 3 in. plus 6 ft 9 in. The diameter of the six coupled wheels was 5 ft 2½ in. and of the trailing wheels 3 ft 9 in. The trailing axle was supported in Webb's radial axleboxes, and the driving axle was provided with three bearings, two in the main frames, as usual, and the third in an auxiliary frame mounted longitudinally between them. The overhangs were 4 ft 3 in. at the front and 3 ft 9 in. at the back.

The boiler was made in three rings, 4 ft 1 in., 4 ft 2 in., and 4 ft 3 in. dia., respectively, and the barrel was 9 ft 10 in. long. There were 198 tubes of 1⅞ in. dia., their heating surface amounting to 980 sq. ft; the firebox heating surface was 103 sq. ft, making the total 1,083 sq. ft. The centre line was 7 ft 5½ in. from rail level and the working pressure

was 150 p.s.i. The grate area was 17.1 sq. ft.

This boiler was one of Webb's standard types and first appeared in 1894 on the 2-4-0 engines of the Precedent class. It replaced one that was introduced 20 years before for use on certain other classes, including the earlier three-cylinder engines of the Compound class, the 18 in. Cauliflower 0-6-0 goods engines, the 2-4-0 engines of the Whitworth class and, finally, the Watford tanks. During more than 25 years, its basic design and dimensions remained unaltered, and it was one of the earliest boilers to be made of steel.

The tank capacity of the Watford tanks was 1,420 gallons and when, about 1902, coal rails were added to the bunkers, about three tons of coal could be carried. In working trim, the weight was 52 tons 6 cwt, distributed into 12 tons 6 cwt on the leading wheels, 15 tons 10 cwt on the driving wheels, 14 tons on the trailing coupled wheels and 10 tons 10 cwt on the radial wheels.

Withdrawal of these engines began as long ago as 1920; but such was their quality and usefulness that

about 70 became LMSR property in 1923 and 15 survived to be taken over by British Railways in 1948. The class became extinct in 1953, the last survivor being 51 years old. In their last years, most of these engines had the Ramsbottom safety-valves replaced by Ross " Pops "; otherwise, little alteration was ever made to their details during the 55 years of their existence.

That reminds me of the stolid consistency with which Crewe perpetuated the basic design of nearly every detail on its many different types and classes of locomotives. For instance, the characteristic Webb chimney-cap, first introduced in 1874, remained basically unaltered until 1923, when LNWR locomotives ceased to be built. The only alterations were with capuchons, or deflectors, which first appeared in 1903. For many years, they were made of plate and fixed by setscrewing to the inside of the bore of the cap casting. Many years later, they became integral with the casting; meanwhile, they tended to vary in height from 1⅝ in. to 4½ in., and eventually were standardised at the former figure.

GENERAL SPECIFICATION

CYLINDERS				TUBES			
Diameter	...	...	17 in.	Number	...	...	186
Stroke	...	...	24 in.	Diameter	...	...	1¾ in.
BOILER							
Length, between				**HEATING SURFACE**			
tubeplates	...		10 ft	Tubes	...	860 sq. ft	
Maximum dia-				Firebox	...	91 sq. ft	
meter	...	...	4 ft	Total	...	951 sq. ft	
FIREBOX LENGTH							
Inside	...	4 ft	11 in.	**GRATE AREA**			
Outside	...	5 ft	6 in.	Square feet	...	16.62	

NORTH LONDON TANKS

THE old North London Railway was one which, in some ways, resembled the District and the Metropolitan Railways. It was, essentially, part of London's own railway system; its locomotive stock consisted entirely of tank engines, and its passenger rolling stock was in sets of close-coupled four-wheeled coaches. It was all very clean, however, and in my young days, I used to regard my rare trips in a North London train as quite important adventures.

Perhaps, my most vivid memory of the line is the piercing, high-pitched squeal of the NL locomotive whistle. Fifty years ago the whistles of Great Western, London and South Western, London and North Western, Great Northern, Metropolitan and District engines were all high-pitched; but the North London beat them all, by what could not have been less than a fifth in the musical scale! And it was the only locomotive whistle known to me in which the "bell" portion was literally *bell*-shaped; I have shown it in my drawing.

With the exception of a curious and ancient crane-engine used at Bow Works, the engines of the North London line were of two types: 0-6-0 tanks for goods work and 4-4-0 tanks for passenger traffic. The latter were sub-divided into two different classes, one with inside cylinders and the other of the more usual outside-cylinder variety. My drawings depict No 20,

and it can be taken as typical of the outside-cylinder passenger engines as they were when I knew them. They were neat, trim little engines with, I recall,

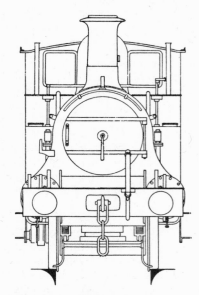

quite remarkable pulling power, as the following incident shows.

One afternoon, many years ago, I was out on Wormwood Scrubbs when a heavy goods train,

coming up from the Chelsea direction on the West London Extension Railway, attracted my attention because of the laboured exhaust of its engine, a London and North Western Webb 0-6-0 coal locomotive. Up the incline from North Pole Road to the big girder bridge carrying the WLR over the Great Western Railway, this train gradually came to a standstill, and the engine was unable to re-start it.

After about 40 minutes, North London 4-4-0 tank engine No 20 arrived from Willesden Junction; she was duly coupled up to the Webb 0-6-0 and with both engines working flat out the train was successfully hauled up the gradient, over the bridge and disappeared. It was obvious that the NLR engine was doing the greater part of the work in re-starting.

The principal dimensions of these engines were: cylinders: 17 in. dia. by 24 in. stroke; diameters of wheels, coupled 5 ft 5 in., bogie 2 ft 9 in.; wheelbase, 5 ft 8 in. plus 7 ft 0¼ in. plus 8 ft, totalling 20 ft 8¼ in.; leading overhang 1 ft 4 in.; trailing overhang 5 ft 6¾ in.; total length over buffers, 31 ft 4 in.; the oak buffer-beams were 8 ft long, 1 ft 5 in. deep and 6 in. thick, each having a ¼ in. flitchplate on the outer face; the width across the tanks was 7 ft 7½ in., and the height from rail to the top of the chimney was 12 ft 11½ in. In working order, the weight was 44 tons, while the working pressure was 160 p.s.i.

In my time, there were 74 of these 4-4-0 tank

engines, and they all lasted long enough to be taken over by the London Midland and Scottish Railway at the time of the grouping in 1923. In the previous year, the London and North Western Railway, which had had virtual control of the North London since 1909, seemed suddenly to wake up to the fact that the NLR engines were still carrying their NLR numbers, although they had been LNWR property for about 20 years! So the LNWR introduced a scheme of renumbering for the NLR engines, but had not fully completed it during the 12 months immediately preceding the grouping.

The LMSR, of course, introduced another re-numbering scheme in which these 4-4-0 engines became Nos 6435 to 6512 inclusively, whereas in the LNW scheme, they were to have been 2800 to 2873.

My most frequent sight of NLR engines was of those that worked the trains from Willesden Junction (High Level) station to Kew and Richmond. They passed well within sight of Friar's Junction (Old Oak Lane) where the Great Western Birmingham line via High Wycombe diverges from the West of England main line, and was a favourite vantage point for train-spotting in my young days. The NLR trains were on their own road as far as Gunnersbury Junction (Chiswick), whence they exercised running

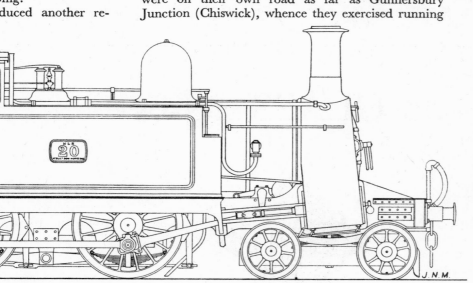

powers over the London and South Western's line from Addison Road and Hammersmith to Kew Gardens and Richmond.

Like their contemporaries on the District Railway, the NLR engines had acquired a standardised external appearance, at the time I came to know them. But I always thought that their cabs must have been extremely draughty, being designed apparently on the principle of allowing unrestricted and probably violent circulation of air, taking little or no account of the fact that, often, heavy driving rain could be mixed with the air. Things must have been even worse in earlier days, when the upper part of the sidesheets was about half the width that I have drawn it.

I must also report that, in later years, the pitch of the sound of the whistle was very considerably lowered; I should think it came down by almost an octave, which made it much more comfortable to hear. At the same time, the very distinctive and old-fashioned bell shape was discarded in favour of a cylindrical shape.

The original design was prepared in 1868 by William Adams and it was so far up-to-date that only slight, superficial modifications were afterwards made, right up to 1929 when the last of the class was scrapped.

A very fine model of one of these engines stands in a glass case in the circulating area of Broad Street station, the old North London Railway's principal terminus. The model was built, exactly to the proto-type working drawings, by apprentices at Bow Works more than 60 years ago and it is one of the finest of the official collection of locomotive models.

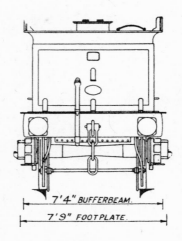

7'4" BUFFERBEAM.

7'9" FOOTPLATE.

GENERAL SPECIFICATION

CYLINDERS			TUBES		
Diameter	...	18 in.	Number	... ...	223
Stroke	...	24 in.	Diameter	... ...	1¾ in.
BOILER			HEATING SURFACE		
Length, between			Tubes	...	1,115 sq. ft
tubeplates	10ft	6 in.	Firebox	...	110 sq. ft
Maximum dia-			Total	...	1,225 sq. ft
meter	...	4 ft 3 in.			
FIREBOX LENGTH			GRATE AREA		
Inside	...	5 ft 9 in.	Square feet	...	17.5
Outside	...	6 ft 4 in.			

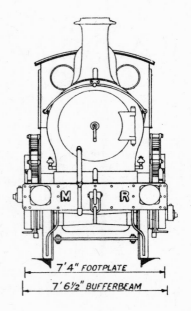

7'4" FOOTPLATE

7'6½" BUFFERBEAM

800 CLASS 2-4-0s

THESE engines were among the classics of English locomotive design, and their history is a long and honourable one. The original design was due to Matthew Kirtley, and 48 engines were built —30 by Nielson and Co. of Glasgow, and 18 at the Midland Railway's own factory at Derby, in 1870-1.

They were at once set to work on the Midland's best express traffic and immediately proved their worth. The enginemen soon found that the engines were capable of being worked extremely hard, when necessary, without becoming short of steam, with the result that they were popular favourites with everyone concerned.

In 1875, Kirtley was succeeded by Samuel Johnson, who promptly turned his attention to the 800s; he was much impressed with their work, but it seems that he was somewhat dubious as to how long the engines could be kept at work without undergoing heavy repairs. Also, I am convinced that their somewhat ungainly appearance did not meet with Johnson's approval; for in 1875, an 800, then not quite six years old, was subjected to some alterations

118

more in keeping with Johnson's meticulous " artistic eye."

She was given a new and slightly larger boiler of typical Johnson design with what came to be, for many years, standard Midland mountings and fittings; no alterations were made to frames or motion, but a cab was put over the footplate and a new and larger tender was provided. In this way, the engine was transformed into one of England's loveliest 2-4-0s —that is, according to my way of thinking !

During the next five years all the rest of the class were similarly treated and they remained unaltered until about 1904 when R. M. Deeley changed the smokebox and chimney in a way that did not enhance the Johnson neatness. When I first knew these engines, they were as Johnson left them and as I preferred them; my drawing shows No 815 in that style, and I suggest she would make a lovely model.

The cylinders were 18 in. by 24 in., but in 11 of the engines the stroke was altered to 26 in.; the leading wheels were 4 ft 2 in. dia., and the four coupled wheels 6 ft 9 in.; the pitch of the boiler was 7 ft 3 in. from rail level; the barrel had a maximum diameter of 4 ft 3 in. outside (4 ft 8½ in. outside the clothing plates), and contained 223 tubes of 1¾ in. dia., giving a heating surface of 1,115 sq. ft to which the firebox added 110 sq. ft, making the total 1,225 sq. ft.

The capacity of the tender was 2,755 gal. and 4 tons of coal. The body was mounted on massive plate frames carried on six 4 ft 2 in. wheels. It is worth noting that the heights of engine and tender running plates were not alike, and that a short length

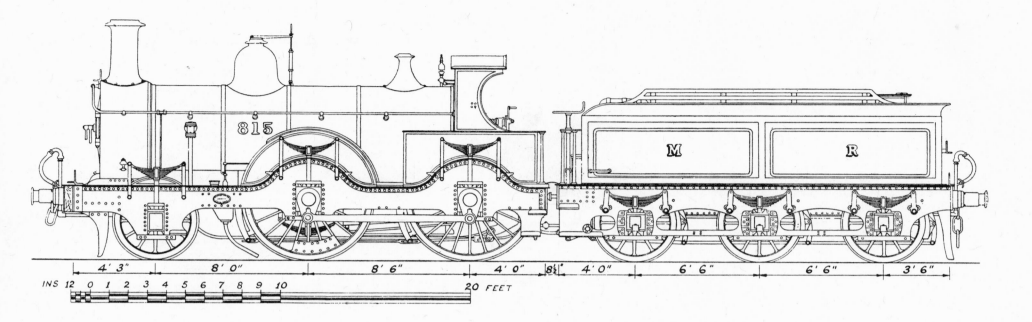

of thick wooden planking was fitted at the cab end of the engine so as to level things up a bit! The heavy wooden bufferbeam, 6 in. thick with a ¾ in. steel flitchplate on its front face, was a characteristic feature that was never altered.

The cylinder centres were spaced at the unusual distance of 2 ft 6 in., and the valves were driven by a beautifully-designed Stephenson link motion, reversed by screw and turncrank. These details probably had much to do with the ability these engines possessed to attain very high speed.

That great locomotive historian E. L. Ahrons, in an article published in *The Railway Magazine* in 1919,

described these engines as " one of the most celebrated classes of express engines that ever ran in this country "; farther on in the same article he remarks: " I believe that many of them are still capable of giving a good many later and larger engines a good start and a bad beating." It was around 1919 when I came to know these engines really well, and the comment by Ahrons exactly reflects my own impression of them; at that time, they were still largely employed on main-line express work, usually as pilots for assisting other engines, and it almost seemed as though they were well set for at least another 20 years on such work. Things did not pan out quite

like that, however; in 1928, all except one had been withdrawn for scrap. They left behind them a reputation that was not equalled by any other class of Midland locomotives except the Deeley three-cylinder compounds of much later years.

The last survivor of this class was old No 827, later No 60; she was broken up as LMSR No 20060, in July 1936, having outlived all her sisters by about eight years and reaching the ripe age of 55. The reason for this was that in 1923 she was fitted with a secondhand boiler in comparatively new condition, and it lasted until the engine's running gear became unfit for further service.

BETWEEN 1887 and 1900 no fewer than 95 lovely 4-2-2 engines were built at Derby Works.

They were divided into five distinct classes: (1) with 7 ft 4 in. driving-wheels, 18 in. by 26 in. cylinders and 160 lb. boiler pressure; (2) with 7 ft 6 in. driving-wheels, 18½ in. by 26 in. cylinders and 160 lb. boiler pressure; (3) with 7 ft 6 in. driving-wheels, 19 in. by 26 in. cylinders and 160 lb. boiler pressure; (4) with 19 in. by 26 in. cylinders, 7 ft 9 in. driving-wheels, and 170 lb. boiler pressure (the Spinners), and (5) with 19½ in. by 26 in. cylinders, 7 ft 9 in. driving-wheels and 180 lb. pressure.

There were 18 engines of the first class, 42 of the second, 10 of the third, 15 of the fourth and 10 of the fifth; the last two classes had piston valves instead of the usual flat valves. My drawing shows one of the second class which was the most numerous and, therefore, the most commonly seen.

The first four classes were very much alike to look at; the fifth, which was the truly grand Princess of Wales class was much larger than its predecessors. Strictly from the point of view of good looks, however, my personal preference was for the fourth class, the notorious Spinners, so called because they were holy terrors for slipping, being noticeably worse than all the others in this respect. No 118 of this class is now a BTC museum piece.

But the engines of the second class were also favourites of mine; this was partly due to No 1855 having been at the head of the first Midland train I ever rode in, and also because I knew that her sister, No 1853, had won the Grand Prix at the Paris Exhibition in 1889, a fact which, for some reason or other, I found tremendously impressive.

Neat, trim, sleek, racy are adjectives that these engines deserved in full measure, though the noble dignity of my prime favourites, the GWR Dean 4-2-2s, was lacking. The gracefulness and undeniable elegance of the Midland singles, however, were hard to beat, and were a tribute to that eye for locomotive beauty that made Samuel Johnson famous, even if he *did* mix up styles.

As was usual about 50 years ago, these engines were kept in spotless condition. The sumptuous coaches that made up the best Midland trains at that

GENERAL SPECIFICATION

CYLINDERS			TUBES		
Diameter	...	... 18½ in.	Number	...	242 & 2
Stroke	...	... 26 in.	Diameter	...	1⅝ & 1½ in.
BOILER					
Length, between			HEATING SURFACE		
tubeplates		10 ft 7½ in.	Tubes	...	1,123.6 sq. ft
Maximum dia-			Firebox	...	117 sq. ft
meter	...	4 ft 2 in.	Total	...	1,240.6 sq. ft
FIREBOX LENGTH					
Inside	...	5 ft 11 in.	GRATE AREA		
Outside	...	6 ft 6 in.	Square feet	...	19.68

SAMUEL JOHNSON'S
7 ft. 6 in. Singles

time were also beautifully clean; moreover, these trains were of strikingly uniform aspect from one end to the other, and the sight of one headed by a single-wheeler produced an effect that few other trains could match.

The engine and train were uniformly painted that somewhat elusive shade of crimson lake known as " Midland Red " and the result was extraordinarily pleasing, especially in bright sunlight.

Engine No 1855 and her sisters were capable of running at very high speed when they had opportunities of doing it. There were no expresses actually booked at an average speed of 60 m.p.h. in those days, but it was by no means unknown for these engines to run the 99¼ miles from London (St Pancras) to Leicester, or vice versa, in anything between 100 and 105 minutes, in good weather, with trains of up to 180 tons.

Unfortunately, I had no actual experiences of this kind on the Midland at that time; my trips were confined to semi-local trains to such places as Radlett,

St Albans, or Bedford. But singlewheelers were often on these turns and usually ran well between stops.

I remember an evening non-stop train from St Albans to St Pancras that was allowed 29 min. for

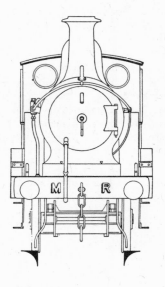

the 20 miles and gave a singlewheeler some scope for showing what she could do, especially between Elstree and Cricklewood, a stretch over which the average speed was often as high as 70 m.p.h., though the maximum did not as a rule exceed 75 m.p.h.

The Midland Railway's faith in its singlewheelers was extraordinary, if not unique. But the engines must have justified it, for they were in constant use on the main line until 1925, and were then gradually withdrawn until the last one was taken out of service in 1928.

It is interesting to recall, however, that the main reason why Johnson decided in 1887 to make the singlewheeler his principal express passenger engine was the invention of the steam sanding gear by a Derby engineer, F. Holt. This apparatus, by blowing a stream of sand right into the line of contact between the driving-wheel and the rail, enabled a single-wheeler to obtain a better grip on the rail when starting from rest.

Incidentally, the first engine ever to be fitted with this device was Caledonian Railway No 123 (see page 132); but in her case it was operated by compressed air and not by steam.

The dimensions of No 1855 and her 41 sisters were: cylinders, 18½ in. dia., 26 in. stroke; diameters of wheels were, bogie, 3 ft 6 in., driving, 7 ft 6 in., and trailing, 4 ft 2½ in. The wheelbase was 21 ft 10½ in. divided into 6 ft plus 7 ft 1½ in. plus 8 ft 9 in., while the overhang was 2 ft 3 in. at the leading end and 3 ft 8 in. at the back.

The boiler was a very good one; it was made in three rings, the diameter of the largest of which was 4 ft 2 in. The barrel contained 242 tubes of 1⅝ in. dia., and two of 1½ in. dia., the heating surface of which amounted to 1,123.6 sq. ft; to this the firebox added 117 sq. ft, so that the total heating surface was 1,240.6 sq. ft. The grate area was 19.68 sq. ft.

There were three safety-valves, two of the Salter spring-balanced type being mounted on the dome, and a single direct-loaded valve placed on the top of the firebox and enclosed in a very shapely cover of brightly polished brass.

The Salters were set to blow off at the normal pressure of 160 p.s.i., while the firebox valve came into operation if the pressure should happen to reach 162 p.s.i. I often saw all three valves working merrily, showing that those Johnson boilers could make

plenty of steam; and it usually happened just before the driver was given " Right Away " from a station platform.

The tender had 4 ft 2 in. wheels on a wheelbase of 13 ft equally divided; its overhangs were 4 ft at the front and 3 ft 6 in. at the back.

It is interesting to recall that 93 of the Johnson 4-2-2 engines survived to become the property of the London Midland and Scottish Railway in 1923, and therefore were among the last singlewheelers, including one or two on the Cheshire Lines, a few on the North Eastern and the ex-Caledonian No 123, to work on British railways after the grouping.

During the next five years, the majority were used for piloting express passenger trains on the London-Derby-Manchester and the Derby-Bristol routes. I do not think that any of them ever worked north of Derby to Carlisle, as the gradients on that line were too severe for them.

I must mention that in the war period 1914 to 1918 it was not unusual to see some of these normally swift locomotives piloting heavy goods trains and coal trains from Toton to Cricklewood sidings, a job for which they were obviously unsuited.

INS. 12 0 1 2 3 4 5 6 7 8 9 10   20 FEET.

GENERAL SPECIFICATION			
CYLINDERS		**TUBES**	
Diameter	19½ in.	Number	228
Stroke	26 in.	Diameter	1⅝ in.
BOILER			
Length between		**HEATING SURFACE**	
tubeplates	10 ft 10½ in.	Tubes... ...	1,070 sq. ft.
Maximum		Firebox ...	147 sq. ft.
diameter ...	4 ft 4⅛ in.	Total	1,217 sq. ft.
FIREBOX LENGTH			
Inside... ...	7 ft 3 in.	**GRATE AREA**	
Outside ...	8 ft 0 in.	Square feet	24.5

THE MIDLAND'S LAST SINGLEWHEELERS

In the last ten years of the nineteenth century there was a marked revival of interest in the inside-cylindered 4-2-2 type of express passenger engine, the first normal examples of which had been built by Beyer, Peacock and Co. for the Great Northern Railway of Ireland, in 1885. Two years later, S. W. Johnson brought out the first and smallest of his 4-2-2 engines on the Midland Railway, while the celebrated Caledonian No 123 went into service in the same year.

Except on the Midland, no more were built until William Dean brought out the first of his Achilles class, eventually to number no fewer than 80, on the Great Western Railway, in 1894. Four years later came a class of ten by James Holden for the Great Eastern Railway, followed in 1900 by Harry Pollitt's ten for the London extension of the Great Central Railway and, finally, 12 by H. A. Ivatt for the Great Northern Railway in 1901. After that, no more for any British railway.

Meanwhile, in 1900, Johnson on the Midland had brought out ten which were not only the last, but the finest of his singlewheelers, at least so far as their looks were concerned. They were larger than any of his previous engines of this type which, since 1887, he had progressively enlarged and multiplied until he had no fewer than 95 in service. I feel that

he might have built another five, just to complete the century! The ten built in 1900 were numbered 22, 23 and 2601 to 2608; I wish that I could add that their work was as good as their looks, but it was no better, if as good, as that of any of their earlier sisters. Perhaps we expected too much of them in view of

their large size, and although in August 1900, Mr Johnson published some interesting particulars of the work done by No 2602 between London and Nottingham during a five-day trial, it was soon apparent that the earlier and smaller engines were easily capable of doing exactly similar work. It is possible that in increasing certain dimensions, Mr Johnson

spoiled some hitherto quite satisfactory ratios and proportions, to the detriment of the engines' capabilities.

However, this must not be taken to imply that these fine engines were failures; far from it, for they did good work for some 20 years. But there was an indefinable something about them that was not all that it might have been. In the early 1920s, they could often be seen laid aside at their sheds, out of use unless there was some pressing need for engines. And they were among the earliest of Johnson's singlewheelers to be withdrawn for scrapping, while their earlier and smaller contemporaries were still busily at work, in numbers, on main line duties.

No 2601 was named *Princess of Wales*, the second of only two Midland engines to be named in Johnson's time, the other being a slender looking racer of a 4-4-0 named *Beatrice*, No 1757. No 2601 was exhibited at the Paris Exhibition in 1900; and in connection with this, Johnson brought out quite an elaborate brochure containing a complete description of the engine, four fine photographs and a beautifully-executed diagram. The engine won the Grand Prix.

For their time, the dimensions of these ten engines were generous; the cylinders were 19½ in. dia., 26 in. stroke and fitted with 8 in. piston valves. The ports were 17¾ in. long and 1⅜ in. wide; the valves

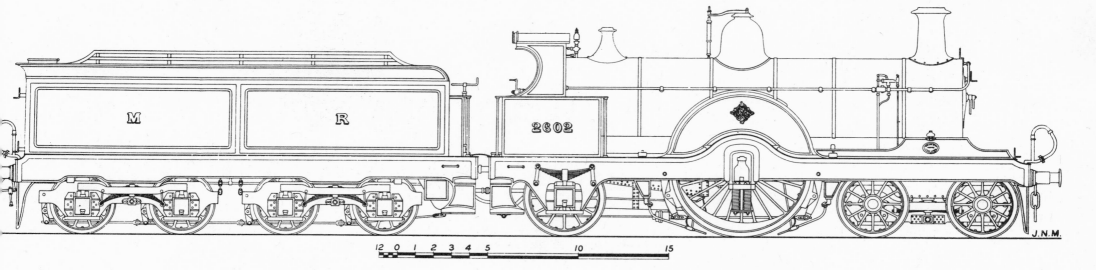

had a lap of $1\frac{1}{8}$ in. and were set to give $\frac{1}{8}$ in. lead in full gear, while their maximum travel was $3\frac{7}{8}$ in. The valve gear was a perfectly normal Stephenson link motion with direct drive, the steam chests being slightly inclined to permit of this.

Wheel diameters were: bogie, 3 ft 10 in.; driving, 7 ft $9\frac{1}{2}$ in.; trailing, 4 ft $4\frac{1}{2}$ in., and tender, 3 ft $6\frac{1}{2}$ in. All tyres were 3 in. thick on tread, made of cast steel, shrunk on to the wheel centres and studded by a hexagon stud inserted between each pair of spokes. The driving wheels were provided with long, crescent-shaped balance weights cast integral with the centres.

The engine wheelbase was 22 ft $11\frac{1}{2}$ in. divided into 6 ft plus 7 ft $2\frac{1}{2}$ in. plus 9 ft 9 in. Overhang was 2 ft $6\frac{1}{2}$ in. at the front and 4 ft 1 in. at the back.

A fairly good boiler was provided; it was made of steel plate $\frac{9}{16}$ in. thick, in two rings, 4 ft 3 in. and 4 ft $4\frac{1}{8}$ in. outside diameter, respectively. It was pitched 8 ft 1 in. above rail level. There were 228 copper tubes of $1\frac{5}{8}$ in. dia. The dome, on which two Salter spring-balance safety-valves were mounted, was set exactly on the vertical centre-line through the driving axle. A lock-up valve, adjusted to blow at a pound or two more than the normal working pressure, was enclosed in the handsome brass casing on the firebox. I have shown the original form of smokebox, the diameter of which, 4 ft 7 in., was flush

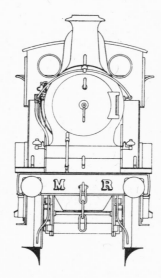

with the boiler cleading; it was much neater than R. M. Deeley's drumhead type with which nearly all Johnson and Kirtley engines were subsequently fitted.

The firebox casing was 8 ft long and the inner shell was 7 ft $3\frac{5}{8}$ in. long and 3 ft $4\frac{1}{4}$ in. wide; the grate area was 24.5 sq. ft. The heating surface of the

firebox was 147 sq. ft, and of the tubes 1,070 sq. ft, making a total of 1,217 sq. ft. This figure is surprisingly small and may be a pointer to what was wrong with these engines.

The tender was a big novelty for the Midland, in more ways than one; its capacity was for 4,000 gallons of water and $5\frac{1}{2}$ tons of coal. It was a veritable watercart carried on two four-wheeled bogies; its wheelbase was 16 ft 9 in. divided into 5 ft 6 in. plus 5 ft 9 in. plus 5 ft 6 in., while the leading overhang was 5 ft and the trailing 3 ft 8 in. Fully loaded, it weighed 50 tons 12 cwt 1 qr, and was, therefore, heavier than the engine.

In working order, the engine weight was 50 tons 3 cwt divided into 16 tons 17 cwt on the bogie, 18 tons 10 cwt on the driving axle and 14 tons 16 cwt on the trailing axle, making the total weight of engine and tender 101 tons 2 cwt 1 qr.

A contemporary journal remarked: "The engines of this class are finished in the usual splendid standard always adopted by the Midland, and *Princess of Wales*, the exhibition engine, looks a perfect picture."

I can add that she was kept in that beautiful condition for some years after the exhibition, standing out even against the scrupulously clean engines of her time; those were the days when engines were kept really *clean*.

GENERAL SPECIFICATION

CYLINDERS		
Diameter	19 in. inside, 21 in.	
	outside	
Stroke	...	... 26 in.

BOILER		
Length between		
tubeplates ...	11 ft 11 in.	
Maximum		
diameter ...	4 ft 9⅛ in.	

FIREBOX LENGTH		
Inside...	...	8 ft 5¾ in.
Outside	...	9 ft 0 in.

TUBES	
Number	Not available
Diameter	Not available

HEATING SURFACE		
Tubes...	...	1,320 sq. ft.
Firebox	...	153 sq. ft.
Total ...	...	1,473 sq. ft.

GRATE AREA		
Square feet	...	... 28.4

MIDLAND RAILWAY
4-4-0 COMPOUNDS

THE compound locomotive, in which the steam is used twice before being discharged into the atmosphere, was never widely adopted in Britain. Among several reasons for this apparent neglect of a very attractive form of motive power, the chief was that coal was plentiful and comparatively cheap, and so there was no paramount necessity for any rigorous economy in its use.

Nevertheless, a number of British locomotive engineers experimented with compounding for its own sake, but only one—Richard M. Deeley of the Midland Railway—can be said to have achieved an outstanding success with it, though he had an excellent foundation on which to work, in five very fine three-cylinder 4-4-0 compound engines built at Derby in 1902-3 to the designs of S. W. Johnson.

These five engines were based on the principle adopted by W. M. Smith of the North Eastern Railway, who, under Wilson Worsdell, had converted a two-cylinder engine, No 1619, into a very successful three-cylinder compound with one high-pressure cylinder inside and two low-pressure cylinders outside. Johnson's inside cylinder was provided with a piston valve underneath, and the two outside cylinders had vertical slide valves. The diameter of the inside cylinder was 19 in., and of the outside cylinders 21 in., the stroke of all three being 26 in.; the boiler pressure was 195 p.s.i.

While the outside cranks were set at 90 deg., with the left-hand one leading, the inside crank was set at 135 deg. to each of the other two, all on the leading coupled axle, which had six eccentrics for three sets of Stephenson link motion. The high-pressure and low-pressure cut-off controls were independent. there was no receiver between the high-pressure and low-pressure cylinders, the high-pressure exhaust passing directly into a large steamchest common to the two low-pressure cylinders.

The engine could be worked as a simple, a semi-compound, or a compound, according to requirements. Simple working was usually applied at starting, boiler steam at full pressure being admitted to the high-pressure steamchest directly, and to the low-pressure steamchest through a reducing valve controlled by a spring-loaded regulating valve which could be adjusted by the driver to vary the pressure in the low-pressure steamchest. The reducing valve was so designed that when the maximum pressure permitted in the low-pressure steamchest was attained, boiler steam was shut off automatically. Non-return valves ensured that steam could pass into either end of the high-pressure cylinder.

If, in starting, the high-pressure piston valve was in a position that closed its ports, the non-return valve lifted to allow steam to pass to either end of the high-pressure cylinder; if the ports were open, the non-return valve was kept shut by the pressure in the cylinder exceeding that in the low-pressure steamchest. The engine would start with 160 lb. pressure in the low-pressure steamchest and a slight differential pressure in the high-pressure cylinder.

In 1905, Deeley simplified and modified this some-what complicated arrangement by designing a special regulator valve through which the changes from simple to semi-compound, or compound working could be effected, according to the driver's manipulation of the regulator handle. He also abandoned the dual reversing gear and used only one for varying the cut-offs in the high-pressure and low-pressure cylinders; his scheme was ingenious, but the drivers took some time to get used to it.

The boiler pressure was increased to 200 p.s.i. and the regulator was provided with an additional

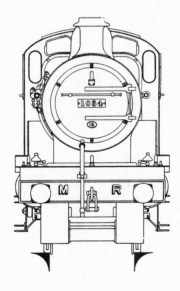

chamber and port from which a pipe gave direct connection to the low-pressure steamchest. The cylinder arrangement, with its non-return valves, was the same as before, except for minor alterations in some of the details. In starting, the regulator handle was pushed over to an angle of about 20 deg. to open the additional port, allowing boiler steam to pass direct to the low-pressure steamchest. At the same time, the pilot valve opened a small port through which steam flowed to the high-pressure steam-chest, and the engine worked as a simple.

After the lapse of the few moments required to get the train well started, the driver pushed the regulator handle further over; this closed the auxiliary port and opened the main port, causing the engine to work as a compound. Semi-compound working could be brought into use only when the engine was running. For this, the regulator handle was placed in the starting position; but owing to the speed, there was a big drop of pressure in the pipe connecting the auxiliary port to the low-pressure steamchest, and the engine worked as a semi-compound, useful in climbing a heavy gradient. But there must have been times when differential h.p. and l.p. cut-offs would have been an advantage.

Deeley built 40 of these grand engines and rebuilt the Johnson compounds to make them similar to his own, in all respects. They were excellent workers, very popular with their drivers, and could indulge in some very high speed when they had the opportunity. Their long, sleek outline, with the beautiful proportions of all its visible details, was suggestive of nothing but the racehorse; and I have endeavoured to capture something of this effect in my drawing, basing it on a photograph I took of No 1034 at Kentish Town in August 1920 when she was still in her original condition.

She had one high-pressure cylinder 19 in. dia., and two low-pressure ones 21 in. dia.; the common stroke was 26 in. There were three sets of Stephenson link motion, one for each valve. The boiler was in two rings, 4 ft 7⅞ in. and 4 ft 9⅛ in. in diameter; the barrel was 11 ft 11 in. long, with its centre-line 8 ft 6 in. above rail level. Particulars of tubing of the original non-superheated boilers are not to be had, but the tube heating surface was 1,320 sq. ft. The firebox shell was 9 ft long, the inner box was 8 ft 5¾ in. at the grate, and the heating surface was 153 sq. ft, making the total 1,473 sq. ft. Grate area was 28.4 sq. ft and working pressure 220 p.s.i. after 1908.

In diameter the bogie wheels were 3 ft 6½ in. and the coupled ones 7 ft. The wheelbase was 6 ft 6 in. plus 8 ft 3 in., plus 9 ft 6 in., a total of 24 ft 3 in.

With a wheelbase for the tender of 13 ft 9 in., equally divided, the total wheelbase, engine and tender, was 48 ft 3¼ in.; while the total length over the buffers was 57 ft 7½ in.

When in working order, the engine weighed 59 tons 18 cwt, of which 20 tons 16 cwt rested on the bogie. The tender, loaded with 3,500 gallons of water and 7 tons of coal, weighed 45 tons 18 cwt 2 qr, making the total weight 105 tons 16 cwt 2 qr.

In 1914 Deeley introduced superheating, adding it to the earlier engines and including it in further batches. Longer smokeboxes were fitted, and the boiler tubing was 148 tubes of 1¾ in. dia. and 21 of 5 in. dia., their heating surface being 1,169 sq. ft and that of the firebox 147.3 sq. ft. The pressure was reduced to 200 p.s.i. and the cylinder diameters were increased, at first, to 19¾ in. and 21¾ in., but were soon altered back to the original figures.

In 1924, Sir Henry Fowler began the construction of further batches for the LMSR until, in 1927, the total number reached no fewer than 240. In the later engines, the driving wheels were reduced to 6 ft 9 in., and the boiler length to 11 ft 9½ in. Shorter and deeper tenders with 13 ft wheelbase were also introduced, making the total wheelbase 47 ft 1½ in.

The first of the class, No 1000, has been beautifully restored and preserved by the BTC.

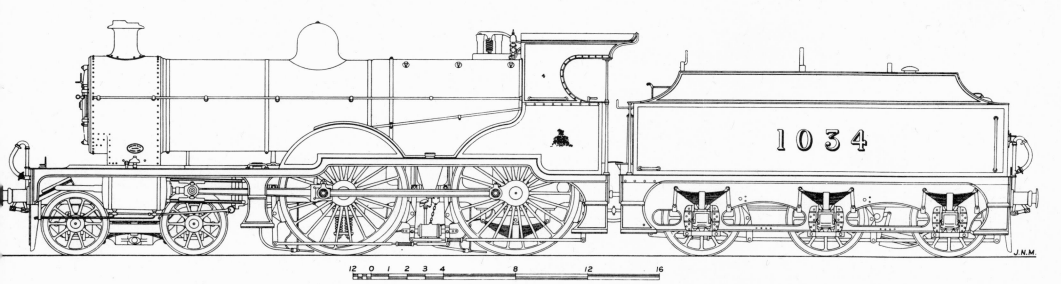

GENERAL SPECIFICATION

CYLINDERS				TUBES			
Diameter	...	...	17 in.	Number	...	...	244
Stroke	...	...	24 in.	Diameter	...	...	1⅝ in.

BOILER

				HEATING SURFACE			
Length, between							
tubeplates			10 ft 6 in.	Tubes	...		1,141 sq. ft
Maximum dia-				Firebox	...		110 sq. ft
meter	...		4 ft 2 in.	Total	...		1,251 sq. ft

FIREBOX LENGTH

				GRATE AREA			
Inside	...		4 ft 11 in.				
Outside	...		5 ft 6 in.	Square feet		...	16.1

KIRTLEY TANKS

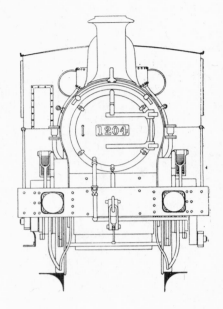

T HESE very attractive engines were designed by Matthew Kirtley and built in 1869-70 for London suburban traffic on the old Midland Railway. The last survivors were broken up in 1935, so the average age of the engines when the class became extinct was not far short of 55 years.

During all that time, the general appearance remained remarkably little altered. The cab, such as it was, was the most conspicuous addition, compared with the original design and was put on by S. W. Johnson when he reboilered the engines in the 1880s. From 1907 on, R. M. Deeley modified the smokebox door and changed the chimney to one of his own standard design. Except for minor details such as lampirons, vacuum brake fittings and so on, the engines remained virtually unchanged.

I came to know them during the last 20 years of their existence and they fascinated me by their quaint appearance, their suggestion of fussiness and efficiency and their unquestionable liveliness, in spite of their old age. My drawing depicts No 1204, *circa* 1920, when some of these engines could still be seen working suburban passenger trains to and from St Pancras, though the majority had, by then, been relegated to local parcels trains and empty coach duties. In their original condition, they were fitted with condensers for condensing the exhaust steam when working trains over the underground lines between Kentish Town and Moorgate. At one time,

they worked semi-fast and stopping trains between St Pancras and St Albans, and even as far as Bedford, taking turns with the later Johnson 0-4-4 tanks.

I recall that, in later years at least one of them went to the London, Tilbury and Southend Railway, for working the Upminster-Romford branch; but I understand that sometimes the engine could be seen working stopping trains between London (Fenchurch Street) and Upminster! I myself saw one, one day, leave St Pancras on a train for Southend.

An engine of this class could often be seen on a parcels train at Victoria, South Eastern and Chatham Railway; there was a regular service of such trains from the Midland line to Victoria, in those days. And I even remember seeing one on a goods train, going in a westerly direction through Hammersmith station, District Railway, probably on the way to Chiswick, or Gunnersbury, while an engine of this class, shunting in the Kensington High Street goods yard was by no means unusual. But it was out on the Midland main line that these engines were most entertaining, when seen on local passenger trains passing such places as Hendon, or Mill Hill. At speed, they were quite amusing to watch, and although

they put up some really good speeds, they never gave the impression that they were being forced to it.

In their last years, several of them took turns at station pilot duties at St Pancras and became a sort of " permanent institution " there. From 1915 until 1935, I frequently visited that station and always found one or more of these engines fussing about with vans and coaches being shunted from one platform to another. To me, the place has never been the same since these engines were withdrawn.

The leading particulars of these engines were: cylinders 17 in. by 24 in.; coupled wheels, 5 ft 2½ in.; bogie wheels, 3 ft 0½ in.; wheelbase, 8 ft, plus 9 ft 10½ in., plus 5 ft; overhang 4 ft 11¾ in. front, 1 ft 6½ in. at the back; the front bufferbeam was of oak, 8 ft 10 in. by 1 ft 4½ in. by 6 in., with its front face covered by a ½ in. flitchplate; the rear bufferbeam was of steel, 8 ft 4½ in. by 1 ft 2 in. by 1 in. The footplating was 8 ft 8 in. wide at the back, but just ahead of the cab panel it narrowed to 7 ft 9 in. and remained thus right to the front, where it butted up to the back of

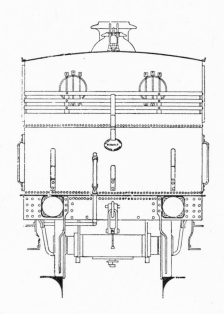

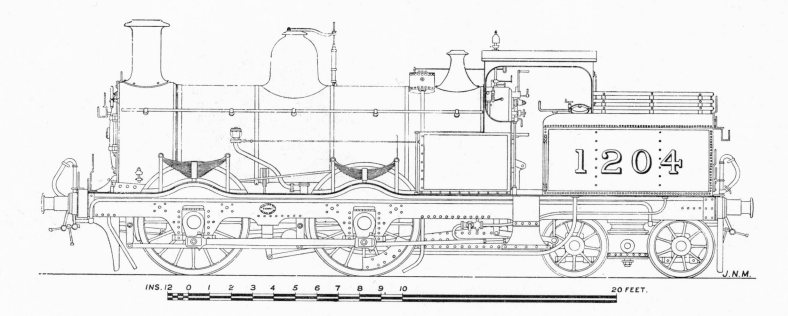

the bufferbeam. The boiler centre-line was 6 ft 10½ in. above rail level; the diameter outside the clothing plates was 4 ft 8 in. The height from rail to the top of the chimney was 12 ft 1 in.

I should add that the first six of these engines were built by Beyer Peacock and Co., of Manchester; they were followed by 20 more by Dübs and Co., of Glasgow. There were slight differences of detail between the two batches; on the Beyer Peacock engines, the bunkers had straight sides and back, from top to bottom, as seen in the drawing; but on the Dübs engines the bunkers were provided with a flared coping on the sides and back.

Another very noticeable difference was that Beyer Peacock provided coupling rods with adjustable brass, at each end, held by gib and cotter, whereas the Dübs engines had plain, circular, bushed ends of much simpler design.

During the time that these engines normally worked in the London area, the condensing gear was retained. Later, some of them were transferred to provincial areas and had the condensers removed. In their last years, some of these " provincials " came back to the London area, but the condensing gear was not restored, owing to the engines being put to empty-coach and shunting duties that did not take them into the Metropolitan tunnels.

CALEDONIAN ROYAL TRAIN PILOT

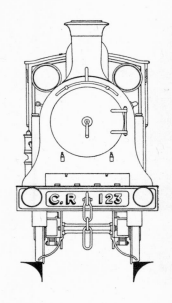

THIS was, and happily, still is, an interesting locomotive with a worldwide renown which, until March, 1958, always appeared to be a little exaggerated. But she has now more than vindicated her claim to fame and is an honoured member of the British Transport Commission's collection of locomotive relics, preserved, let us hope, for all time.

She was built in the extraordinarily short time of 66 days by Neilson & Co., of Glasgow, to the order of the Caledonian Railway, for display at the Edinburgh Exhibition in 1886. Manifestly, her design was by Dugald Drummond, but one wonders what he had in mind in designing such an engine, or how he was able to obtain its approval by the directors. Possibly, the idea was to introduce a 4-2-2 type to supersede the aged and obsolescent Conner 2-2-2s on the main line; but it did not materialise, and Drummond subsequently reboilered some of the Conner engines to keep them in service for a few years longer.

Incidentally, No 123 was the first locomotive to be fitted with F. Holt's power-operated sanding gear; but in her case it worked by compressed air instead of steam.

In 1887 No 123 was actually bought by the Caledonian Railway, but for what reason has never been very clear; there was never a great deal of work that she could do on that line, yet she became known all over the world, chiefly for the part she played in

GENERAL SPECIFICATION				
CYLINDERS			**TUBES**	
Diameter	... ... 18 in.		Number 196	
Stroke	... ... 26 in.		Diameter ... ... $1\frac{3}{4}$ in.	
BOILER				
Length, between			**HEATING SURFACE**	
tubeplates	10 ft 7 in.		Tubes ... 973 sq. ft	
Maximum diameter	... 4 ft 4 in.		Firebox ... 112 sq. ft	
			Total ... 1,085 sq. ft	
FIREBOX LENGTH				
Inside	... 4 ft 11$\frac{5}{8}$ in.		**GRATE AREA**	
Outside	... 5 ft 5$\frac{7}{8}$ in.		Square feet ... 17.4	

the great "races" to Scotland in 1888. By running some of the racing trains from Carlisle to Edinburgh, 100 miles, in times that varied from 101 to 105 minutes, she became famous; but that was the only spectacular work she ever did.

For many years after the races her normal duties were the running of the West Coast Postal trains between Glasgow and Carlisle, and vice versa, and she was nearly always given the job of Royal Train Pilot when Queen Victoria travelled to or from Balmoral. In the early 1900s the engine was semi-retired and was relegated to working directors'

specials, inspection trains, and the like; but in May 1930, wonderful to relate, No 123, by then renumbered 14010 in the LMS list, was reinstated in active service!

For about four years she worked express trains between Perth and Dundee, and did it with considerable credit, although the trains were normally light ones. In this way, she worked up her mileage before being finally withdrawn; also, she won further distinction in being the last singlewheeled express passenger engine to run regularly in Britain.

In 1935, soon after her withdrawal, No 123 was restored as far as possible to her original condition and repainted in the old Caledonian colours for permanent preservation. Her present boiler dates from 1924 and is quite different from her original one; it is not even derived from D. Drummond, but we must be content to have her thus rather than not at all.

I made my first acquaintance with her at Carlisle about 35 years ago when she was on one of her " inspection " trips, and I was glad to meet an engine about which I had read and heard so much.

In July 1953, this engine came to London, as an exhibit in the fascinating Royal Journey exhibition at Battersea; it was the first time she had ever come south of Carlisle, and, of course, I paid her a visit. In spite of her odd boiler, she looked quite nice, painted in what purports to be the original Caledonian livery.

Her original tender has been restored to her, which I must say is rather remarkable, in view of the fact that it was replaced by a standard Caledonian tender in 1888 and, so I understand, remained out of use until recently.

In March, 1958, No 123 was brought out of her retirement to run some enthusiasts' excursions, and is likely to continue at this for some years to come.

The chief dimensions of this fine engine were as follow: wheel diameters, bogie, 3 ft 6 in., driving, 7 ft, trailing 4 ft 6 in.; the wheelbase was 21 ft 1 in., divided into 6 ft 6 in. plus 6 ft 7 in. plus 8 ft; the overhang at the front was 2 ft 1 in., and at the back 3 ft 6 in. The boiler was pitched 7 ft 6 in. above rail level; its barrel was made in two rings, the larger of which was 4 ft 4 in. dia.; the length between tube-plates was 10 ft 7 in. There were 196 tubes of $1\frac{3}{4}$ in. external dia.

The water capacity of the tender was 2,850 gallons, and there was space for about 5 tons of coal. The total length of engine and tender over buffers was 52 ft 3 in.

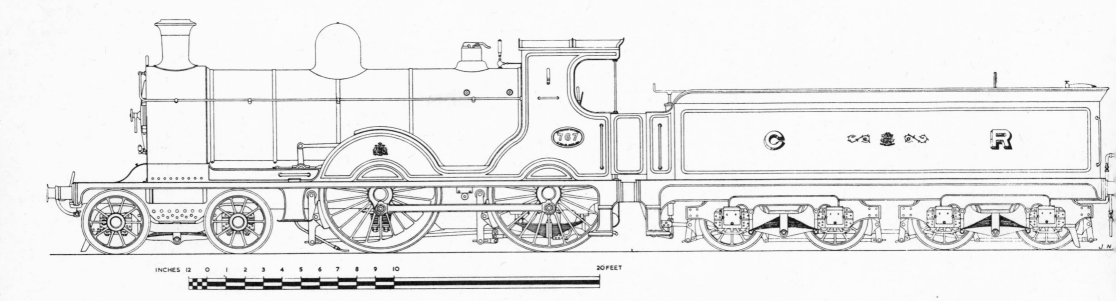

In *Locomotives I Have Known* I dealt with the Caledonian Railway's famous singlewheeler No 123; but that engine did not represent any Caledonian standard type, and was certainly not typical of the company's locomotive policy.

However, No 767, was a horse of a very different colour, so to speak; she certainly was representative of a standard type and typical of her designer's policy. My own direct acquaintance with No 767 was made on the same occasion as when I first met the singlewheeler No 123, though I had already familiarised myself with the history of Caledonian locomotive development.

No 767 was one of a class of 15 fine 4-4-0 engines designed by J. F. McIntosh, six of them built in 1897 and nine in 1898. They were known as the Dunalastair 2nd class, since the first one, No 766, was named Dunalastair 2nd, because the design was a direct development of the famous Dunalastair class of 1896, a class which I regard as a successful mixture of the ideas of John Lambie and J. F. McIntosh, whereas 767 and her sisters were pure McIntosh.

The Caledonian's main line from Carlisle to Glasgow is not unduly difficult with regard to gradients, except for the formidable Beattock Bank,

a 10-mile climb at an average of 1 in 80, which down trains from Carlisle have to surmount. Obviously, the engines for working the heavy Anglo-Scottish trains over this line had to possess a fair reserve of power, and to this end, McIntosh produced four

successive classes of 4-4-0 engines in progressive development between 1896 and 1904.

He was a pioneer in the big boiler idea; but, unlike some other experimenters in this direction, he seems to have understood that a big boiler is of little use

CALEDONIAN RLWY No 767

GENERAL SPECIFICATION

CYLINDERS				TUBES			
Diameter	...	...	19 in.	Number	...	...	—
Stroke	...	...	26 in.	Diameter	...	...	—
BOILER							
Length between				HEATING SURFACE			
tubeplates	...		11 ft 0 in.	Tubes...	...	1,381.22 sq. ft.	
Maximum				Firebox	...	118.78 sq. ft.	
diameter	...		4 ft 9¼ in.	Total ...	...	1,500 sq. ft.	
FIREBOX LENGTH							
Inside	...		—	GRATE AREA			
Outside	...		—	Square feet	...	...	20.63

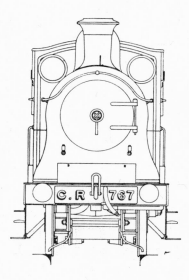

unless its proportions are right. From the start, his boilers were well proportioned and, for that reason, his engines were eminently successful.

To me, No 767 was a most impressive engine, with her massiveness combined with neat, simple lines and a most attractive style of painting. That I was not alone in thinking this way is clear from the fact that certain officials of the Belgian State Railways were so taken with the trim exterior as well as the fine work of these engines, that they ordered a number, built by Neilsons of Glasgow, for service in Belgium.

I sometimes think that this transaction may have

been, at least in part, a reaction against the design of the then latest engines in Belgium, which were probably among the most repulsive looking loco-motives ever built!

The Caledonian engines had cylinders 19 in. dia. × 26 in. stroke; coupled wheels 6 ft 6 in. and bogie wheels 3 ft 6 in. dia.; wheelbase 23 ft 1 in. divided into 6 ft 6 in. plus 7 ft 7 in. plus 9 ft. The tender wheelbase was 5 ft 6 in. plus 5 ft 9 in. plus 5 ft 6 in., totalling 16 ft 9 in. while the total wheelbase of engine and tender was 49 ft 2½ in.

The diameter of the boiler was 4 ft 9¼ in. outside the larger ring; the barrel was 11 ft long and pitched 7 ft 9 in. from the rails. The heating surface was 1,500 sq. ft being 1,381.22 sq. ft for the tubes and 118.78 for the firebox; the grate area was 20.63 sq. ft. The capacity of the tender was for 4,125 gallons of water and 4½ tons of coal. In working order, the engine weighed 49 tons and the tender 49 tons 10 cwt, a rare case of the tender being heavier than the engine. The weight on the four coupled wheels was 32 tons 14 cwt, and the tractive force, calculated at 85 per cent. of the 175 lb. boiler pressure, amounted to 17,900 lb.

For the period, the dimensions were outstanding and so thoroughly up-to-date that the entire class became the property of the LMSR in 1923. Four of the class were rebuilt in the early 1930s, but the other engines remained unaltered. The last survivor of this class was withdrawn for scrap in October 1947.

Two intriguing details, which were characteristic of all Caledonian mainline engines, may be men-tioned; the first was the deep-toned hooter that did duty for the usual whistle of other lines; the second

was the long, single link attached to the leading draw-hook. When working trains, this link was carried turned upwards and leaning slightly backwards, against the front footplating. I have been told this link business was quite a ritual, and no Caledonian driver would have started his train unless that link had been properly upturned.

There is sometimes quite a lot of argument as to what was the true colour of Caledonian blue; officially, it was described as Prussian blue, though there was a tendency, in later years, to lighten this colour by mixing it with white. The lining consisted of black striping with a white line on each edge. Foot-plate edging, footsteps and the outside frames of the tender were crimson lake, bordered in black, with a white line between the lake and the black. The tender axleboxes and springs were black and the tyres of all wheels were also black with a white line all round the inner edge. In the middle of the back of the tender the engine's number appeared in gilt figures, 5 in. high, and shaded in red picked out in white.

These fine locomotives marked the beginning of a long period of steady and progressive development in Caledonian express passenger locomotive design. For they were fairly quickly followed by two suc-cessive enlargements of this very handsome design before McIntosh finally decided to abandon the 4-coupled type in favour of the 4-6-0 type which culminated in the famous "Cardean" class. But the Dunalastairs also set a fashion that is usually referred to as the cult of the big boiler, which was rapidly taken up by other locomotive designers and served as a sort of stop-gap policy until superheating was introduced.

I T was 1920 before I made acquaintance with the old Lancashire and Yorkshire Railway, and it was during a number of visits to Manchester that the acquaintance was made and developed. Previously, my knowledge of the line had been gained from railway journals and talking about the line and its engines, and I had picked up a fair amount of book knowledge about it; so I was able to identify, at a glance, any of its several classes of locomotives and many other features.

In 1899, the L & YR produced the first examples of what was, in most respects, its most outstanding and, for Britain, unique design—the famous Aspinall Atlantics, colloquially known as " Highfliers " and unique because they were the only British 4-4-2 tender engines with inside cylinders. The first one I saw was No 718, depicted in my drawing, and I was immediately impressed by the large size of the coupled wheels, the neat, simple outlines and, above all, what seemed to me to be the unusual height of the engine.

To my mind, the engine's appearance was the complete embodiment of the story published many years before to the effect that No 1392 of this class on a Liverpool-Southport express on 15 July 1899 passed the seventeenth milepost from the start in 12¾ minutes; this means an average speed of 80 m.p.h., and the engine is reported to have reached a maximum speed of 100 m.p.h., but there has never been any conclusive proof that she did so. All the same, the maximum must have been uncommonly high, in the circumstances.

There were 40 of these engines, 20 built in 1899, and another 20 in 1902. At the time they were the largest express passenger engines in Britain, and they quickly established a reputation for high speed. The earlier examples originally had the cab-side cutaway brought down to the level of the top of the handrail on the tender side; but the men soon complained of the draught, not to mention the grave risk of falling out if the engine rolled at speed ! So the cutaway was altered to the shape seen in my drawing.

It is a fact, however, that these engines tended to roll badly when travelling fast, and it was blamed on to the swing-link bogie and inside trailing bearings originally fitted. After the bogie had been altered to

ASPINALL ATLANTICS

the Adams type with transverse slide controlled by powerful side springs, and the trailing wheels fitted with outside instead of inside bearings, the engines were much steadier.

And mention of springs reminds me that the L & YR engines, generally, were fitted with double laminated springs of an unusual type, each being virtually two ordinary leaf-springs one above the other, the upper one being upside down. Their length was only 2 ft 4 in., but the camber was more than usual and the springs were amply resilient. For the trailing wheels, however, a single spring of ordinary type and 3 ft 3 in. long was used.

For the period, the dimensions of these engines were decidedly " big "; the cylinders were 19 in. dia. by 26 in. stroke; the wheel diameters were: bogie 3 ft 0⅞ in., coupled 7 ft 3 in., and trailing 3 ft 7⅝ in.; the throw of the coupling rods was only 10 in.; the wheelbase was 5 ft 6 in. plus 7 ft 5½ in. plus 7 ft 6 in. plus 7 ft 3½ in., totalling 27 ft 9 in.; the overhang was

GENERAL SPECIFICATION

CYLINDERS				TUBES			
Diameter	...	...	19 in.	Number	...	...	239
Stroke	...	...	26 in.	Diameter	...	...	2 in.
BOILER							
Length, between				HEATING SURFACE			
tubeplates	...	15 ft		Tubes	...	...	1,877 sq. ft
Maximum dia-				Firebox	...	...	175.8 sq. ft
meter	...	4 ft 9 in.		Total	...	...	2,052.8 sq. ft
FIREBOX LENGTH							
Inside	...	7 ft 5⅝ in.		GRATE AREA			
Outside	...	8 ft 1 in.		Square feet	...	...	26.05

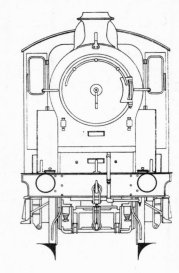

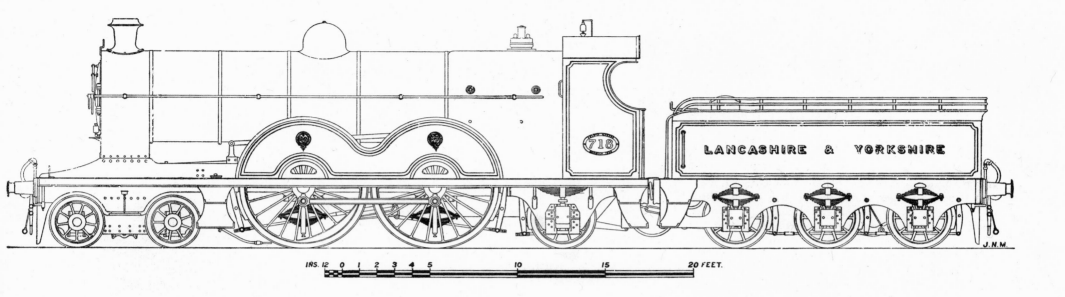

2 ft 1¼ in. at the front and 4 ft 10½ in. at the back.

The boiler was of considerable interest; its diameter was 4 ft 9 in. (5 ft 4⅜ in. outside the lagging plates) and its length was 15 ft between tubeplates, the front one of which was recessed 3 ft 9¾ in. behind the centre line of the chimney to provide a very deep smokebox internally. The Belpaire firebox had a narrow grate 7 ft long, and the grate area was 26.05 sq. ft. The working pressure was 180 p.s.i. There were 239 tubes of 2 in. diameter, the heating surface of which was 1,877 sq. ft, to which the firebox added 175.8 sq. ft, making the total 2,052.8 sq. ft. The pitch of the boiler was 8 ft 11 in., and the engine weighed 58.75 tons, the adhesion weight being 35 tons.

The later history of these engines did not involve any rebuilding, or other alterations, except in one respect; the majority were deprived of their original chimneys which were replaced new ones of shorter and fatter type similar to those used for George Hughes' 4-6-0 engines. This chimney looked very well on the engines for which it was designed, but utterly ruined the appearance of the Atlantics. It is strange how seldom that modifications like this ever came off with complete success.

It is interesting to note the reason why the original inside bearings for the trailing axle were replaced by outside ones. It was *not* because the inside bearings were too close to the fire. The inside bearings of

coupled trailing wheels were always much closer to the fire, and gave no greater trouble on that account. If we stop to think a moment, how many French, Belgian, German, or other Continental 4-4-2, 4-6-2 or 4-8-2 engines had outside bearings to the trailing wheels ? But in matters of this kind, our Continental contemporaries have always seemed more logical than we have ever been !

These very distinctive L & YR engines had all been withdrawn from service by 1934; and that was mainly because, eleven years before, the LMSR decided not to adopt them as a standard type. The last survivor was No 711, renumbered 10316 in the LMSR list, withdrawn in February, 1934.

133

THE 'KLONDYKES'

THIS engine is of more than usual interest, and for a number of reasons. It was Britain's first 4-4-2, or Atlantic-type engine; it was a perfectly logical development of the celebrated 8 ft singles which, when No 990 was built, were still the principal main-line express passenger engines on the Great Northern Railway.

The true Atlantic-type locomotive is one which has the 4-4-2 wheel arrangement, outside cylinders, and a boiler with a wide firebox. In this connection, No 990 did not possess a wide firebox; in fact the only British Atlantics which, in later years, embodied all the features just mentioned were H. A. Ivatt's later 4-4-2s for the Great Northern Railway and D. E. Marsh's for the London Brighton and South Coast.

It follows, therefore, that no other British 4-4-2 type engines were strictly " Atlantics "; yet the type

had quite a vogue during the first 10 years of this century, and GNR No 990 was the first of them all. She was built in 1898 and caused quite a sensation when she was put into traffic, since she was so unlike anything seen before on British railways.

I made my first acquaintance with her in 1903, by which time she had been named *Henry Oakley*, after the then chairman of the GNR company, and was the only named engine on the line until 1922. She had proved her worth five years before to such purpose that by 1903 no fewer than 22 engines of the class had been built; in fact, the last few came out simultaneously with the first examples of Mr Ivatt's

big-boilered 4-4-2s, very similar to the 990s but with very much larger boilers.

As was to be expected, 990's dimensions were exceptional for the period; her cylinders were 18¾ in. dia. by 24 in. stroke, and they were slightly inclined downwards towards the back. They drove the second pair of coupled wheels by connecting rods which were no less than 10 ft long. The port widths were 1½ in. for admission and 3½ in. for exhaust, the common length being 16 in. The maximum valve travel was 4½ in. The bogie and trailing wheels were 3 ft 7½ in. dia., and the coupled wheels 6 ft 7½ in. dia. The wheelbase was 6 ft 3 in. plus 5 ft 3 in. plus 6 ft 10 in. plus 8 ft, while the frame overhang was 2 ft 5 in. at the front and 4 ft 3¾ in. at the back.

The boiler possessed some unusual features: it was pitched 7 ft 11 in. above rail level; the barrel was made in three rings, the first and third of which were 4 ft 8 in. dia., the middle one being 4 ft 6⅞ in. dia., and the total length was 14 ft 8⅝ in. The distance between the tubeplates, however, was only 13 ft, due to the front tubeplate being recessed into the barrel

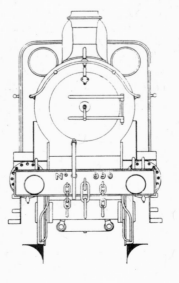

GENERAL SPECIFICATION			
CYLINDERS		**TUBES**	
Diameter ... ... 18¾ in.		Number 191	
Stroke ... ... 24 in.		Diameter ... ... 2 in.	
BOILER			
Length, between		**HEATING SURFACE**	
tubeplates ... 13 ft		Tubes ... 1,302 sq. ft	
Maximum dia-		Firebox ... 140 sq. ft	
meter ... 4 ft 8 in.		Total ... 1,442 sq. ft	
FIREBOX LENGTH			
Inside ... 7 ft 4 in.		**GRATE AREA**	
Outside ... ... 8 ft		Square feet ... 24.5	

1 ft 11¼ in., so as to provide a backwards extension to the smokebox. The grate was 7 ft 4 in. long and 3 ft 4¼ in. wide, giving an area of 24½ sq. ft; 191 tubes of 2 in. outside dia. provided 1,302 sq. ft of heating surface to which the firebox added 140 sq. ft, making the total no less than 1,442 sq. ft. The working pressure was 175 p.s.i.

It is worth mentioning that the bogie was of the swing-link type and had the main pin set 1½ in. to the rear of the true centre, so as to provide differential sideplay to the two axles. Such bogies have not been very commonly used by British locomotive engineers; when they have been used, it has been because of their comparative simplicity. The majority of British engineers, however, have preferred bogies of the Adams sliding type with spring-controlled slides, which make for a steadier running engine when entering or leaving a curve.

In working order, No 990 weighed 58 tons, of which the bogie carried 15 tons, the leading coupled wheels 15 tons, the driving wheels 16 tons and the trailing wheels 12 tons. The tender, loaded with 5 tons of coal and 3,670 gallons of water, weighed 40 tons 18 cwt, making the grand total 98 tons 18 cwt.

Another interesting point is that No 990 reverted to having the regulator placed in the dome and operated by a two-handled upright lever in the cab. This was a great change from the Stirling arrangement of having the regulator placed in the smokebox and operated by a pull-push lever in the cab, which had been standard GNR practice for more than 20 years.

I would add that in the subsequent engines of this class, the frames were slightly modified to provide for the fitting of a much larger boiler; but the boilers were never altered in these particular engines, except for being provided with superheaters. The proposed big boilers, however, appeared on an entirely new class of GNR Atlantics which first appeared in 1903.

It is interesting to recall that, in 1909, No 988 of this class was fitted with a Schmidt superheater, to become the first superheated locomotive possessed by the GNR. For this purpose, an extended smokebox was fitted and the boiler tubing was considerably modified. There were 104 small tubes of 2 in. dia. and 18 large tubes of 5¼ in. dia. for housing the superheater elements. The heating surface of the small tubes became 706.5 sq. ft, and of the large tubes 321 sq. ft; the firebox heating surface was

reduced to 135.5 sq. ft, making the total evaporative surface only 1,163 sq. ft, compared with the original 1,442 sq. ft. At the same time, the boiler pressure was reduced to 160 p.s.i., as was customary for superheated engines in those days, and new cylinders, 20 in. dia. by 24 in. stroke and provided with 8 in. piston valves, were fitted.

No 988 was given an extended trial, during which she was painted dark grey with white numbering and lettering She was so successful that all the other engines in the class were similarly superheated; but the boiler pressure became 170 p.s.i., and the standard GNR livery was restored.

During the time when these engines were being built, the famous gold rush to the Klondyke Valley in the Yukon was in full swing. As a consequence, the " 990 " class Atlantics of the GNR were nick-named " Klondykes " and remained known as such until the end of their days. The class became extinct in 1940, except for No 990, *Henry Oakley*, which is preserved in York Museum; she was brought out, with No 251, in September, 1948, to run the " Plant Centenarian " special train from Kings Cross to Doncaster, in connection with the works' centenary.

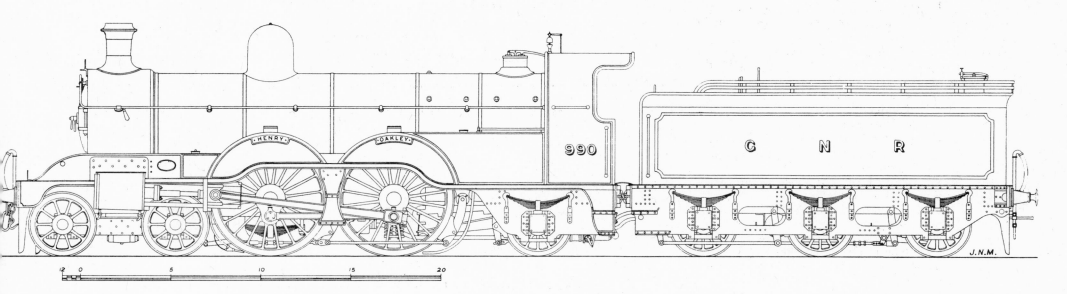

I suppose that locomotive enthusiasts all over the world must have known, or at least heard of, the famous GNR large-boilered Atlantics.

The design was by Mr H. A. Ivatt, and the first example, No 251, was put into traffic in January 1903; she was a true Atlantic in that she combined the 4-4-2 wheel arrangement with outside cylinders and a boiler with a wide firebox.

There is reason to believe that Ivatt, when designing his small-boilered 990 class, had in mind the large-boilered version because, as I mentioned in the previous chapter, the frames of the later 990s were so designed that a larger boiler could be fitted. However that may be, the change was never made on those engines, and the apparent hesitation may possibly have been due to the fact that for some years the 990s would persist in showing themselves to be the better engines ! Yet, construction of the larger-boilered engines continued, and the class eventually numbered 93.

It was at about this time that Ivatt made his well-known statement that the power of a locomotive depended upon its ability to boil water.

This is probably one of the most unfortunate statements ever made by an eminent locomotive engineer. I am not denying its accuracy, but it is unfortunate in so far as it has been misinterpreted by professional and amateur locomotive men ever since. It does *not* mean that the boiler should be the largest that can possibly be accommodated within the limits of the loading gauge !

If any proof of my statement is needed it can be found in the locomotives that Ivatt himself designed for the Great Northern Railway; only on his large Atlantics did he provide anything remotely approaching an outsize in boilers, yet *none* of his boilers failed to produce the required amount of steam at any time. In size, they were perfectly normal, but their *proportions* were always adequate.

In the first few months of 1903 No 251 was kept under constant observation and was subjected to a certain amount of experiment, the smokebox arrangements coming under special surveillance.

At one period during her " probation " she was fitted temporarily with a stovepipe chimney, which did not enhance her appearance, but in due course, everything was put right, and between 1904 and 1908 a further 80 engines of the class were built. They took over the working of all the best and heaviest expresses on the old Great Northern and became firm favourites with the drivers and public alike.

I remember seeing No 1442 when she was on show at the Imperial International Exhibition, White City, London, in 1909, She stood side by side with the old Stirling 8-ft single-wheeler No 1, and a most

interesting pair they made, typifying, between them, nearly 30 years of GNR locomotive development.

No 1442 was then one of the latest of her class and had done very little work before being sent to the exhibition. For years afterwards she was looked upon as being something rather special and was distinguished from all other GNR locomotives by having the company's coat of arms on her driving splashers. She was also always used for working Royal trains on the GNR and had tyres and axle-ends polished.

Up to that time Ivatt had not adopted superheating; he was not against it, but he was not convinced that the lubrication troubles that accompanied it had been overcome.

However, in 1910, he relented and ordered ten new Atlantics, Nos 1452 to 1461, generally similar to their forerunners but fitted with Schmidt superheaters, following tests with that apparatus on No 988, one of the small-boilered Atlantics.

I am fairly certain that it was Ivatt's chief assistant, Nigel Gresley, who was primarily responsible for the

LARGE BOILERED ATLANTICS

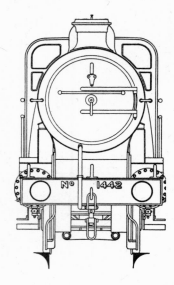

GENERAL SPECIFICATION					
CYLINDERS			**TUBES**		
Diameter	...	20 in.	Number	...	161 & 24
Stroke	...	24 in.	Diameter	...	2¼ & 5¼ in.
BOILER					
Length, between			**HEATING SURFACE**		
tubeplates	15 ft	6⅜ in.	Tubes	...	2,454 sq. ft
Maximum dia-			Firebox	...	143 sq. ft
meter	5 ft	6 in.	Total	...	2,597 sq. ft
FIREBOX LENGTH					
Inside	...	5 ft 2 in.	**GRATE AREA**		
Outside	...	5 ft 11 in.	Square feet	...	31

decision to superheat these engines; at any rate in 1911, when Gresley succeeded Ivatt as chief mechanical engineer, he began to introduce some important detail improvements, which had the effect of placing all these engines among the very best in the world.

Some of their performances with such trains as the Yorkshire Pullman and the Queen of Scots—even the Silver Jubilee on one occasion—must rank for ever among the very finest exploits ever recorded with steam locomotives. Be it noted, too, that these extraordinary performances were achieved during the last years of these engines.

These statements of mine may seem exaggerated, but I claim that they are fully vindicated by just one almost incredible and duly authenticated effort by Atlantic No 4404 one day in 1936 on the down afternoon Scotsman. She was on pilot duties at Grantham on that particular day, when the Scotsman, comprising 17 very crowded coaches and weighing at least 585 tons, arrived. It was headed by a Pacific which was suffering badly from a hot bearing and had to come off the train.

No 4404 was substituted, and after an uncanny and almost superhuman effort at persuasion on the part of Driver Walker, of Gateshead, that huge train

was got under way. Then, believe it or not, she ran the 82¾ miles to York, in 87½ minutes—2½ minutes *less* than the scheduled 90 minutes—and during the run covered a distance of 60 miles at an *average* speed of 64 m.p.h.

This effort was all the more remarkable because the engine was in a run-down condition and by no means ready for such a venture, but the performance is typical of the spirit of these redoubtable engines and their equally redoubtable drivers.

I have been told that one of the signalmen at Selby was so astonished at the sight of 4404 and those 17 coaches passing his box, that he rang up Grantham locomotive depot saying: " She passed here two minutes before we expected her, and is going well." I think that speaks for itself.

My drawing shows 1442 in the altered condition, typical of the class after 1911. In this form the dimensions were: bogie and trailing wheels diameter 3 ft 8 in.; driving and coupled wheels diameter, according to the official drawings and specification, 6 ft 8 in. dia.

This dimension may be nominal because the distance between the driving and coupled centre lines is given on the drawings as 6 ft 10 in., which would not leave enough room for the normal 1¼ in. depth

of the flanges. I think the wheel diameter is more likely to have been 6 ft 7½ in. and the flange depth 1⅛ in., or perhaps 1 3/16 in., similar to the 990 class engines otherwise the flanges would have touched each other.

The wheelbase was 26 ft 4¼ in. divided into 6 ft 3 in. plus 5 ft 3¼ in. plus 6 ft 10 in. plus 8 ft.

The boiler was made in two rings, the back one of which was 5 ft 6 in. dia. inside. The length of the barrel was 15 ft 6⅜ in. and the pitch was 8 ft 8¾ in. above rail level. Outside, the firebox casing was 5 ft 11 in. long and 6 ft 9 in. wide, while its depth at the front was 5 ft 0½ in. The grate area was 31 sq. ft.

There were 161 tubes of 2¼ in. dia. and 24 superheater flues of 5¼ in. dia., their respective heating surfaces being 1,884 and 570 sq. ft, while the firebox added 143 sq. ft to make a total of 2,597 sq. ft. The working pressure was 170 p.s.i.

In working order the engine weighed 69 tons 8 cwt, the bogie carrying 18 tons 12 cwt, the four coupled wheels 36 tons equally distributed and the trailing wheels 14 tons 16 cwt.

The pioneer engine of this outstanding class, No 251, is preserved at York, along with No 990, *Henry Oakley*, the first of the small-boilered Atlantics; they make a very attractive pair.

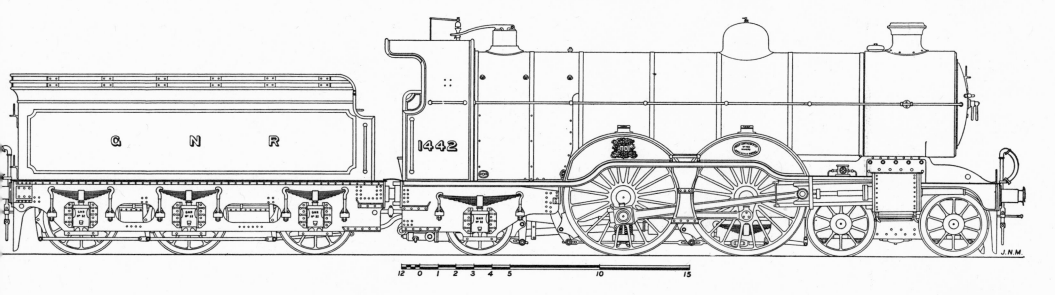

I HAVE mentioned before that the Board of Trade, in control of railways before the Ministry of Transport and Civil Aviation took over, had a rooted dislike of the 0-4-4 tank locomotive; but, in spite of official censure, many railways employed large numbers of such engines, in most cases without trouble. Officialdom tried to make out that the type was unstable when running; in practice, there was little reason for that idea.

Nothing daunted Patrick Stirling in this matter; that deliberate, forthright, level-headed Scotsman would not tolerate interference, official or otherwise, from any quarter whatever. He liked 0-4-4 tank engines, and nobody was going to stop him from using them. Only a major disaster would have caused him to change his mind. He built more than one class of 0-4-4 tanks, and never was one involved in any kind of mishap for which this type of engine could be blamed.

Like most others, Stirling's engines were steady, efficient and reliable. Many were employed on the London suburban services between Moorgate Street or Kings Cross and Hatfield, Barnet and Hertford, at one time, and I can just remember them when they were on these duties. Others were to be found on the old Great Northern Railway, working local trains in every important district between London, Lincoln and York.

Stirling's first examples of the 0-4-4 side tank type of engine were built in 1881; they were a development of the 0-4-4 well-tank engines, 68 of which had been built in 1872 and 1877. The 1881 engines, of which there were 16, were of similar dimensions to their predecessors, but had side-tanks and—a startling innovation—covered-in cabs instead of scanty bent-over weatherboards; they were officially designated class O. In 1889, came the R class, similar to the O class but of slightly larger size.

The 25 Rs that were built included No 767, the subject of my drawing. In 1895, four more were built, as class R2. They had much shorter side-tanks, the water capacity being made up by the addition of a well-tank under the bunker, a feature that seemed to be a return to 1872. But Stirling was inclined to do things like that.

<table>
<tr><td colspan="4" align="center">GENERAL SPECIFICATION</td></tr>
<tr><td>CYLINDERS</td><td></td><td colspan="2">TUBES</td></tr>
<tr><td>Diameter ... ...</td><td>18 in.</td><td>Number ... ...</td><td>174</td></tr>
<tr><td>Stroke ... ...</td><td>26 in.</td><td>Diameter ... ...</td><td>1¾ in.</td></tr>
<tr><td>BOILER</td><td></td><td></td><td></td></tr>
<tr><td>Length, between</td><td></td><td colspan="2">HEATING SURFACE</td></tr>
<tr><td>tubeplates</td><td>10 ft 1 in.</td><td>Tubes ...</td><td>830 sq. ft</td></tr>
<tr><td>Maximum dia-</td><td></td><td>Firebox ...</td><td>92.4 sq. ft</td></tr>
<tr><td>meter ...</td><td>4 ft 2½ in.</td><td>Total ...</td><td>922.4 sq. ft</td></tr>
<tr><td>FIREBOX LENGTH</td><td></td><td></td><td></td></tr>
<tr><td>Inside ... ...</td><td>5 ft</td><td colspan="2">GRATE AREA</td></tr>
<tr><td>Outside ...</td><td>5 ft 6 in.</td><td>Square feet ...</td><td>16.25</td></tr>
</table>

PATRICK STIRLING'S 0-4-4 TANKS

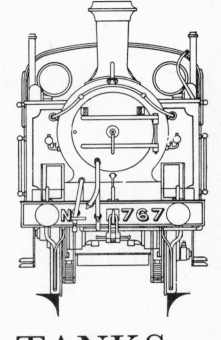

When I came to know these GNR 0-4-4 tank engines, their reign as the principal type for working the suburban services from Kings Cross had ended long before. H. A. Ivatt had begun to supersede them, in 1898, with his 4-4-2 tank engines, and by 1908 the old Stirling engines that remained in the London area were on secondary duties, such as working empty coaching stock between Kings Cross and the Finsbury Park sidings, or running purely local milk and parcels trains in the London district. This kept a number of R class engines occupied until 1914, when the first world war put me out of touch with GNR matters for some years.

In 1919, I found that two of the old R class engines, 767 and 931, were still to be seen at Kings Cross station. They were still in their original condition, except that they were painted dark grey and lined, lettered and numbered in white. They were engaged on station pilot duties.

Just about that time, I discovered a third engine of this class, No 770; but she had been rebuilt with an Ivatt domed boiler. She was stationed at Kings Cross running sheds, where she seemed to be used as shed pilot. As a rebuild she was not quite so interesting as her two sisters at the station. The only occasion on which I saw her away from shed duties was one day when she was working a milk train at Clapham Junction LSWR Windsor line platform. In H. A. Ivatt's time the classification of this class was altered to G1, and in 1923, 12 of the engines, out of the original 16, became LNER class G1.

The dimensions, when in the condition depicted in my drawing of No 767, were: cylinder diameter 18 in., stroke 26 in. and inclination 1 in 8¾ in. The diameters of the wheels were: coupled, 5 ft 7½ in., bogie, 3 ft. The wheelbase was 22 ft 6 in. divided

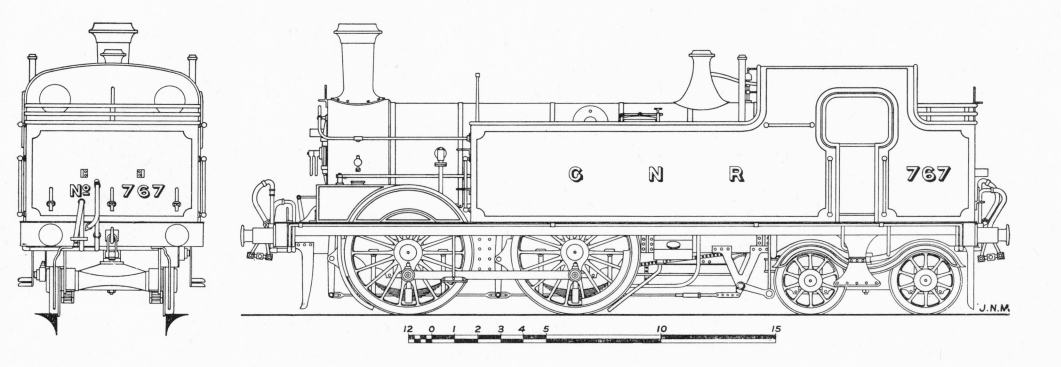

into 7 ft 3 in. plus 10 ft 3 in. plus 5 ft, and the overhangs were 5 ft 3 in. at the front and 1 ft 9 in. at the back. The upper part of the bogie wheels was covered by a neat curved splasher, or mudguard, fixed to the bogie frame and decorated with a simple, flat brass beading, 1½ in. wide, following the top curve continuously. The driving-wheel splashers were fitted with a flat brass semicircular beading 2 in. wide. The top surface of the running plate was 4 ft 2¼ in. above rail level.

The boiler was made in three rings, the outside diameter of the smallest being 4 ft 0½ in. The length of the barrel was 10 ft 1 in. and of the firebox 5 ft 6 in. outside; there were 174 tubes of 1¾ in. dia., their heating surface being 830 sq. ft, to which the firebox added 92.4 sq. ft, making the total 922.4 sq. ft.

This boiler, like most of Stirling's design, seemed small; but it was an excellent steamer, quite adequate for the job, and was used successfully on more than one class of engine, without alterations. The grate

area was 16.25 sq. ft and the working pressure was 160 p.s.i. The tank capacity was 1,000 gallons. In working order, the weight totalled 53 tons 9 cwt, divided into 17 tons 7 cwt 2 qr on the leading axle, 17 tons 16 cwt on the driving axle and 18 tons 5 cwt 2 qr on the bogie.

The drawing depicts No 767 in the condition she was in July 1919, when she was painted grey and lined with a single white line. At that time, No 931 was in exactly the same condition, except that she carried the full condensing apparatus, with cast iron connecting pipes between the smokebox and the tanks, and she had a plain Stirling chimney slightly shorter than the one on No 767.

At the end of 1919, both engines disappeared from Kings Cross; but after about two months, they came back to their former duties and a wonderful thing had happened; they had both been repainted in the full GNR livery of bright emerald green, with dark green bordering, black striping double-lined in white,

gilt initials and numbers shaded in black and red picked out in white, and with the valances and footsteps painted a dark maroon edged with a vermilion line. A further and most intriguing detail was that, in the process of recovering all their pre-war glory, they had exchanged chimneys. At first, I thought that their boilers and smokeboxes had been switched from one engine to the other; but this could not have been, because No 767's smokebox showed no sign of ever having been fitted with condenser pipes, whereas No 931 still retained her full condensing apparatus.

All this, coming when it did, when the long fore-shadowed grouping of the railways was but a matter of months ahead, struck me as being a happy conclusion to the careers of these two interesting old engines. They were the last unrebuilt Stirling engines I ever saw regularly working in their original GNR colours. No 931 was scrapped in 1923, and No 767 in the following year.

F OR something like 70 years in the history of British railways, the 2-4-0 type of locomotive was extremely popular, at first for freight and general mixed traffic and later for all classes of passenger traffic, even to the fastest expresses of the period.

The type was a convenient one on which to design a compact, simple, powerful and speedy engine, and in the 1870s and 1880s several railways produced examples that became famous for the excellent work which they did. In my *Locomotives I Have Known* I have already dealt with some of the more notable of them.

Here was a class of fine 2-4-0 engines which I wish I had known better, for I have always admired them. Not only did they become celebrated for the good, not to say outstanding, work which was always got out of them, but the circumstances of their coming into existence are probably unique in locomotive history.

In 1884 Alexander McDonnell, locomotive superintendent of the North Eastern Railway, suddenly resigned. He had held the post for only about twelve months, having succeeded the redoubtable Edward Fletcher in the previous year. In that short time, McDonnell's only notable achievement was to have made himself so unpopular with the stolid Northumbrians and Yorkshiremen with whom he had to deal that his position became quite untenable.

This unfortunate situation arose just after the NER directors had publicised their intention of running certain of their expresses non-stop each way between Newcastle and Edinburgh. They had no locomotives which could be relied upon to make that 124¼-mile non-stop trip successfully!

William Henry Tennant, the NER general manager, hurriedly called together a committee of locomotive officials and instructed them to prepare a new design immediately. The result was the "Tennant" class of 2-4-0 express passenger engine, 20 of which were built in 1885. They were numbered 1463 to 1479, 1504, 1505 and 1506. Ten of them were built at Darlington and the other ten at Gateshead. In spite of all the hurry in which they were designed and built, the Tennants were outstandingly successful; they had no trouble whatever in working the Newcastle-Edinburgh non-stop trains;

GENERAL SPECIFICATION

CYLINDERS			TUBES		
Diameter	...	... 18 in.	Number	...	... 205
Stroke	...	... 24 in.	Diameter	...	... 1¾ in.
BOILER			HEATING SURFACE		
Length between			Tubes...	...	1,026 sq. ft.
tubeplates ...		10 ft 7 in.	Firebox	...	107 sq. ft.
Maximum diameter 4 ft 3 in.			Total ...	...	1,133 sq. ft.
FIREBOX LENGTH			GRATE AREA		
Inside...	...	5 ft 1⅝ in.	Square feet ...	...	17.3
Outside	...	5 ft 10 in.			

but in 1888 some of them made several record runs between York and Newcastle during the London-Edinburgh races of that year, when No 1475 seems to have been quite a star performer. On August 25, 29, 30 and 31, she is reported to have run 100-ton

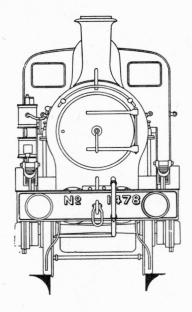

trains over the 80¼ miles from York to Newcastle in 80, 81, 82 and 78 minutes.

On the 28th of the month, No 1505 ran the entire distance of 124¼ miles from Newcastle to Edinburgh non-stop in 127 minutes, a performance which, for the period, was unequalled. In fact, the Newcastle-Edinburgh non-stop booking was the longest in the country then, and the Tennants proved that such a run gave no trouble from the locomotive point of view, provided that the engines were suitably designed.

The dimensions of the engines were: cylinders 18 in. dia., 24 in. stroke; leading wheels, 4 ft 7¼ in.; coupled wheels 7 ft 1¼ in.; wheelbase, 16 ft 8 in. divided into 8 ft and 8 ft 8 in. The overhangs were 4 ft 1 in. at the front and 4 ft 2 in. at the back. The tender wheels were 3 ft 9¼ in. dia. and the wheelbase was 12 ft 8 in. equally divided; overhang was 4 ft 2 in. at each end. The total wheelbase of engine and tender was 38 ft 7¾ in. and the total length over buffers was 49 ft 11¾ in. Water capacity was 2,651 gallons, and there was space for five tons of coal.

The boiler barrel was 10 ft 7 in. long, and the distance between tubeplates was 10 ft 11⅛ in.; the diameter was 4 ft 3 in. outside, the barrel being

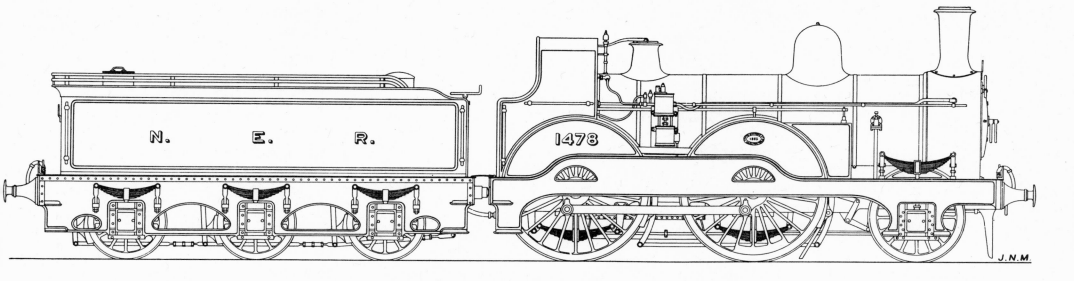

made, apparently, in one ring with a butt-strip along the bottom. The centre-line was pitched 7 ft 2½ in. above rail level.

There were 205 tubes of 1¾ in. dia. the heating surface of which was 1,026 sq. ft. The firebox casing was 5 ft 10 in. long and the inner box was 5 ft 1⅝ in. long at the grate, tapering to 5 ft 0⅜ in. at the crown; its heating surface was 107 sq. ft, making the total 1,133 sq. ft. The grate area was 17.3 sq. ft, and the working pressure 160 p.s.i.

According to the official diagram, from which all these particulars are taken, the Stephenson valve gear was designed to give a maximum valve travel of 4¼ in. and a full-gear cut-off of 60.3 per cent. The valves were flat with 1¼ in. lap and no exhaust lap or clearance. Particulars of port sizes are not given, but it is clear from the other information that the engines were deliberately designed to run fast. It is generally conceded that the design as a whole was mainly attributable to Wilson Worsdell, then a comparatively new member of the staff.

In working order, a Tennant weighed 42 tons 2 cwt, divided into 12 tons 12 cwt on the leading axle, 15 tons 14 cwt on the driving axle. The tender, full, weighed 32 tons 2 cwt, so that the total weight was 74 tons 4 cwt.

Other useful dimensions are: width over cab sides and rear splashers, 7 ft 1 in.; over the footplating, 8 ft; diameter of boiler clothing, 4 ft 7½ in.; and outside diameter of smokebox, 4 ft 11¾ in., its length being 2 ft 7⅛ in. On some of these engines, when new, the safety valves were uncased; but later the entire class acquired handsome, polished brass casings of the shape shown in the drawing. The cab roof radius was 16 ft, dropping to the sides by radii of 1 ft.

I have chosen to illustrate No 1478 simply because she was the only one of the class I ever had a run behind, so far as I am aware. One day in May 1920 when I was stationed in Birmingham, I had to go to Hull to investigate some trouble in lift machines. It was a somewhat tortuous journey; but trips of that sort did not very often come my way, and when they did they were all the more welcome because they usually involved my travelling over railway routes that were new to me. On this occasion I went from New Street, Birmingham, to Leeds via Derby by the Midland Railway, and at Leeds caught a North Eastern train to Hull via Selby.

Returning two days later, I was surprised and delighted to find that the engine from Hull to Leeds was Tennant No 1478. She certainly knew how to run. During the non-stop journey to Selby her speed

was well into the middle 70s at several places, but after that we stopped at the principal stations between Selby and Leeds and had no opportunity to indulge in high speed.

I noted that 1478's acceleration with a train of six corridor coaches was very different from what I was more used to behind Stirling 7 ft 4-4-0s on the SECR! Her work was altogether excellent and particularly pleasing because, at that period, the Tennants had long ceased to be used as main-line express engines and were chiefly employed on secondary passenger trains around York, Darlington and Newcastle. But even on this sort of work they were very good, the equal of several other and bigger locomotives with which they shared these duties.

Withdrawal of this famous class began in September 1926, the first one to go being, oddly enough, the last one to be built in 1885, No 1506. The entire class had been withdrawn by March 1929; but the pioneer engine, No 1463, withdrawn in August 1927, was saved. She was thoroughly refurbished and repainted at Darlington and then placed in the Railway Museum at York, where she can still be seen, a lasting memento of one of Britain's most celebrated locomotive classes, known and admired far outside their home territory.

RACING ENGINES

┌───┐

GENERAL SPECIFICATION

CYLINDERS				TUBES			
Diameter	...	...	20 in.	Number	...	...	201
Stroke	...	...	26 in.	Diameter	...	...	1¾ in.

BOILER				HEATING SURFACE			
Length, between tubeplates		11 ft 6 in.		Tubes	...	1,089 sq. ft
Maximum diameter	...	4 ft 4 in.		Firebox	...	127 sq. ft
				Total	...	1,216 sq. ft

FIREBOX LENGTH				GRATE AREA			
Inside	...	...	6 ft 5 in.	Square feet	...	20.75
Outside	...	...	7 ft			

└───┘

P ROBABLY the only instance of locomotives being designed and built specially for racing was to be found in the two fine 4-4-0 type engines that are the subject of these notes.

The design was prepared in 1895 and the original order was for five engines. But the anticipated "races" from London to Aberdeen, which were to have taken place in the summer of 1896, were abandoned, so the construction of three of the engines was cancelled and only two were completed.

Visually they were very striking engines, with their huge coupled wheels and general balance of proportions. I shudder to think of what some designers would have made of engines of similar dimensions! The snag, of course, was the 7 ft 7¼ in. diameter of the coupled wheels—the largest in the world, for an otherwise normal design. But Wilson Worsdell, the designer, had a really outstanding sense of proportion, and he so blended the size, position and proportion of each visible detail of the engine to produce a harmonious, beautifully-balanced effect in which no single detail overpowered any other.

As a boy I often gazed at photographs of these two engines, fascinated by every detail, but especially by those big wheels; and I longed to be able to see the actual engines, but the opportunity for that did not come until 1925.

These engines, which were given the running numbers 1869 and 1870, were built at Gateshead Works and were put into traffic early in 1896. They had cylinders 20 in. dia. by 26 in. stroke with the valve chests on top. Originally ordinary flat valves were provided and driven by the Stephenson link motion having launch-type links; the drive was indirect via rocking shafts. I believe that this arrangement was subsequently altered to direct-driven piston valves.

The boiler was made in three rings, butt-jointed and 4 ft 4 in. dia.; the length of the barrel was 11 ft 6 in. There were 201 tubes of 1¾ in. dia., providing 1,089 sq. ft of heating surface, to which the firebox added another 127 ft to make a total of 1,216 sq. ft. The grate area was 20.75 sq. ft, and the working pressure was 175 p.s.i.

The diameter of the bogie wheels was 3 ft 7¼ in.; the engine wheelbase was 23 ft 9 in. divided into 6 ft 6 in. plus 7 ft 9 in. plus 9 ft 6 in. The overhang at the leading end was 2 ft 9 in., and at the back it was 4 ft 8 in. The tender was carried on six wheels with a wheelbase of 12 ft 8 in. equally divided; the wheel diameter was 3 ft 9 in., and the overhang at each end was 4 ft 3 in. The capacity was for 3,940 gallons of water and five tons of coal.

The arrangements made for coupling the engine and tender were unusual. They consisted of a huge screw-coupling, the links of which were no less than

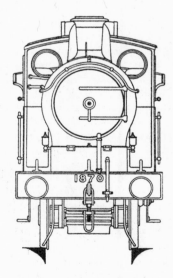

2 ft 10 in. long, and it was flanked on each side by a massive double eyebolt. This suggests the Gateshead people thought that when these engines were racing there would be more than an ordinary tendency for

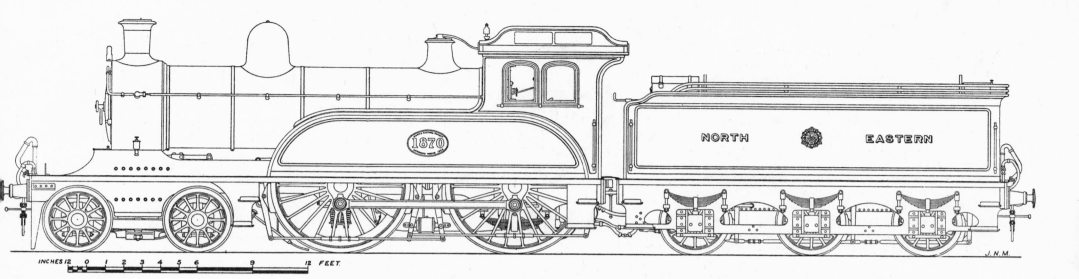

INCHES 12 0 1 2 3 4 5 6   9   12 FEET.

J.N.M.

engine and tender to come apart—and it had to be counteracted at all costs!

The cab was of the usual Worsdell pattern, but with a raised portion with ventilators mounted on the roof.

In working order the weight of the engine was 50 tons 16 cwt, while that of the tender was 41 tons 2 cwt. The adhesion weight was 34 tons 8 cwt.

These engines were painted a light green with black bands and white lines. The chimney cap, safety-valve casing and the beading on the front and side windows of the cab were polished brass, as was the 2 in. flat brass edging to the splashers. The numberplate was a brass casting, the numerals, border and lettering being in relief and polished on a black background.

The smokebox door hinges and rim, all handrails and the coupling-rods were of polished steel, but the flutes of the coupling rods were separated by a broad black band.

The frames, footsteps and valances were black edged with fine red lines. The buffer-beams were vermilion with a narrow black edging and fine white line; the front beam carried the engine's number placed as shown on my drawing, the figures being in gilt shaded in black and white. The general effect of all this was very attractive and pleasing.

In spite of there being no official races for these engines to take part in, their work was quite good on such trains as the well-known "flyers" between York and Scarborough until the loads became too much for them. They lasted until 1930, when both were withdrawn for scrap.

In 1925 I paid a visit to the Railway Centenary Exhibition at Darlington. To get there I travelled overnight by the 10.10 p.m. from Kings Cross. As sleep in a train has never been possible for me—day or night—I spent most of the journey seeing as much as I could from the carriage window . . . Then as

we were running into York station, somewhere about 2 a.m., I spied a perishable goods train, at the head of which was No 1869—my first sight of one of these engines. So, what had been a long-felt want was satisfied.

But the story isn't quite finished. For as we pulled out of the station, there—believe it or not—stood No 1870. Double satisfaction for me!

By that time, however, the original finery of these engines had been replaced by sombre black paint; even so, they succeeded in retaining much of their impressiveness. I saw both again during the next three years or so, though I was not fortunate enough to travel on either of them. It is enough that I was able to see them, and in that way to have made the acquaintance of two fine locomotives.

At one time they were popular subjects for models, and I seem to remember that there was a fine 1 in. scale example in the 1925 Railway Centenary Exhibition at Darlington.

My acquaintance with these elegant locomotives was, perhaps, somewhat slender because I was not very often on the old Great Eastern Railway in those days. It was only between 1898 and 1901 that the engines were regularly to be seen at Liverpool Street station; after that they were removed from the London area to work in the Fen districts of East Anglia, and their visits to London became very rare.

Yet I have a clear recollection of seeing some of them, and of being in trains hauled by No 12 on the outward journey and No 10 in the reverse direction, when accompanying my mother on a visit to some friends at Ingatestone some time around 1903.

There were only ten of these engines, numbered 10 to 19, all built in 1898 and put to work the best Great Eastern expresses of the day. Their chief interest was that they were the first Holden locomotives to be fitted with a bogie. All ten were originally equipped for burning oil fuel and were provided with the very characteristic Holden "oil-tank" tender. The general dimensions were really very moderate, yet the engines virtually monopolised the best main-line trains of their day; but only for two years, because in 1900 Holden introduced his splendid Claud Hamilton 4-4-0 express engines which immediately superseded the single-wheelers on the main line.

Seen in retrospect, the success of the singlewheelers was astonishing, short-lived though it was. Like their Great Western counterparts, the singlewheelers really could pull, and there are published records of their timing trains of 270 tons, or more, *tare* weight, on the Cromer Express between Liverpool Street and North Walsham. We have only to think of the Bethnal Green bank beginning almost immediately outside Liverpool Street station, and the steadily rising line, culminating in the distinctly formidable Brentwood bank before Shenfield, and we are left to wonder how these singlewheelers ever managed to work the trains they did. They must have been very well driven, but I can imagine that there were some ticklish moments sometimes.

Externally, the design was of interest in that it was such an extraordinary mixture of styles. James

GENERAL SPECIFICATION

CYLINDERS				TUBES			
Diameter	...	...	18 in.	Number	...	...	227
Stroke	...	...	26 in.	Diameter	...	...	1¾ in.
BOILER							
Length, between				HEATING SURFACE			
tubeplates		11 ft	4 in.	Tubes	...	1,178.5	sq. ft
Maximum dia-				Firebox	...	114.23	sq. ft
meter	...	4 ft	4 in.	Total	...	1,292.73	sq. ft
FIREBOX LENGTH							
Inside	...	6 ft	3⅞ in.	GRATE AREA			
Outside	...	...	7 ft	Square feet	...	...	21.3

JAMES HOLDEN'S 4-2-2s

Holden was very decidedly conservative in outlook and a strict-living man; therefore, he could hardly be regarded as a mere plagiarist.

But his No 10 class engines had scarcely an original feature; basically the design was S. W. Johnson's of the Midland Railway; there was the same framing scheme; the cab was Johnson's, very much enlarged —too much to be pleasing; the driving-wheel splasher was Johnson's, but smaller; that great sweeping curve of the footplating below the splasher was William Dean's of the Great Western, but too exaggerated; and the chimney was an almost exact copy of Dean's, even to the manner in which it was built up.

It might almost seem that Holden was hypnotised by the artistic abilities of Johnson and Dean, and strove " to do likewise "; but he missed the mark. All the same, the No 10 class possessed an elegance that was their own and just saved them from being downright ungainly ! I still possess a copy of the fine coloured plate of No 10 published as a supplement to the *Locomotive Magazine* in 1899; it shows that much of the elegance of the engine was due to the livery in which she was painted. And that particular coloured plate was the first and most accurate reproduction of the old Great Eastern colours ever made.

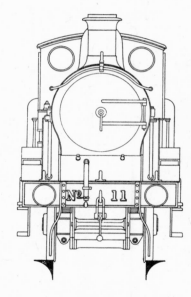

No 12, in her later years, was fitted with an extended smokebox; but the results obtained from it did not appear to justify a similar alteration being made to any others of the class. In due course also the oil-burning apparatus was removed and the engines were altered to burn coal, because the cost of the oil became prohibitive after the chemists had discovered that what had been regarded as a waste material actually

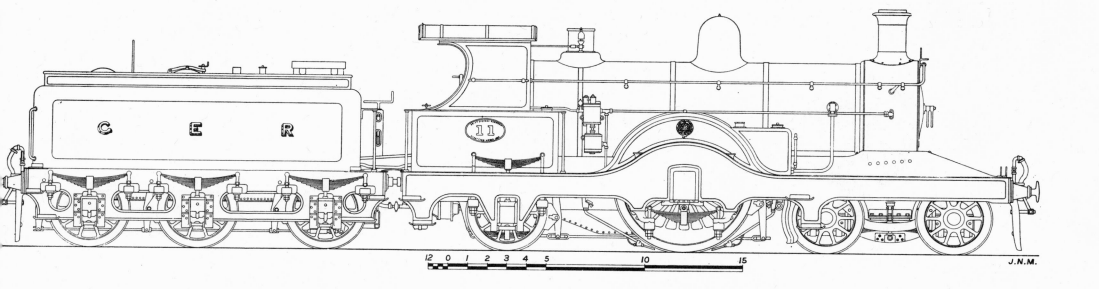

contained several valuable by-products. This led the Great Eastern Railway to abandon Holden's ingenious and successful oil-burning system for locomotives; but it meant that a fillip was given to certain other industries, especially the manufacture of aniline dyes.

Nevertheless, the Holden apparatus was tried out on one or two other railways. Although it gave satisfactory results, the cost of the fuel proved to be too much.

The GER 4-2-2 engines were officially designated Class P43. Their cylinders were 18 in. dia. by 26 in. stroke, and were inclined upwards at an angle of 1 in 14; the steamchest, which was below the cylinders, was inclined at a similar angle, but downwards, and the slide valves were directly driven by Stephenson link motion with locomotive-type links suspended in the middle. Reversing was effected by wheel-and-screw gear, though the arrangement was such that the reach-rod was drawn back for forward running.

The wheelbase was 22 ft 9 in., divided into 6 ft 6 in. plus 7 ft 3 in. plus 9 ft and the overhangs were 2 ft 9 in. at the front and 5 ft 4 in. at the back, the length of the main frames being 30 ft 10 in. The

wheel diameters were: bogie, 3 ft 9 in.; driving, 7 ft; and trailing, 4 ft.

The boiler was of two rings, 4 ft/3 in. and 4 ft 4 in. dia. respectively, and the barrel was 11 ft 4 in. long between the tubeplates; its centre line was 7 ft 9 in. above rail level. There were 227 tubes of 1¾ in. dia. The length of the firebox casing was 7 ft, and the grate area was 21.3 sq. ft, while the working pressure was 160 lb.

The heating surface was 1,292.73 sq. ft, made up of 1,178.5 sq. ft for the tubes and 114.23 sq. ft for the firebox, the latter figure being smaller than that of any other contemporary 4-2-2 engine.

The official figures for the weight of the engines in working order gave 16 tons 14 cwt 2 qr on the bogie, 18 tons on the driving axle and 15 tons 5 cwt 2 qr on the trailing axle; but there is reason to believe that the weight on the driving axle was actually more like 20 tons. Several authorities have suggested this, if only because of the fact that the engines were able to haul *unassisted* a train of 275 tons weight up the Bethnal Green bank almost immediately after starting from Liverpool Street station.

True, steam sanding gear was provided and undoubtedly played its part in making the feat possible; but the noticeable lack of any tendency to excessive slipping, in all ordinary circumstances, strongly suggested that there was more than 18 tons on those driving wheels.

When the engines were oil-fired, the tenders carried 2,790 gallons of water and 750 gallons of oil. The wheelbase was 12 ft, divided into 6 ft 6 in. and 5 ft 6 in. with an overhang of 3 ft 3 in. at each end. The weight of the tender, full, was 37 tons 1 cwt. After the abolition of oil-firing, these tenders were replaced by ordinary ones with capacity for 2,640 gallons of water and 5 tons of coal. The wheelbase and its divisions were as before, but the overhangs were 3 ft at the front and 3 ft 3 in. at the back; the weight was 30 tons 12 cwt 2 qr.

The official figure for the tractive effort of the engines, at 85 per cent of the 160 lb. boiler pressure, was 13,157 lb.; this, when worked out by the usual formula, certainly indicates an adhesion weight of no more than 18 tons—but I have already mentioned the doubt !

GREAT EASTERN RAILWAY

No I

2-4-0

MY acquaintance with this engine, and with several of her sisters, dates back to quite early childhood and summer holidays at Blakeney, Cromer and Clacton. The chief attraction, of course, was the magic " I " on the numberplate; it was the second of the No Is I eventually came to know, and they have all had the same fascination.

This particular No I belonged to a class of 40 diminutive tender engines that were originally designed by S. W. Johnson in 1867. They were built between that year and 1872, 10 of them at the G.E.R. factory at Stratford, and 30 by Sharp Stewart and Co. at Glasgow. In 1881, James Holden began the reboilering of the whole class and made certain alterations to the appearance; my drawing shows what they looked like when I knew them, from 1900.

I remember that the journey to Blakeney was long and tedious, especially for children; we had to change at Wells (Norfolk) into a train for Holt, the nearest station to Blakeney, and on the first occasion it was No I which took us over this last stage. In later years, I saw her again several times, usually in or near Norwich; but meanwhile I got to know some of her sisters, all in that part of the country.

I found that these engines, in spite of their small size, were quite popular, and they certainly seemed to do very well on passenger trains and some goods trains in the counties of Norfolk and Suffolk. Essex, also, knew some of them; but their visits to the London area were rare, at least in my time. The engines were essentially suitable for working on branch lines, some of which, on the Great Eastern Railway were quite extensive.

The principal dimensions of these most attractive little engines were: cylinders, 16 in. × 22 in.; leading wheels, 3 ft 7 in.; coupled wheels, 5 ft 7 in.; the boiler barrel was 4 ft 2 in. dia., pitched 6 ft 4½ in. above rail level; it was 9 ft 1 in. long and contained

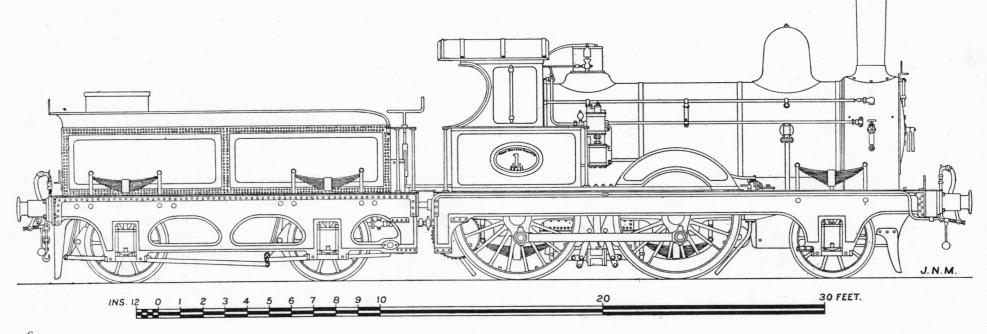

INS. 12 0 1 2 3 4 5 6 7 8 9 10   20   30 FEET.

223 tubes $1\frac{5}{8}$ in. dia.; the length of the firebox, outside, was 4 ft 10 in.; the wheelbase was 14 ft, divided into 6 ft 11 in. plus 7 ft 1 in., while the overhangs were 4 ft 2 in. at the front and 3 ft 8 in. at the back.

The delightful little tender ran on four wheels, 3 ft 8 in. dia., and axles spaced 9 ft centre to centre; its capacity was 1,184 gallons of water and $2\frac{1}{2}$ tons of coal; the overhang was 4 ft at the front and 3 ft at the back. The weight of engine and tender in working order was 49 tons 5 cwt, the engine accounting for 30 tons 15 cwt and the tender for 18 tons 10 cwt.; adhesion weight, I believe, was 21 tons.

I can recall that these little engines were remarkably speedy when they had a chance; but the branch-line trains on which they were normally employed did not give many opportunities for speeding. I am perfectly certain that, in spite of the small dimensions, an engine of this type would make an attractive and successful model for any gauge from $3\frac{1}{2}$ in. upwards, and it would have the advantage of being small enough to transport without much difficulty.

For some indefinable reason the prototype engines were most fascinating to watch when they were running. And that Westinghouse pump, as made at Stratford for all Great Eastern engines, was much more noisy than the one used on the London, Brighton and South Coast locomotives with which I was so familiar at that time. These noticeable differences always added so much interest to the study of the locomotives of various railway companies.

Incidentally, the tender, with its 445 rivets per side, would provide a nice little exercise to try the patience and skill of the modeller. I know what it was like to draw! It adds another point of interest to a fascinating class of locomotives, if only because four-wheeled tenders were but rarely provided for locomotives after about 1870, at least in England.

There is a further point about the Great Eastern example that always rather intrigued me; it is that, in the early 1900s all Great Eastern locomotives, passenger as well as freight, were painted in the beautiful ultramarine blue with black bordering and red lining. All the six-wheeled tenders carried the initials G.E.R. in gilt figures shaded in red with white highlights.

Now, the four-wheeled tenders had a raised sheet-iron bordering, about $\frac{1}{4}$ in. thick of the same type as used by S. W. Johnson on all the tenders he provided for his engines on the Midland Railway, after he had left the Great Eastern. This bordering divided the tender side into two panels and I have always marvelled that the Great Eastern authorities did not appear to think of the idea of relieving the spaces inside those panels with the letters G. and E. I am certain Johnson would have done it, as it is just what he did with the letters M. and R. on the Midland.

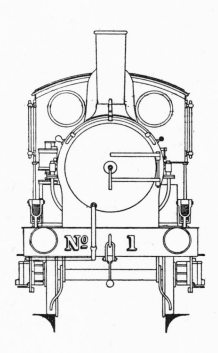

GENERAL SPECIFICATION			
CYLINDERS			**TUBES**
Diameter ... ... 16 in.			Number 223
Stroke ... ... 22 in.			Diameter ... ... $1\frac{5}{8}$ in.
BOILER			**HEATING SURFACE**
Length between tubeplates ... 9 ft 1 in.			Tubes... ... ... —
Maximum diameter 4 ft 2 in.			Firebox ... ... —
			Total ... ... —
FIREBOX LENGTH			
Inside ... ... —			**GRATE AREA**
Outside ... 4 ft 10 in.			Square feet ... ... —

HOLDEN'S T 19 Class

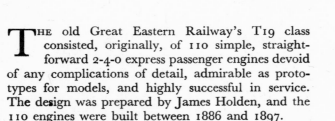

THE old Great Eastern Railway's T19 class consisted, originally, of 110 simple, straightforward 2-4-0 express passenger engines devoid of any complications of detail, admirable as prototypes for models, and highly successful in service. The design was prepared by James Holden, and the 110 engines were built between 1886 and 1897.

They were intended to supersede the 2-4-0 compound engines designed by T. W. Worsdell, which were of very similar dimensions and appearance; but Holden's engines accomplished more by being so efficient and reliable as to become the GER standard main-line type for several years. They were quite up to date and in keeping with the prevailing practice of their time; for the great majority of the top-link express passenger engines on the railways of Britain were then of 2-4-0 type, and remained so for about another ten years.

In spite, or perhaps because of, the extreme simplicity of their design, the T19 class engines were very soundly and solidly built. They gave a remark-

able impression of massiveness, and I have always understood that they were unusually light on repairs. But, in those days, the GER timetables did not call for any abnormally high speeds, and this was obviously reflected in the satisfactorily high mileages run by the engines between major overhauls.

In addition, the engines were kept clean and looked very well in their deep ultramarine blue, with black bordering and having a prominent red line, $\frac{1}{4}$ in.

wide, between the blue and the black. A peculiarity of the GER painting, however, was that the front spectacle plate of the cab, on every class of engine, was painted a plain, unlined black on the outside. I suppose the idea behind this was that the plate was liable to become smoke-stained, in any case, so it might just as well be painted black, rather than any colour, in the first place.

The principal dimensions were:— cylinders, 18 in. by 24 in.; coupled wheels, 7 ft, leading wheels, 4 ft; boiler barrel, 10 ft long by 4 ft 4 in. dia.; tubes, 254 by $1\frac{5}{8}$ in. dia.; heating surface, tubes 1,116.18 sq. ft and firebox 100.9 sq. ft, making a total of 1,217.08 sq. ft; grate area 18 sq. ft; pitch of boiler centre-line 7 ft 6 in.; height from rail level to top of chimney 12 ft 11 in.

The wheelbase was 7 ft 9 in. plus 8 ft 9 in.; the leading overhang was 5 ft and the trailing 4 ft 3 in. The tender's capacity was for 2,640 gal. of water and 3½ tons of coal; its wheelbase was 12 ft, divided into 6 ft 6 in. plus 5 ft 6 in., and the total length of engine and tender over buffers was 48 ft 2 in.

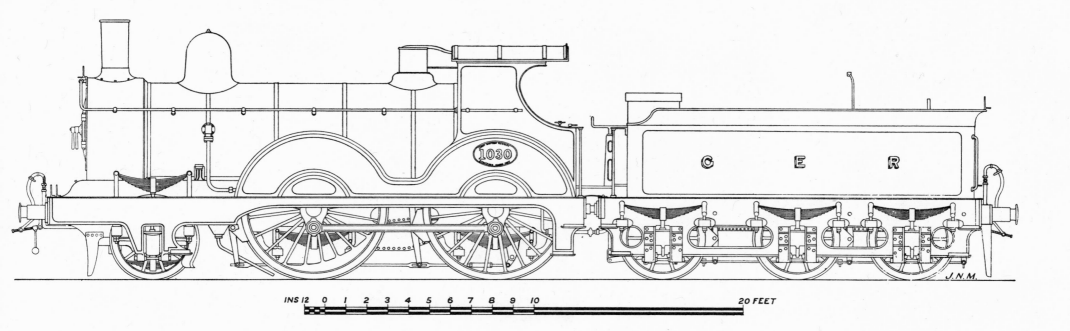

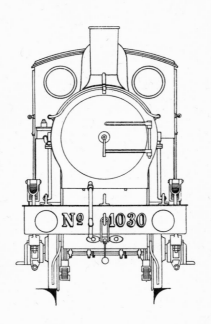

The overhang of the tender was 3 ft at the front and 3 ft 3 in. at the back. In working order, the engine weighed just over 42 tons and the tender 30 tons 12 cwt 2 qtr., totalling 72 tons 12 cwt 3 qtr.

These engines were used chiefly on the heaviest and fastest trains between London, Ipswich, Norwich, Cromer, and York and they were regarded as being most successful. GER locomotive policy, however, always strove to be right up to date and in 1903 a start was made on the rebuilding of 20 of the T19 class by fitting a larger type of boiler having a Belpaire firebox.

The pitch of the boiler was raised to 8 ft 6 in.; a new type of cab with a single window in each side replaced the earlier one and the dome—which now became a somewhat squat, slightly flattened protuberance on the boiler barrel—was placed well forward, as before. This resulted in a rather humped-up appearance which earned for the engines the nick-name " Humpty-dumpties."

Ten years later, a rather more extensive rebuilding

was put in hand; for this, the " Humpty-dumpty " cab and boiler were used, except that the dome was placed about midway along the barrel. At the same time, the main frames were lengthened at the front end to accommodate a leading bogie. Sixty of the engines were transformed in this manner and were set to working secondary main-line traffic, though they were sometimes employed for piloting top-link express trains.

Fifty-eight of these 4-4-0 rebuilds, all superheated, survived to become LNER property in 1923, as Class D13. From then on, their numbers gradually diminished until, on 29 May 1943, the last survivor, LNER No 8039, was withdrawn from service.

In LNER days, certain minor detail alterations were made; the old brass-capped chimney was replaced by a plain, but shapely, casting; the brass beading round the splashers and cab windows was either removed or painted over; the Gresley snifting-valves replaced the superheater dampers, and the old Ramsbottom safety valves made way for Ross " pops."

It was in the summer of 1901 that a younger brother and I were taken by our nurse to spend a fortnight's holiday at the then almost unknown and decidedly remote, Norfolk village of Blakeney. It was my first journey on the old Great Eastern main line and I vividly recall catching sight of No 1900, *Claud Hamilton*, as we slowly drew out of Liverpool Street station.

Here was a noble engine, if ever there were one: I had read about her in the *Locomotive Magazine* not long before and learned that she had been an exhibit at the Paris Exhibition the previous year. That fact was plain to see in the engine herself, for she retained that true " exhibition finish " which her cleaners bestowed upon her for some years afterwards and made her a rewarding sight for locomotive enthusiasts; and in those days it was *some* finish, the art of attaining which has long since been forgotten.

Claud Hamilton was the first of a class of no fewer than 111 fine 4-4-0 express passenger engines designed by James Holden for working the principal express trains of the Great Eastern Railway, and these splendid engines were destined to become known all over the world for the outstanding quality of their performances.

Stationed at Stratford, Ipswich and Norwich, handled by enginemen whose names are remembered and whose deeds are recalled to this day, these engines were literally the pride of the line for several years. In fact, it was not until 1911 that they were displaced by a 4-6-0 type, 1500 class, on the heaviest trains. A Claud at the head of the 400 ton *Norfolk Coast Express*, climbing the Brentwood bank, provided spectacle and sound effects that can never be forgotten.

The dimensions of these engines were fully abreast of the prevailing practice, and certain changes and improvements were introduced, almost from batch to batch, as the engines were built. The numbering was peculiar in that it progressed backwards: the first 10 were 1900 to 1891; the next 1890 to 1881, and so on to the last one, which was No 1791. *Claud Hamilton* was the only one to have a name, a distinction it shared with only two other GER locomotives.

GENERAL SPECIFICATION

CYLINDERS			**TUBES**		
Diameter	...	19 in.	Number	...	274
Stroke	...	26 in.	Diameter	...	1¾ in.
BOILER					
Length, between			**HEATING SURFACE**		
tubeplates	12 ft 1 in.		Tubes	...	1,516.5 sq. ft
Maximum dia-			Firebox	...	114 sq. ft
meter	...	4 ft 9 in.	Total	...	1,630.5 sq. ft
FIREBOX LENGTH					
Inside	...	6 ft 3⅞ in.	**GRATE AREA**		
Outside	...	7 ft	Square feet	...	21.3

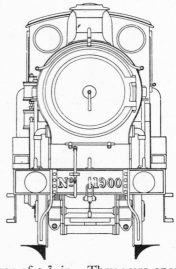

No 1900
CLAUD
HAMILTON

The reason for the retrograde progress of the numbers was: the number 1900 had been chosen to mark the year in which the engine was built as well as the fact that she was exhibited at the Paris Exhibition in that year, and the number was nearly 800 above the highest then in use on the GER—0-6-0 No 1119. It left a lot of blanks to be filled.

The cylinders of No 1900 were 19 in. dia. by 26 in. stroke and had the steamchest below. Balanced slide valves were used; they had a steam lap of ⅞ in. and

a travel in full gear of 3 7/16 in. They were operated by a well laid out Stephenson link motion; the inclination of the cylinders was 1 in 16, which gave plenty of clearance above the bogie. The lead was ⅛ in. and an exhaust clearance of 3/16 in. was provided. The length of the ports was 16¾ in. and their widths were 1⅝ in. for the steam ports and 3½ in. for exhaust.

The boiler was made in two rings, the larger of which had an outside diameter of 4 ft 9 in., the plates being ½ in. thick. The barrel was 12 ft 1 in. long between the tubeplates and its centre line was pitched 8 ft 3 in. above rail level. The firebox casing measured 7 ft long and 4 ft 0½ in. wide, outside, and the grate area was 21.3 sq. ft. A total heating surface of 1,630.5 sq. ft was made up of 1,516.5 sq. ft for the tubes and 114 sq. ft for the firebox; the working pressure was 180 p.s.i.

A driving-wheel diameter of 7 ft had been used successfully on a number of previous classes of GER express locomotives, single and coupled, and was adopted on the Claud Hamilton class, though for the last time on the GER; the bogie wheels were 3 ft 9 in. dia. A total wheelbase of 22 ft 6 in. was divided into 6 ft 6 in. plus 9 ft, while the front and back overhangs were 2 ft 9 in. and 4 ft 4 in., respectively.

The tender was of a type that had been developed for use on those engines which were equipped for burning oil fuel on Holden's system; its corners and top edges were rounded, and the fuel space was provided with a raised coping on three sides. The wheelbase was 12 ft, equally divided in the case of *Claud Hamilton*; the wheel diameter was 4 ft 1 in. and the overhang at each end was 3 ft. The tender's capacity was for 2,790 gallons of water and 750 gallons of oil.

This fine engine weighed 50 tons 6 cwt 1 qr, in working order, the tender 35 tons 1 cwt, while 37 tons 3 cwt 3 qr rested on the coupled wheels, thereby providing adhesion which surpassed that of most other four-coupled express engines of that time; in fact, it was only just under the prevailing maximum permissible limit of 40 tons for two axles.

James Holden was responsible for the general design, but the details were worked out by W. V. Russell, A. M. Bell and A. J. Hill. The result was a veritable triumph which won its due reward at the Paris Exhibition; for Holden was awarded the Grand Prix, Russell and Bell a silver medal each, and Hill a bronze medal.

Years later, Bell told me that they would dearly have loved to try the engine out on a French railway but the necessary arrangements could not be made. Bell was of the opinion that the underlying reason was that the engine was too heavy for the French track. He may have been right; but he was obviously proud of *Claud Hamilton*, and I am sure that the same applies to everybody who had anything to do with the design, construction and subsequent running of this splendid engine and her sisters.

Bell's periodical, *The Locomotive Magazine*, devoted much space to *Claud Hamilton* in 1900 and published a very fine coloured plate of the engine. In 1901 *The Railway Engineer* published the working drawings, a complete specification and a large engraving. All these have been freely used in the preparation of my drawing and these notes.

Although I was never a frequent visitor to East Anglia, I have recollections of runs behind Clauds; and in each case it was a good if not specially spectacular performance. The loads were always quite heavy, but the engines ran well and usually managed to gain a minute or two on schedule.

My second encounter with *Claud Hamilton* herself was at, of all places, the Midland Railway's London terminus, St Pancras, where I was surprised to find her standing in the middle siding one afternoon waiting to take a train to Southend-on-Sea. This was some time in 1905, when there was a regular GER service to Southend from St Pancras, worked by GER engines and stock.

But it was not often that a top-link GER express passenger engine could be seen on this job, and I fancy that *Claud Hamilton* was either being run-in after some repairs or was making up some mileage on secondary work before being sent to Stratford for an overhaul. But I clearly recall that the engine had a plain smokebox door without the prominent and decorative bright-polished steel rim. Strange how such a prominent detail is so noticeable when it isn't there!

Claud Hamilton was withdrawn from service, as LNER No 2500, in May 1947; like the majority of the class, she was never rebuilt, but she had been reboilered with a boiler having a Belpaire firebox. Her name was later transferred to No 2546 of the same class.

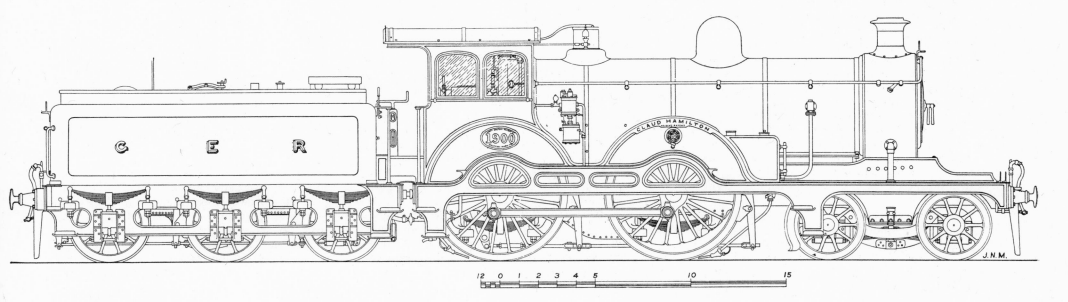

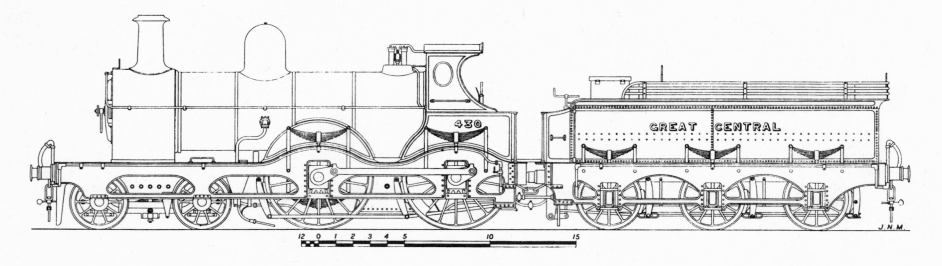

CHARLES SACRÉ'S 437 CLASS 4-4-0 ENGINES

THE most striking feature about these stalwart old engines was the peculiarity of the design, in which, at first glance, the main purpose of the massive outside frames was merely to accommodate outside bearings for the coupled wheels !

There was, of course, much more in it than that, but I doubt if a more extraordinary arrangement was ever applied to a locomotive. It attracted the attention immediately, and it gave rise to a number of quite irresponsible explanations on the part of uninitiated enthusiasts. I remember that, as a boy, I was considerably puzzled by it when reading descriptions and looking at photographs of these unique engines; but my first acquaintance with any of them was made in 1913, when I spent a few days in Manchester as the guest of a fellow enthusiast.

He and I spent most of the time at certain railway vantage points in and around that city. At the Central station we found some of these curious engines busily engaged on passenger trains on the Cheshire Lines, for which the old Great Central Railway provided the motive power.

Just after the 1914-18 war No 430 for a short while became a fairly frequent visitor to London (Neasden) locomotive depot; I cannot recall where she was then stationed, but she appeared to work exclusively on perishable freight and fish trains. She caused quite a sensation among London enthusiasts, most of whom had never seen her like before; and it has been a matter of some surprise that, apparently, nobody succeeded in obtaining a photograph of her while she was engaged on this turn. I believe it was the only occasion on which an engine of this class was ever seen in London.

Originally, there were 27 of these engines, built for the Manchester, Sheffield and Lincolnshire Railway at Gorton in the years 1877-1880. For many years, they were used on express trains to and from Manchester, Retford and Grantham in connection with the Great Northern Railway's expresses between London (Kings Cross) and Manchester, through coaches being conveyed in each direction. These trains were sharply timed and won a considerable reputation for punctuality. In fact, it was essential for them to run strictly to time, as they were in direct competition with the London and North Western and Midland services from London to Manchester, and had farther to go in the same or, in some cases, less time. This meant that the MS and LR engines had to work really hard, but they stood up to it well.

When the MS and LR became the Great Central Railway, in 1900, Charles Sacré retired. All his locomotive designs had been distinctive and original, in appearance at least, and it is to the credit of his successor, J. G. Robinson, that little alteration was made to them in after years. One noticeable feature was that, although the Sacré engines were repainted in the *colours* adopted for the Great Central locomotives, the *style* remained that of the MS and LR and was never exactly like that of the GCR.

The 437 class were soon taken in hand by Robinson, who rebuilt them with new boilers having slightly longer smokeboxes and fitted with chimneys and other details of his design. It is in this form that I have drawn No 430, simply because I did not know her, or any of her contemporaries, in their original condition. But they retained much of their former

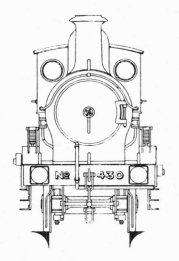

GENERAL SPECIFICATION

CYLINDERS					TUBES				
Diameter	...	... 17½ in.			Number	...	...	...	—
Stroke	...	... 26 in.			Diameter	...	...		—
BOILER					HEATING SURFACE				
Length between					Tubes	...	...	...	—
tubeplates	10 ft 10⅝ in.				Firebox	...	...	...	—
Maximum diameter 4 ft 6 in.					Total	...	...	...	—
FIREBOX LENGTH					GRATE AREA				
Inside...	...	...	...	—	Square feet	...	...	...	—
Outside	...	...	...	—					

distinctiveness and, moreover, gave many more years of useful service. In fact, 12 of the class survived long enough to become LNER property after the railway grouping in 1923, and they were reclassified Class D12, after having been Great Central Class 6B for more than 20 years.

These 12 engines were Nos 128, 423, 425, 428, 430, 434, 439, 440, 441, 442, 443 and 446. For several years previously, they had all been on the duplicate list and had the suffix B added to their numbers. The LNER renumbered seven of them, Nos 128, 425, 428, 430, 439, 442 and 443, which became LNER 6460 and 6468 back to 6463, in that order. Their withdrawal began with Nos 423, 434, 440, 441 and 446, in 1923; then followed 6463, 6465 and 6468 in 1925; 6460, 6466 and 6467 in 1926, and 6464 in 1930, after about 50 years of service.

These engines were not, and never had been exactly alike; there were minor differences of detail to be noted, particularly in the tenders of which there

appear to have been two types, one slightly shorter than the other. Official information, however, indicates no difference in the capacities of the tenders; photographs show that they were apparently changed from engine to engine occasionally. For example, No 430, in GCR days, had a long tender as shown in my drawing; but as LNER 6466 she had a short one. The official diagram for the class, incidentally, shows a long tender, but photographs showing this are rare.

No 434 of this class had the great misfortune to break her crank axle when travelling at speed near Penistone on July 16, 1884. The result was a most disastrous smash in which 24 persons were killed and many injured. Among those who lost their lives was Massey Bromley, locomotive superintendent of the Great Eastern Railway. The engine was subsequently repaired and lasted long enough to become one of the LNER D12 class.

The dimensions of these engines were: cylinders

17½ in. dia., 26 in. stroke and 2 ft 5 in. apart, centre to centre. Wheel diameters were, bogie 3 ft 3½ in., coupled 6 ft 3½ in. and tender 3 ft 9½ in.; the wheelbase was 20 ft 9½ in. divided into 6 ft plus 6 ft 9½ in. plus 8 ft. The leading overhang was 2 ft 5 in. and the trailing 3 ft 6 in.

Available boiler particulars are meagre. The barrel was 10 ft 10⅝ in. long between tubeplates; it was made in three rings, 4 ft 4 in., 4 ft 5 in. and 4 ft 6 in. dia. and the centre line was 7 ft 1¾ in. above rail level. The pressure was 140 p.s.i., but heating surfaces and firebox sizes do not seem to have been recorded in any published description. Even the copy of the official diagram I have been using does not include them, which is unusual.

That diagram, however, shows two obvious errors; one is the height to the top of the chimney, which is given as 12 ft 6 in., whereas it was more like 13 ft; the other is the width over platform, shown as 8 ft 9 in. This is much too wide and I think it is intended to be the distance across the coupling-rod pins. Many years of experience with official diagrams has taught me to be on the alert to spot errors of this kind; they do crop up, but only occasionally.

The tender had an equally divided total wheelbase of 12 ft; its leading overhang was 3 ft 8 in., and the trailing 3 ft 10 in. The capacity was for 1,800 gallons of water and 2 tons 15 cwt of coal.

The maximum weight of the engine was 43 tons 19 cwt, with 13 tons 19 cwt on the bogie, 17 tons 12 cwt on the driving wheels, and 12 tons 8 cwt on the trailing wheels. The tender, all found, weighed 25 tons 14 cwt, so the total weight of engine and tender was 69 tons 15 cwt in working trim.

Finally, those massive frames provided a very strong and rigid foundation on which to support the engine. Incidentally, the tender also was mounted on double frames, which was a comparatively rare feature in British locomotive practice.

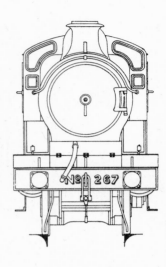

GENERAL SPECIFICATION

CYLINDERS			TUBES		
Diameter	....	19 in.	Number	... ...	221
Stroke	... ...	26 in.	Diameter	... ...	2 in.

BOILER					
Length, between			HEATING SURFACE		
tubeplates	15 ft	4⅜ in.	Tubes	...	1,777.9 sq. ft
Maximum dia-			Firebox	...	133.1 sq. ft
meter	... ...	5 ft.	Total	...	1,911 sq. ft

FIREBOX LENGTH					
Inside	...	7 ft 9 11/32 in.	GRATE AREA		
Outside	...	8 ft 6 in.	Square feet	...	26

GREAT CENTRAL ATLANTICS

IN the early years of the present century, the Atlantic type of locomotive had quite a vogue in Britain. The title is American and signifies a locomotive with 4-4-2 wheel arrangement and, properly speaking, outside cylinders; but 4-4-2 engines with inside cylinders are by no means unknown and have also been referred to as " Atlantics."

Of the several British examples, those designed for the old Great Central Railway by J. G. Robinson, and built between 1903 and 1906, to my mind were the most handsome; many people do not agree with me on this point, but I will leave my drawings to speak for themselves ! The general design was bold, neat, massive and beautifully proportioned, and if that does not add up to a handsome locomotive, then I do not know one when I see it !

There were 31 of these engines on the GCR, four of them being three-cylinder compounds, while the rest were two-cylinder simples. In service, it was found that there was little to choose between the work of the simples and that of the compounds; all were excellent engines and appeared to be equally powerful and speedy. In any case, they were popular with the enginemen and public, and they rapidly built up a splendid reputation for speed and punctuality.

My own experiences of their performances were, unfortunately, severely limited. My observations of the engines were confined almost wholly to the London end of the line, and I often used to see GCR expresses with these Atlantics on them passing such places as Neasden, Wembley Park and Harrow. These trains seldom had more than six coaches on, however, so the engines were not being seen at their best, though they always seemed to be in a terrific hurry. But on the cross-country runs from Manchester to Sheffield, York, Lincoln or Grimsby, the work done by these engines was little short of marvellous. The trains were really heavy and the road extremely difficult; and if the schedules were not nearly so sharply timed as those to and from London, they called for first-class locomotive work which the Atlantics could give in full measure.

For the period, the dimensions of these fine engines were thoroughly up to date; they were—cylinders, 19 in. dia. by 26 in. stroke; wheel diameters, bogie, 3 ft 6 in., coupled, 6 ft 9 in., trailing, 4 ft 3 in.; the wheelbase was 27 ft 9½ in., divided into 6 ft 6 in. plus 5 ft 9½ in. plus 7 ft 3 in. plus 8 ft 3 in,; the overhang was 2 ft 5 in. at the front and 6 ft 1 in. at the back. The diameter of the boiler barrel, outside the cleading, was 5 ft 6½ in.; its pitch was 8 ft 6 in. from rail level. The firebox was of the Belpaire type, the grate area of which was 26 sq. ft.

The boiler barrel contained, originally, 221 tubes of 2 in. dia., and there was no superheater, as this did not come into general use until about 1908. All the GCR Atlantics, however, were eventually superheated. The total heating surface of this boiler amounted to 1,911 sq. ft, towards which the tubes contributed 1,777.9 and the firebox 133.1 sq. ft. The working pressure was 180 lb. p.s.i. for the simple engines and 200 lb. for the compounds.

The height from rail level to the top of the chimney was 13 ft 3 in. The width over the cab sides and splashers was 7 ft 6 in.; over the footplating it was 8 ft 3 in. at the cab end and 8 ft 9½ in. at the front, the increase being by means of a gentle S-curve just ahead of the leading splasher, on each side of the engine. The tender was carried on six 4 ft wheels, the wheelbase being 13 ft equally divided; the overhang was 4 ft at each end.

The chimney for the Atlantics, as built, was, of course, one of Robinson's standard pattern; but, like

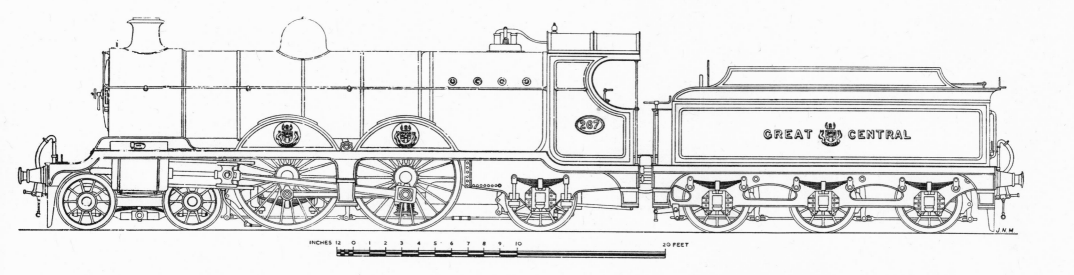

INCHES 12 0 1 2 3 4 5 6 7 8 9 10   20 FEET

many other chimneys of the early 1900s, how subtle was its shape ! I doubt if many people—especially model makers—realise that, except for the horizontal lines of the flange and the lip, there is not a *straight* line anywhere on its outer surface. The barrel between the underside of the flange and the flare into the smokebox wrapper not only increases in diameter from top to bottom, but is also very slightly curved.

I will admit that I did not know this until, in 1939, I came into possession of a copy of the official chimney drawing. This consists of a 3 in. scale drawing of a very short chimney, together with a full-size cutaway view of part of the top, while below is a table of dimensions giving the different sizes for quite a lot of GCR chimneys, all of them with very slightly curved barrels. It is most interesting, but, in those days, designers took a pride and delight in this kind of thing, though very few went to the length of designing curved barrels for chimneys. Not all Robinson's chimneys were curved, however; it seems to apply only to those which were less than 1 ft 6 in. high. Moreover, no definite dimensions are indicated for the curve; but it is there, nevertheless, very slight though it is. All other Robinson chimneys seem to have had a straight-sided taper from top to bottom.

These splendid engines were painted and lined in a most attractive colour scheme. The main colour was a rich green for boiler, tender and wheels, and purple-brown for the tender frames, valances and cylinder clothing. The lining was in black, red and white, with vermilion buffer beams and gold-leaf lettering. The whole effect was very striking and thoroughly worthy of the engines. The last survivors of this class were withdrawn and scrapped in 1950.

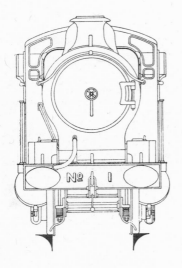

GENERAL SPECIFICATION

CYLINDERS			TUBES		
Diameter	...	21 in.	Number	...	110 & 22
Stroke	...	26 in.	Diameter	...	2 in. & 5¼ in.
BOILER					
Length, between			HEATING SURFACE		
tubeplates	15 ft	4¾ in.	Tubes	...	1,349 sq. ft
Maximum dia-			Firebox	...	154 sq. ft
meter	...	5 ft	Total	...	1,503 sq. ft
FIREBOX LENGTH					
Inside	...	7 ft 9⅜ in.	GRATE AREA		
Outside	...	8 ft 6 in.	Square feet	...	26.24

ROBINSON'S 2-8-0 ROD ENGINES

BEFORE 1911, the only British railway to have built 2-8-0 type heavy freight, or mineral engines was the Great Western, on which line G. J. Churchward had introduced the type in 1903, for working the South Wales coal trains to London and other parts of the GWR system. Subsequently, they became the principal freight type on the GWR.

In the latter part of 1911, however, J. G. Robinson of the Great Central Railway, who had only just completed a numerous class of 0-8-0 engines begun in 1902, decided upon an enlargement to 2-8-0. In doing so, he produced a masterpiece which, in time, was to achieve a fame and popularity that could scarcely have been foreseen. Not that there was anything remarkable, or outstanding in them; they were good, sturdy engines, solidly built and possessed of plenty of pulling power. Eventually, the GCR built 127 of them for its own use.

At the beginning of the 1914-18 war, however, some of these engines were commandeered by the War Office for service overseas. They proved to be so handy and useful that the Government ordered no fewer than 521 of them to be built for the Railway Operating Division of the British Army. Before long the engines were to be found all over Europe, the

Middle East and in China, in company with their much older and smaller contemporaries, the Dean and Armstrong 0-6-0 engines of the GWR as well as many of the Adams 0-6-0s from the LSWR. Because of this, the Robinson engines were known ever after as the RODs.

After the war, about 300 of them were returned to England and eventually sold by the Government Disposals Board. At first, some were loaned to various railways such as the London and South Western, the South Eastern and Chatham, the London and North Western and the Great Western; but after 1922, the Great Western bought 100, while the London and North Eastern bought the remainder. Those left overseas continued to work in the countries where they had seen military service, and some may still be there; others were transferred to Australia.

The Great Western Railway immediately scrapped 50 of their hundred and by so doing obtained a store of spare parts which were used for the purpose of keeping the other 50 in arduous service for more than 30 years. The three survivors of this lot were withdrawn for scrap in December 1958, after 36 years' service, ten of which were spent under British Railways' ownership; it was a remarkable record.

The LNER possessed about 440 of this type, more than half of which became British Railways' property in 1948, and about half of these are still working. Some of them, including a number of the original engines rebuilt, had larger boilers. It is interesting to note that several of these rebuilds reverted to the original size of boiler in their later years, as they were more satisfactory in that form. This shows, once more, that large boilers are not always successful; in this case, it is all the more remarkable because the smaller-boilered RODs won unstinted praise wherever they went, at home or abroad, whereas the larger-boilered engines were generally regarded as being " nothing to write home about," as they were rather inclined to run short of steam !

The RODs were Great Central Railway class 8K, but after 1923 they were reclassified O4 by the LNER and were renumbered by having 5000 added to the original GCR numbers. Those built by the Government were given an entirely separate set of numbers, but after the war, the LNER lot were renumbered 6253 to 6642 inclusive.

In the original GCR series was one of the several No 1s that I have known, and I have chosen her as the subject of my drawing. I do not think she was

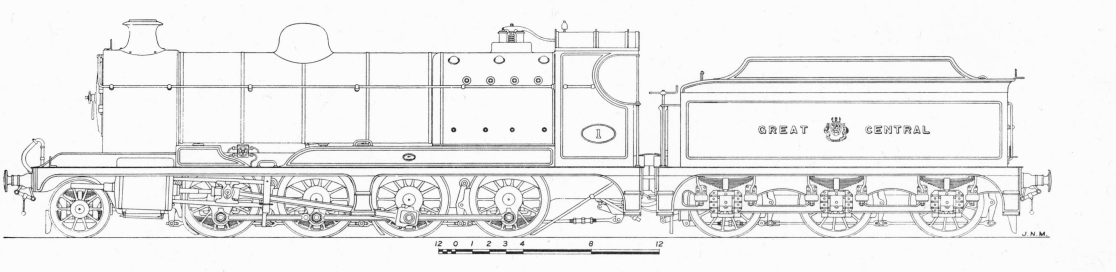

ever stationed in, or near, London, but she was well known on that exceedingly difficult line between Manchester, Sheffield and Grimsby, where her prodigious hauling power stood her in good stead; she needed it when hauling those heavy trains of good Yorkshire coal between the mining towns and the docks, over those terrific gradients through the Pennines, and through those 3½ mile, single line Woodhead tunnels.

It is there—in their home waters, so to speak— that this engine and most of her 126 sisters did some of their finest work; and it is certain that no finer work was ever done by any other locomotives. Add to that the fact that they were so easy to handle, so responsive to a driver's control, and there can be no wonder that they were popular. When occasion demanded it, they would willingly submit to really merciless thrashing and emerge none the worse for it, quite ready for more, if needed.

An O4 is supposed to have been involved in that delightful story told of a volunteer driver, during the strike of 1926. This man, evidently somewhat lacking in footplate experience, was detailed to work a passenger train between two important stations, 40 miles apart. The train duly departed, and the engine, finding herself on a most unaccustomed duty, gave of her best by running like mad, mile after mile. Conditions on the footplate are best left to the imagination !

Strange to relate, they arrived safely at their destination, after failing to make a number of stops that should have been made on the way. However, after the train had come to rest at the terminal station, a somewhat agitated stationmaster strode up to the engine and asked the driver: " Do you know, young man, that you are about 36 minutes before time ? " Came the disarming reply: " I know, old thing, but I have only just found out how to stop this damn bus " ! It is something of a miracle that he did not run into far worse trouble.

The cylinders of these engines were large, 21 in. dia. by 26 in. stroke, and were provided with 10 in. piston valves situated behind the frames. The centre lines of the cylinders and the valve chambers, seen in elevation, were all in the same plane and inclined at an angle of 1 in 24. The valves were driven by Stephenson link motion, the eccentrics of which were fixed to the driving axle, while the expansion links were centre-suspended about 18 in. ahead of the second coupled axle.

The boiler was made in three rings of $\frac{5}{8}$ in. plate, the diameter of the largest ring being 4 ft 10¾ in. inside. There were 22 superheater flues of 5¼ in. dia. and 110 fire tubes of 2 in. dia., the combined heating surface being 1,349 sq. ft. The firebox added 154 sq. ft making the total heating surface 1,503 sq. ft. The length between tubeplates was 15 ft 4¾ in., the pitch of the centre line was 8 ft 6½ in., and the working pressure 180 p.s.i. The grate area was 26.24 sq. ft.

The leading wheels were 3 ft 6 in. dia. and the coupled 4 ft 8 in.; the wheelbase was 25 ft 5 in. divided into 8 ft 4 in. plus 5 ft 8½ in. plus 5 ft 5½ in. plus 5 ft 11 in., and the overhang 2 ft 8 in. at the front and 7 ft 10 in. at the back. In working order, the weight was 73 tons 4 cwt, of which 66 tons 4 cwt was available for adhesion, while the tractive effort was 31,326 lb.

The tender was carried on six 4 ft 4 in. wheels with an equally divided wheelbase of 13 ft; its overhang was 4 ft 1 in. in front and 4 ft 3 in. at the back. The capacity was for 6 tons of coal and 4,000 gallons of water, the full weight being 48 tons 6 cwt. An unusual feature of these tenders was that the wheels had 13 spokes.

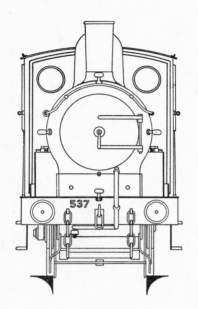

537

The JUBILEES

GENERAL SPECIFICATION						
CYLINDERS				**TUBES**		
Diameter	...	...	18 in.	Number	...	216
Stroke	...	...	26 in.	Diameter	...	1¾ in.
BOILER				**HEATING SURFACE**		
Length, between tubeplates	...		11 ft	Tubes	...	1,121 sq. ft
Maximum diameter	...		4 ft 4 in.	Firebox	...	110 sq. ft
				Total	...	1,231 sq. ft
FIREBOX LENGTH						
Inside	...	...	5 ft 5 in.	**GRATE AREA**		
Outside	...	...	6 ft	Square feet	...	17

ANY reader who is fortunate enough to have access to the Proceedings of the Institution of Civil Engineers for 1885 will know that they include William Stroudley's paper on the "Design and Construction of Large Locomotive Engines."

Stroudley deals very fully with his own 0-4-2 Gladstone class of the L.B. & S.C.R. The interesting point is that in the discussion that followed the paper some eminent locomotive engineers of the time were openly critical of Stroudley's engines—and among the critics was William Adams, locomotive chief of the London and South Western Railway.

Something must have happened during the next two years, however, to cause Adams to alter his views, because in 1887 he produced some 0-4-2 engines of his own, and very good engines they were. In fact, they were so successful that no fewer than 90 were built between May 1887 and May 1895.

The first 30 engines, all built at the railway company's own factory at Nine Elms, had cylinders with steam-chests underneath as in Stroudley's engines; but the next 60 engines had the steam-chests between the cylinders and were fitted with lever reversing gear instead of screw gear.

My drawing shows one of the first of these engines, unofficially known as "Jubilees" because the year 1887 marked the silver jubilee of Queen Victoria. The chief dimensions were: cylinders, 18 in. dia. by 26 in. stroke, coupled wheels, 6 ft dia. and trailing wheels 4 ft.

It is interesting to note that the trailing axleboxes had the springs placed behind the frames in all the engines except the first one, No 527, which, when new had the springs in front of the frames. The wheelbase was 8 ft plus 9 ft, and the leading and trailing overhangs were 5 ft 11½ in. and 4 ft 2 in., respectively.

The boiler was 4 ft 4 in. dia. and 11 ft long, the pitch of the centre line being 7 ft 6 in. The working pressure was 160 p.s.i. The barrel contained 216 tubes of 1¾ in. outside dia., the heating surface of which was 1,121 sq. ft; to this the firebox added 110 sq. ft, making the total 1,231 sq. ft. The grate area was 17 sq. ft, and the engine weight was 43 tons 8 cwt in working order.

The 60 engines built between 1892 and 1895—40 by Neilson and Co., Glasgow, and 20 at Nine Elms —had brass beading on the splashers, an adornment

that was missing from the earlier engines. It was on this class, however, that Adams first introduced to the L.S.W.R. in 1887 his well-known cast number-plate with its highly-polished figures, border, etc., on a bright red ground.

No 537, depicted in my drawing, was an engine I knew well when she worked in the London area, usually on Waterloo-Reading trains. This would be about 1904; but in those days these engines seemed to work mainly on Portsmouth and Reading trains. There were many then stationed at Nine Elms, Guildford, Portsmouth, Reading and Basingstoke, and I think that I must have seen practically the whole class during those early years working trains through Clapham Junction.

They were fascinating engines and always seemed to do their work well. They were never altered very much in later years, though Drummond put a boiler of his own design on about a dozen of them, and his chimney on a great many more. Personally, I much disliked a Drummond chimney on an Adams engine —the effect always seemed to me to be like that of a lifeguardsman in full ceremonial rig but wearing a cloth cap!

The Adams Jubilees, or, to give them their official designation, A-12s, had a fairly long life. Withdrawal began in 1928, but was not completed until 1948.

In their later years these 90 engines became widely scattered over the L.S.W.R., but the last examples were withdrawn from the London area where, 61 years previously, the first examples had started work. These sturdy, solidly built, hardworking engines were always great favourites of mine, though they could not compare with the easy stateliness and quietness of movement that were so characteristic of Stroudley's Gladstones.

For the benefit of modellers I must add a few words about the Adams stove-pipe chimneys that were used on these engines. There were three varieties: the first was a built-up chimney, the main barrel of which had a slight, almost imperceptible taper above the separate base into which it fitted; the second was similar but had a very pronounced and rather ugly taper and the third was a cast-iron one-piece chimney with an amount of taper that was a sort of compromise between the other two.

This last, in spite of the inherent plainness and austerity of its design, was a real work of art—there was some subtle quality about it that lifted it right out of the commonplace and turned it into a master-piece.

This may possibly account for my personal aversion to the Drummond chimney being substituted for the Adams stove-pipe. On the other hand I have met many people who solemnly declare that the substitution actually *improved* the look of an Adams engine. There is no accounting for taste!

Unless my imagination was playing me tricks, I formed the impression in later years that the earlier engines of this class were rather livelier than the later ones. Whether this apparent difference was due to the change that Adams made in the arrangement of the steam-chests and valve-gears, I would hesitate to say; but it might be possible, because the original arrangement with the steam-chest underneath the cylinders would provide a less cramped space for the valves to work in than when the steam-chest was between the cylinders.

In addition, the fact that the earlier engines had screw reversing-gear instead of the lever would permit of much finer adjustment being made when notching up—and that might well result in a livelier performance from the engine. This kind of thing was ever an intriguing feature of the study of locomotive design; a slight alteration in the dimensions or arrangement of some particular part of the machinery would sometimes make a great, and even unexpected, difference to the performance of the engine.

I have never been able to find out the details of the valve events on the Adams Jubilees. They must have been good, however, judging by the power these engines could develop on occasions, and the speeds at which they could run.

The first 20 engines of this class were equipped with the automatic vacuum brake complete; all the others had a steam brake and an ejector for working the vacuum brake on trains. Nos 529, 534, 538, 543, 555 and 556 were fitted with the Westinghouse air brake in addition to the standard brakes, and, therefore, could be used when required for working Westinghouse-fitted stock from other railways.

Finally, it is worth mentioning that No 654, completed in April 1895, was never altered in any way except for her paintwork; she was still in her original state, Adams chimney and all, when withdrawn in 1947, aged 52.

As drawn, No 537 is shown painted in the Drummond style, but still in the original state, as I remember her like that.

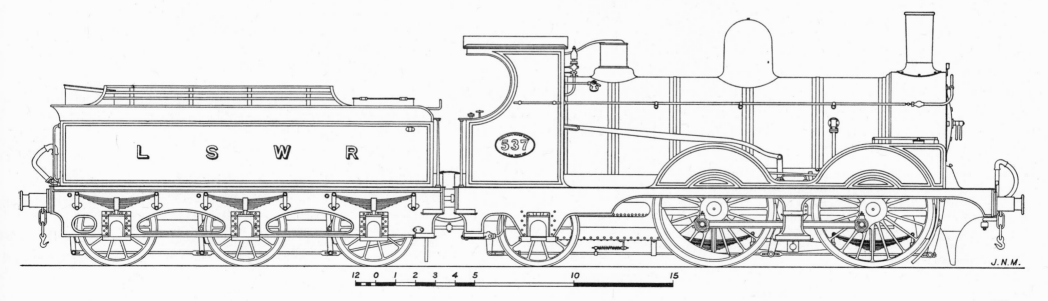

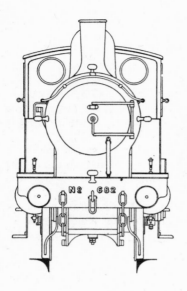

```
                    GENERAL SPECIFICATION

CYLINDERS                              TUBES
   Diameter   ...    ...   19 in.         Number   ...    ...   220
   Stroke     ...    ...   26 in.         Diameter  ...   ...   1¾ in.

BOILER
   Length, between                     HEATING SURFACE
      tubeplates    ...    11 ft          Tubes    ...   1,141.7 sq. ft
   Maximum dia-                           Firebox  ...   122.1 sq. ft
      meter   ...    4 ft 4 in.           Total    ...   1,263.8 sq. ft

FIREBOX LENGTH
   Inside    ...    6 ft  1 in.         GRATE AREA
   Outside   ...    6 ft 10 in.           Square feet   ...   19.65
```

THE ADAMS FLYERS Class T6

WILLIAM ADAMS of the London and South Western Railway was a strong advocate of the 4-4-0 type passenger locomotive, and designed several series of such engines.

His usual custom was to have these engines built in two series at a time, one with 6 ft 7 in. driving-wheels for working over the heavily graded routes west of Salisbury, and the other with 7 ft 1 in. driving-wheels for working east of that town.

This custom began in 1883 and it terminated, so far as the Adams engines were concerned, in 1896 with the building of Classes T-6 and X-6. Engine No 682 was one of the T-6 class which, to my mind, were the finest of all the Adams engines. They were designed on the massive scale; their proportions were excellent and they were very solidly built. On the road they were speedy and powerful, and they well-merited their nickname of Adams Flyers.

There were 10 of them, and when I first came to know them they were about four years old; they were numbered 677 to 686, and I think they were all stationed at Nine Elms.

If my recollection is accurate, No 682 was the only one of the 10 still in the original Adams livery;

all the others had been repainted in the style introduced by Dugald Drummond. In fact, I believe that the last four engines of this class, dating from March and May 1896, were painted in Drummond's livery when they were new.

I have shown No 682 in the Adams style because she was like that when I first knew her, and I copied it from her official photograph. It was plain, neat and simple, and I rather preferred it to the Drummond livery.

However, no matter what the livery, in the T-6 class, Adams produced some really grand 4-4-0 express passenger engines that could hold their own against any others of their type and period; and they remained unchallenged on their home road until Drummond's celebrated T-9 class appeared in 1899.

Compared with the earlier Adams 4-4-0 engines, the T-6 class had slightly longer smokeboxes and fireboxes, the latter necessitating a 6 in. addition to the coupled wheelbase. These slight alterations, however, considerably enhanced the appearance and gave the engines an air of noble dignity that the earlier engines did not quite reach.

The opportunity was taken to introduce a cast-iron

stovepipe chimney with a perfectly smooth exterior, which added its quota to the generally pleasing effect of the other modifications.

The principal dimensions were: cylinders, 19 in. dia., 26 in. stroke; wheels, bogie 3 ft 9¾ in., coupled 7 ft 1 in. dia.; wheelbase, 23 ft 6 in. divided into 7 ft 6 in. plus 7 ft plus 9 ft; overhang 3 ft 1 in. at the front, 4 ft 3 in. at the back.

The centre-line of the boiler was pitched 7 ft 9 in. above rail level, and the height to the top of the chimney was 13 ft 2¾ in. The diameter of the barrel was 4 ft 4 in. and its length was 11 ft; it contained 220 tubes of 1¾ in. dia., the heating surface of which was 1,141.7 sq. ft. To this, the firebox added 122.1 sq. ft, making the total heating surface 1,263.8 sq. ft. The grate area was 19.65 sq. ft, the outside length of the firebox being 6 ft 10 in.

The tender, carried on six 3 ft 9¾ in. wheels, had a wheelbase of 13 ft equally divided and the total wheelbase of engine and tender was 45 ft ⅛ in.; at least, that is the official figure, and I have often wondered if it remained constant and unaltered when the engine was pulling !

In any case, I have been unable to discover what

accounted for that odd ⅛ in. There must have been something somewhere, because the total length of engine and tender over buffers is given as 54 ft 5⅜ in. With 5 tons of coal and 3,300 gallons of water, the tender weighed 33 tons 4 cwt. Incidentally, it was on these engines that tender coal rails made their first appearance on the L.S.W.R.

The engine weighed 50 tons 2½ cwt, so that, ready for the road, engine and tender scaled 83 tons 6½ cwt. The working pressure was 175 p.s.i., which was common to all the later Adams 4-4-0 engines. An official figure for the tractive effort does not appear to have been published.

For several years these fine engines worked the best expresses between London and Southampton, Bournemouth and Salisbury; they were seldom to be seen at Exeter, Plymouth or other places west of Salisbury.

Only one of this class, No 680, was ever fitted with a Drummond boiler, but in later years the Drummond chimney appeared on most of them; No 684, however, retained the Adams chimney until she was withdrawn in 1940. The withdrawal of these fine engines began with Nos 677 and 683 in 1933; Nos 678, 682, 685 and 686 followed in 1936; Nos 679 and 680 in 1937; 684 in 1940, and No 681 in 1943.

The last-mentioned gave me a pleasant surprise one afternoon in 1937; I happened to be on Wimbledon station when she came through at a good 65 m.p.h. at the head of the up Atlantic Coast Express, about 20 min. late. For that, I thought she deserved all honour in her old age; but it showed the stuff that was in her.

I cannot think of many other engines which, at the age of 42 years, would tackle a train like that, non-stop from Salisbury to Waterloo. I can only suppose that the King Arthur or Nelson that should have worked the turn had failed, and No 681 was the only substitute available. But what a contrast.

Later, I discovered that she had worked down to Salisbury on a local train from Basingstoke, her home station, and was preparing to work a similar train back when she was suddenly called upon to work the A.C.E. to London instead. It was an all the more meritorious performance when we remember that the water capacity of her tender was only 3,300 gallons; and there are no water troughs on the line, or ever have been.

In the last years of this class, No 686 was always conspicuous because the brass beading on her splashers had never been removed, or painted over,

and it was kept brightly polished. I never discovered the reason for this but feel that there must have been one simply because most other Adams engines had had the beading removed during Drummond's regime; those that had not had it removed had had it painted over.

Finally, I would suggest that, even at this late date, an Adams T-6 would make a fine model, especially in 5 in. or 7¼ in. gauge. Many years ago, models of Adams 4-4-0 engines were fairly numerous; but curiously enough never a T-6, and I have often wondered why. To be frank, however, most of those models were hideous and entirely unnecessary caricatures of Adams' beautiful designs, and I have been told that, because of this, William Adams regarded model locomotive builders as lunatics!

When, in the late 1890s, the two Coates brothers approached him for information to enable them to build a model of one of the X-6 4-4-0s, he at first refused to have anything to do with them. But Messrs Coates persisted and sent him examples of their previous work; then he relented and gave them the particulars they wanted. The result was the superb model that is to be seen and admired in the Science Museum, South Kensington.

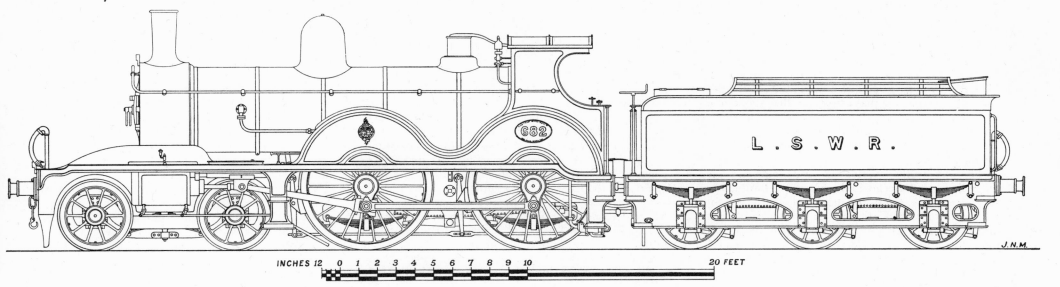

INCHES 12 0 1 2 3 4 5 6 7 8 9 10   20 FEET

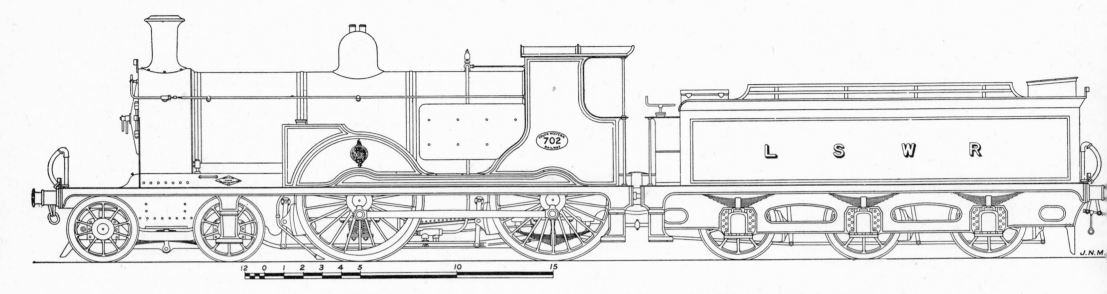

DRUMMOND'S GREYHOUNDS

HE various nicknames that have been so often bestowed upon locomotive types and classes were usually singularly apt, and I know of none that was more appropriate than the soubriquet of "Greyhounds," as applied to Dugald Drummond's celebrated 4-4-0 engines of the T9 class on the London and South Western Railway.

There was something about the appearance of these engines, and not a little about their capacity for speed, that was suggestive of nothing but greyhounds. It was behind No 702 that I first recorded a maximum speed of 80 m.p.h. during a glorious but much too short sprint from Battledown summit, through Micheldever towards Winchester, one day in the summer of 1912.

She was badly overloaded and had struggled doggedly from Waterloo to the summit at Battledown; but, once over the top, the driver seemed to give her head, and she accelerated at a remarkable rate, with speed mounting into the 80s in a distance of about five miles. She held it until steam was shut off and the brakes applied for a stop at Winchester; to me, it was most exciting.

162

After that, my regard for the T9 class, hitherto not so very high, changed; in due course, I developed quite an affection for the engines, and it has persisted to this day. The class originally consisted of 66 engines; but they were not all exactly alike, and they could be divided into three different varieties: (1) with no water-tubes in the firebox, and with six-wheeled tender; (2) as seen in my drawing, exactly similar to (1) but fitted with a nest of 61 water-tubes in the firebox, necessitating a prominent casing being fitted on each side of the firebox, immediately in front of the cab and (3) similar to (2) but with wider cab

and splashers and fitted with large, double-bogie tenders.

The running numbers were: variety (1), 113 to 122 and 280 to 289; variety (2), 702 to 719, 721 to 732 and 773; variety (3), 300 to 305, 307, 310 to 314 and 336 to 338. The engines of variety (2) were built by Dubs and Co., of Glasgow; all the others were built at Nine Elms Works.

Their dates ranged from June 1899 to October 1901, and the general dimensions were: cylinders, 18½ in. dia. and 26 in. stroke; bogie wheels, 3 ft 7 in. dia.; coupled wheels 6 ft 7 in. dia., wheelbase, 23 ft 3 in., divided into 6 ft 6 in. plus 6 ft 9 in. plus 10 ft; this last figure was the longest coupled wheel-base in Britain at the time the engines were being built.

The boiler was made in two rings, 4 ft 5⅛ in. and 4 ft 6 in., respectively, in outside diameter; its length was 10 ft 6 in., and its centre line was 7 ft 9 in. above rail level. The working pressure was 175 p.s.i.

Originally, there were 280 tubes of 1½ in. dia., the heating surface of which amounted to 1,187 sq. ft; 21 years later, when these engines were fitted with

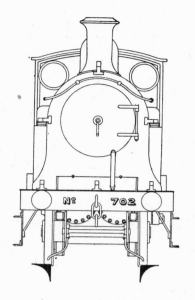

GENERAL SPECIFICATION

CYLINDERS			TUBES		
Diameter	...	18½ in.	Number	...	280
Stroke	...	26 in.	Diameter	...	1½ in.
BOILER					
Length, between			HEATING SURFACE		
tubeplates		10 ft 6 in.	Tubes	...	1,187 sq. ft
Maximum diameter		4 ft 6 in.	Firebox	...	148 sq. ft
			Total	...	1,335 sq. ft
FIREBOX LENGTH					
Inside	...	6 ft 8 in.	GRATE AREA		
Outside	...	7 ft 4 in.	Square feet	...	24

superheaters, the boiler tubing was considerably modified and the heating surface reduced, for there were now 115 tubes of 1¾ in. dia. and 21 flues of 5¼ in. dia., giving, respectively 610 and 311 sq. ft of heating surface, the combined figure being only 921 sq. ft.

The firebox heating surface was 148 before, and 142 after superheating, so that the respective totals were 1,500 and 1,063 sq. ft. These figures do not take into account the effect of 61 water-tubes of 2¾ in. dia. fitted in the fireboxes of the engines of varieties (2) and (3); these tubes added about 165 sq. ft to the total heating surface, but their value as such is rather dubious. They were later taken out.

As might be expected, the weights of these engines rather tend to take on the character of a set of permutations, according to the inclusion or omission of superheaters, firebox water-tubes and double-bogie tenders; but the following is an honest attempt to present the facts:

With no water-tubes and with six-wheeled tender, the engine weight was 46 tons 4 cwt and the total 86 tons 8 cwt. With water-tubes and six-wheeled tender, the engine weighed 48 tons 17 cwt and the total was 89 tons 1 cwt. With water-tubes and double-bogie tender, the engine weighed 48 tons 17 cwt and the tender 44 tons 17 cwt, totalling 93 tons 14 cwt. With no water-tubes but with double-bogie tender, the total was 91 tons 1 cwt.

In later years, after 1922, superheaters and extended smokeboxes were fitted, and with the double-bogie tender—which, by this time, had been fitted to all the engines of the class—the total weight was 96 tons 13 cwt. About 15 years later still, the bogie tenders were commandeered for use on certain 4-6-0 engines, and the T9s reverted to the original six-wheeled variety. On all the survivors of this class, however, the double-bogie tenders have re-appeared !

Engine No 773 was exhibited by Dubs and Co. at the Glasgow Exhibition in 1901, and was given a special external finish for the occasion; she retained it for several years after she was taken over by the LSWR when the exhibition closed. I remember it well, if only because of the little extra embellishments to the lining.

She was immediately recognisable by reason of the almost glass-like surface of her paint and the bright steel tyres of her wheels. In those days, the cleaners seemed to revel in the task of keeping her in absolutely spotless condition. In 1925, this engine was renumbered 733, so that her original number could be used to preserve a sequence for the new King Arthur class engines then on order.

In their prime, the T9 class were often to be seen working west of Salisbury on expresses from London to Exeter and Plymouth. Unlike the Adams 7 ft 4-4-0s, the T9s had no difficulty in working trains over the severe gradients met with in Devon and Cornwall, though it was not very frequently that they proceeded farther than Plymouth.

At the moment of writing, about two dozen T9s are still in active service in the Southern Region, chiefly on local passenger work. When they get the opportunity, however, they are even now capable of running in a manner that justifies their nickname of "Greyhounds."

Incidentally, the six-wheeled tenders used on these engines were unusually long for such vehicles; their wheelbase was 13 ft, equally divided, and there was a 5 ft overhang at each end.

It is not without interest to note that the numberplate of No 702 carries the title "South Western Railway" while the tender carries the initials LSWR. The story behind that apparent discrepancy is a little involved and dates from Drummond's early days at Nine Elms.

The Adams cast numberplates had displayed the company's full title, "London and South Western Railway" which was spread along the upper edge of the plate, inside the border. Along the lower edge was the legend "Nine Elms Works" followed by the year of the engine's construction. Like a lot of people in much later times, Drummond seems to have taken a dislike to what he considered to be ponderous verbiage; but he could not make up his mind as to what to use instead. His earliest engines were lettered SWR, some with a full stop after each letter, others without the stops. This was followed by a number of engines lettered LSW, again with and without full stops. The numberplates on all these engines were lettered "South Western" above the number and "Railway" below it.

Then, one day the company's Chairman quietly drew Drummond's attention to the strictly correct title as rendered on the Adams numberplates. Drummond took his revenge for this by bringing out a few engines lettered "L. & S.W.R." but left his numberplates unchanged. After some quite heated discussion between Drummond and the Chairman, it was agreed that a plain "LSWR" was enough, and this became the standard until 1923. But there were still the numberplates to be dealt with, and Drummond, properly fed up, finally decided to do away with them entirely and adopt painted or stencilled figures !

DUGALD DRUMMOND'S
D15 CLASS

IN February 1912, the Eastleigh Works of the London and South Western Railway turned out the first of ten really find 4-4-0 express passenger locomotives, officially styled class D15; the design was by Dugald Drummond who, during the preceding six years, had made five more or less abortive attempts to produce a successful 4-6-0 and then reverted to a 4-4-0 design which, beyond all question, was his masterpiece.

Unfortunately, Drummond did not live long enough to witness the work of these, his last locomotives, when they were at their best, for his sudden death in November 1912 occurred just one month before the final engine of class D15 was completed. Had he designed and built nothing else, these splendid engines would have been enough to ensure that his abilities and ingenuity would give him a place for all time among the great locomotive engineers. But he had scored a former triumph in his T9 class 4-4-0 engines 13 years before, and the D15 class was the final development of the basic design first seen in the T9s.

For some five or six years, the D15s worked mainly on West of England expresses between Waterloo and Salisbury; then they took over the principal Bournemouth trains. From about 1920 until 1937, however, they were employed on the Portsmouth line, almost exclusively, and added to their reputation for fast running. They were at least as speedy as the T9s and, being larger and more powerful, they could take, on the average, two or three more coaches without difficulty.

In the summer of 1913, I was one of a party of members of the Stephenson Locomotive Society on their annual visit to Eastleigh Works—the first time that I had ever been there. From London we travelled by a Bournemouth express headed by No 464 which was apparently being tried out on the best LSWR expresses other than West of England trains. She ran well and treated us to a steady and exhilarating 80 m.p.h. between Micheldever and Winchester. It was here that, not many months before, I had timed 80 m.p.h. for the first time in my life, behind a T9, No 702.

No 463, at first, differed from the others in being fitted with a hooter instead of a whistle; but in 1915, an ordinary whistle was substituted because, so it is said, the hooter was liable to be mistaken for an air-raid warning! After the war, however, the hooter was put back on the engine and she sported it until the end of her days. At a station like Clapham Junction, if a blast from a hooter heralded the approach of an express train, the engine was certain to be No 463. But a batch of M7 0-4-4 tank engines built in 1897 ran, for a short time, with similar hooters, soon replaced by ordinary whistles.

An interesting little feature, common to all Drummond's inside-cylinder engines, was the short throw of 9 in. for the coupling-rods. This was inherited from William Stroudley, of the Brighton line, and was seldom used by other designers; but Drummond employed it consistently for nearly 40 years on all the inside cylindered coupled engines he

GENERAL SPECIFICATION			
CYLINDERS		**TUBES**	
Diameter ...	... 19½ in.	Number ...	... 247
Stroke ...	... 26 in.	Diameter ...	... 1¾ in.
		HEATING SURFACE	
BOILER		Tubes... ...	1,406 sq. ft.
Length between		Firebox ...	148 sq. ft.
tubeplates ...	12 ft 0 in.	Total	*1,724 sq. ft.
Maximum			
diameter ...	4 ft 10½ in.	**GRATE AREA**	
		Square feet ...	... 27
		*Including additional heating	
FIREBOX LENGTH		surface provided by 66 water	
Inside... ...	—	tubes of 2¾ in. dia. contained in	
Outside ...	8 ft 4 in.	firebox.	

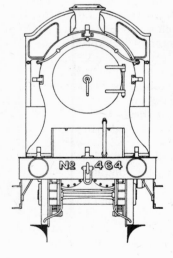

designed for the North British, Caledonian and London and South Western Railways. The idea was that the short throw tended to minimise the disturbing forces set up in the vertical plane by heavy coupling-rods, especially at high speed.

The dimensions of these engines were decidedly bold, though it is noteworthy that no superheater was incorporated; instead, Drummond used his steam drier which he preferred because it got rid of much of the moisture in the steam, thereby reducing the tendency for condensation in the cylinders, and it gave him no trouble with the lubrication. The cylinders, which were 19½ in. dia. and had a stroke of 26 in., had the valves on top actuated by Walschaerts valve gear which was driven by eccentrics mounted on the driving axle. Since only two eccentrics were required, instead of the four that would have been needed for Stephenson gear, Drummond, for once, took advantage of the extra room available and provided good, big main bearings.

The wheel diameters were: bogie, 3 ft 7 in. and coupled, 6 ft 7 in. The wheelbase was 24 ft 9 in. divided into 6 ft 6 in., plus 8 ft 3 in., plus 10 ft. Overhang was 2 ft 1 in. at the front and 4 ft 1 in. at the back.

The boiler centre line was 8 ft 9 in. above rail level. The barrel was 12 ft long and made in two rings, the larger of which was 4 ft 10½ in. dia., inside.

There were 247 tubes of 1¾ in. dia., which gave 1,406 sq. ft of heating surface. A large firebox was provided, 8 ft 4 in. long outside and adding 148 sq. ft to the heating surface; it contained 66 water tubes of 2¾ in. dia., increasing the heating surface still further by 170 sq. ft to make a total of 1,724 sq. ft. The grate area was 27 sq. ft and the working pressure 200 p.s.i.

The original tender was of 4,500 gallons capacity and had space for 4 tons of coal; it is shown in my drawing. It was carried on two bogies, the wheels of which were 3 ft 7 in. dia., the wheelbase being 14 ft 6 in., divided into 5 ft plus 4 ft 6 in., plus 5 ft. The leading overhang was 5 ft 8 in., and the trailing 4 ft 4 in. Over bufferheads, the total length of engine and tender was 59 ft 2¼ in., and the total wheelbase was 49 ft 7 in. In working trim, the engine weight was 59 tons 15 cwt, with 20 tons 15 cwt on the bogie and 19 tons 10 cwt on each of the coupled axles. The tender, full, weighed 49 tons, so that the total for engine and tender was 108 tons 15 cwt.

In 1915, R. W. Urie began to modify these engines by doing away with the firebox water-tubes and replacing the steam drier by the Eastleigh superheater, which necessitated a considerable extension of the smokebox. These alterations did not improve the appearance, and so far as could be seen, they made little difference to the performance; but there

may have been some gain in economy. During these alterations, No 468 had her boiler mountings modified; her safety valves were taken off the dome and moved to the firebox, and she acquired a dome and safety valve casing of King Arthur pattern which made her look rather strange. None of the other D15s was altered in this manner.

In 1925-6, R. E. Maunsell removed the Eastleigh superheaters and replaced them with new ones of his own design. At the same time, he replaced the double-bogie tenders with Drummond six-wheelers of only 3,500 gallons capacity. The D15 class became extinct in 1956.

A detail that is worth mentioning is that the balancing of these engines appears to have been subject to some variations. Judging by photographs, the majority of the class had the balanceweights in the upper quadrant of the driving wheels; No 463, and possibly one or two others, had wheels which were similar to those of the T9 class, in which the balanceweights were in the lower quadrant. I have been unable to discover whether there was any particular significance in this, as no previous writer seems to have even mentioned the matter.

Incidentally, the " steering-wheel " on the tender, for operating the hand-brake, probably caused a few firemen to mutter unprintable oaths until they got used to it !

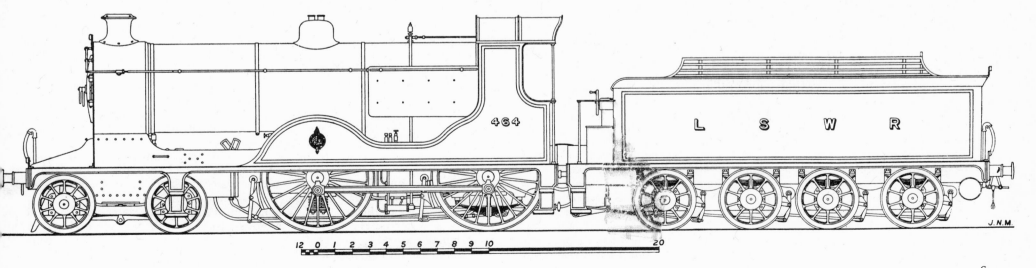

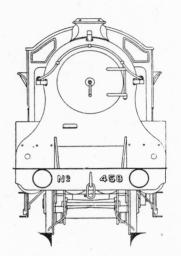

GENERAL SPECIFICATION

CYLINDERS			TUBES		
Diameter	...	15 in. (four)	Number	...	247 & 84
Stroke	... ...	26 in.	Diameter	1¾ in. &	2¼ in.
BOILER			HEATING SURFACE		
Length, between			Tubes	...	1,580 sq. ft &
tubeplates		14 ft 2 in.			200 sq. ft
Maximum dia-			Firebox	...	140 sq. ft
meter	...	4 ft 10¾ in.	Total	...	1,920 sq. ft
FIREBOX LENGTH			GRATE AREA		
Inside	... ...	9 ft.	Square feet	...	31.5
Outside	9 ft	6 in.			

DRUMMOND'S T14 Class

DUGALD DRUMMOND was a man who, in his time, designed some very fine locomotives, but in his last years his skill appeared to fail him.

His 4-4-0, 0-6-0 and 0-4-4T engines on the North British, Caledonian and London and South Western railways stood second to none of their kind and were far better than some; but when, in 1905, he tried his hand at 4-6-0 engines, he seemed to go to pieces. And although he persisted until 1911, none of his 4-6-0 designs was entirely successful.

There were four successive designs—three for mixed traffic, and one for heavy express passenger work. It is the last-mentioned which is the subject of my drawing; the class was officially designated T14 and consisted of ten engines built in 1911-2 for working heavy express passenger trains from London to Bournemouth and to Salisbury.

I well· remember when the first of these engines came out in March 1911. What a huge thing we all thought her. A closer acquaintance, however, soon showed that she was *not* so big as she seemed to be; the effect of large size was owing to the very high pitch of the boiler, due to four cylinders, with piston valves on top, being arranged all in line under the smokebox.

These engines were promptly dubbed Drummond's Babies, but eventually became known as Paddleboxes

because of the big combined splasher, with its " port-hole " over the coupled wheels.

Incidentally, that porthole, which was provided with a nice, brass, hinged frame, was made to open so as to give access to the steam-operated Walschaerts valve gear which was almost hidden by the big splasher.

I can well imagine that, in spite of the porthole, the whole arrangement was conducive to quite a number of new words and phrases in the unofficial locomotive vocabulary ! It is almost incredible that the mind which was responsible for the M7 class 0-4-4 tank engines should have thought up these Paddle-boxes ! However, I suppose it is always easy to be wise after the event.

That the T14 class engines were not wholly bad is clear from the fact that both of Drummond's successors, R. W. Urie and R. E. L. Maunsell, devoted considerable thought to the problem of making the engines more successful.

Urie, in 1915, decided to superheat them by equipping them with extended smokeboxes and his standard Eastleigh superheaters in place of the former steam drier which Drummond had put on six of the engines. Urie also removed the firebox water tubes with which all the engines were originally fitted.

But these alterations made little difference; in fact,

in some ways they made things worse, particularly with what had, up till then, been the main trouble—hot boxes.

In 1930 Maunsell turned his attention to the engines, and he made some quite drastic alterations. He removed the Eastleigh superheater and replaced it with one of his own design; at the same time, in order to cut down weight as well as to provide better ventilation to the bearings, he discarded the paddle-box splashers, substituting small, separate splashers on a raised footplating.

These alterations did achieve some improvement which, however, was made better still a little while later when forced lubrication was provided for the bearings. But the engines were made to look more gawky than ever !

Probably as a result of the alterations just mentioned, the T14s managed to exist, on the average, for some 40 years.

The first one to be broken up was No 458, which had the misfortune to receive a direct hit from a bomb during an air-raid in 1940, and it just about reduced her to scrap on the spot !

It was not until eight years later that normal official withdrawal began with Nos 445 and 459 in 1948, and all the nine remaining engines had gone by 1952. In their last years these engines did most of their work during the summer months, as they were regarded as stand-by engines for use when required in busy holiday periods.

My drawing depicts the original Drummond design, the dimensions of which were: cylinders (4), 15 in. dia., 26 in. stroke; wheel diameters, bogie, 3 ft 7 in., coupled 6 ft 7 in.; wheelbase, 27 ft 7 in., divided into 6 ft 6 in. plus 6 ft 9 in. plus 7 ft 2 in. plus 7 ft 2 in.; the overhangs were 2 ft 1 in. at the front and 5 ft 3 in. at the back.

The boiler, pitched 9 ft 3½ in. above rail level, was none too large for steaming four 15 in. cylinders; its diameter was 4 ft 10¾ in. outside the larger ring, and its length was 13 ft 9 in. The firebox was 9 ft 6 in. long, outside, and 4 ft 1 in. wide. The grate was 9 ft long and 3 ft 7 in. wide, the area being 31.5 sq. ft; it was slightly sloped and, for so large an engine, very shallow.

The working pressure was 200 p.s.i., and there cannot be much doubt that the fireman was hard pressed to maintain such a pressure for any length of time, especially if the engine was being worked hard.

There were 247 fire tubes of 1¾ in. dia. and 84 water tubes of 2¼ in. dia. The heating surface for the fire tubes was 1,580 sq. ft, and for the water tubes 200 sq. ft; that of the firebox was 140 sq. ft so that the total amounted to 1,920 sq. ft.

In engines 447 and 458 to 462, the smokebox was fitted up with Drummond's steam drier, which consisted of grids of 2 in. tubes communicating with the boiler tubes and, therefore, exposed to the heated gases from the firebox; these grids were housed in chambers through which the steam was passed on its way to the valve chests.

This arrangement raised the temperature of the steam to some 400 deg. F, which was thought to be enough without leading to any serious lubrication troubles. It could not have achieved an outstanding success, however, as Urie soon replaced it with a proper superheater.

This, however, *did* lead to lubrication troubles, as the engines suffered worse than ever from overheated main bearings, a disease that was not alleviated until Maunsell installed his system of forced lubrication. But even this was not the perfect cure because the root cause of the trouble was that the main bearings were too small.

The engines weighed, in working trim, 74 tons 10 cwt, with 52 tons resting on the coupled wheels. The original tender, loaded, weighed 49 tons, making the total 123 tons 10 cwt. This tender was of the 4,500 gal. pattern carried on two bogies, the wheels being 3 ft 7 in. dia. and the wheelbase 14 ft 6 in. divided into 5 ft plus 4 ft 6 in. plus 5 ft.

No 462, however, was fitted, in 1912, with a 5,800 gal. tender, and the other nine engines of the class were provided with similar tenders in 1913; it is one of these that I have shown in my drawing.

This larger tender, with its 8 ft wide body, was the biggest that Drummond designed. Its wheelbase was 16 ft 6 in., divided into 5 ft 6 in. plus 5 ft 6 in. plus 5 ft 6 in., and it weighed 60 tons 8 cwt in working order.

A T14 starting away with a train was always interesting to watch; it was usually a slow business—sometimes painfully slow—with the engine giving out ponderous, muffled-sounding exhaust beats suggesting that she nursed a rooted objection to being obliged to start at all!

This was particularly noticeable when leaving Waterloo, or northwards from Winchester. Possibly, the layout of the valve gear, combined with a valve setting that was not as good as it might have been, had something to do with those lethargic starts while a contributing cause of the muffled sound was that half the exhaust was turned back, Stroudley fashion, into the tender to heat the feed water.

All the same, to be able to remember these " babies " in their prime recalls happy days for me: and, whatever their faults, the engines were very imposing in their original condition, though I would hesitate to place them among England's most handsome 4-6-0s.

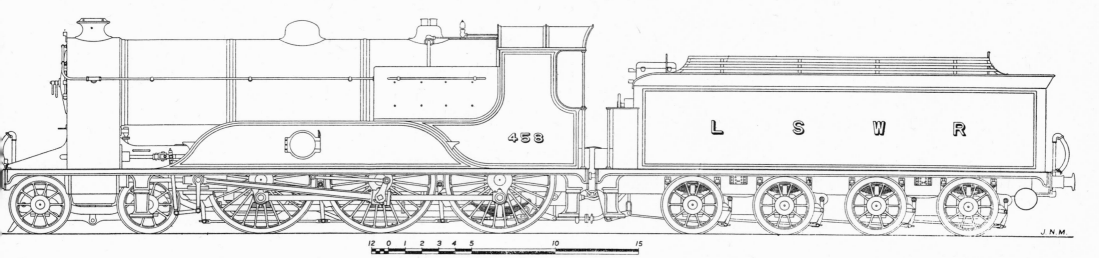

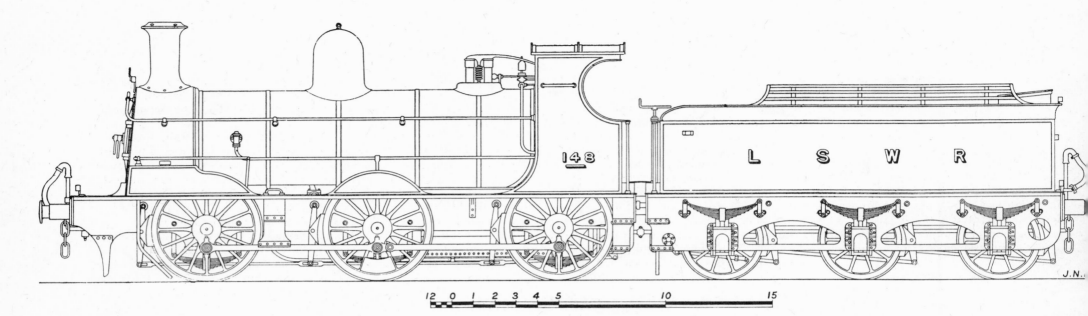

12 0 1 2 3 4 5   10   15

THE
ADAMS GOODS ENGINES

GENERAL SPECIFICATION

CYLINDERS			TUBES		
Diameter	...	... 17½ in.	Number	...	... 218
Stroke	...	... 24 in.	Diameter	...	... 1¾ in.
BOILER			HEATING SURFACE		
Length between			Tubes...	...	1,079 sq. ft.
tubeplates	...	10 ft 6 in.	Firebox	...	108 sq. ft.
Maximum diameter	4 ft 4 in.		Total	...	1,187 sq. ft.
FIREBOX LENGTH					
Inside...	...	5 ft 2¼ in.	GRATE AREA		
Outside	...	5 ft 10 in.	Square feet	...	... 17.8

I BELIEVE I am right in thinking that the Adams Goods Engines were the first and only 0-6-0 tender freight engines that William Adams ever designed. Very excellent examples they were !

They were all built by Neilson & Co., of Glasgow, in batches: five in 1881, seven in 1882, twenty-four in 1883, thirty in 1885 and four in 1886, making seventy in all.

Pretty well every main line locomotive depot on the London and South Western Railway had its quota of them; yet it is surprising how rarely they were to be seen. The reason for this was that the LSWR was primarily a passenger-carrying line and nearly all its freight traffic ran during the night hours when all decently brought-up boys like me were in bed— or should have been. But provided that you knew where to go, you could find one or more of these engines shunting or marshalling in the larger goods yards during daylight hours. I used to see them at Nine Elms, Wimbledon and Aldershot; there was a considerable amount of military traffic at Aldershot where No 0148 was often to be seen shunting, or working trains of Government stores and sometimes troop specials, in the years before the 1914-18 war.

In 1916, 50 of these fine old engines were commandeered by the Government and, during the next two years, were sent out to the Middle East for war service in the Railway Operating Division behind the various battle fronts. Of 36 of them sent to Palestine, four were lost when the s.s. *Arabic* was torpedoed in the Mediterranean Sea in 1918.

Five went to Serbia in 1916 and nine to Mesopotamia in 1917; none of the 50 ever came home again. As late as 1930, some were still working in the countries to which they had been sent nearly 15 years before, and a few had migrated to Greece, Turkey and Egypt, where they seemed to have become popular with the local railwaymen.

Of the 20 that were not taken over by the Government in 1916, all continued to work until 1933, when two—Nos 0153 and 515, then 3153 and 3515 in the Southern Railway list—were withdrawn. The remaining 18 lingered on to become the property of British Railways in 1948, and were renumbered 30564 to 30581 in the BR list. They put in about another 10 years of work on local goods traffic until the last survivor, No 30567—old No 154 of 1883—was withdrawn in September 1959, at the ripe old age of 76!

Let people scoff as they will at anything Victorian and Edwardian, these old goods engines were typical of the times in being very carefully designed and built. Apart from having been reboilered four times, No 30567 was almost in her *original* condition when she was withdrawn. Compare this with the record of certain Bo-Bo and 0-6-0 diesel locomotives built from 1945 to 1950 and now withdrawn for scrap!

My drawing shows No 0148 in the condition in which she was when I knew her at Aldershot. She had been little altered since she first went into service in 1885. Her original stovepipe chimney had been replaced by a cast-iron one of Drummond's standard pattern; her tender had lost the handrail and footboard with which it had been built and had been fitted with coal-rails. In other respects, she was in nearly her original condition, except that she had been given a boiler with a taller dome than the original one.

No 0148 was built as No 148 in 1885 and was transferred to the duplicate list in 1904, which accounts for the bar under her number. This was the usual LSWR method of numbering duplicate engines at that time; it had the merit of simplicity and was certainly convenient, as it readily identified the engines.

No 0148 was one of 14 of her class that were sent out to Palestine in 1916—the first batch to go. She was employed on purely military duties while the war lasted, and then, when hostilities ceased in November 1918, she was taken over by the War Department and was used for rehabilitating the

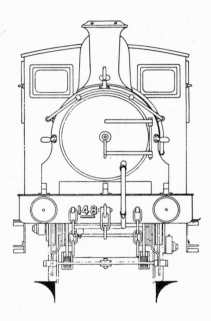

railways of Egypt and Palestine, working out there until 1929, when she seems to have been sold for scrap. I did not see her again after 1914, but a friend of mine, who was in the Middle East during 1924, reported having seen her working on the Egyptian State Railways, still carrying her British number.

No 3509 was an engine of some interest, her animated image must have been seen by many thousands of people; for, in June 1937, she was temporarily taken out of traffic, fitted with a short LBSCR Marsh chimney, and given a prominent part in that hilarious Will Hay film *Oh, Mr Porter!* To locomotive enthusiasts, No 3509 flaunting that short chimney, was quite as amusing as any of the other characters in the film, and she certainly played her part very well.

These engines, officially designated the 395 class, had cylinders of 17½ in. dia. × 24 in. stroke, inclined at 1 in 9, to clear the leading axle. The wheels were 5 ft 1 in. dia., with a wheelbase of 16 ft 6 in. divided into 8 ft plus 8 ft 6 in. For the engines built before 1885 the leading overhang was 4 ft 9 in.; for those built in 1885-6 it was 6 ft. The rear overhang for all was 3 ft 6 in.

A very good boiler was provided; its diameter was 4 ft 4 in. outside and its length of barrel 10 ft 6 in.; its centre-line was pitched 7 ft above rail level. A rather unusual feature was the sloping front to the smokebox, evidently to avoid an awkward joint with the cylinder block, whose front was inclined. In later years some of the engines were given new smokeboxes with vertical fronts; but most of them retained the old type to the end.

In the boiler barrel were 218 tubes of 1¾ in. dia., of which the heating surface was 1,079 sq. ft; the firebox added 108 sq. ft, making the total heating surface 1,187. The outer shell of the firebox was 5 ft 10 in. long, and the inner box 5 ft 2¼ in. Grate area was 17.8 sq. ft and working pressure 140 p.s.i.

The tender wheels were 3 ft 9¾ in. dia., and the wheelbase was 13 ft equally divided. At the front the overhangs were 3 ft 6 in., and at the back 3 ft, while the total length of engine and tender over buffers was 48 ft 0¾ in. for the engines built before 1885 and 49 ft 4¼ in. for the later ones. Water capacity was 2,500 gallons.

Between the earlier and later engines the weights, of course, varied. For the earlier, the distribution, in working order, was 12 tons 16 cwt on the leading axle, 13 tons 12 cwt on the middle axle and 11 tons 4 cwt on the trailing axle, a total of 37 tons 12 cwt. For the later engines the corresponding figures were: 13 tons 17 cwt, 13 tons 16 cwt and 11 tons 1 cwt, a total of 38 tons 14 cwt. For all, the tender weighed 28 tons 13 cwt loaded, so that the weight of engine and tender was 66 tons 5 cwt for the earlier lot and 67 tons 7 cwt for the later.

The last survivor, BR 50567 of Guildford, had an old London, Chatham and Dover boiler and an Adams 3,300-gallon tender.

2-4-0

TANK ENGINE

No 298

GENERAL SPECIFICATION

CYLINDERS			TUBES		
Diameter	...	... 16½ in.	Number	...	... 224
Stroke	...	... 20 in.	Diameter	...	... 1⅝ in.
BOILER					
Length, between			HEATING SURFACE		
tubeplates		9 ft 10 in.	Tubes	...	753 sq. ft
Maximum dia-			Firebox	...	94 sq. ft
meter	...	3 ft 10 in.	Total	...	847 sq. ft
FIREBOX LENGTH					
Inside	...	5 ft 6 in.	GRATE AREA		
Outside	...	6 ft	Square feet	...	14.8

THIS FASCINATING little engine is as old as it looks, but it has a most interesting history. I use the present tense deliberately because the engine is still in service in the Southern Region of British Railways—and for a special reason that will be apparent later.

Between 1863 and 1875 Joseph Beattie ordered eighty-five engines of this type for working suburban passenger traffic, chiefly in the London area but also around Exeter, Salisbury, Bournemouth and other important centres on the London and South Western Railway.

In their original condition these engines must have been very pleasing, judging by pictures of them. They were not only nicely finished, but were decorated with plenty of polished brass, copper and other bright metal work.

In later years, however, their appearance was considerably modified by William Adams, who re-boilered most of the engines and drastically toned down the former decoration, though a smart finish was retained in keeping with the Adams tradition. The withdrawal of these engines began as far back as 1890 and was completed by 1900, with the exception of three engines—L.S.W. Nos 0298, 0314 and 0329.

Believe it or not these three survivors are still in active service as British Railways' Nos 30585, 30586 and 30587, respectively. They are employed in the

Bodmin area of Cornwall, where they work exclusively on the short branch line to Wenford quarries.

Odd as it may seem, those three aged little sisters are the only engines—out of all the Southern Region's considerable locomotive stock—that can work the Wenford quarry traffic without giving trouble, either to the track or to themselves! So it comes about that

for more than 50 years after all the other engines of their class had been scrapped the three old maids have been carefully maintained specially for working on the Wenford line.

It was in 1913, I believe, that I first met No 0298 at Eastleigh, where she had just undergone a periodical overhaul, and my drawing shows her as she was

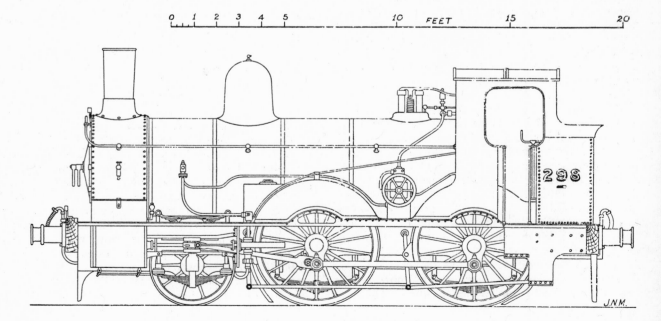

then. She had an Adams boiler and an unusually short stovepipe chimney, giving her a rather stocky look that cannot be described as typical of her class.

Since then further detail changes have taken place, with the result that the general appearance of these engines has been very considerably modified.

There have been a few other instances of old locomotives being kept specially for working certain duties, but none, I think, covering so long a period as that of these three Beattie tank engines. In practically all cases where this has happened the reason has been that the flexibility of the wheelbase and the light axle-loading of the engines concerned have been particularly suitable for the particular lines over which the engines have had to run.

Until 1871 the cylinder diameter was $15\frac{1}{2}$ in., but later it was increased to 16 in. and then to $16\frac{1}{2}$ in. The stroke remained unaltered at 20 in. The diameter of the leading wheels was 3 ft $7\frac{3}{4}$ in., and of the coupled wheels 5 ft 6 in. The wheelbase was 5 ft 6 in. plus 7 ft.

The boiler had a maximum diameter of 3 ft 10 in and contained no fewer than 224 tubes of $1\frac{5}{8}$ in. dia. The grate area was 14.8 sq. ft, and the working pressure was 130 p.s.i. In full trim, ready for traffic, the weight was $34\frac{1}{2}$ tons. Water was carried in two well-tanks, one under the boiler, the other under the

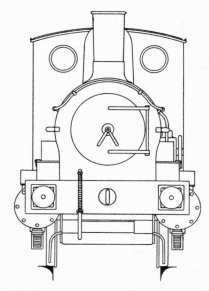

bunker. Their combined capacity was 550 gallons.

An interesting feature of these engines is that they were fitted with Alexander Allen's straight-link valve gear while No 0298 at least was still equipped with Beattie's steam-driven boiler feed pump (see drawing) as late as 1930.

The arrangement of the leading springs was very

unusual though typical of Beattie; in fact, I cannot recall any other quite like it. The outside axlebox took a bearing on the lower slidebar, to which, also, the spring hangers were attached, the spring itself being below the axlebox. The inside springs were above their respective axleboxes which were mounted in horned slots in the inside frames—a perfectly normal arrangement. There was nothing unusual about the underhung springs for the driving and coupled axles.

I have always understood that the underlying reason for this uncommon springing arrangement was to check the " boxing " motion that is very likely to arise from the use of outside cylinders combined with such a short wheelbase. The scheme appears to have been very successful.

How much longer the three survivors of this interesting class will remain at work seems to depend entirely on how long the Wenford quarries remain productive. But it must be one of the curiosities of British railway history that these three engines have, in their particular field, withstood the onslaughts of more modern forms of motive power unit for over half a century.

I cannot recall anything to compare with it; and into the bargain these engines date from 1874 and 1875, so they are now nearly 90 years old.

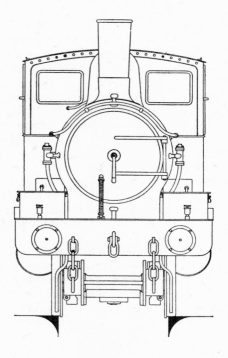

GENERAL SPECIFICATION

CYLINDERS			TUBES		
Diameter	...	... 17½ in.	Number	...	... 201
Stroke	...	... 24 in.	Diameter	...	... 1¾ in.
BOILER					
Length, between			**HEATING SURFACE**		
tubeplates		... 10 ft	Tubes	...	944.7 sq. ft
Maximum dia-			Firebox	...	111.2 sq. ft
meter	...	4 ft 2 in.	Total	...	1,055.9 sq. ft
FIREBOX LENGTH					
Inside	...	5 ft 6 in.	**GRATE AREA**		
Outside	...	6 ft 2 in.	Square feet	...	18.14

In the 1880s, when the suburban passenger traffic on most railways was being worked by 6-wheeled or 8-wheeled tank engines, the London and South Western Railway went one better and introduced 10-wheelers.

They were designed by William Adams, but they were all built by private builders such as Beyer Peacock & Co., Neilson & Co., Dubs & Co. and Robert Stephenson & Co. The class eventually numbered 71 engines—officially styled the "415" class—built between March 1882 and December 1885.

My drawing shows No 60, which was originally No 78, built by Stephensons in 1885 and renumbered in 1890; she is depicted in her original condition, except for the number, because that is how she was when I first came to know her and many of her sisters in 1899 and 1900.

They were handsome engines and wonderful workers on many of the London suburban services operated by the L.S.W.R. I remember seeing many of this class at work on trains to Epsom, Leatherhead,

Guildford, Hampton Court, Shepperton, Windsor and Reading.

Not every train stopped at all stations—and the engines had opportunities of showing their paces on non-stop sprints to such places as Richmond, Surbiton and even Guildford. It was on such work as this that their capacity for speed was frequently noted. No 60, on one occasion, was at the head of a Reading train and was timed to Richmond, 11½ miles from Waterloo, in exactly 14 minutes, start to stop. The maximum speed, just before steam was shut off for the Richmond stop, was 63 m.p.h.

On another occasion, No 487 on a semi-fast train from Alton, started from Woking with such vigour as to reach 60 m.p.h. in less than four miles, and sustained it continuously for about eight miles before stopping at Surbiton. Several similar examples of such sprints with these engines could be quoted; for it seems that the drivers had no compunction in letting the engines go as they would, if conditions were favourable. This was largely owing to the fact that these engines rode very steadily and comfortably at any speed;

they would negotiate points and crossings and glide smoothly round curves without indulging in unpleasant oscillations. Their flexible wheelbase and the equalisers between the springs of the coupled wheels contributed largely to these excellent riding qualities.

There were some differences of detail between the various batches built, but there now seems to be no information available as to the precise reasons for the changes.

For example, the 12 engines built by Beyer Peacock in 1882, and the 18 by Stephensons in 1883, had a water capacity of 1,000 gallons whereas in all the others the capacity was 1,200 gallons. Again, in 10 engines by Stephensons and 10 by Dubs in 1885, the trailing wheels were 3 ft 6 in. dia., while in 10 built by Neilsons in the same year this diameter was 3 ft, as in all the earlier engines of the class.

Apart from these variations, the general dimensions of this class were : cylinders, 17½ in. dia. 24 in. stroke; coupled wheels 5 ft 7½ in. dia. when new; bogie wheels, 3 ft dia.; wheelbase 29 ft 5 in., divided into 7 ft plus 6 ft 5 in. plus 8 ft 6 in. plus 7 ft 6 in.

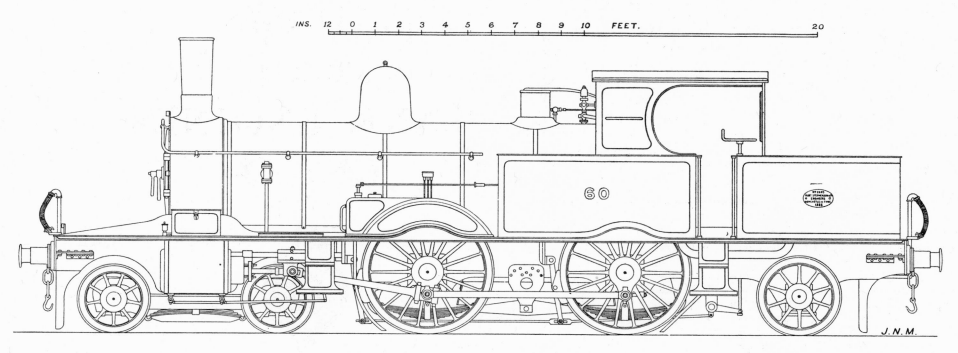

J. N. M.

The boiler was 4 ft 2 in. dia. and 10 ft long, pitched 7 ft above rail level. There were 201 tubes of 1¾ in. dia., the firebox was 6 ft 2 in. long, and the grate area was 18.14 sq. ft. The heating surface was 944.7 sq. ft for the tubes and 111.2 sq. ft for the firebox, totalling 1,055.9 sq. ft. The original working pressure was 140 p.s.i., later increased to 160 p.s.i.—rather a jump!

The total weight in working order was 54 tons 2 cwt, of which 30 tons 16 cwt was imposed upon the coupled wheels and therefore available for adhesion. The tractive effort was 14,920 lb., quite a respectable amount for such engines.

The withdrawal of this class began in 1921, but was halted in 1928 when only two of the engines remained in service; these were originally Nos 125 and 520, and they were kept specially for working the Axminster-Lyme Regis branch where they are still at work.

In 1946, they were joined by a third engine, old No 488, which had had an interesting history: She was sold to the Government in September 1917, for working at the General Salvage Depot near Sitting-bourne, Kent, and two years later she was sold to the

East Kent Railway. In 1946 she was resold to the Southern Railway by whom she was numbered 3488. She was taken into Eastleigh Works where, like her two sisters, she was provided with new frames made to the original drawings, and her bogie was altered to give extra side play. After this she was sent to Exmouth Junction motive power depot as a spare engine for the Axminster branch.

So, here we have another instance of old engines being renovated and kept in good repair specially for working a particular service simply because no other proved so satisfactory on the same service.

In the British Railways books these engines are numbered 30582, 30583 and 30584, respectively, and I hope they may be kept at work for some years.

A further point of interest is that during the 1914-18 war—for about 18 months—four of this class, Nos 480, 481, 485 and 487, were lent to the Highland Railway for working light-passenger traffic, and so became familiar far from their native haunts.

My last trip behind one of these engines occurred in the summer of 1921, when I had gone down to

Staines one day. For my return to London I chose to travel by an up fast train from Windsor, rather than by a local stopping at all stations. When my train came in I was surprised to see that the engine was No 0490.

At that time very few of these fine old engines were left in service, especially in the London district; those that did remain were used on empty-carriage working between Waterloo and Clapham Junction, and it was rare indeed to see one on a regular passenger service.

I believe that No 0490 was then stationed at Strawberry Hill (Twickenham) and was probably the last one of the class to work London suburban trains; she was withdrawn for scrap in 1926.

Another interesting detail is that the trailing wheels of these engines were mounted in radial axleboxes, and in this respect were unique on the L.S.W.R. After 1885, however, Adams abandoned the 4-4-2 type in favour of the 0-4-4, of which he designed two different classes between 1888 and 1896; but for many years his 4-4-2 tanks continued in full force to give very satisfactory service.

ADAMS
0-4-4
TANK ENGINES
Class O2

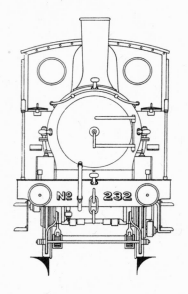

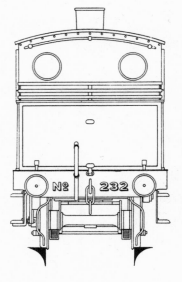

THESE were delightful little engines and great favourites with everyone who had anything to do with them. William Adams built the first examples in December, 1889, and Dugald Drummond the last lot in March, 1895.

There were 60 of them, numbered from 177 to 236, and they were designed expressly to work on branch lines and for general light passenger duties. It should be noted that the last ten, Nos 227 to 236, had cabs which were 6 in. higher than those in the rest of the class; otherwise, the engines were all alike, and when I first saw them about 1900, many of them were finding plenty of work to do in the London area on local passenger and parcels trains. In spite of their small size they were sturdy, powerful and capable of running at surprisingly high speeds.

When the electrification of the London suburban lines was completed in 1929, the local contingent of O2-class engines was put on to empty-coach duties between Waterloo station and Clapham Junction carriage depot, and many of them were thus employed for several years. They were used for marshalling steam express trains, hauling them to Waterloo and bringing back to Clapham Junction the empties of steam main line trains that had terminated at Waterloo.

Engine No 232 was employed on this kind of work for a long time, and was a familiar object in the Clapham Junction scene. She was especially noticeable because, unlike the other O2s that shared her duties, she retained the Adams stovepipe chimney; the others had Drummond chimneys.

It always fascinated me to see one of these diminutive engines hauling a long and heavy train of main line corridor stock either to or from Waterloo. It looked rather incongruous, but the engines seemed to have little difficulty and seldom faltered.

Another intriguing and slightly amusing feature of these engines, in common with other Adams engines, was the husky sound given out by their whistles. They seemed quite unable to sound a clear note, and therefore always gave the impression that they suffered from bad colds. This attracted some attention at Clapham Junction, because there was always a lot of whistling when the engines were engaged on marshalling work, and the sound was such a contrast to the sharp, rather piercing note of a Drummond whistle.

I suppose the chief reason why these engines were so extraordinarily attractive was that, compared with their designer's fine and massive T1 class, or the later Drummond M7 class, they were so small. That there was more in this impression than some people might admit, became abundantly clear in 1923, when a number of the O2 class were withdrawn from their normal duties. They were taken to Eastleigh Works to be thoroughly overhauled, fitted with much larger bunkers, deprived of their vacuum and steam brakes which were replaced by the Westinghouse air brake, and then sent to the Isle of Wight where, for more than 35 years, they have performed yeoman service.

In all, 21 of the class were involved in this transformation, the last to go to the island being sent over in 1947. They were warmly welcomed by the islanders, whose train services they completely revolutionised. The majority are still there, working as well as ever. I am sorry to have to add that their condition is not now what it was; for some 15 years after they first went to the Isle of Wight, they were kept in a wonderful state of cleanliness and good order which was well worth a trip across The Solent to see.

All that now belongs to the past, unfortunately; but the size and light weight of these engines made them completely suitable for running on the none-too-robust, though well kept track of the Isle of Wight railways, while at the same time, the engines were considerably more powerful than those they replaced.

These 21 engines were all renumbered into a separate list, 14 to 34 inclusive, each with the prefix W, to distinguish them from engines on the mainland. After 1931, however, the prefix was discarded, because the general renumbering scheme brought in by the Southern Railway made it unnecessary.

In 1929 came the added distinction of names for all the Island engines; the nameplates were of cast brass with raised letters and border on a red background, adding quite a smart touch of colour to the general effect. The names were all after towns, villages and places of interest in the Isle of Wight, and they enhanced the individuality and popular appeal of the engines. None but the most prosaic of holiday-makers, who poured into the Island during summer months, could possibly fail to notice the names of the trusty little engines so busily and efficiently taking away crowded train after crowded train from Ryde Pier station. It was an unforgettable sight and experience.

The dimensions of the O2 class were: cylinder diameter, originally 17 in., but in 1891 this was increased to 17½ in.; the stroke was 24 in. The wheel

diameters were, coupled 4 ft 10 in., bogie 3 ft. The wheelbase was 20 ft 4 in. divided into 6 ft 10 in. plus 8 ft 6 in. plus 5 ft, and the overhang was 5 ft 6¼ in. at the front and 1 ft 11½ in. at the back. The total length over buffers was 30 ft 11 in., the buffers being 1 ft 6 in. long and the bufferbeams ⅝ in. thick.

A well proportioned little boiler was provided, made in two rings, 4 ft 2 in. and 4 ft 3 in. dia., and the length of the barrel was 9 ft 5 in.; the height of the centre line above rail level was 6 ft 10½ in. The firebox casing was 5 ft long outside and the grate area was 13.83 sq. ft.

There were 201 tubes of 1¾ in. dia., and the total heating surface was 987 sq. ft made up of 898 sq. ft for the tubes and 89 sq. ft for the firebox, and working pressure was 160 p.s.i.

In working order, the weight was originally 44 tons 11½ cwt, but the official diagram gives 48 tons 8 cwt for those engines which were altered for service in the Isle of Wight. The adhesion weight was 30 tons, and the official figure for tractive force was 17,245 lb. The tank capacity was 800 gallons, and the original bunker was for 2 tons of coal, but was increased to 3 tons for the Isle of Wight engines. The width across the footplating was 8 ft 3 in.

It is of interest to note that the O2 class were the only Adams engines to be named. The first occasion was the opening of the Brookwood-Bisley branch on July 12, 1890, and the first meet of the National Rifle Association at the Bisley ranges. HRH the Princess of Wales (afterwards Queen Alexandra) attended the event, and No 185 hauled the special train, the first on the branch.

The engine bore the name *Alexandra* painted in block letters on the side tanks, with a representation of the Prince of Wales' feathers above it and an elaborate monogram of the letters LSWR below it. The engine retained this unusual decoration until November, 1896. The other named engines were Nos W14 to W34 in the Isle of Wight; their names, in order of numbers, were: *Fishbourne, Cowes, Ventnor, Seaview, Ningwood, Osborne, Shanklin, Sandown, Brading, Totland, Calbourne, Godshill, Whitewell, Merstone, Ashey, Alverstone, Shorwell, Chale, Bonchurch, Bembridge* and *Newport*. That is a nice list that will probably awaken nostalgic memories for some readers.

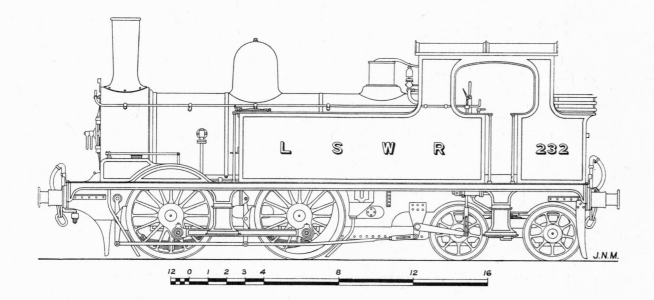

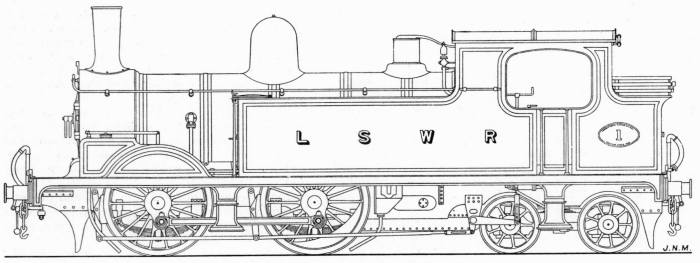

WILLIAM ADAMS T1 Class

ALTHOUGH William Adams adopted the 4-4-2 type for his initial design of suburban tank engines for the London and South Western Railway, he abandoned the type in 1888 when new engines were needed for suburban work, and adopted the 0-4-4 type instead; it gave him a much more compact design with greater capacity for water and coal.

Adams designed two classes of 0-4-4 tank engines. The first was the T1 class which was intended for suburban passenger work, and the second the O2 class, a much smaller design for working on light branch lines.

The T1 class comprised 50 fine engines built between June 1888 and August 1896, the last ten being completed under Dugald Drummond, who introduced a few alterations to minor details. The boilers, cylinders and valve gear were interchangeable with those of the 0-4-2 tender engines of class A12, described in Chapter 16, but the boiler height was lower, due to the smaller diameter of the coupled wheels.

I first saw the T1s about 1900, when many were engaged on suburban work in the London area. I admired them for their simplicity, neatness and compactness. By that time, I think, they had been repainted in the Drummond style, as I do not recall

ever seeing one in the original Adams livery. This seems a little odd, as I can clearly remember seeing some of the earlier Adams 4-4-2 radial tank engines in their original colours. However, I have depicted No 1 as she was when painted according to the ideas of Dugald Drummond, as that is how I remember her.

No 1 was a familiar engine in the London area when I was a small boy; but she disappeared after a few years, and I did not see her again until 1919, at Eastleigh. Surprisingly, she was still in her original condition, Adams chimney and all, a distinction she shared with at least two others, Nos 8 and 19.

The 50 engines of this fine class were built in the following order: Nos 61 to 67 in 1888; 68 to 75 in 1889; 76 to 80 in 1890; 1 to 10 in 1894; 11 to 20 in

1895, and 358 to 367 in 1896. They were excellent workers, and I would place them among the finest 0-4-4 tank engines ever built. On those turned out in 1896, the brass beading on the splashers was omitted, and plain brass numberplates with sunk, black lettering and numerals replaced the Adams handsome cast plates. In the same group the safety valves were at first left uncased, but later they were enclosed in the normal casings.

The stationing of the T1 class was widely spread over the LSWR system, including Plymouth, Salisbury, Andover, Eastleigh, Bournemouth and Portsmouth, as well as the London area. When the electrification of the London suburban district was completed in the 1920s, the London contingent of the T1 class was transferred to provincial depots and continued to do useful work for about another 20 years.

Coal rails on the bunkers first appeared on the engines built in 1896. They were added to the earlier engines as they passed through the works for overhaul. The coal capacity was thereby increased by about 10 cwt.

Throughout the whole of their existence, these engines remained virtually in their original condition, apart from the substitution of Drummond chimneys

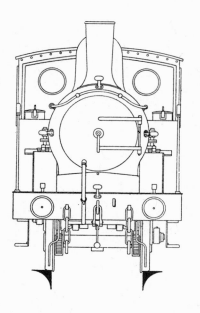

GENERAL SPECIFICATION

CYLINDERS				TUBES			
Diameter	...	...	18 in.	Number	...	...	216
Stroke	...	...	26 in.	Diameter	...	...	1¾ in.

BOILER							
Length, between				HEATING SURFACE			
tubeplates		...	11 ft	Tubes	...	...	1,121 sq. ft
Maximum dia-				Firebox	...	...	110 sq. ft
meter	...	...	4 ft 4 in.	Total	...	...	1,231 sq. ft

FIREBOX LENGTH							
Inside	...	...	5 ft 5 in.	GRATE AREA			
Outside	...	...	6 ft.	Square feet	...	...	17

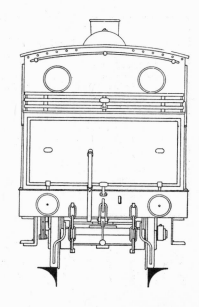

for the Adams stovepipes. But four of the class, at different times, were rebuilt with the Drummond boiler; these were Nos 63, 11, 15 and 361, and since never more than one engine in service was treated like this at any time, the inference is that only one Drummond boiler was used for all four engines. It seems to have made little difference to the capabilities of the engines, or more would probably have been rebuilt in this way. In any case, there may have been enough Adams boilers in stock for replacements when the older boilers wore out.

The dimensions of these engines were thoroughly up-to-date, if not actually in advance of their time The four coupled wheels were 5 ft 7 in. dia., the bogie wheels 3 ft. The wheelbase was 23 ft divided into 8 ft plus 10 ft plus 5 ft, with overhangs of 6 ft 1½ in. in front and 2 ft 7½ in. at the back, while the total length over the buffer heads was 35 ft 1½ in.

Two different arrangements of cylinders were used; the first group of engines, Nos 61 to 80, which were class T1 proper, had cylinders with the steam chest underneath, and all the others, which were originally class F6, had the steam chest between the cylinders. In both classes the cylinder diameter was 18 in. and the stroke 26 in.; the slide valves were operated by Stephenson link motion. In later years, both classes

were amalgamated under the classification T1, though the difference in the cylinders was never altered.

The boiler barrel was 4 ft 4 in. dia. and 11 ft long; it was pitched with its centre line 7 ft 3½ in. above rail level. There were 216 tubes of 1¾ in. dia., with a heating surface of 1,121 sq. ft; the firebox, 6 ft long outside, added 110 sq. ft, making the total heating surface 1,231 sq. ft. The working pressure was 160 p.s.i. and the grate area 17 sq. ft.

In the case of the Drummond M7 0-4-4 tank engines, there was a curious difference that occurred in the weights of two batches of those engines. An even more curious difference was to be noted in the weights of the Adams T1 and F6 classes. The official particulars give the following: class T1, on the leading axle, 17 tons 3 cwt; on the driving axle, 18 tons; on the bogie 17 tons 17 cwt; total 53 tons. Class F6, on the leading axle, 16 tons 6 cwt; on the driving axle, 18 tons 6 cwt; on the bogie, 20 tons 10 cwt; total 55 tons 2 cwt.

These figures show that the adhesion weight of the T1 class was 35 tons 3 cwt, and for the F6 class it was 34 tons 12 cwt; yet the latter engines were 2 tons 2 cwt *heavier* than the former. How did this come about? The only known difference between the two classes is that the F6s had the steam chest between instead

of underneath the cylinders; but a possible explanation would be that the F6 class had a heavier dragplate and drawgear arrangement than that of the T1 at the rear end. Examinations of the engines failed to reveal any differences in the drawgear. It is all somewhat mysterious !

The estimated tractive effort of these fine engines was 17,100 lb., which made them eminently suitable for their job, and was especially useful for working heavy trains that stopped at every station on a journey. On short distance semi-fast trains, these engines were equally satisfactory and were frequently employed on such work, at which there was little to choose between them and the Drummond M7 class.

Nos 1, 4, 5, 8, 18, 359 and 361, about 1910-14, were fitted for push-pull autotrain working, on which they were employed chiefly in Hampshire. During the war, the apparatus was removed and the engines reverted to normal duties.

Withdrawal of the 50 engines of this class began in 1931, but was not completed until 1951 when the class became extinct. They had a long and useful career amounting, on the average, to more than 50 years per engine, which does not appear to lend much support to the Board of Trade's censure of the 0-4-4 tank type of locomotive.

GENERAL SPECIFICATION

CYLINDERS				TUBES			
Diameter	...	...	18½ in.	Number	...	...	213
Stroke	...	...	26 in.	Diameter	...	...	1¾ in.

BOILER			
Length, brtween			
tubeplates		10 ft 6 in.	
Maximum dia-			
meter	...	4 ft 6 in.	

HEATING SURFACE			
Tubes	...	...	1,067 sq. ft
Firebox	...	...	124 sq. ft
Total	...	...	1,191 sq. ft

FIREBOX LENGTH			
Inside	...	...	5 ft 8 in.
Outside	...	...	6 ft 4 in.

GRATE AREA			
Square feet	...	...	20.35

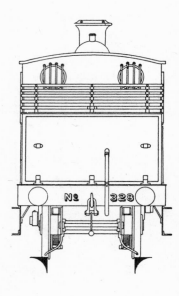

DRUMMOND'S M7 0-4-4 TANKS

THE 105 engines of this well-known class were built between March, 1897 and November, 1911; they were Dugald Drummond's standard design for LSWR suburban work, and were obviously derived from the very similar engines he had built for the North British and Caledonian Railways some years before.

I have always felt that these M7s have never attracted the widespread interest they deserve, though they are very popular with Southern Region enthusiasts. Without question, they must be placed among the best engines of their type, and I have no hesitation in claiming them as masterpieces. After all, their construction was in progress for more than 13 years, a long enough time in which to have designed and built a better type, had it be desirable; but basically, the last one built was the same as the first one, so there was obviously no need to make any alterations, except in very minor details.

The first three, Nos 242, 243 and 244, were completed at the Nine Elms works in March, 1897, and it is of interest to recall that No 244 was the 500th engine to be built at Nine Elms.

The class can be divided into two lots, the first of which consisted of 55 engines, all built at Nine Elms and finished by October, 1900. The second lot was made up of 40 engines built at Nine Elms between February, 1903 and March, 1906 and ten completed at Eastleigh by November, 1911.

This second lot differed from the first in having their total length increased from 35 ft 0¼ in. to 36 ft 3¼ in., the whole of the increase being in the leading overhang; also, the second lot were fitted with feed-water heaters in the side tanks.

These engines were the first to be designed by Drummond for the LSWR, and were not very popular when new, as Drummond placed the driver on the left-hand side of the footplate and so reversed a position that had been standard practice on the LSWR for 45 years. When the men eventually got used to the change, the M7 class became very popular and settled down to good steady work on suburban services for upwards of 40 years; the fact that so many of the class are still in service is its own testimony to the quality of the engines.

Some of the engines were to be found at almost every shed on the LSWR. In the Plymouth area, a few of them were employed for a while on secondary express passenger trains; but an accident at Tavistock, where one of these engines became derailed at speed while working an express train from Exeter to Plymouth, caused their relegation to local traffic, and a few were sent to Barnstaple to be tried out on the truly formidable Ilfracombe branch.

The line from Barnstaple to Ilfracombe abounds in sharp curves and some terrific gradients. The M7s did so well on this line that some of them were employed on it for many years. To be in a train of three corridor coaches behind an M7, climbing the terrific Mortehoe bank, was an experience which nobody with any love for locomotives could forget.

In the reverse direction, the trains were usually heavier and banking assistance was taken, because the 1 in 36 gradient at that end is entered almost immediately outside Ilfracombe station.

In whatever district they worked, it was the same story of good, steady reliability that gained the M7s popularity. And I must add that they were quietly and frequently put to work on fast, heavy outer-suburban trains; and so far as I know they never came to any harm after the Tavistock mishap.

Some of the London engines worked far afield, particularly to Reading and such places as

Basingstoke, Alton, Leatherhead and Guildford; and I have even seen them at the head of semi-fast trains labelled "Portsmouth." These trains, of course, were not expresses, and stopped at the principal stations on the way; but the trip to Portsmouth and back entailed a total mileage of about 165 miles— a good day's work for a suburban tank engine, even if it *did* take about three hours each way.

On the 26 April, 1923, No 58 of this class had the unusual distinction—for a suburban engine—of working a Royal special, for she hauled the train conveying the then Duke and Duchess of York (afterwards King George VI and Queen Elizabeth) from Waterloo to Bookham on the first stage of their honeymoon.

In May, 1948, No 672 achieved distinction of a very different order, by falling down the lift shaft leading from a reception siding beside Waterloo station down to the Waterloo and City Line. Fortunately, the driver and fireman were able to jump clear before the engine plunged; but as a result of the accident, there was no alternative but to scrap No 672 where she lay, and in this way she became the first of the class to be broken up, though she was not the first to be withdrawn.

The latter doubtful honour belonged to No 126.

This engine had been rebuilt with an extended smokebox and Eastleigh superheater in 1921, and it added 2 tons 15 cwt to her total weight; nearly the whole of the increase came on the leading end. In this condition, and in spite of the addition of a heavy dragplate at the back end, the engine was unsatisfactory and was found to be too heavy for most of the suburban lines on which she was expected to work.

This episode shows that attempts to "modernise" a good design do not always bring the desired results.

The dimensions of the M7s were: Cylinders, 18½ in. dia. by 26 in. stroke; wheel diameters, coupled 5 ft 7 in., bogie 3 ft 7 in.; wheelbase, 7 ft 6 in. plus 9 ft 7 in. plus 6 ft 6 in., total 23 ft 7 in.

The overhang in the second lot was 6 ft 7 in. in front and 2 ft 9 in. at the back. No 328 was one of the second lot, and, therefore, my drawing conforms to the dimensions just given; the engines of the first lot had a leading overhang of only 5 ft 6 in.

The boiler proportions of the M7s were excellent and very closely followed Stroudley's practice, but on a larger scale. The two rings of the barrel were, respectively, 4 ft 5⅛ in. and 4 ft 6 in. dia. outside, and the centre line was 7 ft 6 in. above rail level. The barrel length was 10 ft 6 in.; it contained 213

tubes of 1¾ in. dia. giving 1,067 sq. ft of heating surface.

With 124 sq. ft of firebox heating surface, the total amounted to the respectable figure of 1,191 sq. ft.

The grate area was 20.35 sq. ft, and the working pressure was 175 p.s.i., at 85 per cent of which the tractive effort amounted to 19,750 lb. 1,300 gallons of water could be carried in the tanks, and three tons of coal in the bunker.

The weights, as given on the official diagrams are something of a mystery. Diagram No 29 for the first lot of M7s gives the following: on leading axle, 17 tons 8 cwt; on driving axle, 18 tons; on bogie, 24 tons 16 cwt, which adds up to 60 tons 4 cwt. Diagram 29A for the longer engines shows 17 tons 5 cwt on the leading axle, 18 tons on the driving axle and 24 tons 18 cwt on the bogie, which totals 60 tons 3 cwt. In other words, the engine with the longer and, presumably, heavier frame is 1 cwt lighter than the shorter engine. How does this come about when all the other dimensions of the two engines are alike?

Some years ago, I put this poser to the Southern Railway's Locomotive offices at Waterloo, but nobody could supply the answer. I am still waiting for it.

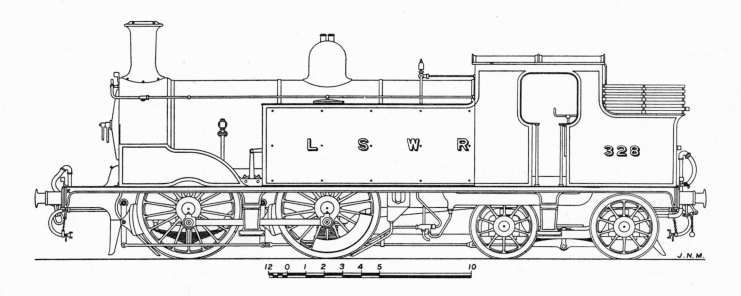

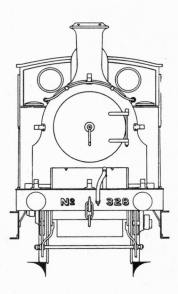

SOUTH EASTERN AND CHATHAM RAILWAY

2-4-0   No 512

Formerly No 53 EUROPA

FROM 1903 until 1909 my parents rented a bungalow facing the sea at Seasalter, near Whitstable, Kent. There, the youngest members of the family spent most of the year, while we older ones went there at holiday times.

At the end of the back garden ran the South Eastern and Chatham Railway's main line to Herne Bay, Margate and Ramsgate, and I, of course, took a great delight in the locomotives that worked the frequent trains along there. Among these engines were two grand old 2-4-0s, Nos 512 and 513, which, because of their wonderful array of springs, double frames and outside cranks, fascinated me beyond words!

No 513, however, was comparatively rarely seen; she was, I think, stationed at either Faversham or Sittingbourne, and did not appear to have a regular turn of duty past our cottage. No 512, on the other hand, was frequently to be seen; she was stationed at Ramsgate and worked local trains between there and Faversham, or Chatham, usually making two—sometimes three—double trips per day.

Although I probably did not realise it at the time these two fine old engines were not only members of a formerly famous class, but merely making up their mileage prior to being withdrawn for scrapping. In

the two or three years during which I saw her so often, No 512 certainly showed no signs of decrepi-

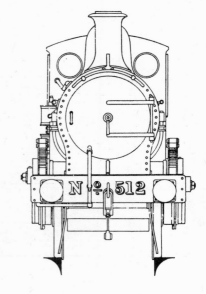

GENERAL SPECIFICATION

CYLINDERS			TUBES		
Diameter	...	17 in.	Number	...	205
Stroke	...	24 in.	Diameter	...	1¾ in.
BOILER					
Length, between			**HEATING SURFACE**		
tubeplates	10 ft 8 in.		Tubes	...	1,078 sq. ft
Maximum dia-			Firebox	...	102 sq. ft
meter	...	4 ft 3 in.	Total	...	1,180 sq. ft
FIREBOX LENGTH					
Inside	...	4 ft 11 in.	**GRATE AREA**		
Outside	...	5 ft 6 in.	Square feet	...	16.5

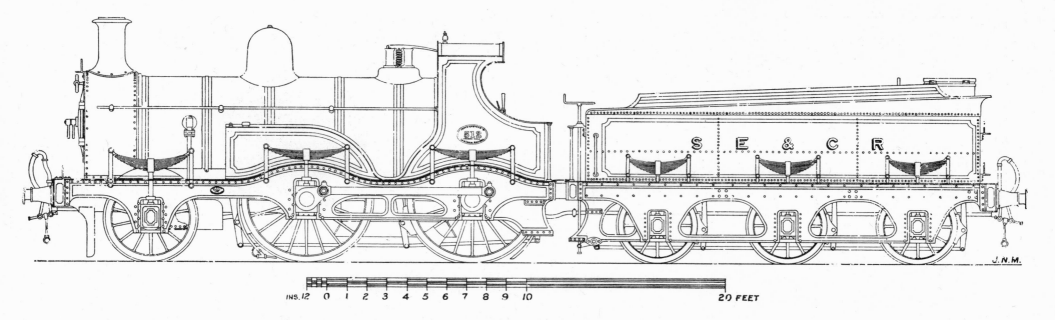

INS.12 0 1 2 3 4 5 6 7 8 9 10   20 FEET

tude; she went about her work in a calm, efficient manner without any fuss, and she was always kept in smart condition.

About this time I read an article in *The Locomotive Magazine*, describing four 2-4-0 engines built by Sharp, Stewart and Co., in 1873, for the London Chatham and Dover Railway, specially for working the Dover boat trains and Continental mail traffic. These engines were: No 53, *Europa*; 54, *Asia*; 55, *Africa*, and 56, *America*. Two more were built at the LCDR factory at Longhedge, Battersea—Nos 57 and 58—but had no names. These six engines won fame for the excellent work they did between London and Dover. In 1899, when the South Eastern Railway and the LCDR combined to form the South Eastern and Chatham Railway, the Europa class were renumbered 512 to 517, consecutively, and the names were removed. In this way I discovered that my old friend No 512 had been none other than No 53, *Europa*, 40 years before, and my respect for her duly increased !

My drawing shows what she looked like when I knew her. It cannot give much idea of the splendid style in which she was painted, with her Brunswick green boiler, cab and tender tanks, dark red framing

—all panelled and lined in sea-green, black, red and yellow.

This style of painting had been introduced in 1899 by H. S. Wainwright as the locomotive livery for the SE and CR, and it was certainly very attractive. Wainwright's standard cast-iron chimney, too, was rapidly replacing those formerly used on the SER and LCDR engines, and both 512 and 513 had acquired it when I knew them.

Some of the leading dimensions of these engines were: cylinders, 17 in. by 24 in.; coupled wheels, 6 ft 6 in.; leading wheels, 4 ft 6 in.; wheelbase 16 ft, divided into 7 ft 9 in. plus 8 ft 3 in.; the overhang was 4 ft 3 in. at the front and 4 ft at the back.

The front bufferbeam was of wood, probably oak, 7 ft 8 in. long, 1 ft 4½ in. deep, 6 in. thick and faced with a ¾ in. flitchplate. The boiler centre-line was 7 ft 2 in. above rail level, and the diameter of the barrel was 4 ft 8 in. outside the clothing plates; the smokebox was 5 ft 1½ in. diameter outside. The width across the cab sides and coupled-wheel splashers was 5 ft 10 in., and over the footplate it was 7 ft 6 in.

The tender wheelbase was 13 ft, equally divided; the diameter of the six wheels was 4 ft.

The designer of these engines was William Martley, whose successor, William Kirtley, reboilered them all and generally modernised them in the 1890s. Subsequently, Wainwright made only slight alterations to details, but had scrapped the whole class by 1907.

In their original condition, judging by photographs, these six engines were probably the prettiest ever owned by the old LCDR, and they were certainly the largest on that line, at the time. They were built without cabs, but very soon acquired a rather scanty form of cab which was remarkably like some of S. W. Johnson's efforts in this direction on the Midland Railway.

These engines quickly established an excellent reputation for reliability and punctuality, and they were put exclusively to working the boat trains for several years. They were eventually superseded by some of William Kirtley's celebrated M class 4-4-0 engines, and then put in many years of work on main line duties between London and the Kent coast holiday resorts. Except for No 512, they ended their careers by working semi-fast trains between London, Chatham, Faversham and Maidstone, and occasionally on the boat trains in connection with the Queenborough-Flushing service to the Continent.

KIRTLEY'S 4-4-0 Ms

I FIRST came to know the Kirtley 4-4-0s in 1903 when my parents rented a week-end cottage at Whitstable, Kent, on the old London, Chatham and Dover main line between Faversham and Rams-gate, where these engines worked most of the passenger trains.

They were fascinating machines; rather small in size, but distinctly lively and powerful. Their design was by William Kirtley, and Neilson and Co., of Glasgow, built six of the engines in 1877. Longhedge Works, Battersea, produced two in 1880, two in 1881 and a further two in 1885, while Dübs and Co., of Glasgow, delivered six in 1884. The Vulcan Foundry, of Leeds, built another six in 1891, and between 1892 and 1901 Longhedge made 20 more, two at a time, to bring the total number to 44. There were slight variations of detail and dimensions from batch to batch, and the class was officially divided into four —M, M1, M2 and M3—though the engines were all very much alike in appearance.

My drawings show No 651, of class M3, chosen for a reason that will be clear later. For the M3 class, cylinders were 18 in. dia. bore × 26 in. stroke and were inclined at 1 in 24. Stephenson link-motion actuated the valves. I have been unable to discover any details of the port sizes and valve events, but the steamchest was between the cylinders, and the valves were the ordinary flat ones; their setting must have been good.

Bogie wheels were 3 ft 6 in. in diameter; coupled wheels 6 ft 6 in., and tender wheels 3 ft 9 in. The wheelbase was 21 ft 0½ in., divided into 5 ft 9 in. plus 6 ft 11½ in. plus 8 ft 4 in., while the overhang was 1 ft 11½ in. at the front and 4 ft at the back. From the trailing coupled axle to the leading tender axle

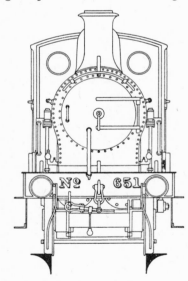

the distance was 8 ft 8¼ in. The tender wheelbase was 12 ft equally divided, and the length of engine and tender over buffers was 50 ft 4 in.

The boiler was made of $\frac{7}{16}$ in plate, in two rings of 4 ft 2⅛ in. and 4 ft 3 in. dia. Its barrel was 10 ft 3 in.

long and the distance between tubeplates was 10 ft 7 in. There were 207 tubes of 1¾ in. dia., with a heating surface of 1,003.2 sq. ft. Working pressure was 150 p.s.i., and the pitch of the centre-line 7 ft 2 in. from rail level. The length of the firebox shell was 5 ft 9 in.; the inner box was 5 ft 0½ in. long and 3 ft 4½ in. wide. Grate area was 17 sq. ft; the heating surface was 107 sq. ft, making the total 1,110.2.

There was room in the tender for 4¾ tons of coal and 2,600 gallons of water. In working order, the engine weighed 42 tons 9 cwt, divided into 13 tons 12 cwt on the bogie, 15 tons 13 cwt on the driving axle and 13 tons 4 cwt on the trailing axle. With 34 tons 3 cwt for the tender, the total was 76 tons 12 cwt.

Class M3 had 26 engines built from 1891 to 1901. The eight in class M2 were turned out in 1884-5; they differed from the others in having 200 tubes, 17½ in. cylinders, 1,070 sq. ft total heating surface, 16.5 sq. ft of grate area, an engine weight of 43 tons, and a tender capacity of 2,470 gallons.

Unlike M2, M1 had 199 tubes, 1,069 sq. ft of heating surface, a working pressure of 140 p.s.i., and an engine weight of 42 tons.

Class M was similar to M1 except that it had a tender of 2,550 gallons capacity. Class M1 consisted of four engines constructed in 1880-1, and class M of six engines constructed in 1877.

It is also worth noting that all except four were designed and produced for the London, Chatham and Dover Railway. The exceptions were the last four of class M3, built from 1899 to 1901; they did not belong to that line, but were SECR property from the beginning. All 26 of class M3 survived to become Southern Railway property in 1923; their withdrawal began in 1925 and was completed in 1928.

The work of the Kirtleys was always good, if not particularly outstanding; the old Chatham road, on which they ran almost exclusively, was relatively mountainous, and the trains were usually heavy, but the timetable seldom, if ever, called for overall average speeds as high as 50 m.p.h. until the Ms were well past their prime. They occasionally put up some runs that were rather above the ordinary. On June 12 1896, No 16, later 475, of class M3 made a record run with the down Continental Night Mails train. The details published in certain technical periodicals at that time show that the load was a light one of 70 tons, including mails and passengers. But the engine was driven with considerable vigour, especially in the early stages; and achieved an overall time of just under 82 minutes for the 78½ miles to the stop at Dover Pier, at an average speed of 57.5 m.p.h. over a markedly switchback road.

Another M3, No 651, gave me an unexpected and quite brilliant run on the evening of July 31 1926. I had been to Chatham and had decided to return by the 7.24 p.m. non-stop to Victoria. While I was waiting for my train, I watched 651 (by that time renumbered A-651 in the SR list) marshalling some coaches in the sidings alongside the station; and I recalled with nostalgia how she had been when I knew her 20 years before—a smart, game little engine. She appeared to be anything but smart and game, on that fine warm evening at Chatham!

At 7.24, there was no sign of my train. It arrived about eight minutes later—eight corridor coaches and a Pullman car, fully 245 tons, behind No 487, one of Harry Wainwright's D-class 4-4-0s, then newly rebuilt to D1-class. I noticed that the signalman had either guessed or had been warned, that there was trouble, for he stood at his cabin window gazing at the train as it arrived, and he continued to gaze after it had stopped. The driver got down from his cab, made a quick examination of the engine's front end from which an ominous cloud of pale blue smoke was issuing, and then signed to the signalman that the engine would be detached. She drew forward and was backed into the sidings, alongside 651. The two crews exchanged engines, and 651 came off

the sidings and backed on to my train, which I boarded with mixed feelings.

After the tender had been topped-up with water and the " right-away " given, 651 started that heavy train without difficulty. Slowly we passed into the tunnel west of Chatham station. Gaining speed to pass Rochester we ran over the Medway bridge and round the great curve to the foot of the formidable five mile Sole Street bank of 1 in 100, at 35.5 m.p.h. So well was the engine driven that we reached the top of the bank, seven miles from Rochester, in 16 min. 35 sec. at 20 m.p.h., before attaining speeds of 74 at Fawkham, 72 at Farningham, 63 at St Mary Cray, 66 at Bickley, 55 at Shortlands, 50 at Beckenham Junction, 44 at Catford, 44 at Nunhead, 38 at Peckham Rye and 36 at Brixton. We stopped in Victoria in 50 min. 10 sec. from Chatham—booked time 56 min., gain on schedule 5 min. 50 sec., average speed 40.5 m.p.h.

No 651 stood there, dirty, but apparently none the worse for her exertions. With only a few months to go before she was sent to the scrap-heap early in 1927, she had shown me that she was still the same game little engine that I had always known her to be. She was Vulcan Foundry No 1322 of 1891.

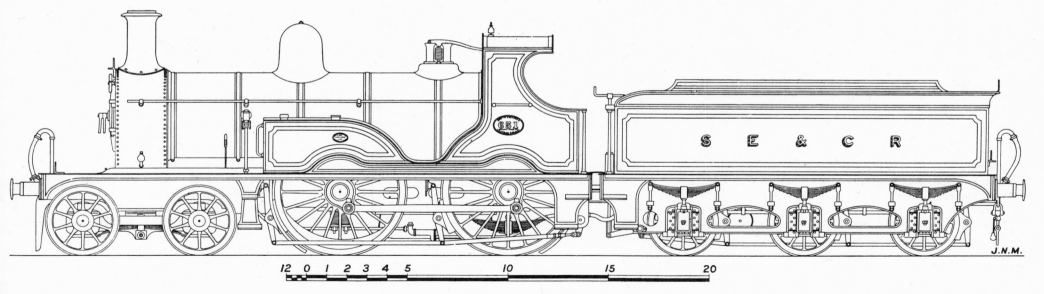

JAMES STIRLING'S Class F 4-4-0

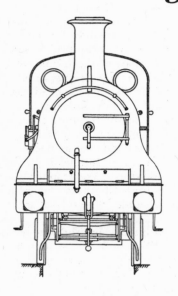

GENERAL SPECIFICATION			
CYLINDERS		**TUBES**	
Diameter ... ... 19 in.		Number 202	
Stroke ... ... 26 in.		Diameter ... ... $1\frac{5}{8}$ in.	
BOILER			
Length, between		**HEATING SURFACE**	
tubeplates 10 ft $4\frac{1}{2}$ in.		Tubes ... 917 sq. ft	
Maximum dia-		Firebox ... 103 sq. ft	
meter ... 4 ft 4 in.		Total ... 1,020 sq. ft	
FIREBOX LENGTH			
Inside ... 5 ft 2 in.		**GRATE AREA**	
Outside ... 5 ft 9 in.		Square feet ... 16.78	

During the railway strike in 1919 I was one of a number of volunteers who tried their hands at keeping the wheels turning on the old South Eastern and Chatham Railway.

Through my acquaintance with Mr David Sheppey, who was then the local District Locomotive Superintendent, I became " night shedmaster " (unofficial title !) at Cannon Street locomotive shed and my job, with the help of two other enthusiasts and one of the regular foremen, was to keep steam up in some ten or a dozen locomotives that would be required to work the meagre train services.

All the locomotives under my charge were of either old South Eastern, or South Eastern and Chatham design; there was none from the London Chatham and Dover Railway. One of them was No 198, a J. Stirling Class F 4-4-0, still in almost her original condition, much to my delight because I had a great affection for these engines.

No 198 was one of a class of 88 engines designed for the S.E.R. by James Stirling and built at Ashford Works between 1883 and 1898; for some reason that has never been very clear these attractive engines were known as " Jumbos " to the men; but for many years they were the mainstay of the SER locomotive department, and they certainly did some good work.

James Stirling was a brother of Patrick of Great Northern Railway fame, so there were certain features that were common to the designs of both: big wheels, big cylinders, a none-too-generous boiler and the characteristic Stirling cab which seemed very scanty but actually gave quite a lot of protection from wind and the weather, as I know from my own experience with it. But that is another story.

I have drawn her in the condition in which she was then, although I had known her for about ten years dating from the time when she had boasted the beautiful green-and-dark-red livery and elaborate lining introduced by H. S. Wainwright in 1900.

I knew and loved these engines for many years, chiefly through being so often on the SECR in my early life. But in my time the whole class was engaged principally on secondary passenger duties and were seldom to be seen on an important express train. In my Edenbridge days, No 2, still in her original condition, was regularly engaged, for some time, on the through train from Folkestone and Dover to Birmingham and Wolverhampton via Reading and Oxford. She worked it between Ashford and Redhill, and it was the only really important train on which I can remember an F being regularly employed. She was later replaced by a Wainwright D class engine on this turn.

Several of her unrebuilt sisters, in those days, were frequently to be seen at Edenbridge, working between Redhill, Tonbridge and Ashford, and they also ran westwards from Redhill to Reading. They appeared to be handicapped by their big wheels which tried them sorely on any up-grade, and it was very seldom that they could be coaxed into attaining anything like a high speed.

The dimensions of this very distinctive class of engine were: cylinders, 19 in. dia. × 26 in. stroke, though the diameter was reduced to 18 in. some years later. All the wheels reflected the Stirling liking for large diameters, the four coupled wheels being no less than 7 ft, and the bogie wheels 3 ft 9¼ in. One of the main ideas of this preference for large wheels was that they revolve at less speed than smaller wheels would, and therefore the wear and tear of bearings was less.

The bogie design was unusual in that the king-pin was placed 1 in. *forward* of the centre; a lateral sliding movement of 1½ in. was provided and controlled by rubber pads in lieu of springs. The wheelbase was uncommonly short for a bogie, at 5 ft 4 in. instead of the more normal 6 ft or more.

The boiler was made in two rings arranged telescopically, the larger ring having an outside diameter of 4 ft 4 in. The pitch of the centre line was 7 ft 5 in. above rail level. True to the time-honoured practice of the Stirlings, there was no dome; but James' ideas differed from Patrick's in that the safety-valve was mounted on the back ring of the boiler barrel instead of on the firebox. The regulator was in the smokebox and took steam from a perforated pipe mounted in the steam space in the boiler barrel.

The length of the boiler barrel was 10 ft 4½ in.; there were 202 tubes of 1⅝ in. dia., giving a heating surface of 917 sq. ft. The firebox added 103 sq. ft, to make the total heating surface 1,020 sq. ft; the grate area was 16.78 sq. ft, and the engine weight in working order was 42 tons 10 cwt, of which 28 tons 2 cwt rested on the coupled wheels.

The total wheelbase of the engine was 23 ft 9¼ in. divided into 5 ft 4 in. plus 9 ft 10¼ in. plus 8 ft 6 in. The overhang at the front was 2 ft 7¼ in. and at the back 4 ft 4 in., the total length of the frames being 30 ft 8½ in. The chimney shown in the drawing was a cast-iron one introduced by H. S. Wainwright after 1900, and its top was 13 ft 4½ in. above rail level. The original Stirling chimney was of a rather different shape but the same height.

The capacity of the tender was for 4 tons of coal and 2,650 gal. of water. The wheels were 4 ft dia. and the wheelbase 12 ft equally divided; the overhang was 4 ft 2½ in. at the leading end and 3 ft 10 in. at the back. The weight in working order was 30 tons 10 cwt.

The shape of the cab, seen end-on, was important; its height was 7 ft above the running plate and its width was 6 ft. The radius of the roof was 11 ft 4 in. with a 1 ft 1½ in. radius at each side, struck from the centres of the windows, the glasses of which were 12 in. dia. The depth of the roof and sides was 3 ft.

It is worth recalling that James Stirling introduced the inside-cylinder 4-4-0 type express passenger engine for the first time in Britain in a class of engine built for the Glasgow and South Western Railway in 1874, though there had been one or two attempts by other designers before. Thereafter, the type was widely adopted by other British locomotive designers. In fact, it became very much a standard British type of express passenger engine for many years.

These South Eastern engines of Stirling's were a modernisation of his GSWR engines; most of them were rebuilt with domed boilers by Wainwright, from 1902 onwards, and many of them continued to give good service until the last one was withdrawn in 1949.

My drawing represents No 198 in the severely economical wartime livery which came into use about 1915; dark grey all over, except for black smokebox and chimney, vermilion bufferbeams, white numerals and lettering. This engine was one of the few of her class that were not rebuilt.

My personal acquaintance with her was not concerned with the particular coat she wore, so to speak; I enjoyed looking after her during the nights of duty at the old Cannon Street shed, and I should not be surprised if I gave her rather more attention than my other charges received! They were more modern and, therefore, less attractive to me!

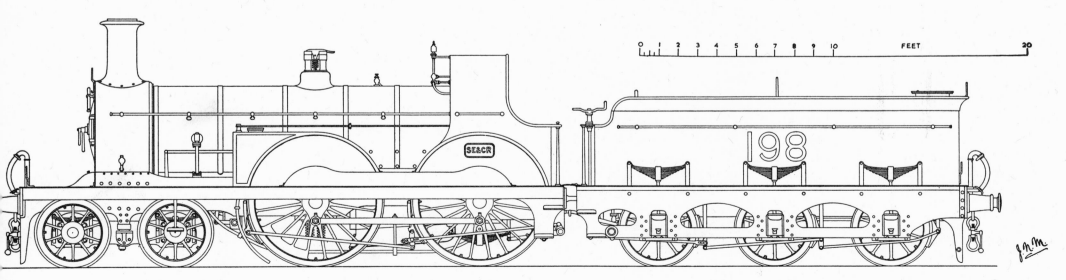

185

H. S. WAINWRIGHT'S
D Class 4-4-0s

GENERAL SPECIFICATION

CYLINDERS
    Diameter ... ... 19 in.
    Stroke ... ... 26 in.

BOILER
    Length, between
        tubeplates 11 ft $5\frac{5}{8}$ in.
    Maximum dia-
        meter ... 4 ft 9 in.

FIREBOX LENGTH
    Inside ... 5 ft $10\frac{13}{16}$ in.
    Outside ... 6 ft 6 in.

TUBES
    Number 263
    Diameter ... ... $1\frac{3}{4}$ in.

HEATING SURFACE
    Tubes ... 1,381 sq. ft
    Firebox ... 124 sq. ft
    Total ... 1,505 sq. ft

GRATE AREA
    Square feet ... 20

How well I remember the sensation that was caused when the first of these beautiful engines was put into traffic in 1901.

In the previous year, the South Eastern and the London Chatham and Dover Railways were combined under a management committee to become the South Eastern and Chatham Railway. The two former locomotive superintendents of the separate companies, James Stirling and William Kirtley, retired, and the combined departments were placed under the charge of Harry S. Wainwright, who had been carriage and wagon superintendent of the former South Eastern Railway under Stirling—but was not then regarded as a locomotive man.

Yet within 18 months he produced, first, some 0-4-4 tank engines for local work, followed by his C-class 0-6-0 goods engines and, then, the pioneer examples of his truly spectacular 4-4-0 express passenger engines of Class D.

The drawing can do no more than give a bare idea of the graceful outline and extremely pleasing proportions of this design. Painted and lined out in the elaborate livery adopted by Wainwright, and additionally embellished by the provision of copper caps to the chimneys, the whole was kept spotlessly clean. These engines, and the very similar E class which followed, were almost the last examples of Victorian and Edwardian finery.

The modern generation can have no conception of the effect produced by the sight of a locomotive

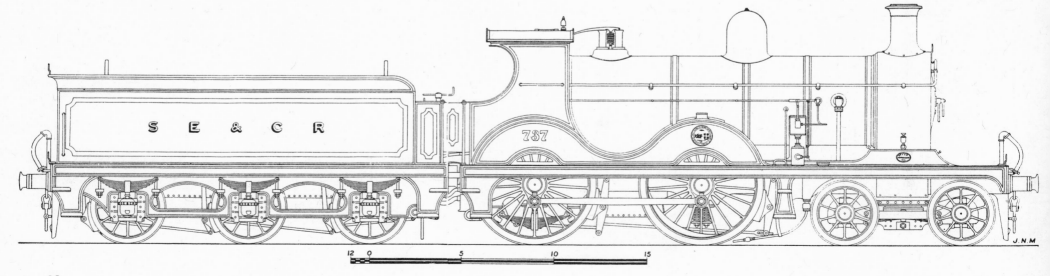

finished in this style; it was almost breathtaking, but not in the least garish or flamboyant. I am glad to be able to add that engine No 737 has been saved from the scrap heap and is being restored to her original condition.

If the work is carried out with anything like the care and skill that were devoted to the decoration of the original engines, then No 737 will, indeed, be a sight worth seeing. It should not present any serious difficulty; all the necessary information exists at Ashford.

Very little structural alteration will be required because this engine, withdrawn in November, 1956, is virtually in her original state. So far as I can see, little need be done except for the removal of the raised coalplates from the top of the tender coping and the provision of a new copper-topped chimney of the original pattern.

The rest, to restore her exactly to her pristine beauty, is merely a matter of repainting.

When new, these engines, of which there were 51, at once took over the working of the best express trains of the SECR, including all the Continental traffic between London, Dover and Folkestone.

The engines soon proved that their virtues were not all wrapped up in good looks. The routes were heavy and difficult compared with most other British main lines. It used to be said that nowhere on the SECR was there even so much as one level mile, and I believe that to be true. Yet these fine engines could haul greater loads at higher speeds—and on less coal—than their predecessors.

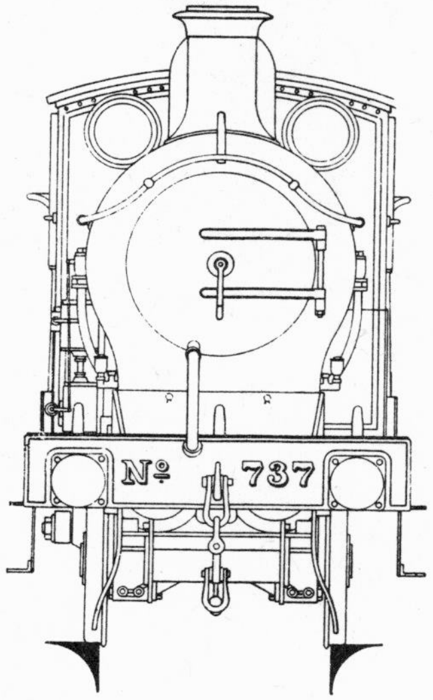

Models of these engines can be very attractive, but for the really meticulous modeller there was one big snag: the driving and coupled wheels had 21 spokes instead of the more usual 22. The only model of a D known to me in which the number of spokes has been correctly represented is the beautiful 7 mm. scale model of No 735 owned by my friend Mr W. S. Norris.

The 51 engines of this class were built in the following order: In 1901, ten, Nos 726 to 735, by Sharp Stewart and Co., of Glasgow; five, Nos 741 to 745, from Robert Stephenson and Co., of Newcastle; five Nos 736 to 740, from the SECR works at Ashford. In 1902, five, Nos 57, 246, 487, 488 and 490, from Ashford. In 1903, ten, Nos 75, 92, 145, 247, 489, 492, 493, 494, 501 and 502, from Dubs and Co., of Glasgow, and five, Nos 746 to 750, from the Vulcan Foundry Ltd, of Leeds. Ashford built the final 11, delivering five, Nos 470, 509, 545, 549 and 577, in 1906, and six, Nos 477, 496, 505, 574, 586 and 591, in 1907.

It will be seen from this list that 737, when she was withdrawn in November 1956, was one of the oldest, having reached the ripe old age of 55 years —a resounding tribute to her quality. She had never been rebuilt, and finished her days at Guildford whence she generally worked local trains to Reading.

She shared this duty with her sister, No 75 (BR No 31075), which was two years younger and was actually the last active survivor of the D class, being withdrawn in December 1956.

The original dimensions were quite typical of the practice of those days: cylinders, 19 in. dia. by 26 in. stroke; the coupled wheels were 6 ft 8 in. dia., and the bogie wheels were 3 ft 7 in. The wheel base was 22 ft $11\frac{1}{2}$ in. divided into 6 ft 3 in. plus 7 ft $8\frac{1}{2}$ in. plus 9 ft. The leading overhang was 2 ft 4 in. to the back of the bufferbeam, which was $1\frac{1}{8}$ in. thick; the rear overhang was 3 ft $11\frac{3}{4}$ in.

The boiler, pitched 8 ft from rail level, was made in two rings, the larger of which was 4 ft 9 in. dia. outside, the smaller (front) one being 4 ft $7\frac{7}{8}$ in. dia. There were 263 tubes of $1\frac{3}{4}$ in. o.d.; according to the original specification they were made of "Kora" metal, but whether this was some form of brass or steel I have been unable to discover.

The length between tubeplates was 11 ft $5\frac{5}{8}$ in., and the tubes were cambered $1\frac{5}{8}$ in.; that is to say they were not dead straight, but were higher in the middle than they were at the ends.

The outside firebox casing was 6 ft 6 in. long and 4 ft $\frac{1}{2}$ in. wide; the inner box was 5 ft $10\frac{13}{16}$ in. long and 3 ft $5\frac{3}{8}$ in. wide, the grate being horizontal, 6 ft 6 in. below the top of the box. The grate area was 20 sq. ft.

Stephenson link motion with locomotive-type links was employed. The throw of the eccentrics was $3\frac{1}{4}$ in., but the valve travel in full gear was $4\frac{1}{8}$ in. The valves were provided with $1\frac{1}{16}$ in. lap, and there was no lap or clearance on the exhaust side, according to the drawings. The steam ports were $1\frac{5}{8}$ in. wide, exhaust ports $3\frac{1}{2}$ in. wide, their common length being 18 in. The connecting-rods were 6 ft 10 in. long, and the eccentric rods 4 ft 10 in.

A total heating surface of 1,505 sq. ft was made up of 1,381 sq. ft for the tubes and 124 sq. ft for the firebox; the working pressure was 180 p.s.i.

In working order, the engine weighed 50 tons, with 17 tons on the bogie, 16 tons 17 cwt on the driving wheels and 16 tons 3 cwt on the tailing wheels. The reversing gear was operated by steam power, and other equipment included automatic vacuum brakes and steam sanding apparatus.

The tender was mounted on six 4 ft wheels, the wheel base being 13 ft equally divided. Loaded with 3,300 gallons of water and $4\frac{1}{2}$ tons of coal, the weight was 39 tons 14 cwt.

The total length of engine and tender over buffers has been variously recorded; on the official weight diagram it is given as 54 ft $11\frac{7}{8}$ in. whereas the specification gives it as 54 ft $10\frac{3}{4}$ in.

My drawing, worked out from the official drawings, agrees with the latter figure, so where the difference arises is a mystery. Possibly, the buffers and draw-gear have been altered since the engines were built; this, coupled with the fact that the weight diagram is of much later date than the working drawings, may be the explanation.

To the end, the D class did their work punctually and with precision, even with very heavy trains.

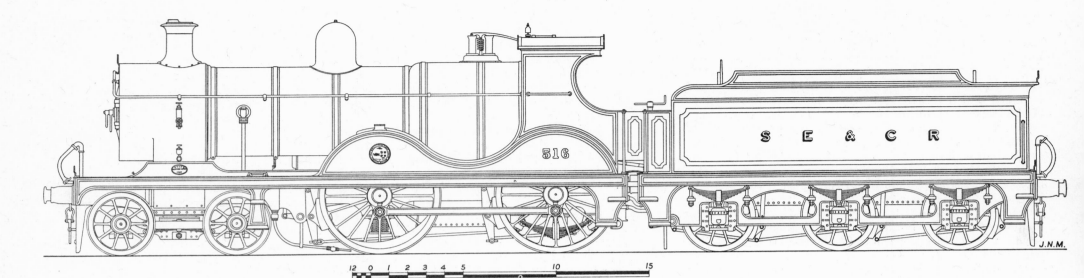

H. S. Wainwright's second design of 4-4-0 express passenger engines consisted of 26 engines, the first of which, No 273, came out in 1905; she was followed by Nos 275, 504, 506 and 511 in 1906; 157, 160, 165, 166, 176, 491, 497, 514, 515 and 587 in 1907; 19, 36, 67, 159, 175, 179, 507, 516 and 547 in 1908, and 163 and 315 in 1909.

The design was similar to that of the D class, except for the facts that the Es were fitted with Belpaire fireboxes and those built in 1908-9 had extended smokeboxes, while the coupled wheels were

2 in. smaller in diameter, and the wheelbase 6 in. longer. Exhibited at the Franco-British Exhibition held at the White City, during the summer of 1908, No 516 was afterwards usually reserved for working royal and other special trains.

The elaborate livery and spotless cleanliness that I mentioned when dealing with the Ds applied also to the Es, and No 516, for some years, was regularly turned out looking as if she was about to work a royal train.

At the big White City exhibition she was a truly

4-4-0 EXPRESS ENGINES

Class E

breath-taking spectacle. Probably instructions were issued that the degree of extra finish given to make her suitable for the exhibition should be carefully maintained. However that may be, No 516 retained her original livery for a long time after all her sisters had been repainted in the drastically simplified livery adopted in 1912.

GENERAL SPECIFICATION

CYLINDERS			TUBES		
Diameter	...	19 in.	Number	...	266
Stroke	...	26 in.	Diameter	...	1¾ in.
BOILER			HEATING SURFACE		
Length, between			Tubes	...	1,396 sq. ft
tubeplates	11 ft 5⅝ in.		Firebox	...	136 sq. ft
Maximum dia-			Total	...	1,532 sq. ft
meter	...	4 ft 9 in.			
FIREBOX LENGTH			GRATE AREA		
Inside	...	6 ft 4¹³⁄₁₆ in.	Square feet	...	21.15
Outside	...	7 ft			

None of these engines was superheated at first, but in 1912 No 36 was fitted with a Robinson superheater and No 275 with the Schmidt apparatus; oddly enough, the rest of the class remained non-superheated until 11 of them were rebuilt in 1920, to class E1.

The original height to the top of the chimney was 13 ft 4 in., but from 1910 and onwards this was lowered to 13 ft, a change that applied to the D class as well. I understand that this was done to enable the engines to work over certain cross-country routes and all sections of the SECR where the vertical clearances in some places were less than on the main line.

There was a story told that one of the D class, while working a train to Maidstone one day, had the misfortune to knock her chimney off when passing under one of the bridges on the way! If this is true, it seems strange that such a mishap should not have been foreseen. It did not happen again, however.

It will be noted that the construction of the first engines of the E class was in hand concurrently with that of the last batch of engines of the D class. This was because there was no intention that the Es should supersede the Ds, but that the two classes should be complementary. With their slightly superior tractive force, the Es were almost entirely confined to the

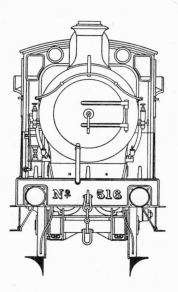

Chatham routes, while the Ds were fairly evenly distributed over the whole of the SECR main lines. Both classes superseded the old Kirtley and Stirling 4-4-0s on the best express passenger trains. For some years, the Es had almost the monopoly of the Continental boat trains between Victoria and Dover, and did some splendid work on these duties. The Ds were not often to be seen on these trains, but they did a great deal of work on less important expresses over the same route.

My introduction to the E class took place at our seaside cottage at Whitstable; I mentioned in a previous chapter that the main line to Margate and Ramsgate passed the end of our garden. On this line, in those days, Sundays always provided opportunities for the first sight of new engines; the National Sunday League had a number of trains run each Sunday for day-trippers to Whitstable, Herne Bay, Margate and Ramsgate. These trains seem to have been used by the SECR locomotive department as running-in turns for new engines, and I always was made aware of any new locomotive construction, because the NSL trains were so often headed by brand new locomotives.

The trains were usually made up of a heterogeneous collection of rolling stock—some of it remarkably ancient—filled to capacity with noisy excursionists bent on enjoying a day by the sea. These amenities were then to be had for as little as 5s or less, return between Victoria and Ramsgate. I must add that, so far as the down trains in the mornings were concerned, they kept excellent time. I am unable to record what the timekeeping was like on the up trips in the evenings, except to say that the trains passed or departed from Whitstable punctually. I must have had my first sight of nearly every engine of the E class, except No 516, on one of these excursion trains.

No 516 did no work until after the White City exhibition had closed. She spent the early months of her career standing to be admired, and was so successful at this job that she was awarded a gold medal. So far as I am aware, she never worked an NSL excursion; she was far too aristocratic for that! But joking apart, she fully deserved her prize, because of all the railway exhibits in the show, she was by far the most impressive to the majority of visitors.

At that time there was a considerable coming and going of foreign kings, presidents and other important

people requiring special trains, and No 516 was delegated to this traffic. Between times, the engine was kept in good running order by working secondary passenger trains which did not require her to exert herself unduly, and she was thus employed for some years. During that period—1909-1913—I had one or two trips behind her on Charing Cross-Tonbridge semi-fast trains via Redhill, or Oxted, when I was travelling daily to London from Edenbridge. The engine was, at that time, stationed at Bricklayer's Arms. During the 1914-18 war this arrangement ceased, and No 516 was transferred to the ordinary rota of passenger traffic duties, in which she remained for the rest of her existence.

The original diameter of the cylinders was 19¼ in., but was subsequently reduced to 19 in.; the stroke was 26 in. Ordinary slide valves were arranged between the cylinders and were driven by Stephenson link motion identical with that of the D class engines. The coupled wheels were 6 ft 6 in. dia., and the bogie wheels 3 ft 7 in.; the later engines, however, had the bogie wheel diameter reduced to 3 ft 6 in. The wheelbase was 23 ft 4½ in., divided into 6 ft 3 in. plus 7 ft 8½ in. plus 9 ft 6 in. and the overhangs were 2 ft 4 in. at the front end and 3 ft 8¾ in. at the back end. The coupling rods were fluted, and were the first instance of this on the SECR.

The boiler was 11 ft long and made in two rings, 4 ft 7⅞ in. and 4 ft 9 in. dia.; its centre line was 8 ft above rail level. With no superheater, there were 266 tubes of 1¾ in. dia., giving 1,396 sq. ft of heating surface. To this, the firebox added 136 sq. ft, making the total heating surface 1,532 sq. ft. The grate area was 21.5 sq. ft.

The engine weight in working order was: 17 tons 7 cwt on the bogie, 17 tons 12 cwt on the driving axle and 17 tons 6 cwt on the trailing axle, totalling 52 tons 5 cwt.

The tender was slightly wider than that of the D class and carried 3,450 gallons of water and 4 tons of coal. It weighed 39 tons 2 cwt full; therefore the total weight of engine and tender was 91 tons 7 cwt.

In 1919-20, 11 of these engines, Nos 19, 67, 160, 163, 165, 497, 504, 506, 507 and 511 were rebuilt to class E1 by Beyer, Peacock and Co., Manchester, to the specification of Mr R. E. L. Maunsell. Most of these are still running, but the last of the unrebuilt engines was withdrawn in 1953, as BR No 31166.

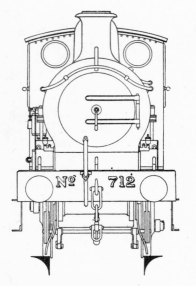

WAINWRIGHT'S S Class 0-6-0

SPECIFICATION

CYLINDERS			TUBES		
Diameter ...	...	18½ in.	Number ...	...	214
Stroke	...	26 in.	Diameter ...	...	1¾ in.
BOILER			HEATING SURFACE		
Length	...	11 ft 1⅝ in.	Tubes	...	1089.32 sq. ft
Maximum diameter			Firebox	...	110.68 sq. ft
		4 ft 7 in.	Total	...	1,200 sq. ft
FIREBOX			GRATE AREA		... 17 sq. ft
Outside length		0 ft 0 in.	WORKING PRESSURE		
Inside length		5 ft 1⅝ in.			160 lb. per sq. in.

THE first tender locomotives to be designed by Harry S. Wainwright for the SECR, immediately after his appointment as Locomotive Superintendent in 1900, were his singularly fascinating 0-6-0 goods engines of Class C, now to be described. My recollections of them date from 1904, when they were often to be seen on excursion trains and, sometimes, on ordinary passenger trains at Whitstable.

There were 109 of them, the first examples being put into traffic in 1900 and the last in 1908. They were simple, straightforward 0-6-0s with nothing specially remarkable about them; yet they have worked steadily on goods, and not a little passenger traffic for nearly 60 years.

Fifteen of these engines were built by Neilson, Reid and Co., Glasgow, in 1900; another 15 by Sharp, Stewart and Co., Glasgow, also in 1900, while nine were constructed at the old Longhedge Works of the London Chatham and Dover Railway, two in 1902 and seven in 1904. All the rest were built at Ashford.

This class largely superseded the Stirling O class which was designed by James Stirling for the old South Eastern Railway, and first built in 1878. Incidentally, these Stirling engines were noteworthy in having no balance weights in the wheels, and, although Wainwright discontinued this practice, his

C Class engines were rather unusual in having balance weights in the middle pair of wheels only.

My drawing shows No 712, an engine which was under my charge at Cannon Street during the strike of 1919. She was typical of the class except that she was one of a number that were fitted with short blastpipes and, consequently, had much shorter chimneys than normal for the class. As a result of this short chimney, the height of 13 ft 1⁷⁄₁₆ in. from rail to chimney top was reduced to 12 ft 6⅜ in., and gave the engines a very sturdy appearance.

They appeared to be ready to tackle any job that offered itself, and were frequently used for working heavy excursion trains to Kent Coast resorts at holiday times. At work, they were inclined to be noisy, but in a subtly different way from that of some other noisy locomotives. For these Wainwright engines always gave the impression that they were really getting down to good hard work, and not to some sort of drudgery.

The principal dimensions of this class were: cylinders 18½ in. dia., 26 in. stroke; the steamchest was between the cylinders, and the valves were operated by Stephenson link motion which was interchangeable with that on the H Class 0-4-4 tank engines (page 48). The same valve setting was used in the two classes, and it certainly appeared to enable the

engines to reach and sustain quite high maximum speeds when necessary.

The wheel diameter of the C Class was 5 ft 2 in., and the wheelbase was divided into 8 ft plus 8 ft 6 in.; the front overhang was 6 ft and the back 3 ft 4 in., the total length of the main frames being 25 ft 10 in.

The boiler was pitched 7 ft 7 in. from rail level; it was made in two rings, the maximum diameter of the larger ring being 4 ft 7 in. There were 214 tubes of 1¾ in. dia., giving 1,089.32 sq. ft of heating surface; to this the firebox added 110.68 sq. ft, making the total heating surface exactly 1,200 sq. ft. Inside, the firebox measured 5 ft 1⅝ in. long and 3 ft 4⅜ in. wide, the grate area being 17 sq. ft. I must add that the boiler barrel was 11 ft 1⅝ in. long between tubeplates; the tubes were cambered 1⅝ in. and the working pressure was 160 p.s.i.

In working order the engine weight was 43 tons 16 cwt, all of which was, of course, available for adhesion. It was divided into: leading, 14 tons 15 cwt; middle, 15 tons 5 cwt, and trailing, 13 tons 16 cwt.

Originally, these engines presented an unusually smart appearance for goods engines because they were painted in Wainwright's standard livery with all its elaborate lining, and were provided with a polished brass dome, safety-valve cover and fillet at the junction of the smokebox and boiler barrel.

In 1912, this elaboration was replaced by a very much simpler livery, and a few years later, during the 1914-18 war, this simpler style gave way to a plain dark grey all over—without any lining whatever —though the chimney and smokebox were black as before. The lettering and the number were white. My drawing indicates this war-time style of painting, which remained the standard style for all SECR engines until after 1923.

The tender was similar to the one described for Wainwright's D Class engines on page 54, with capacity for 3,300 gallons of water and 4½ tons of coal. Several were subsequently fitted with raised coping at the sides of the coal space to increase the capacity to about five tons.

All these engines were equipped with the automatic vacuum brake, steam reversing gear, steam sanding apparatus and Stone's patent sight-feed lubricators for cylinders and valves. Most of the engines had sandboxes arranged as seen in my drawings, but in some, additional sandboxes were provided below the running plate just ahead of the leading wheels.

Nos 711 to 725, built by Sharp, Stewart and Co. in 1900, were fitted with the Westinghouse air brake, as well as the normal vacuum brake; the air pump was mounted on the right-hand side of the engine, between the cab and the middle splasher.

The cabs of these engines were quite roomy and comfortable, the roofs being provided with sliding ventilators, while the spaces at the sides, between engine and tender, could be closed by double-folding doors for lessening the draught on the footplate when running.

It is worth recalling that in 1919 No 686 was given an extended smokebox, the front of which was brought to within 3 in. of the leading buffer beam. Apparently, the results obtained did not justify a general adoption of this feature, as no other engine of this class was similarly treated and, after a year or two, 686 was restored to her original condition.

A more extensive alteration, however, was made to No 685 which, in 1918, was rebuilt into a 0-6-0 saddle-tank shunting engine. In this form, she was re-classed S, but she remained the sole example of that class until she was broken up in 1955.

The rebuilding entailed no alterations to the boiler, cylinders, wheels or valve gear, but the frames were extended at the rear end to accommodate the bunker and enlarged cab, the trailing overhang being increased from 3 ft 4 in. to 8 ft. A large semicircular saddle tank, of 1,200 gallons capacity, was slung over the boiler barrel, and I believe I am right in stating that this was the first and only saddle tank built at the Ashford works.

In her altered form 685 weighed 53 tons 10 cwt in working trim, 17 tons 10 cwt resting on each of the leading and driving axles and 18 tons 10 cwt on the trailing axle. Bunker capacity was for two tons.

A sort of "accidental pimple" of a dome was mounted on top of the saddle tank, and a pair of Ross pop safety valves replaced the original Ramsbottom type. The engine was equipped with powerful steam and hand brakes in addition to the usual vacuum brake, and was used exclusively for shunting and marshalling goods trains and passenger stock in the sidings at Bricklayers Arms. She was withdrawn in the latter part of 1954.

No other alterations worth mentioning were made to any other engines of the class, the survivors of which still find plenty of work to do in various localities in the Eastern section of the Southern Region.

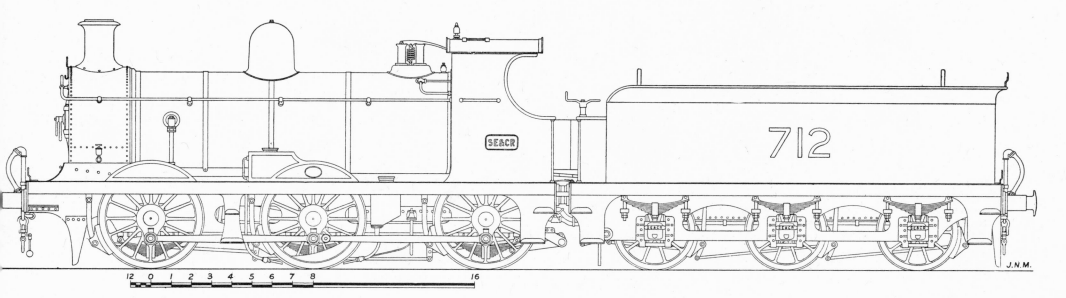

Q CLASS
TANK
ENGINES

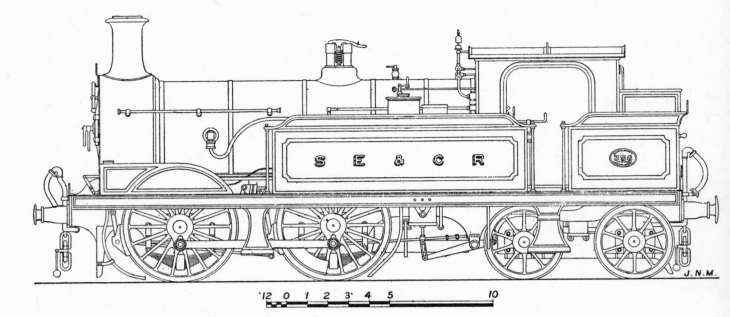

J.N.M.

THESE engines were, originally, James Stirling's standard type for suburban passenger duties on the old South Eastern Railway; but I did not know them until after 1900, when they had become the property of the SECR Managing Committee.

There were 118 of them built between 1881 and 1897, 45 by Neilson and Co., Glasgow, between 1881 and 1897, ten by Sharp Stewart and Co., Glasgow, in 1893, and all the others, 63 in all, at Ashford. They are an interesting comparison with the 0-4-4 tank engines designed by James Stirling's brother, Patrick, for the Great Northern Railway, which I have already described. I have always had the impression that James' engines were somewhat less robust than his brother's, but there was certainly little to choose between the two types, so far as their work was concerned.

Until September 1907, there was a service of SECR local trains working through from London Bridge via Ludgate Hill, Kings Cross and Finsbury Park to Wood Green, on the Great Northern Railway, and to work this service 12 of James Stirling's 0-4-4

tank engines were built with condensing apparatus for use when running through the tunnels of the Metropolitan Railway between Snow Hill and Kings Cross. The height to the tops of the chimneys on these 12 engines was reduced from the standard 13 ft 4 in. to 12 ft 6⅝ in., to clear the Metropolitan height gauge; also, for some unexplained reason, their bogies had wheels of only 3 ft dia. and a wheelbase of only 4 ft 10 in. This type of bogie, however, was fitted to 22 engines of the non-condensing series, so it seems to have been experimental. All the other engines of this Q-class had standard Stirling bogies with wheels 3 ft 9½ in. dia. on a wheelbase of 5 ft 4 in.

This reminds me of a rather peculiar event. In 1890, J. J. Hanbury, locomotive engineer of the Metropolitan Railway, wanted some new engines and he suggested designing an 0-4-4 tank type, of which he thought half a dozen would meet requirements. The chairman of the Metropolitan was Sir Edward Watkin, who was also chairman of the South Eastern and nothing if he was not an economist. He was about to sign an order on Neilson and Co., of Glasgow, for ten new engines of Stirling's Q-class

for the SER; he summoned Hanbury and showed him Stirling's drawings, remarking: "These are the engines you want."

Hanbury studied the drawings and said he thought Stirling's design was satisfactory, except that it was much too high, and he preferred to have a dome on the boiler. Sir Edward promptly altered Stirling's order from 10 to 14, at the same time specifying that four of the engines were to have the standard Hanbury chimney, and their boilers were to have a dome on which two Salter safety valves were to be mounted in accordance with normal Metropolitan practice of that period.

The 14 engines were delivered in 1891, the four with Hanbury's alterations going to the Metropolitan and the rest to the SER. And that is how the Metropolitan obtained four useful 0-4-4 tank engines, the first of their type on that line, at a price considerably cheaper than it might have been! It also explains why, except for the chimneys and domes, the Met's C-class 0-4-4 tank engines were precisely similar to Stirling's Qs.

In 1890, Stirling began the reboilering of a number

of Qs, using new boilers similar to the originals, but fitted with deeper fireboxes, which necessitated raising the pitch of the centre line from 7 ft 1½ in. to 7 ft 8⅞ in. My drawing shows No 356 reboilered in this way; she was built by Neilsons in 1891 and reboilered in 1902. I knew her well, frequently seeing her and riding behind her when I was an engineering apprentice at Vickers Ltd, at Erith from 1911 to 1913. She was stationed at Bricklayer's Arms and, together with many more of the class, worked London-Dartford local trains. I cannot say that their work was in any way outstanding; they plodded along, keeping good time on the sort of work they were doing, and they looked well in Wainwright's SECR livery, generally kept very clean. It seems a little odd that, for some reason, Stirling made use of a square-shaped cab for these engines; in fact, until 1898, they were the only Stirling engines so distinguished. All the others—tender and tank—had the familiar Stirling rounded-roof type.

Another peculiar detail was that, when Wainwright applied his livery to Stirling's engines, of all classes, he did not put their numbers on the bufferbeams, whereas all his own engines together with all the former London, Chatham and Dover engines displayed their numbers on their bufferbeams; this feature did not appear on any Stirling engine until about 1912. Also, the bufferheads at the front were 1 ft dia. while at the back they were 1 ft 4 in., which seems strange because the engines did about as much running backwards as they did forwards, and one would have thought that the buffers should have been interchangeable.

The following dimensions apply to the Q-class when reboilered, as shown in my drawing: cylinder diameter 18 in., stroke 26 in., inclination 1 in 9.

The boiler had three rings, the middle one being 4 ft 5 in. dia., outside, the other two being 4 ft 4 in.; the barrel was 10 ft 7 1/16 in. long between tubeplates. The inside firebox was 5 ft 6 in. long, 3 ft 4 in. wide

and 5 ft deep below the centre line; the grate was horizontal.

There were 185 tubes of 1⅝ in. dia. giving 883.3 sq. ft of heating surface, to which the firebox added 89.25 sq. ft, totalling 972.55 sq. ft. The grate area was 15.5 sq. ft and the working pressure 140 p.s.i.

The coupled wheels were 5 ft 6 in. dia. and the bogie wheels 3 ft 9 in., on a wheelbase of 22 ft 1 in. divided into 7 ft 5 in. plus 9 ft 4 in. plus 5 ft 4 in., and the overhang was 5 ft 3 in. in front and 2 ft 1 in. at the back.

In working order, with 1,050 gallons of water in the tanks and 1 ton 10 cwt of coal in the bunker, the weight was 46 tons 4 cwt, though how this was distributed is not known.

In 1902, H. S. Wainwright reboilered 55 of these engines with his H-class boiler and reclassified them Q1.

Both classes have become extinct, class Q in 1919 and class Q1 in 1930.

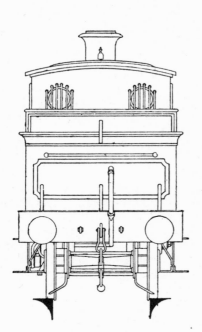

GENERAL SPECIFICATION

CYLINDERS			TUBES		
Diameter	...	... 18 in.	Number	...	... 185
Stroke	...	... 26 in.	Diameter	...	... 1⅝ in.
BOILER			HEATING SURFACE		
Length between			Tubes...	...	883.3 sq. ft.
tubeplates	10 ft 7 1/16 in.		Firebox	...	89.25 sq. ft.
Maximum diameter	4 ft 5 in.		Total ...	...	972.55 sq. ft.
FIREBOX LENGTH					
Inside...	...	5 ft 6 in.	GRATE AREA		
Outside	...	—	Square feet ...	...	15.5

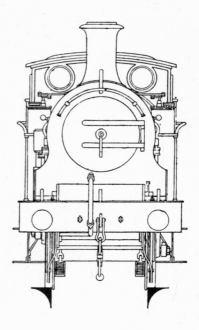

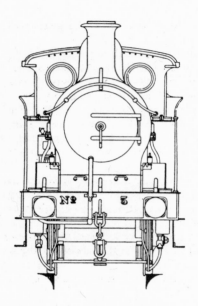

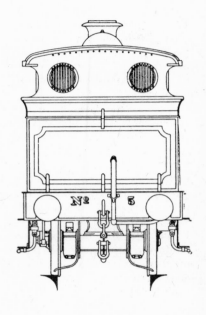

GENERAL SPECIFICATION

CYLINDERS			TUBES		
Diameter	...	18¼ in.	Number	... ...	205
Stroke	...	26 in.	Diameter	...	1¾ in.

BOILER		
Length, between tubeplates		10 ft 3½ in.
Maximum diameter	...	4 ft 4 in.

HEATING SURFACE		
Tubes	...	1,002.45 sq. ft
Firebox	...	102.2 sq. ft
Total	...	1,104.65 sq. ft

FIREBOX LENGTH		
Inside	...	4 ft 11 18/18 in.
Outside	...	5 ft 8 in.

GRATE AREA		
Square feet	...	16.66

WAINWRIGHT'S
H Class 0-4-4 TANKS

In the course of the history of steam locomotive development in Britain, there have been many different types and classes of engines that never attracted any particular attention outside the railway for which they were built. Usually, they worked steadily and well at the tasks for which they were designed, but their fame, if any, was confined within the limits of their own territory.

Among such engines were the 0-4-4 tanks first brought out in 1904 by Mr Harry S. Wainwright as Class H for the South Eastern and Chatham Railway's suburban services. They were quite attractive engines in their original condition—stolid, sturdy and powerful—and they have always given satisfaction.

I remember when they were new, and in course of time I got to know the entire class; they were to be found all over the SECR system, though the majority were to be seen in the London area, whence, in addition to working on purely local suburban trains, they often ran through to such places as Redhill, Reigate, Guildford and Tonbridge on semi-fast outer suburban trains.

My acquaintance with this class began at Whitstable in 1905, and was much increased when we moved to

a new country home at Edenbridge in 1909. At the latter place there are two railway stations situated about a mile apart; one, Edenbridge Town, was a former LBSCR station on the Tunbridge Wells direct line, the other belonged to the SECR on the Redhill-Tonbridge line.

Much of my time at weekends and holidays was fairly evenly divided between these two stations which, to me, were a kind of paradise !

The H-class tanks were very much in evidence in the Edenbridge area. Some were stationed at Tonbridge, others at Redhill, and they frequently worked stopping trains to and from London. One of them

was No 5, the subject of my drawing, and I particularly remember her because of a curious experience I had when going home to our London house one Sunday evening.

I went from Edenbridge SECR station; the train arrived with engine No 5, and I got in, only to discover that I was in coach No 5 ! On arrival at Charing Cross, I went down to the Underground to take a train to West Kensington, and—yes !—I got into District car No 5, and then to cap all when I arrived at West Kensington I was just on the point of handing my ticket to the collector when I happened to catch sight of its number—it was 5005 !

There were 66 engines in this very useful class, all built at Ashford in the following batches: nine in 1904; 17 in 1905; 11 in 1906; five in 1907; six in 1908; 12 in 1909; four in 1910 and two in 1915.

Why these last two should have been built after a lull of five years is because R. E. L. Maunsell discovered that 66 engines had been ordered, but only 64 had been built. He demanded that the outstanding two should be completed forthwith !

The leading particulars of the H class were given in great detail in the official specification, which was

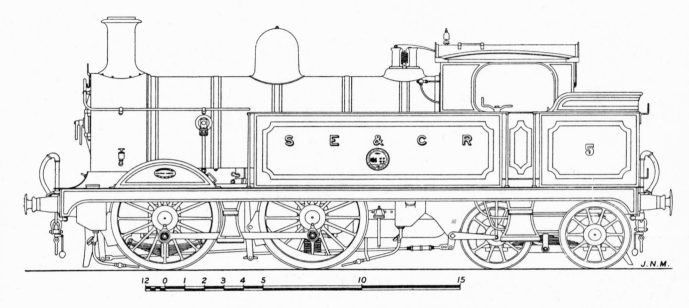

The tank capacity was 1,200 gallons and the bunker would take 2¼ tons of coal. Fully loaded, the engine weighed 53 tons 18 cwt, 33 tons 10 cwt resting on the four coupled wheels, evenly distributed, and 20 tons 8 cwt on the bogie. The tractive effort was 16,777 lb.

These engines were equipped with the automatic vacuum brake and steam sanding apparatus, and the smokeboxes were fitted up with Stone's patent spark arrester and fuel economiser. I must add that the height from rail level to the top of the chimney was 13 ft 2¾ in., and tip-up seats were provided for drivers and firemen.

It is rather curious that the 0-4-4 tank engine should have been so often criticised, if not condemned, by Board of Trade inspectors. True, there were several accidents involving 0-4-4 tank engines in different parts of the British Isles, and the BOT inspectors seldom failed to blame the 0-4-4 tank if the accidents should have occurred while the engines were travelling at speed.

Yet, in spite of the dictates of inspectors, the 0-4-4 tank was a popular and very reliable type found on most British railways, especially for suburban work. The Wainwright H-class engines were among the steadiest and most infallible suburban locomotives I have ever known, and I cannot recall a mishap that could be in any way blamed on to their design.

At the moment of writing, more than 40 of these stalwart engines are still in service—some of them far from their native haunts. They are largely used on push-pull auto-trains on branch lines or in provincial suburban areas; they can still be seen occasionally on ordinary stopping passenger trains, while there are several engaged on empty coaching-stock workings at large stations in different parts of the Southern Region.

They are officially classed as equal to the similarly-respected Drummond M7 engines of the same wheel arrangement. In fact, in some districts they work turn-and-turn-about with them.

I have always had the impression that of the two classes the Wainwright engines were the sturdier and more robust; and I would not be surprised to learn that they had amassed a greater average mileage per engine.

printed in full in *The Engineer* of 25 August 1905 to supplement the working drawings; some of the dimensions are very interesting, more especially those of the valves, valve-gear and valve events. The cylinders had a diameter of 18¼ in. and a stroke of 26 in. and their centres were 2 ft 4½ in. apart; they were inclined at 1 in 9 to clear the leading axle.

The width of the steam ports was 1¼ in. and of the exhaust ports 2½ in., their common length being 16 in. The steamchest was between the cylinders, its centre line, in side elevation, coinciding with those of the two cylinders. The lap of the valves was 1 in. on the steam admission side, but there was no lap or clearance on the exhaust side. Due to the rather steep inclination of the cylinders, the leads differed, being ¼ in. for the front port but only $\frac{1}{16}$ in. for the back port.

Ordinary Stephenson link motion was provided and was arranged so that it gave a full-gear valve travel of 4 9/32 in. over the front port, but only 4$\frac{1}{16}$ in. over the back port. These figures are according to the official specification.

The eccentric sheaves were 1 ft 3¼ in. dia., and their throw was 3¼ in. The eccentric rods were 5 ft 2¾ in. long, and they were attached to the top

and bottom of the expansion links which were 1 ft 6 in. long between the eccentric-rod pins. The length of the connecting-rods was 5 ft 11 in.

Leading and driving wheels were 5 ft 6 in. and the bogie wheels were 3 ft 7 in. dia. The wheel base was 21 ft 10 in. divided into 7 ft 6 in. plus 9 ft 4 in. plus 5 ft. Leading and trailing overhangs were 5 ft 3 in. and 2 ft 1 in., respectively, and the total length over buffers was 32 ft 10⅝ in.

A thoroughly up-to-date and well-proportioned boiler was provided; it was pitched 7 ft 9¼ in. above rail level. The barrel was 10 ft 3½ in. long and was made in two rings, the larger (back) one of which was 4 ft 4 in. dia. outside, the thickness of the plates being ½ in.

There were 205 brass tubes of 1¾ in. outside dia.; they were cambered 1⅝ in. as was usual in Wainwright boilers. The firebox was of copper, 4 ft 11$\frac{15}{16}$ in. long, and 3 ft 4 in. wide at the bottom. The casing was of steel, 5 ft 8 in. long, 4 ft wide and 5 ft 11 in. deep, below the centre line. The total heating surface amounted to 1,104.65 sq. ft, made up of 1,002.45 sq. ft for the tubes and 102.2 sq. ft for the firebox. The working pressure was 160 p.s.i. and the grate area was 16.66 sq. ft.

GENERAL SPECIFICATION				
CYLINDERS			**TUBES**	
Diameter	17 in.		Number	164
Stroke	24 in.		Diameter	2 in.
BOILER				
Length, between			**HEATING SURFACE**	
tubeplates	10 ft 3 in.		Tubes ...	903 sq. ft
Maximum dia-			Firebox ...	90 sq. ft
meter ...	4 ft 2 in.		Total ...	993 sq. ft
FIREBOX LENGTH				
Inside ...	4 ft 10½ in.		**GRATE AREA**	
Outside ...	5 ft 7 in.		Square feet ...	16

BEYER PEACOCK 'DISTRICT' TANKS

Before the days of electrification, the trains on that part of London's underground railway system officially titled " The Metropolitan District Railway," but known to all and sundry as the " District," were worked by a squad of 54 Beyer Peacock 4-4-0 tank engines.

It was in 1902, when I was what is now called a locospotter, that I first took any notice of these engines, but by 1906, thanks to frequent visits with school friends to such places as Ealing Common, Acton Town and Earls Court, I had " copped " the lot of them. At that time, the engines were all alike outwardly, but there had been minor differences of detail between the various batches when built. All the engines remained in service until 1905, when 52 of them were withdrawn for scrap, leaving two survivors, Nos 33 and 34, which were transferred to the Works and Maintenance Department at Lillie Bridge, West Kensington, as odd-job engines.

In 1923, I paid a visit to those two old engines at Lillie Bridge and found them in very good condition. They were still in the condition in which I had always known them, except that No 33 had been

fitted with sleet-brushes for removing frozen sleet or snow from electric conductor rails—a task which she performed where needed during severe winter weather.

This engine was scrapped in 1925, but No 34 lingered on, working occasional track maintenance trains and doing certain marshalling jobs, until 1928, when she was broken up.

The 54 District tanks must not be confused with the 66 very similar engines which belonged to the Metropolitan Railway; the two sets, as well as the two railways, were separate and quite distinct, though they did join forces in working the traffic on the Inner Circle of the Underground line. The District engines worked trains from Ealing Broadway, Hounslow, Richmond, Putney Bridge and Wimbledon to Earls Court, Kensington High Street, Mansion House and Whitechapel. On the Inner Circle line, they worked trains via Aldgate, Kings Cross, Baker Street, Notting Hill Gate, Victoria and Charing Cross in a counter-clockwise direction, while the Metropolitan engines worked the same route, but in the opposite direction. Again, both railways ran trains through to New Cross

on the London Brighton and South Coast Railway via the East London line.

Quite an intensive service was maintained on all routes and the old engines certainly worked well and earned their cost and keep many times over. The trains were not remarkable for comfort, those of the District being close-coupled sets of four-wheeled stock, providing the then usual three classes of accommodation.

Modern writers often stress the discomfort of the smoky atmosphere that prevailed on the Underground in those days. I remember it quite well and I assert that it was not nearly so bad as some people would have us believe. True, there was the characteristic smell, which was not so very unpleasant, and everyone was used to it !

There was plenty of ventilation, however, and the trains did a great deal of their own ventilating by the very fact of moving through the tunnels. Moreover, all the engines condensed their exhaust steam and always ran with the blower on, so there was comparatively little smoke.

No ! It was only in very hot weather that conditions became at all unpleasant but even then, they were not unbearable. All the same, when electrification came and the old steam locomotives ceased to work the traffic, there was a considerable improvement in the general atmospheric conditions. In the old days, some passengers may have grumbled but I have never known a time when passengers didn't grumble !

The original specification for these engines was prepared by Sir John Fowler, who also planned the whole of the London Underground Railways, among other notable engineering feats. The engine design was standardised by Beyer Peacock & Co., and examples, with very minor differences, were sold to the District, the Metropolitan, the London and South Western, the South Eastern, the Midland and the London and North Western Railways, as well as to certain countries abroad.

Some tender engines and some 4-4-2 tank engines, both directly derived from this design, were sent to South Australia, and they became the inspiration of a number of later developments that took place in that country. So the design may be said to have had a wide application.

I would just add that the above-mentioned South Eastern examples, of which there were three, were virtually on loan and not actually sold to that line; later they went to the Metropolitan.

Beyer Peacock & Co. report that, between 1864 and 1889, no fewer than 148 of the 4-4-0 tank engines were built; of these, 120 were for the London Underground Railways. Typical dimensions are: cylinders, 17 in. by 24 in., steeply inclined, so as to clear the leading truck. The valve-gear was of Allan straight-link type.

The four leading wheels, originally, were carried in a Bissell truck which was pivoted at a point 6 ft 8 in. behind its centre-line; its wheelbase was 4 ft, and the diameter of its wheels was 3 ft. It had the merit of being simple and cheap, but there seems to have been something about it that was not entirely satisfactory, because on all the engines of this type built after 1879, an Adams bogie was substituted, still with 3 ft wheels and 4 ft wheelbase.

The coupled wheels had the comparatively large diameter of 5 ft 9 in. and their wheelbase was 8 ft 10 in., the total for the engine being 20 ft 9 in.

The boiler was made in three rings, the smallest of which was 4 ft 2 in. in diameter, outside, and had the dome mounted on it. There were 164 tubes of 2 in. diameter, giving 903 sq. ft of heating surface to which the firebox added 90 sq. ft, the total being 993 sq. ft. The working pressure, at first, was 130 p.s.i. but was later raised to 160 p.s.i. The tank capacity was 1,000 gallons, while the bunker carried 1½ tons of coal.

In working order, the total weight was 42 tons 3 cwt, with 31 tons resting on the four coupled wheels.

My drawing shows engine No 34 because, not only was she the last survivor of her class, but she was, in her last years, the one I knew best. In the last few months of her existence, she was fitted with a cab over the footplate; it did not improve her appearance, so I have omitted it, and left the drawing to show the form in which these engines did most of their work.

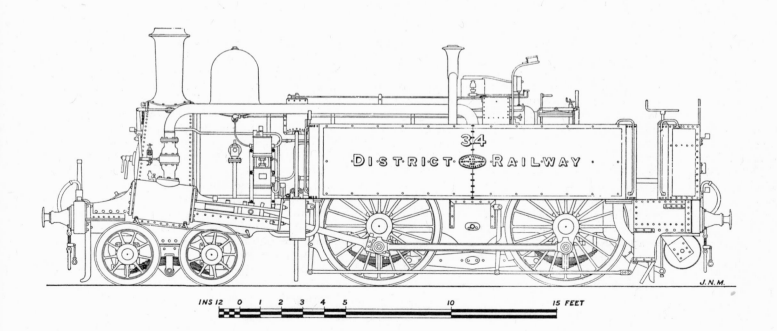
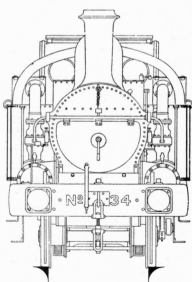

INS 12 0 1 2 3 4 5   10   15 FEET

J.N.M.

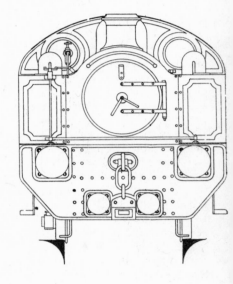

GENERAL SPECIFICATION			
CYLINDERS		**TUBES**	
Diameter ... ... 14½ in.		Number 129	
Stroke ... ... 18 in.		Diameter ... ... 1⅞ in.	
BOILER			
Length, between		**HEATING SURFACE**	
tubeplates 7 ft 9 in.		Tubes ... 511 sq. ft	
Maximum dia-		Firebox ... 51 sq. ft	
meter ... 3 ft 8½ in.		Total ... 562 sq. ft	
FIREBOX LENGTH			
Inside ... 2 ft 9 in.		**GRATE AREA**	
Outside ... 3 ft 4 in.		Square feet ... 8.5	

'TUPPENNY TUBE' TANKS

I WONDER how many readers ever saw either of these two extraordinary little engines. If it comes to that, how many readers even know that the Central London Railway, originally the " Tuppenny Tube " and now the Central Line of the London Transport Executive, ever possessed *steam* locomotives at all ?

When I was going to school, between 1905 and 1911, I used the Metropolitan and Great Western joint line to Hammersmith, and passed the CLR power-generating station at Shepherds Bush, at least twice a day, and rarely failed to see one or other of these two little engines.

At a later date I had the opportunity of inspecting and riding on both of them, during a private visit to this power station; as I am over six feet tall, standing in the cabs of these engines involved a working knowledge of the " knees bend " exercise, which was, I believe, the sole form of athletics at which I acquired any notable proficiency !

The two engines, which were Nos 1 and 2 on the CLR books, were specially designed and built by the Hunslet Engine Co. Ltd, Leeds, in 1899, and carried makers' numbers 635 and 636. Due to the fact that the working clearance in the tube tunnels was only 10 ft 6 in. dia., the dimensions of these engines were extremely " compressed " externally; the cab had plenty of width, but was severely restricted in height and depth. This did not matter very much as the driver was provided with a seat of sorts. Usually, there was only one man in the cab. The engines were oil-fired and normally, there was no need for a fireman.

I recall that when I visited the Shepherds Bush power station, the man in charge of these engines pointed out to me that, when running through the very restricted " tube " tunnels, steam engines had their disadvantages. The heat and fumes from the chimney, combined with the normal heat of the cab, made things unpleasant for the engineman. Therefore, it was preferable to work the engine bunker-first; but this condition could only apply to one direction of running, as there were no turntables below-ground on the CLR. It was the custom, when working chimney-first, to make frequent stops at stations to take the air !

That this particular difficulty was not entirely overlooked during the design stage, is suggested by the fact that the view rearwards from the cab was entirely unobstructed. The forwards view was not nearly so clear, as may be seen in the drawings.

The engines were painted a distinctly brownish oilve-green, panelled with black striping having a red line on its outer edge and a pale yellow line on the inner one. The wheels slightly varied this scheme by being painted olive-green, with black tyres, black axle ends outlined in yellow and the bosses outlined in red. Smokebox, chimney and front plate, between the tank ends, were black; dome, safety-valve casing and the whistle were polished brass, and the coupling-rods were bright steel. All this looked quite nice, especially as the engines were kept very clean.

The design of these engines is not without interest because though they were used chiefly above ground, shunting wagons of coal from the reception sidings to the power-house bunkers, they were also used for working maintenance and engineers' trains through the tunnels. Therefore an inside-cylinder design was essential, simply because there was absolutely no room for outside cylinders.

The diameter of the cylinders was 14½ in., and the stroke was 18 in.; the steamchest was arranged between the cylinders, and the flat valves were actuated by normal Stephenson valve gear. The wheels were 3 ft 3 in. dia., the leading and trailing

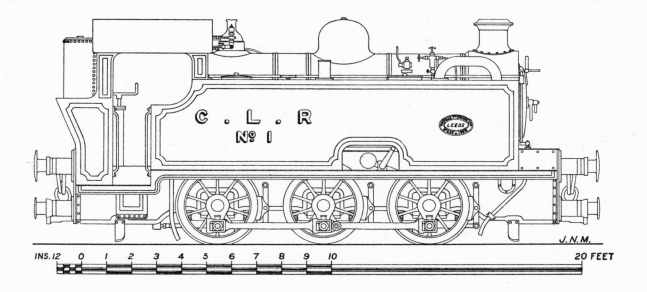

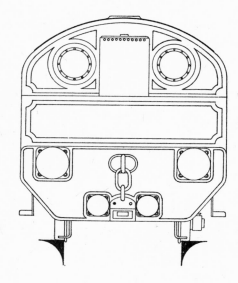

INS. 12   0   1   2   3   4   5   6   7   8   9   10   20 FEET

J.N.M.

pairs being 5 in. wide with flanges, while the middle pair were 6 in. wide without flanges. The wheelbase was 8 ft 6 in., equally divided, and the minimum curve the engines could negotiate was 150 ft radius.

The diameter of the boiler was 3 ft 8½ in. externally, and 4 ft 0½ in. over the lagging; the length of barrel was 7 ft 9 in. between tubeplates. There were 129 brass tubes of 1⅞ in. outside diameter, the heating surface of which was 511 sq. ft; the firebox heating surface was 51 sq. ft, making the total 562 sq. ft. The

grate area was 8.5 sq. ft.

It is obvious that when the engines were working in the extremely confined space of the tunnels, the presence of any quantity of exhaust steam was to be avoided. To meet this requirement, condensing apparatus was provided and part of the side tanks was reserved for 1,000 gallons of water supplied for use in the condenser alone. For the boiler feed a separate supply of 250 gallons of water occupied the rear portion of the tanks.

The fuel tank in the bunker was semicircular in plan view and carried 50 gallons of oil, but there was also space in the bunker for 20 cu. ft —approximately ¾ ton—of coal for use when the engines were at work above ground.

I am not certain when these two very interesting little engines were broken up. The last I saw of either was when No 2 replaced the old District Railway engine No 33 at Lillie Bridge depot, West Kensington, for a few months in 1925.